Encountering Modernity

INTERSECTIONS

Asian and Pacific American
Transcultural Studies

Russell C. Leong
David K. Yoo
Series Editors

Encountering Modernity

« « « « « • » » » » »

Christianity in East Asia and Asian America

Edited by
Albert L. Park and David K. Yoo

University of Hawai'i Press
Honolulu

in association with UCLA
Asian American Studies Center
Los Angeles

Printed in the United States of America
19 18 17 16 15 14 6 5 4 3 2 1

Library of Congress Cataloging-in-Publication Data

Encountering modernity : Christianity in East Asia and Asian America / edited by Albert L. Park and David K. Yoo.

pages cm — (Asian and Pacific American transcultural studies)

Includes bibliographical references and index.

ISBN 978-0-8248-3947-5 (cloth : alk. paper)

1. Christianity—East Asia. 2. East Asians—United States—Religion. 3. East Asian Americans—Religion. 4. Christianity—United States. I. Park, Albert L., editor of compilation. II. Yoo, David, editor of compilation. III. Series: Intersections (Honolulu, Hawaii)

BR1275.E53 2014

275'.082—dc23

2013030109

University of Hawaiʻi Press books are printed on acid-free paper and meet the guidelines for permanence and durability of the Council on Library Resources.

Designed by Josie Herr

Printed by Sheridan Books, Inc.

Contents

Acknowledgments

This book would not have been possible without the generous support from the Henry Luce Foundation to Claremont McKenna College. Funding from the Luce Foundation allowed us to hold the conference "Negotiating the Global with the Local: Translating Christianity in Modern East Asia" from which several papers are included in this book. A special thanks goes to Helena Kolenda, Luce's Program Director for Asia, for her steady help and encouragement. This book project also greatly benefited from the support of several key people at Claremont McKenna College, especially President Pamela B. Gann and Dean Gregory Hess, as well as Christopher Wiedey, now at the University of Southern California, and Abigail Flores.

At the University of Hawai'i Press, we thank Masako Ikeda for her wisdom and guidance throughout the publishing process as well as the two anonymous reviewers whose close readings helped us to improve the manuscript. We also benefited from the copyediting of Susan Stone.

It has been a privilege to work with our contributors, who have patiently journeyed with us through the twists and turns that accompany projects such as this one. We are glad to be able to feature their research here and are appreciative of the goodwill and cooperative spirit that they have extended to us and to each other.

Albert L. Park is extremely grateful to his wife, Jennifer H. Lee, for providing him with the precious love, encouragement, comfort, and guidance that have sustained him throughout the process of editing this book. Lastly, he wants to thank his nephew Andrew Park, who sadly passed away while this book was being completed. Andrew's loving nature and heroic fight against leukemia demonstrated courage and how to live with focus and passion—values and characteristics that helped bring this book to fruition.

David K. Yoo is thankful for the research assistance provided by Christina Lee and Phi Su. The UCLA Asian American Studies Center and Department have been wonderful spaces in which to work, and he gives a shout-out to faculty colleagues, staff, and students. Mahalo to Gary Pak of the University of Hawaiʻi, who has generously allowed us to use his painting *Fish and Eye*, for the cover. Ruth, Jonathan, and Joshua hopefully already know how much they are loved and appreciated.

Introduction

Modernity and the Materiality of Religion

Albert L. Park and David K. Yoo

The story of Christianity in East Asia has been told in detail and with verve, chronicling the introduction and practice of Catholicism and Protestantism in China, Japan, and Korea. The existing literature is especially rich in documenting church and missionary activities. It also relates how varied regions and cultures have translated Christian ideas, practices, and symbols. Less evident, however, are studies that contextualize Christianity within the larger economic, political, social, and cultural developments in each of the three countries and its diasporas. The contributors to *Encountering Modernity: Christianity in East Asia and Asian America* address such concerns and, collectively, provide insights into the role that Christianity has played in the development of the region of East Asia and among East Asians in the United States.

Scholarship in English on East Asian Christianity grew significantly in the nineteenth and early twentieth centuries as Western missionary activities increased in the area. Not surprisingly, missionaries themselves wrote the majority of these studies on Christianity through publishing houses located in various denominations and missionary-built institutions. In the first half of the twentieth century in Korea, for example, presses such as the Christian Literature Society, the Korean Religious Book and Religious Tract Society, and the Chosen Mission Presbyterian Church U.S.A. distributed journals and books such as *Korea Mission Field* (1905–1941), *History of the Korea Mission Presbyterian Church U.S.A.* (1934), and *The Nevius Plan for Mission Work* (1937). During the 1930s and early 1940s, the Board of Foreign Missions of the Presbyterian Church in the United States of America published numerous materials on Christianity in China written by missionaries and Christian workers, such as *China Missions* (1937) and *On the Shantung Front* (1940). After 1945, books and articles on Christianity in China, Japan, and Korea were not only authored by missionaries, but also by native converts who served as pastors, educators, and lay workers in the church. For example, Arimichi Ebisawa, who was a professor of history at International Christian University in Japan, became a leading historian on Christianity in Japan through books such as *Christianity in Japan* (1960) and *Christianity in Japan: A Bibliography of Japanese and Chinese Source* (1960).[1]

These studies by Western missionaries and native converts to Christianity mainly centered on missiological issues and history as well as on the reception of Christian theology by natives and their church activities. Nicholas Standaert points out that the introduction of missiology as a theological discipline in the 1920s and 1930s pushed scholars to ask "whether the Chinese experience was representative of a certain missiological approach."[2] This research agenda was also applied to the examination of missionary movements in Korea and Japan. Many of these studies reviewed missionary activities in foreign settings in order to refine and further develop missionary strategies and methods. Hence, according to Standaert, in the field of Chinese Christian history, writers focused on the work and ministries of missionaries such as Matteo Ricci, Adam Schall von Bell, and Ferdinand Verbiest.[3] Expanding the field of missiology further required studies on how Japanese, Korean, and Chinese converts to Christianity responded to missionary teachings and how they practiced Christianity in their local settings. Examining church activities and movements further helped refine and strengthen the mutual efforts of missionaries and East Asian Christians, contributing to an increased church membership in the three countries.

By focusing so much on the ideas and practices of missionaries and the way Christian theology was interpreted and practiced by natives, studies of Christianity in China, Korea, and Japan have failed to look at this religion within a larger historical context. Put differently, these studies have provided little insight into how Christianity as a system of ideas, practices, and institutions affected and shaped political, social, economic, and cultural structures in East Asia, and what role it played in mediating people's everyday lives as they also experienced modernity and capitalism. Some studies on Christianity in Korea, such as the edited volume *Christianity in Korea* (2006),[4] have analyzed the role the Protestant Church played in terms of Korean nationalism under Japanese colonial rule. A central focus has been how Japanese imperialism affected church activities, as in the 1937–1938 Shinto shrine controversy. Only recently, with the use of postcolonial, critical, and cultural theories and through research conducted by those outside of the church and its institutions have studies illuminated the role Christianity played in political, social, and economic developments in China, Japan, and Korea. Hyaeweol Choi's book *Gender and Mission Encounter in Korea* and Kelly H. Chong's book *Deliverance and Submission* are two examples of studies that have analyzed the relationship between Christianity and social structures such as gender roles. Furthermore, Ryan Dunch's book *Fuzhou Protestants and the Making of Modern China, 1859–1927,* has helped expand Chinese historiography through its examination of Christian ideas and how they informed political thought and movements in modern China.[5] Yet, these books represent the exception, as the scholarship on East Asian Christianity continues to focus on missionary activities and native church practices and developments.

The existing historiography, moreover, has tended to focus on a single East Asian country rather than providing a sense of how Christianity unfolded in the region. *History of Christianity in Asia* in two volumes by Samuel H. Moffett stands in contrast to the trend and is significant in documenting and analyzing the role of Christianity in the broad expanse of the Asian continent. Moffett provides a rich and deep history, rooted in the tradition of church history and missiology. The comparative frame employed by Moffett is less about individuals and communities and more about institutional traditions.[6]

Encountering Modernity contributes to the scholarship by bringing together studies of Christianity in China, Taiwan, Korea, and Japan and their diasporas that expand the field through new perspectives that look at how Christian ideas, practices, and institutions were adopted, translated, and practiced in relation to political, economic, social, and cultural developments in order to negotiate phenomena such as modernity. This mode of analysis not only results in a deeper understanding of Christianity, but also produces more informed and nuanced histories of East Asian countries that take seriously the structures and sensibilities of religion, broadly understood and within a national and transnational context. This volume critically investigates how Protestant Christianity was negotiated and interpreted by individuals in Korea, China (with a brief look at Taiwan), and Japan starting in the nineteenth century as all three countries became incorporated into the global economy and the international nation-state system anchored by the West. People in East Asia from various walks of life studied and, in some cases, embraced principles of Christianity as a way to frame and make meaningful the changes they experienced because of modernity.

For clarity, it is important to explain the term "modernity." According to Raymond Williams, "modern" appeared at first "as a term more or less synonymous with 'now' in the late sixteenth century, and in any case used to mark the period off from medieval *and* ancient times."[7] More specifically, "modern" was a *chronological* term that denoted a new historical period starting in the middle of the fifteenth century in Europe. Several institutional features distinguished the modern period from the earlier period in history. Relying on theories and historical works by Anthony Giddens, Max Weber, Charles Tilly, and Jürgen Habermas, Kim Dong-no argues that these new institutions reshaped the political system, economic system, culture, and social relationships.[8] The first new political feature of the modern period was the nation-state, which "can be defined by its centralized power structure, clearly demarcated boundaries, institutional separation between politics and other realms of everyday life (especially economy), and the monopoly of legitimate means of physical violence."[9] Second, capitalism, especially industrial capitalism, became the dominant economic system, where "mass production and mass consumption prevail for the maximization of profit as opposed to the precapitalist one dominated by the principle of subsistence." Third, in the area of social relationships, the modern period featured the "detachment of the individual from traditional collectives" in order to shift personal loyalty to the nation-state and allow the individual to commodify his or her own labor without inference from any "supraindividual entity." Finally, nationalism emerged as a new cultural force in the modern period, as it "enabled the horizontal integration of individuals by cross-cutting various political, economic, and social interests, thereby replacing the vertical hierarchy of traditional society."[10] Urbanization and rationalization also represented prominent features of the modern period.[11] Far from denying that these features may have appeared earlier in history, scholars emphasize that these elements collectively became dominant features in society that organized people's daily lives in new and powerful ways, thus setting the modern period apart from previous historical periods.

"Modern" lost its meaning as a chronological term that simply denoted a new historical period as it became intertwined with various ideological-based processes that turned it into a normative category. Totalities of history, especially those articulated by Karl Marx and G. W. F. Hegel, configured the modern as an essential stage of history that needed to be reached in order to achieve progress and the unfolding of model personhood and society. These totalities envisioned a linear history with a beginning, middle, and end through which the goals of the respective histories were played out, and, more important, they located the origins of these historical totalities in the West. For both Hegel and Marx, these histories were universal totalities in that their goals applied not only to Westerners, but also to people and societies throughout the world. What was right for Westerners in their present and future was appropriate and right for non-Westerners because these historical totalities were presumed to be based on universal beliefs and categories. These totalities of history ultimately became the authoritative philosophies or ideologies on modernity that promised a positive progression of society.[12]

Framed as "truth" and what "ought" to be and backed by political and military power, theories on modernity were exported to many parts of the non-West through Western colonialism and imperialism. In particular, they forced people in East Asia to organize knowledge in a particular way and to adopt a particular ideological orientation for political, economic, and social development. In terms of the production of knowledge, there are a number of examples of Japanese, Korean, and Chinese scholars in the late nineteenth century using Hegel's theory to dig into the past and identify which institutions and elements to eliminate or cultivate for the purpose of becoming modern. Sinologists and historians in Meiji Japan, for example, constructed new categories for historical investigation, such as Tōyō (Orient) and Shina (China), based on the epistemological framework on modern historical development found in the West. They used these categories to investigate the origins of the nation and Japan's historical development in East Asia in order to validate its ability to become modern and ultimately lead other Asian countries to achieve modernity.[13] As for ideology, a diverse group of people in East Asia during the late nineteenth and early twentieth centuries, including government officials, intellectuals, and social reformers, were guided by the belief that the modern period was the highest stage of humanity and a universal phenomenon that began in the West. Therefore, in order to start the linear development toward modernity in which one stage of development led to another and ultimately ended with "catching up with the West," proponents of modernization recognized it as necessary to adopt the "civilized and enlightened" ideas, practices, and institutions popular in the West.[14] In other words, government leaders, intellectuals, and social reformers in Korea, China, and Japan pursued a process of "modernization" that included reforms such as constructing a strong central state, developing industrial capitalism, fostering nationalism, and promoting urbanization.

As a category to organize knowledge and guide practice, modernity, or more specifically multiple theories on modernity, influenced notions of the ideal form of human subjectivity and society. More than just capturing imaginations and remaining in the world of ideas, these theories pushed intellectuals, politicians, and ordinary citizens to materially organize the world in order to reach the goal of becoming modern—a process that reshaped the political, economic, and social landscapes of East Asia. Before and after 1945, the quest to realize modernity through modernization produced effects in East Asian societies and countries that were far from the promising results guaranteed by these theories: imperialism, colonialism, war, political authoritarianism, social division, ecological ruin, and wide-ranging economic inequality. In effect, modernization has set into motion far-reaching and unanticipated changes that have extended well into the present.

Since the late nineteenth century, Protestant Christianity has been an important source and system of ideas and knowledge for intellectuals, politicians, and everyday people in Korea, China, Taiwan, and Japan to help them negotiate modernity and give them meaning and direction in a changing present, especially as imperialism and colonialism have threatened their countries' sovereignty. Protestant Christianity in East Asia, in particular, was often mediated and understood through the history and the particular cultural and social structures of a local area or a given people. Through this interaction, Protestant Christianity inspired new forms of subjectivity, visions of society, and conceptions of national identity. Moreover, new forms of Protestant Christianity emerged and took on characteristics of "new religions." Today, Protestant Christianity has thrived in China and especially in Korea, which today is the second largest exporter of missionaries in the world.

Although the missionary legacies in East Asia have been an important part of the story, the chapters presented in this volume explore the ways in which Christianity was given shape and form by those who received it. As one of our contributors documented in an earlier study, indigenous forms took root often in direct resistance to missionary efforts that failed to reach deeply into the souls of the people. While understanding indigenous forms of Christianity is important, the contribution of *Encountering Modernity* lies less in parsing out what is native versus foreign and more in the analysis and interpretation of contact and exchange, negotiation, and adaptation. It is in those intersections, tensions, and transitions that we discover a role for this religious tradition as part of its larger context and its societal influence that is greater than numbers of adherents might suggest.[15]

In addition, many of the authors of this volume are attentive to transnational processes, such as how Koreans, Chinese, Taiwanese, and Japanese people "exported" Christianity back to other parts of the world, including the United States, through an investigation of Asian American Christian experience. Increasingly, the line between Asian and Asian American Studies has been blurred, reflecting the movements of people, goods, and ideas that have been taking place for some time between East Asia and the United States. The fields have distinctive legacies, but there is a convergence taking place that is opening up greater opportunities for conversation and dialogue. In that sense, this volume brings together what have often been treated as separate spheres. Ultimately, these chapters introduce new methodologies for the study of the relationship between Christianity and modernity in East Asia and its diasporas that draw up theoretical tools found in the areas of history, sociology, religious studies, and cultural studies.

The transnational approach also complicates long-standing categories and dividing lines such as "East" and "West." Christianity was very much a part of and in some cases directly facilitated the movement and multidirectional flow of labor and capital. How do we make sense of terms like "east" and "west" when a variety of Christianity born out of contact and exchange in East Asia is rerouted to the country that sent the missionaries to East Asia and then is planted in locales marked by different racial, social, and cultural dynamics? In addition, what does it mean that Korea sends so many missionaries throughout the world, including to regions thought to be the core of "Western" Christianity?

In effect, *Encountering Modernity* demonstrates that it makes less and less sense to think of Christianity as a "Western" religion rather than as a world religion. Lamin Sanneh, among others, has pointed to a resurgence of Christianity in the post–World War II period in which Christianity has become the principal religion of the peoples of the world with over 2 billion adherents. This resurgence has been marked by the twilight of the Western phase of Christianity. The dynamic growth of Christianity in Africa, Asia, and Latin America has signaled the early stages of a Christianity centered on regions once considered the edges of the religious tradition, including East Asia and Asian America.[16]

While the theme of religion and modernity underlies and connects the chapter of this book, four more specific themes tie certain chapters together: (1) the links between economy and religion, (2) religion as a medium for social relationships, (3) the sacred and social activism, and (4) national identity and religion. Links between economy and religion are a well-studied theme in various disciplines. Rejecting the notion that economy and religion represent autonomous spheres, scholars such as Max Weber and Karl Polanyi have shown how religious beliefs legitimize and motivate economic practices, and the organization of the economy has often affected religion. Contemporary discourse on the relationship between religion and economy has been significantly shaped by anthropologists, such as Jean and John Comaroff, who have demonstrated that resurgence of religion depends on socioeconomic conditions and that sacred signs and symbols in occult economies have often served as popular means to negotiate and control the forces of capitalism. Contributing to this discourse on the connection between capitalism and religion through multiple historical sources, Albert L. Park examines the process in which capitalism unfolded in Korea through ideas and institutions developed by the Protestant Christian Church after 1885. Specifically, through a study of the Nevius Plan and the Industrial Education Departments, Park argues that the Protestant Christian Church supplied language and practices that exposed Koreans to the principles of capitalism. The Nevius Plan, which promoted a financially self-supporting native church, introduced Korean followers to a new language of money, work, and economy, while Industrial Education Departments became places where young Koreans actually experienced the principles of capitalism by learning business skills and how to manufacture various goods. Park contributes to the scholarship on the history of capitalism in Korea by analyzing the historical links between religion and economics. Eun Young L. Easley's chapter continues the dialogue on the relationship between religion and economy by documenting the growth of megachurches in Korea since the 1990s, especially the impact of neoliberalism on Korean Christians. Within this context, Easley pays attention to what she terms starter megachurches, large congregations that have come into being recently, which represent the latest era of postwar Korean Christianity. The argument forwarded is that these churches reflect a postindustrial society in which leading pastors have embraced an individual orientation geared toward personal responsibility for material success that supports the free flow of capital, less governmental intervention, and the acceptance of social inequality. These starter megachurches have also employed market adaptations such as online stores and themed social services, providing comfort and meaning in times of rapid global change.

Alongside religion and economy, two chapters by a historian and a sociologist examine the theme of religion as a medium for social relationships. Religion's role in cultivating and sustaining social relationships and communities has been a popular subject of study toward understanding how individuals foster means of exchange and contact in the face of capitalist forces that have been known to create social inequality and conflicts. These two chapters skillfully document and analyze the relationship between religion and community formation in relation to changing material conditions within Chinese, Taiwanese, and Taiwanese American Christian communities. Joseph Tse-Hei Lee's chapter draws on Western archival materials, local congregational histories, and fieldwork data to analyze the integration of Christianity into rural China during the latter half of the nineteenth century and into the twentieth century in Guangdong Province in southern China. Lee traces how Christianity spread through lineage networks that adapted and indigenized teachings and rituals to their unique cultural contexts. In the process, these Chinese Christians formed a regional hub of religious activity outside the English Presbyterian Mission headquarters in the treaty port of Shantou. The process of contact and exchange spawned new and reinforced old identities among the village converts, underscoring the linkages between Christianity and Chinese grassroots society. Carolyn Chen connects the development of Christianity among contemporary Taiwanese Americans to both the large-scale twentieth-century political, economic, and social transformations in East Asia, and the individual and communal everyday realities of Taiwanese Americans. Transformations in Taiwan and around the globe created the conditions for the mass migration of an educated Taiwanese population to the United States. Although the majority of Taiwanese Americans came to the United States as nominal Buddhists, many were attracted to Christianity because ethnic churches responded to their practical needs as a displaced population. Taiwanese Americans used their newfound Christianity to reconstruct their communities, families, and selves in the United States. These two chapters give us a nuanced picture of religion as an institution for social relations while providing details that further explain why people value religion in modern society.

The theme of the sacred and social activism connects three chapters, as each one explores the ways in which followers of Protestant Christianity pursued political, economic, and social reforms and the establishment of a heaven on earth as means for advancing the principles and objectives of their religion. Each of the chapters shows how local and global conditions shaped Christian theologies into forces that inspired and undergirded social movements to secure people's bodies, minds, and souls. Kyusik Chang engages the issue of modernity in Korea during the Japanese colonial period (1910–1945) with the city of P'yŏngyang serving as a case study. Chang is less interested in church growth and missions, and focuses instead on how Koreans embraced Christianity as a model of modern Western civilization. Christianity helped to create a public sphere through organizations like the Young Men's Christian Association (YMCA) in which debates took place on a wide range of topics. Leaders like Cho Man-sik envisioned a Christian basis of commerce as a basis for the building of the kingdom of God and an independent Korea against the backdrop of Japanese colonialism. Yunjae Park's chapter also looks at Christianity during the colonial period, tracing the history of the Severance Hospital in Korea as it transformed from a government hospital to a Christian institution. Those associated with the hospital from 1885 to 1945 had to navigate operations under the Korean government and then Japanese colonialism while also addressing differing missionary expectations of how the hospital was to function as an arm of evangelistic efforts in Korea. Medical missionaries as well as mission personnel wrestled with how to frame health care and the practice of medicine as a Christian vocation of compassion in a secular setting and a larger society in which Christianity operated as a distinct minority. Finally, a transnational-based Christian social activism is explored in the chapter by Mark Mullins that follows the expansive career of the progressive Japanese Christian leader Kagawa Toyohiko. Mullins situates Kagawa within a global Christianity in which the trajectory of Japanese Christianity was not limited to or dictated by a missionary agenda. A well-educated and cosmopolitan figure, Kagawa through his writings and activities spawned an international Christian social movement during the 1920s through the 1950s. The United States played a key role for Kagawa, through his experiences as a student but also as a source of support for his ideas and institution building that included Japanese American Christians. Together these three chapters help us understand the factors and reasons behind the rise of faith-based social movements that deemphasize conversion, while Park's chapter specifically gives further insight into why conservative Christian leaders and followers have criticized any movement other than those that directly evangelize and seek to convert people.

Finally, the theme of national identity and religion is explored and investigated in four chapters that cover Japanese, Chinese, and Korean American communities. Studies on the intersection between nationalism and religion reveal that religious ideas and practices have commonly legitimized and reaffirmed nationalist principles and have been used to foster a national body. Studies also show that religion has served as a counterforce to national ideologies by offering principles that question standard political discourse and by cultivating loyalties beyond the boundaries of the nation-state. The two chapters on Christianity in Japan before 1945 shed further light on this complicated area between religion and nationalism. In Garrett Washington's chapter, the focus is on nation-making in Japan during the late nineteenth and early twentieth centuries and how Protestant churches provided one of the many spaces in which Japanese peoples added their own interpretations to those being constructed by the government. In particular, pastors came to embody visions of the nation for Japan's well-educated, well-traveled, and sociopolitically concerned new middle class. Washington moves the discussion of pre–World War II Japan away from a simplistic link between Christianity and a jingoistic nationalism to a more diversified and complex understanding of the relationship between religion and the state. Sermons of pastors preaching during these times provide insights into the process of modernization taking place in Japan and the ways that they used the lens of Christianity to make sense of these issues. Gregory Vanderbilt's chapter assesses the question of what might constitute "Japanese Christianity" that surfaced in the 1930s at a time of military aggression. Increased political controls and mobilization of the populace, recognizable as fascism, were swept up into ideology that promised the "overcoming of modernity" and the purification of the national body. The first generation of Protestant Christians, who were born into samurai families before Christianity's relegalization in 1873, were passing from the scene, and the generation that was assuming leadership had been born into the ideology of the "emperor system." Vanderbilt unpacks the viability of Christianity itself as it traveled to new situations through second-generation Japanese Christians who published a Christian magazine, the *Voice at the Lakeside.*

David K. Yoo's chapter on diasporic Korean Christianity in the earlier decades of the twentieth century specifically explores the transnational relationship between nationalism and Christianity. Focusing on a publication called the *Korean Student Bulletin,* sponsored by the International YMCA, Yoo documents how Korean international and Korean American college and graduate students navigated their times while attending schools in the United States. Protestant Christianity served as a logic and grammar for students. Relational themes of religion and race, migration and exile, and colonialism and independence frame the discussion and analysis. The intersection between nationalism, religion, and politics is also explored in David Ownby's piece, which chronicles the rise of Protestant Christianity in post-Mao China that has been part of a broader religious revival and that has accompanied China's economic and social transformation. In particular, Ownby follows the "house church" movement, which is the least subject to government control and that stands in contrast to the government-sponsored Protestant Church. Moreover, the chapter focuses on the role of Chinese missionary groups in the diaspora such as the China Soul for Christ Foundation and their high-quality docudramas produced in the United States that "educate" Chinese Protestants on their own history and contemporary situation. Ownby suggests that these dramas may serve as a unifying force for Protestantism in China.

Through a multidisciplinary, comparative approach to exploring multiple themes, *Encountering Modernity* grounds and contextualizes religious ideas, practices, and institutions within material conditions and thus sheds light on the processes of interpreting and practically applying religion in relation to modernity. As the chapters below illuminate, Christian leaders and followers in East Asian and Asian American communities continuously conceptualized and reconceptualized traditional religious language, symbols, signs, and practices as ways to interpret and negotiate the forces of modernity and adapt to built environments that were rapidly changing. In effect, for them, religion became a source for developing their visions of the ideal and of means to give value to and control the changing present as they materialized their spiritual visions. These chapters further show that Christians pursued their religious activities and missions with the same objective as all modernist movements from the left to the right. That is, they sought to bridge the gap between material reality and the ideal in order to achieve meaningful experiences and a secure existence and therefore to domesticate modernity. Thus, the ideas, practices, and institutions of Christian leaders, followers, and groups studied in the book and those of modernist movements converged at times because both sides shared similar encounters and experiences of modernity. Yet, at other times, they diverged because individuals and groups used different language to interpret and negotiate modernity and experiences, beliefs, and practices formed according to different local contexts and built environments.

The narratives that compose *Encountering Modernity* represent a broad-based inquiry into the questions and issues posed here, examining the complexities of Christianity as it played out in East Asia and in its diasporic expressions in the United States. The authors provide fascinating glimpses into a lived religion that took many forms through time and place. Moreover, they supply diverse interpretative lenses through which to explore the varied nature of Christianity and religion in East Asian and Asian American communities. In particular, the chapters by Eun Young L. Easely, Kyusik Chang, and Yunjae Park offer excellent representations of Korean historiography on Christianity that pay close attention to details in their investigation and analysis of specific historical issues, events, and developments. These three chapters introduce readers, who may only be familiar with works by US-trained scholars, to another form of scholarship and methodology to help interpret Christian ideas and institutions in East Asia. None of the contributors, including the scholars from South Korea, would claim a comprehensive methodology or perspective, but what does emerge from this book is a fuller and a more contextualized picture of how a particular religion set into motion an encounter with modernity that had long-lasting and significant consequences for all involved. In the end, the chapters in this book provide valuable contributions to a sustained conversation regarding religion and modernity—grounded in a particular region but with broader implications that stretch well beyond East Asia.

Notes

1. Arimichi Ebisawa, *Christianity in Japan,* part 1: *1543–1858* (Tokyo: Committee on Asian Cultural Studies, International Christian University, 1960); and Arimichi Ebisawa, *Christianity in Japan: A Bibliography of Japanese and Chinese Sources* (Tokyo: Committee on Asian Cultural Studies, International Christian University, 1960).

2. Nicholas Standaert, "New Trends in the Historiography of Christianity in China," *The Catholic Historical Review* 83, no. 4 (October 1997): 574.

3. Ibid.

4. Robert E. Buswell and Timothy S. Lee, eds., *Christianity in Korea* (Honolulu: University of Hawai'i Press, 2007).

5. Hyaeweol Choi, *Gender and Mission Encounters: New Women and Old Ways* (Berkeley: University of California Press, 2009); Kelly H. Chong, *Deliverance and Submission* (Cambridge, MA: Harvard University Asia Center, 2008); and Ryan Dunch, *Fuzhou Protestants and the Making of Modern China, 1857–1927* (New Haven: Yale University Press, 2001).

6. Samuel Hugh Moffett, *A History of Christianity in Asia,* vol. 1: *Beginnings to 1500* (Maryknoll, NY: Orbis Books, 1998), and *A History of Christianity in Asia,* vol. 2: *1500–1900* (Maryknoll, NY: Orbis Books, 1998).

7. Raymond Williams, *Politics of Modernism* (London: Verso Press, 2007), 31.

8. Dong-no Kim, "National Identity and Class Interest in Peasant Movements during the Colonial Period" (unpublished paper, Yonsei University, 2004), 5.

9. Ibid.

10. Ibid., 6–7.

11. Dilip Parameshwa Gaonkar, "On Alternative Modernities," in *Alternative*

Modernity, ed. Dilip Parameshwar Gaonkar (Durham, NC: Duke University Press, 2001), 1–9; Marshall Berman, *All That Is Solid Melts into Air* (New York: Penguin Books, 1982), pts. 3 and 4.

12. See Prasenjit Duara, *Rescuing History From the Nation: Questioning Narratives of Modern China* (Chicago: University of Chicago Press, 1995).

13. Stefan Tanaka, *Japan's Orient* (Berkeley: University of California Press, 1995).

14. Andre Schmid, *Korea between Empires* (New York: Columbia University Press, 2002).

15. Mark Mullins, *Christianity Made in Japan: A Study of Indigenous Movements* (Honolulu: University of Hawai'i Press, 1998).

16. Lamin Sanneh, *Disciples of All Nations: Pillars of World Christianity* (New York: Oxford University Press, 2005).

PART I

Economy and Religion

1

A Sacred Economy of Value and Production

Capitalism and Protestantism in Early Modern Korea (1885–1919)

Albert L. Park

This essay argues that Western missionaries contributed to the cultivation of new forms of economic thought and practice through the establishment of ideological and physical structures between 1885 and 1919. Ideologically, through the Nevius Plan, which encouraged the construction of financially self-sustaining churches throughout Korea, missionaries taught church members that they were each stakeholders in their church and had the duty to contribute money constantly to ensure its survival and vitality. This idea helped promote a view of money as a form of productive capital, while it also transformed the definition of labor for Koreans to mean an activity necessary for the accumulation of money. The Nevius Plan also put into place physical structures called Industrial Education Departments (IEDs), factory-like settings where Korean students acquired industrial skills and knowledge, manufactured goods that were sold to the public, and consequently learned and experienced the process of the production, exchange, and circulation of goods for the market. Through the Protestant Church, Korean Christians encountered new language and practices that not only gave spiritual justification for the production of wealth, but also provided the means to acquire and circulate money and capital. Through such processes, Korean Christians learned how to behave as capitalists.

By critically studying missionary activities to produce new forms of economic behavior grounded in religion, this essay seeks both to augment the empirical data and arguments already put forward by economic and religious historians and to expand methods of exploring noneconomic data and historical materials to excavate the processes through which capitalism developed in modern Korea.[1] An important goal of this essay is to push the fields of both economic and religious history to incorporate different ways of thinking about the relationship between religion and economics. Indeed, scholars of Korea's complex economic history such as Kim Yŏng-sŏp, Hong Sŏng-chan, Pang Kie-chung, and Carter Eckert have played important roles in laying out how capitalism originated in Korea during the eighteenth century, owing to internal developments such as technological innovations, and further expanded and transformed when Korea was connected to the global market after 1876 and underwent industrialization beginning in the 1920s under Japanese colonial rule (1910–1945).[2] However, they have paid little attention to the significant role Christian missionaries from the West have played in spreading ideologies and building institutions that fostered capitalist modernity. In particular, these scholars have overlooked individuals at work between the 1905 Protectorate and the start of massive capitalist developments after 1919, when the Japanese colonial state embarked on major initiatives to boost agricultural output. In contrast, scholars of the history of Christianity in Korea such as Kenneth Wells, Jim Yong Kim, and Kyusik Chang have provided valuable information and analyses on the role of missionaries and Korean Christians in cultivating capitalism in Korea. However, works by these and other scholars of Korean Christianity contain little information on how the Nevius Plan and IEDs specifically influenced the development of capitalism in modern Korea.[3] In fact, books and articles about the Nevius Plan and IEDs rarely discuss how they might have played a role in the development of capitalist thought and practices in the everyday lives of Koreans.[4]

While seeking to bridge the gap between economic and religious histories of modern Korean, this essay also seeks to enhance our understanding of how Korean capitalism unfolded through a diverse process that involved multiple institutions and agents by specifically examining the role of the Protestant Church after 1885 in fostering thoughts and behaviors associated with capitalism. This study is indebted to Max Weber's *The Protestant Ethic and the Spirit of Capitalism* and takes seriously Weber's belief that the understanding of capitalist development must include a study of ideas and how they become effective forces in history. Along with Weber, this essay is also influenced by the research and theoretical work of anthropologists, especially the works of Jean Comaroff and John Comaroff. Recently, anthropologists have increasingly conducted detailed ethnographies on the interaction of capitalism and economics in various societies and have come up with categories and arguments that illuminate the relationship between religion and economics, especially the theory that religious language endows money with a sacred or magical quality that sustains efforts to accumulate money and wealth and the understanding that people view religions as reliable sources for meaning and direction in the midst of changes caused by economic forces.[5]

The 1876 Treaty of Kanghwa started the process of moving Korea away from the Chinese-centered tributary system and toward a new international system. The Korean connection to the modern world system not only forced Korean statesmen to contemplate new political measures to deal with the rising threat of Japanese and Western imperialism but soon contributed to the growth and expansion of the emerging native capitalist economy. The political and economic transformations played a large part in the ultimate demise of the Neo-Confucian order in Korea through the Kabo Reforms (1894–1895), which dismantled long-standing structures that embodied Neo-Confucian principles. After the Kabo Reforms, Koreans entered a period of "breakdown," which Charles Taylor defines as being "when people are expelled from their old forms . . . before they can find their way in the new structures."[6] During this time, many Koreans searched for new ideological structures that would not only give them an understanding of present conditions, but also order and make meaningful the shifting material reality in the modern world. Since Neo-Confucianism and other long-standing systems of thought like Buddhism no longer supplied adequate direction to their lives, many Koreans turned to new native religions such as Tonghak and Namhak in rural areas. This turn signified Koreans' desire to find new beliefs that framed the social order and promised the arrival of a better social world.[7]

Protestant Christianity offered a cultural matrix through which Koreans could acquire knowledge about how to have meaningful social lives and navigate a path to modernity. Through this cultural matrix, Christians worked out new ideas about economics or what were appropriate economic practices. New attitudes on economics were institutionally forged and cultivated through the Nevius Plan, designed by John L. Nevius (1829–1893), a Northern Presbyterian missionary. Born in Ovid, New York, and educated at Princeton Theological Seminary, Nevius moved in 1853 to China, where he used his experiences spreading the message of Protestant Christianity in Ningbo and Shandong to develop a blueprint for missionaries on how to establish native churches and a Christian movement that could be maintained without the direct supervision of missionaries.[8] In his plan, Nevius called for a self-propagating, self-governing, and self-supporting church. This three-step approach to building a vibrant Christian movement challenged the typical missionary program in which the missionary assumed the lead role in evangelizing, building churches, funding programs, and expanding the influence of Christianity in society. According to Nevius, if natives took ownership of the Christian movement by organizing church activities, they would feel independent and be motivated to expand Christianity's presence. Stressing this point, he wrote, "The 'New' [Nevius] way . . . believes that the principle of independence and self-reliance, applied from the very beginning, will soonest bring about the establishment of independent, self-reliant, aggressive native churches."[9]

In his plan of action, financial support of all church activities was the basis for fostering self-reliance.[10] Building a church, supporting the pastor and church workers, running educational programs, and providing aid to the poor were activities that had to be funded by money coming from native followers.[11] The traditional model of missionaries paying pastors and funding all church activities only encouraged Korean dependency by making it unlikely that Koreans would ever strive to build a Christian society without the help of missionaries. Recognizing the importance of a financially independent native church, Nevius stressed that the church needed to exert continual pressure on members to increase their gifts, which presumably included money. For Nevius, the church as an institution carried the responsibility to exhort and move its members to give money and other material goods continually in order for the native church to grow and thrive.

Invited by Presbyterian missionaries in Korea, Nevius traveled throughout Korea for two weeks in 1890, and missionaries quickly embraced his message on how to build a self-sustaining, long-lasting native church. Following his visit, various missions adopted his ideas on missionary work as policy and distributed a booklet on Nevius' ideas to new missionaries arriving in Korea.[12] In 1893, the Council of Missions, a governing body for missionaries in Korea, officially adopted the Nevius Plan.[13] Among missionary groups, Presbyterians became the strongest supporter of carrying out Nevius' suggestions. Indeed, even before the ruling by the Council of Missions, Presbyterians institutionalized the self-financing mandate by issuing rules in 1891 and 1893 stating that missionaries were required to press the newly converted Korean Christian to contribute money and other resources to the creation of an "aggressive church."[14] The Presbyterian Church organized a Visitation Committee, made up of Korean ministers and elders, who traveled around Presbyterian churches to set the standards for financial support for churches and to "visit them again if the offerings do not come in, and generally see to it that the situation is covered." Foreign missionaries preferred that Koreans do the work in the Visitation Committees of making sure members continue to support the church financially. According to Charles Allen Clark, "as Koreans, they can exert a pressure which no missionary could apply."[15]

Among the various expenses, church leaders appeared to make a concerted effort to push followers to raise money for a church building. According to Alex A. Pieters, when first organized, churches should immediately conduct an organized campaign to collect money to purchase or construct a church building:

> Begin to agitate the question about purchasing or building a house of worship as soon as the group is organized, and start a church building fund. Have the congregation save as much as possible from their Sunday collections toward that fund; have a special subscription taken up to pay into the fund so much per week, urging the men who have no money, to make a pair of straw shoes a week, or gather a load of brush wood, and the women to save from their rice a little each day. Also teach the people to make contributions toward the fund on special occasions, such as birthday, times of special thanksgiving, etc.[16]

Pieters also suggested that church leaders talk with "financially able men" whose acts of giving could be used as examples for others to follow. Yet

Pieters made it clear that all needed to give money to the church and to perform labor of any kind to raise the money and resources for the church building fund.

Presbyterian financial records reveal that this message of giving money resonated with followers. From 1897 to 1919, the total contributions made to the church increased from $1,042 to $188,674, mostly through contributions made by Koreans.[17] Between 1894 and 1909, financial support from Korean followers led to the construction of 780 new church buildings. Ninety-four percent of the 1,052 Koreans working for the Presbyterian Church in different capacities were financially supported by Koreans. Moreover, by 1934, nearly all of the salaries of three hundred Korean pastors were paid by the Korean Presbyterian Church rather than by funds coming from missionary organizations. The generous support of church activities by Korean congregants even extended into the realm of education, with Korean Christians supporting schools first created by missionaries, such as primary schools, night schools, Bible institutes, and vacation Bible schools.[18]

Numerous stories about Koreans in the Presbyterian Church giving money and resources to strengthen and expand the church added to the statistical evidence detailing the financial generosity of Korean Christians. Although missionaries probably embellished individual stories, that there were so many stories attests to the fact that many Koreans did financially support their churches. Korean Christian leaders and missionaries played a role in urging followers to give money to their churches. For example, Horace G. Underwood wrote about a Korean deacon's challenge to his followers to contribute 1,000 yen to construct a building for Saemunan Church.[19] Leaders often couched their challenges in vibrant religious language. One pastor asked his congregation to give nickel and silver rather than copper coins since Jesus' sacrifice made followers clean: "Now, when through his sacrifice we are white, shall we not give Him white money instead of only the darkest and poorest?"[20] Missionaries also wrote about how Korean followers donated material objects to support church activities rather than money. In the early 1900s, James Gale wrote that, during times of collection to build a church in Seoul, "many a dinner has been foregone that the money might go into the church, and many a new dress, silver hairpins with jade ornaments, and rings, found their way into the collection plate."[21] Alongside money and these objects, Gale remarked, followers also maintained a practice of putting rice, a commodity that was just as valuable as money, into the Sunday offering plate.

The statistical evidence and stories about giving point to the idea that Korean Christians in the Presbyterian Church were ideologically conditioned to give money. The church became a disciplinary site in which the importance of giving was impressed upon followers. Korean Christians responded to this discipline by internalizing new ideas about money. For many Korean churchgoers, money took on new value as a sacred means to achieve positive spiritual results. Indeed, as Korean followers found themselves inundated with charitable demands, they came to believe that money should be valued as a means for spreading God's message and turning Korea into a Christian nation. One article reported that rural Korean women set aside portions of uncooked rice that would otherwise have been consumed by family members and sold them to support church activities.[22] Another article titled "How Korean Women Give" described how two women raised ten chickens, sold them for a profit, then gave the money to their church to support missionary work.[23] The persistence of the women above to obtain money reveals that the underlying logic behind their behavior was the belief that money was the key mechanism for realizing God's plans for Korea. Money was the necessary capital for accomplishing the church's goals. According to Yun Ch'i-ho, a leading Korean Christian leader, "If money is power anywhere it should be in the church, not for pride and luxury but for doing good."[24] For Yun, "doing good" meant supporting activities that would advance the mission of Protestant Christianity to create a Korean Christian kingdom. As the ideas of the Nevius Plan spread to other denominations, and as Koreans witnessed the many social, religious, and cultural advancements made by the various Protestant groups in the late nineteenth and early twentieth centuries, an increasing number of Korean Christians presumably became convinced that money had the magical power to bring about spiritual transformations, thus increasing their motivation to give to the church.

Missionary accounts also strongly suggest that Korean converts discovered a new rationale for making money or accumulating profit—in order to support the native church. After being converted and hearing messages of self-support in his church, a Korean Christian businessman, who cared more about pleasure and passion than work, said:

> *Moksa* [pastor], it does not seem right that I, a strong, healthy man, should be idle. Though I could live without work, these hands of mine are strong and skilful, and I have a good trade. Why should not I work that I might have more whereof to give to God? Since I have no education, and the gift of speech is not with me, I can not preach or teach the people about Jesus their Savior, but I can earn money and give that to send someone who can, and this is my ambition.

The missionary further wrote that the businessman went on to devote regularly a portion of his earned wealth to the church, and "the more he made the more he had to give, and the more he gave the more he enjoyed the services of the Lord."[25] This story reveals that the Korean Christian businessman had reconceptualized labor and hard work as requirements for any Christian wanting to make money and therefore promote God's work or "enjoy" the benefits of a relationship with God. In fact, Presbyterians after 1894 agreed never to live in idleness. Instead, they would be industrious and "diligent in business" since God ordered that all followers live by working.[26] Followers were reminded of this requirement to work vigorously at the baptism ceremony.[27] Practicing faith in the Presbyterian Church and other Protestant denominations entailed practical labor. Work and the process of making money were no longer seen as mundane economic practices in society; instead they became sacred acts.

Through the church, Korean Christians were exposed to the principles of capitalism. Indeed, capitalism functions based on the continual process of money being invested in a commodity that will be bought or sold to make more money and profit (M-C-M). As Marx points out, this process defines the way capital is produced and reproduced.[28] In the case of Korean Christians, making money and producing capital were not solely for material gain but had sacred purposes. The development of new economic ideas and practices via the church in Korea mirrored developments in other areas of the world where missionaries sought to build Christian nations. For example, in their studies of British Methodist missionaries to southern Africa in the eighteenth and nineteenth centuries, Jean Comaroff and John Comaroff identified new ideas and practices that fostered a relationship between Christian enterprise and economic (capitalist) activity. Through this connection, it was thought that the "economy was a part of a sacred order that described the production of value and virtue in the world."[29]

This sacred order determined economic activity, especially the making of money and the accumulation of capital, which was seen as a legitimate way to advance the mission of Protestant Christianity and concretely realize spiritual gifts under Wesleyan theology.[30]

After the 1876 Treaty of Kanghwa, Koreans found themselves caught between two systems of economic thought. On the one hand, Neo-Confucianism viewed money as corrosive to mind and body, and the pursuit of profit and great wealth through commerce as destructive to society. On the other hand, procapitalist ideas promoted the development of a strong money and industrial/commercial economy. Living in this contested ideological environment, Korean Christians discovered a religious language regarding the economy that not only gave them direction on how to live their everyday lives, but also assured them that their actions were correct. Many Korean Christians thought capitalist economic practices were validated by biblical texts, the fundamental source of knowledge.

The Korean church's interpretation of the economy and economic practices may help explain why a large number of Korean merchants and wealthy farmers embraced Christianity. Identified by internal development theorists as the primary force behind the early development of a capitalist economy in Korea from the eighteenth century, merchants, wealthy farmers, and others involved in the burgeoning commercial activities became active members of the Protestant Church. Membership records of churches in Seoul reveal that a considerable number of Koreans who attended church came from the world of commerce. For example, the records of Saemunan Church indicate that the church drew those engaged in industry, farming, trading, and other commercial activities.[31] In P'yŏngyang, one of the leading commercial centers during the Chosŏn period and the center of Presbyterian activities, many merchants and businessmen became associated with Presbyterian churches.[32] Yi Seung-hun (1864–1930) stood out among those associated with both the church and commerce. Yi is mainly known for his nationalist activities in the Sinminhoe and for founding Osan Academy (1907), which became a Christian school. However, as a leading merchant, Yi played an active role in organizing a number of business ventures with fellow Presbyterians. In 1908, for example, Yi helped to start Sangmudongsa (1908), one of the first general merchandise stores in Korea. In 1909, Yi also led the movement to start joint-stock companies through the P'yŏngyang Chagi Chusik Hoesa (P'yŏngyang Porcelain Company), which raised 60,000 won and employed sixty-one Koreans by the time it closed in 1919.[33]

Merchants and figures in commerce also found opportunities to come together at church and organize groups to invest in companies throughout the peninsula. In 1911, merchants and commercial figures in the Presbyterian Church started the P'yŏngyang Chŏkŭm Chohap (P'yŏngyang Savings Cooperative) and supplied capital for a silk-reeling company.[34] Alongside the P'yŏngyang Chŏkŭm Chohap, the Kŭnkŏm Chŏch'uk Siksan Chohap (Cooperative for Thrift, Savings, and Industry) originated in 1917 through the efforts of Korean Christian leaders, missionaries, and Korean lay leaders, who presumably were part of the commercial class, and invested in a factory that manufactured socks.[35]

As capitalist ideas spilled out from the church and infiltrated people's everyday lives in places such as P'yŏngyang and Seoul, they came to be practiced in diverse ways and affected areas in Korea differently based on local conditions, demands, and developments. It could be argued that Korean Christian merchants and businessmen in P'yŏngyang took their knowledge of capitalism and applied it toward organizing new forms of exchange that could develop a community through which individuals cooperatively worked to limit Japanese political and economic influence on the peninsula.[36] More than just serving as tools to advance material interests, economic beliefs learned through the church also appeared to inform and structure political, social, cultural, and nationalistic practices and developments in late-nineteenth and early-twentieth-century Korea.

Though merchants and commercial figures seem to have been drawn to churches to advance their business interests and nationalist causes, they may also have embraced Christianity because of the way religious language helped them reconceptualize their identities and roles in society. In the church, Koreans who worked in business encountered a language based on the principles of the Nevius Plan that legitimized their economic practices instead of criticizing them. Under Christian theology, the economic activities and productivity of businesspeople took on new meanings as sacred rather than destructive acts based on self-interest. Korean businessmen discovered a new identity and purpose in life as productive Christians who could give money and capital to promote God's work in Korea. The impact of a new epistemological order on Korean businessmen and merchants mirrored discursive developments in late Tokugawa

Japan when merchants in Osaka reconceptualized themselves as important agents in maintaining a strong economy that would enable the safe and healthy development of people and society.[37]

As the Presbyterian Church refined the disciplinary structure that encouraged the idea and practice of giving, factors that would enable the operation of a capitalist economy also began to emerge in Korea under the direction of Korean and Japanese officials. The Kabo Reforms dismantled the Neo-Confucian social hierarchy system and turned human labor into a commodity. The Japanese colonial state's wide-scale land survey (1910–1918) officially codified private landownership for the first time in Korea, thus transforming land into a commodity. Currency and banking reforms started by institutions such as Dai-Ichi Bank and the Bank of Chosen transformed lending institutions into capitalist banks. The creation of an elaborate infrastructural system consisting of railways, roads, and ships facilitated quicker circulation and transportation of commodities and labor and connected Korea to a market beyond its borders. These material developments facilitated capitalist development in Korea, but articles and historical documents from 1885 to 1919 strongly suggest that principles and ideas about capitalism were formed at the everyday level through institutions like the Protestant Church. These newly learned ideas not only informed Koreans about how they should engage in economic practices in society but, more important, provided the rationale as to why they should engage in those practices. As Protestant missionary groups besides Presbyterians adopted the principles of the Nevius Plan, conceptions of self-financing, money, and work-for-profit spread throughout the Christian community, which by 1920 had grown to 200,000 members. The Nevius Plan had more than just a religious effect on Koreans. It also made a social and economic impact as it molded followers into workers who produced capital, invested it, and used it in a rational manner to advance their businesses and promote the goals of the church.

The "ideal Korean Christian" was expected to produce for a profit and use his or her earned money to ensure the growth of the church in the present and the future. The question was how would the ideal Korean Christian make money? For many missionaries in Korea, the answer to the question lay in industrial production. Rather than solely focus on the improvement of agriculture and related business in Korea, which was the main occupation for most Koreans, many missionaries called for the development of an industry-based economy. The Western missionaries' firm belief in industrializing Korea was unsurprising considering how they associated industrialization with modernity and being "civilized and enlightened." This line of thinking among missionaries solidified at a time when discourse on modernity in the United States and other Western countries privileged an industry-based capitalist economy as a requirement to become "modern." In the United States, industrialization boomed and became a major component of the economy starting in the mid-nineteenth century. Materializing as an "uneven movement" with textile manufacturing taking place in both homes and factories, industrialization reshaped the American economic and social landscape as it introduced new forms and purposes for labor and turned America into an economically powerful nation.[38] The fast-paced growth of industrialization and its beneficial results convinced Americans that industrialization equaled modernity. The Protestant Christian community, especially in the northern United States, not only associated industrialization with the modern, civilization, and enlightenment, they also believed that Christianity undergirded great developments in Western societies. To them, Christian principles were the driving force behind the development of civilized Western countries like the United States.[39]

A number of American missionaries who experienced industrialization in the United States before arriving in Korea decided to push for the development of an industry-based economy in Korea.[40] A. E. Lucas, a missionary who strongly advocated industrializing Korea, expressed the desire for the birth of an industrialized Korea. According to Lucas, the countries of the world were moving from agrarian-based to industry-based economies—an odd comment to make since a large segment of the world's population still worked in agriculture. Lucas believed that Korea should follow this trend to improve its standing in the world economy. He wrote: "With the whole world highly developed in industry and crafts it becomes imperative for Chosen to do her share or the individual [Korean] will degenerate into the coolie of the orient."[41] Lucas believed Koreans had to embrace economic development or else suffer the consequence of becoming a lowly nation of "manual servants." He further wrote: "If this nation is not to sink into oblivion she must work her way up among the family of nations on the industrial ladder."[42]

Korean Christians agreed with the missionaries' vision for Korea. Starting in the late nineteenth century, many Korean Christians believed industrializing was a requirement for becoming a civilized and enlightened (*munmyŏng kaehwa*) country. Along with Protestant Christianity, an industry-based economy was considered a marker of civilization. Korean Christians assumed that industrialization would create a new, more powerful Korea that resembled "civilized and enlightened" Western countries and that could defeat foreign aggressors. Yun Ch'i-ho (T. H. Yun) became one of the leading Korean Christians to think along these lines. Yun wrote several articles in *The Korea Mission Field* that proclaimed Korea's future lay in industry and commerce. Though not totally opposed to an agriculture-based economy, Yun strongly advocated for and justified the creation of industries as a matter of national security. He believed commerce and industry would bring the money needed to buy goods, especially food, to sustain everyday living. Agriculture alone, according to Yun, could not sustain Korea economically. Yun also wrote that industrial development in Korea had to fit the specific conditions of Korea. For example, Koreans should manufacture goods that meet the needs and demands of Koreans. Stressing this point, Yun wrote, "No sensible man, for instance, would start a factory for the manufacture of knives and forks when the mass of the people use spoons and chop-sticks." Yun also stressed that Korean industries should use the natural resources found in Korea rather than depend on imported resources.[43]

Helping Koreans move from an agriculture-based economy to an industry-based one was an immense task. Among the challenges, which included how to spread the message of industrialization widely and set up a system to teach Koreans new industrial trades and skills, missionaries faced the issue of how to convince Koreans to embrace an industrial arts education when many Koreans hoped to become part of the professional class. A. E. Robb, a prominent Canadian Presbyterian missionary, pointed out that "the youth of Korea" were flocking to government schools and that their parents were "making sacrifices" to send their kids to these school in order for them to obtain an education that would help them "get good salaried position as school teachers or as clerks in government offices; or that they may enter college with a view to entering one of the higher professions which will command good salaries."[44] Many young Koreans and their parents rejected not only farming, but also occupations like factory workers, artisans, and traders because they were menial professions that were low paying; young Koreans held out for the prospect of a secure and prosperous future through a professional occupation that promised steady pay and advancement. Robb and several missionaries, however, argued that Koreans would find advancing in society challenging because of restrictions by the government that were anything but favorable to them.[45] To prevent massive numbers of young Koreans from becoming unemployed and turning into discontented youths "who fell an easy prey to Communistic and Bolshevistic propaganda," missionaries stressed that it was imperative to offer Koreans an education in technical training and in trades.[46]

To indoctrinate Korean followers ideologically about the value of industrialization and technical trades, Yun suggested that churches set aside one sermon a month to preach about the "virtues of industry, of thrift and of saving or no sins of laziness, of extravagance, of improvidence and kindred subjects."[47] Sermons and lectures alone, however, were not sufficient, according to Yun. He also insisted on the establishment of institutions where Koreans could learn different skills pertaining to industrial production. Industrial Education Departments (IEDs) filled this role of helping Koreans experience the ideas associated with industry. Starting in the 1890s, IEDs originated as institutions where young Korean students learned different trades and then made and sold finished products as a way to support their education.[48] As the discourse on creating a new industrialized Korean society expanded and gained more traction in the Protestant Church by the early 1900s, IEDs assumed a new purpose of preparing Koreans to be competitive commercially and industrially rather than only helping them pay for their education.

Missionaries mainly established IEDs at Christian schools throughout the Korean Peninsula. By 1919, Western missionaries had built an elaborate educational system that consisted of primary, secondary, and high schools as well as private universities and colleges, such as Sungsil University, Ewha College, and Choson Christian College. Both Presbyterian and Methodist schools created IEDs in their schools. Some of the better-known IEDs were the Anna Davis Industrial Department (1900, Presbyterian), the John D. Wells Industrial Department (1912, Presbyterian), the Mary Helm Industrial Department (1918, Methodist), the Kwangju Lace-Making Department (1918[?], Presbyterian), and the Textile Department of the Songdo Higher Common School (1914, Methodist). Alongside these IEDs founded in Christian schools, the Young Men's Christian Association

(YMCA), mostly led by Methodists and based in Seoul since 1903, started its own IED that later became one of the largest and most comprehensive industrial education programs in Korea.

From their beginnings, the majority of IEDs were tied to a larger system of global finance in that they got their start through generous donations from wealthy industrialists in the United States. Work at the Anna Davis Industrial Department, for example, began through a $5,000 donation from Samuel Davis of Rock Island, Illinois. Davis owned and operated a major utilities company (People's Power Company) that managed waterworks and constructed electric lighting systems. Horace G. Underwood, one of the first Presbyterian missionaries in Korea, "secured through the generosity of an individual, a large sum to provide land, building equipment and a certain amount of capital for this department, as well as the gift of four large modern power looms" for the John D. Wells Industrial Department in 1912.[49] Though Underwood never revealed the donor's name, John T. Underwood, Horace's brother and president of the Underwood Typewriting Company, most likely provided the initial funding for the Wells Industrial Department. As head of a company that was the leading producer of typewriters in the world, John T. Underwood often donated large sums of money to support his brother's missionary activities in Korea, including the start-up capital for Chosen Christian College that amounted to $25,000. Davis' and Underwood's generous donations were not uncommon, as many wealthy industrial families in the United States, particularly families from the Northeast and the Midwest, funded missionary activities in Korea. Like Korean Christians, these wealthy donors viewed money as a productive form of spiritual capital that should be used to spread Christianity. Thus, through IEDs and other missionary activities, industrialists from the United States made spiritual investments in Korea while also making their presence known there.

By soliciting funds from wealthy industrial families and positioning them prominently in the industrial departments, officials at the IEDs defined their departments as places where industry/commerce and Christianity were connected. IEDs would serve as spaces where young Korean Christians learned about industry and commerce and strived to become like Davis and Underwood, that is, economically and spiritually powerful industrialists. Korean Christians in IEDs were envisioned as future leaders of Korea who would pave the way for the creation of a completely industrialized Korean Christian nation. Missionaries showed their serious commitment to cultivating young Korean Christian leaders when they had to select the types of students who would participate in the IEDs. The selection process was rigorous. John D. Wells School, for example, screened students based on letters of recommendation, which mentioned the applicant's financial status and moral stature, from pastors or church officials. A positive letter of recommendation would move an applicant to the second stage of the application process, in which school officials interviewed the applicant. If the applicant passed the first two stages, he or she was required to make a deposit that was only refundable upon completion of the program.[50] Officials at the Wells School undoubtedly used this application process to make sure the applicant was committed and motivated to forge a new livelihood and make himself or herself into a new person who could positively influence others.

To become future industrial leaders, accepted applicants took part in a rigorous educational process that involved learning new ideas and applying the knowledge they acquired in the classroom. The curriculum in all IED classrooms consisted of not only learning about Christian principles and morals, but also improving basic skills such as reading and writing. The John Wells and the Songdo School bolstered native language skills but also required students to learn foreign languages such as Chinese and Japanese. Learning Japanese was not merely an option for students since the colonial government required Japanese to be taught in all schools, including missionary-founded schools, after 1915 in order to obtain a government license. However, requiring students to study Japanese or Chinese also served the larger purpose of preparing students for international commerce and trade since missionary teachers at the IEDs believed foreign language skills would help Koreans broker successful commercial transactions and would advance their prospects throughout East Asia.

The majority of the IEDs also taught students rudimentary business skills. At the John Wells School, for example, students learned how to use the abacus, perform simple arithmetic, and do elementary bookkeeping.[51] Teachers at the school, according to Underwood, also taught students "modern business methods."[52] The YMCA's IED went even further than the Wells School and other IEDs in molding students into successful businesspeople. The YMCA IED offered lectures on themes such as

"The Dignity of Labor," "The Value of Money," and "Methods in the Modern Business World." The YMCA even offered a specialized class titled "Biographical Lectures on the Lives of Successful Businessmen," in which students apparently learned about how particular businessmen became successful.[53] By providing students with a definition of success and how business could enable individuals to achieve that success, the class promised the YMCA IED students that they too could achieve magnificent financial and social results by modeling themselves after the "successful businessmen" they studied. The class served to motivate Korean students in the YMCA IED to be committed to the program and to building an industrialized Korea.

Finally, in their classes, students in IED programs learned trade and technical skills. Following Yun's call for the production of goods that would meet the needs of Korean consumers, the IEDs concentrated on teaching how to produce goods like undergarments, clothing, and lace, and finished goods such as baskets, mats, shoes, machinery, and Western-style furniture.[54] In addition to learning how to manufacture goods, some students trained to become photographers, tailors, typists, or printers. These trade and technical classes truly exposed students, the majority of whose families worked in agriculture, to the industrial process by exposing them to the transformation of raw resources into finished goods. Students most likely became even more enthralled with the industrial process as they learned how to operate machines that manufactured finished goods. At the YMCA IED and the Songdo IED, students learned to operate machines to produce textiles, furniture, and shoes. To give them a complete understanding of machines and keep them updated about the most current trends in machinery, students attended lectures on machines. At the John Wells School, lectures were given on topics such as "gas-machines," "the knitting machine past and present," and "looms past and present."[55] Manufacturing by hand was also taught, but most IEDs emphasized the use of machines to produce various goods since the common discourse on industrial production throughout the world privileged the use of machines.

The only exception to the trend of teaching IED students to use machines took place in female-oriented IEDs, such as the Mary Helm Industrial Department and the Lace-Making IED in Kwangju. At these institutions, instruction on textile production stressed that women use their hands to produce goods. This line of thinking originated from a gendered view of labor that assumed women would be making these goods at home, rather than in a factory. Both male Korean Christian leaders and Western missionaries imagined that a woman was "an intelligent wife, a sweet daughter-in-law, a good housekeeper" in a Korean Christian society.[56] Both male Korean Christians and Western missionaries shared the patriarchal view that informed gendered forms of space in which a woman's place was in the home taking care of the family while the man worked and socialized outside of the home. With this mindset, IED educators thought it was best for women to learn handicrafts, since they would be staying home and taking care of the family.[57] IEDs also aimed to make female students into "wise mothers, good wives" by teaching women washing and ironing, household economy, physical culture, and flower-making.[58] Women were required to take Bible and ethics classes since they were expected to teach their children about morality and religion at home. This gendered treatment of women in the IEDs revealed the contradictions of Christian practice and thought in Korea. Though they preached religious equality, missionaries and Korean Christians often advanced social and economic inequality by upholding gendered forms of labor.

In IEDs, molding young Koreans into future industrialists and businesspeople extended beyond the classroom and into the practical realm. Students practiced what they learned in factory-like settings established in buildings that housed IEDs. When missionaries designed the buildings for IED programs, they recognized it was critical for students to apply what they learned so that the ideas would be inscribed on their minds and bodies. Consequently, the majority of IEDs devoted space in their buildings to rooms that resembled industrial workshops found around the United States. The largest factory spaces were found at the IEDs in the Anna Davis School, the John Wells School, the Songdo Textile Department, and the YMCA. Since the Anna Davis School, the John Wells School, and the Songdo Textile Department primarily taught how to manufacture textiles, these IEDs set up rows of hand, foot, and power looms on the main floor of the IED buildings. Though the Wells School had more looms (thirty-two) than the Davis and Songdo IEDs, the Songdo IED was the most technologically advanced since all twenty of its machines were up-to-date power looms.[59] Since the YMCA IED promoted various types of industrial programs, different rooms were designed like mini-industrial workshops where students practiced using machines. For example, the carpentry room, where students manufactured furniture, held a power-driven turning lathe and a foot-powered mortiser; the machine room contained different types of power equipment that manufactured machines such as the lathe and mortiser used in the carpentry room. The shoe room was, according to a YMCA official, "the first and only factory in Korea employing modern machinery, other than sewing machines, in the manufacture of shoes."[60]

By setting up machines and supplying tools for student to use regularly, missionary leaders organized IED buildings in ways that would give students the opportunity to apply what they learned and prepare for livelihoods anchored by industrial work. The IEDs even forced students to adhere to a rigorous daily schedule of labor in the factories. After their morning classes, IEDs devoted afternoons to work. Just like any factory, each student was given a machine to work. Like factory owners, IED instructors wanted students to perform their tasks correctly, complete their assignments, and work hard. Instructors closely supervised their students and subjected them to surveillance. Some IED supervisors even set up mechanisms to measure students' industriousness. At the Wells School, for example, students' machines had cards on them that showed how many items were to be made, the number of hours worked by each student, and the number of items produced by that student.[61] Through observation and mechanisms such as the cards described above, missionaries made students accountable for their actions. Supervisors presumably punished those students who failed to accomplish their assigned tasks in various ways, including expulsion from the program.

In this environment, missionaries taught Korean students that they had to be productive laborers. More specifically, Korean students learned how to treat workers. They learned that workers had to be subjected to surveillance, disciplined, and punished in order to ensure that they were industrious and labored in a correct manner. Through their daily schedules, IED students, as future entrepreneurs and factory owners, were trained to replicate this system in any workplace so that time would be carefully managed and not wasted, which would allow owners to extract surplus labor, thus earning greater profit. Missionaries believed it was vital to set up these systems of discipline and punishment in order to inscribe the proper way of laboring on the bodies and minds of Koreans since a strong discourse had emerged among Western missionaries that characterized Koreans as lazy and lacking a work ethic.[62] This thought was captured in the following statement by W. L. Swallen of the Presbyterian mission in Korea: "Generally speaking, Koreans are constitutionally lazy. It is born and bred in them. Their phlegmatic temperaments render them thoroughly indisposed to continued or consecutive labor, whether of physical or mental effort. The Koreans are probably the laziest people among nations occupying a cool zone."[63] Missionaries thought Koreans were lazy and possessed no work ethic for various biological and social reasons, including a lack of incentives to work hard since they were long oppressed by the Korean government. Based on these unsubstantiated claims, missionaries in the IED believed their comprehensive educational programs could instill new work habits in Koreans and teach them how to become independent and industrious. C. H. Deal, who led the Songdo IED, described the impact the IED would have on Korean students:

> The student acquires skill, is taught to bear responsibility, to do business for himself, and to be economical; he learns, gets out of the old Korean way of easing along like the pendulum of a clock, and into the way of hustling like the balance wheel of a watch. He is taught not to expect anything without giving its equivalent in service. . . . He learns to be self reliant, self-confident, self-respecting, and independent.[64]

According to Deal, Korean students underwent a disciplinary process where they shed their old, negative characteristics and identities for new and improved personalities that would allow them to advance not only economically but also socially.

In addition to molding Korean students into hard workers, IED classrooms and factories instructed students on the principles of capitalism. Korean students experienced firsthand the process of turning raw materials into finished products that were then sold to the public for money and profit. All of the IEDs sold the finished goods made by students. The YMCA, for example, found a market for its finished furniture in the missionary community, whereas the Kwangju IED exported its lace products to customers in the United States, and the Wells IED developed a customer base for its uniforms.[65] The Songdo IED became the most commercially successful industrial department as its vibrant textile business earned $20,000 by 1919, thus making it the "leading textile factory of the country."[66] IEDs used the revenue from sales to pay students and instructors wages and to maintain IED operations.[67] Students experienced the most essential aspect of capitalism at IEDs when their manufactured goods were exchanged for money. They saw the worth of materials goods measured by their exchange value rather than their use value.[68] They witnessed the production of tradable commodities intended only for exchange.

As students in IEDs prepared to establish an industrial capitalist society in Korea by learning how to operate a business, manufacture commodities, and market their goods, IEDs also enabled students to conceptualize Korean society as an economic system for producing and exchanging goods and services for money and profit. In fact, IED students could probably imagine the entire world, not just Korean society, as an intertwined economic system as they watched the goods they produced exported abroad. The students encountered new social imaginaries that viewed society as the main space for the performance of capitalist activities. Like the Physiocrats and Adam Smith, IEDs helped promote the belief that "the most important purpose and agenda of society [is] economic collaboration and exchange."[69] Moreover, IED students would have believed that these ideas about economics and society were "correct" since they were validated by religious principles, which were considered the most authoritative and authentic principles.

IEDs furnished young Korean students with the knowledge, practices, and language needed to anchor their everyday lives and helped inform the kinds of social relationships they would develop. One can see the far-reaching effect of IED language and practices in the lives of IED graduates—many of whom went on to set up their own businesses in P'yŏngyang and Seoul following graduation.[70] It was no surprise to see many IED graduates setting up businesses in P'yŏngyang since it was one of the leading centers of commerce on the peninsula. In fact, Presbyterian churches in the city made sure that these graduates would survive economically by adopting various measures:

> In the Pyengyang district, there are a dozen such men running iron shops or carpenter shops as a business. The school work department [IED] does not compete with these men. It gives them the field and takes up other lines. Several companies have started making cheap bells for churches, so the work department of the academy and college

> is now confining itself to the more expensive kind, leaving the cheaper field to the private companies.[71]

Missionaries saw these new businesses as positive developments because the practical ideas and skills learned at IEDs helped graduates advance their commercial interests. Moreover, missionaries had to have been pleased that these Korean Christians were becoming industrious laborers who exhibited types of behavior associated with entrepreneurs. Yet students were taught to understand that the purpose of business was not just material gain but also to sustain a capitalist economic system in which money could be made continuously to support church activities and promote Christianity in Korea. Based on their training, they were highly motivated to live out the ideas and practices they learned about in order to realize an authentic life. At a time when political and economic changes were shaking the foundations of many Koreans, Christian beliefs and practices about the economy became valued as a powerful system that could help people realize the spiritual ideal in society and therefore overcome the disjuncture between material reality and representation.

Into the 1920s and 1930s, alongside the continuation of the Nevius Plan, IEDs continued to train young Koreans for a life centered on industrial capitalism. After 1919, however, new developments and challenges emerged that forced the Protestant Christian movement in Korea to move in new directions. The challenge to the established trends of Protestant Christianity came from the rise of new theologies and from visions of modernity that came forward from Korean Christian leaders after the March First movement of 1919, which became one of the largest mass protests against Japanese imperialism. Ironically, during the 1920s and 1930s, through the Nevius Plan, the Protestant Church grew strong enough to produce a number of native Christian pastors, theologians, and leaders who sought more independence from Western missionaries as they developed their own Christian ideas and practices. During this period, many Korean Christian leaders, including Sin Hung-ŭ, were in conflict with missionaries over the theological direction of the church since many missionaries held onto conservative or fundamentalist theologies, whereas some Korean Christians believed in more liberal, socially progressive theologies. This disagreement soon developed into conflict over the best way to help Koreans and what an ideal Christian society looked like. Many Korean

Christians rejected evangelical campaigns and visions of creating an industrial capitalist society anchored by the bourgeoisie in favor of establishing a spiritual, agrarian utopian kingdom on earth that would be anchored by peasants. They rejected the discourse of civilization and enlightenment and industrial capitalism because of their harmful social and economic effects on people and instead supported an alternative vision of modernity that lay in a cooperative-based agrarian society and economy.

Studying the intersection between Christianity and commerce in the early Korean church by focusing on the Nevius Plan and IEDs provides a way to help unravel the complex and multifaceted history of capitalism in Korea. Additionally, this analysis of Christianity and capitalism contributes to the dialogue on the relationship between religion and economics that continues today at a time when the face of capitalism has changed.[72] Contrary to the beliefs of Marx and Weber, religion has not withered away under modernization. Studies on societies throughout the world have shown that the popularity of religion has increased under modernity. The increased interest in religion can be attributed to the fact that timeless religious ideas and symbols can be comforting and meaningful during periods of change, dislocation, and fragmentation, which are characteristics of modernity. Religious ideas and symbols have long been seen as sacred and immutable, thus legitimate and authentic. Therefore, religion is perceived as a system of ideas and practices that speak truthfully about and explain political, economic, social, and cultural developments and events in the profane world. Hence, more than other ideologies, people have turned to religion in order to help rationalize and inform their material practices. In the last decade, the Comaroffs have shown that "occult economies" have grown significantly as people have looked to religion to grasp and control the "arcane forces intervening in the production of value" under neoliberalism.[73] Followers of any religion use religious language to shape and sustain economic processes. Thus, fully understanding what ideologically and materially powers capitalism in a society requires an analysis of religious language, practices, and institutions.

Analyzing the impact of religion on economic structures, including capitalism, also involves studying how the material world influences and shapes religious language and practice. Far from being immutable, religious language and practice have undergone frequent transformations in response to shifts in the modern lived world. The reconstitution of traditional religious beliefs and customs reflects efforts to adequately grasp and handle new forms of power and knowledge structures in a rapidly changing present. Integrating a materialist frame of study into an investigation of religion provides opportunities to uncover and understand how religious figures and groups transformed religions in order to "creatively adapt" under modernity.[74] In the end, a methodological approach that connects religion and economics is necessary to detect and interpret particular, emergent, and complex social processes and patterns in the "dereification of social life—revealing how apparently blind social forces and dumb social coercions are actually intelligible as products of semiotically generated action."[75]

Notes

1. This essay targets Presbyterian and Methodist activities as its main subjects of study since those groups constituted the largest missionary groups in Korea.

2. This essay is theoretically informed by internal development theory, which argues that capitalism in Korea developed as a *process* that internally originated in late Chosŏn (1392–1910) society and advanced starting in the late nineteenth century with the aid of outside influences and institutions such as the Japanese colonial state. See Michael D. Shin and Pang Kie Chung, eds., *Landlords, Peasants, Intellectuals in Modern Korea* (Ithaca, NY: Cornell East Asia Program, 2005), 7.

3. See Chang Kyu-sik, *Ilche ha Han'guk kidokkyo minjokjuŭi yŏn'gu* (Seoul: Hyean, 2001); Jim Yong Kim, "The Role of Christianity in the Economic Modernization of South Korea" (Ph.D. diss., Florida State University, 1984); Kenneth M. Wells, *New God, New Nation: Protestants and Self-Reconstruction Nationalism in Korea, 1896–1937* (Honolulu: University of Hawai'i Press, 1990), 65–66.

4. For example, see Donald N. Clark, *Living Dangerously in Korea* (Norwalk: East Bridge Press, 2003); George Paik, *The History of Protestant Missions in Korea, 1832–1910* (Seoul: Yonsei University Press, 1970).

5. See Jean Comaroff and John L. Comaroff, "Millennial Capitalism: First Thoughts on a Second Coming," in *Millennial Capitalism and the Culture of Neoliberalism*, ed. Jean Comaroff and John L. Comaroff (Durham, NC: Duke University Press, 2001), 1–56.

6. Charles Taylor, "Modern Social Imaginaries," *Public Culture* 14, no. 1 (2002): 99.

7. Kil-myung Ro, "New Religions and Social Change in Modern Korea History," *Review of Korean Studies* 5, no. 1 (June 2002): 31–62.

8. Though first adopted by the Presbyterians, the Nevius Plan "became the standard mission policy for all Protestant groups in Korea." See Sheridan Gilley and Brian Stanley, eds., *Cambridge History of Christianity,* vol. 8 (Cambridge, UK: Cambridge University Press, 2005), 507.

9. Charles Allen Clark, *The Nevius Plan for Mission Work* (Seoul: Christian Literature Society, 1937), 24.

10. His plan for missionary work included ten points. (1) Its most important aspect is the "voluntary system" in contrast to the "employment system." (2) Yet a few paid laborers—helpers or colporteurs—are in charge of more than twenty substations. (3) The means by which converts are brought to the knowledge of the truth is not street preaching to the masses but efforts to influence individuals. (4) The places of worship are supplied by the natives themselves. (5) Sunday services are conducted by the native Christians themselves. (6) In terms of the way in which the native Christian is taught, all church members are learners and teachers as the same time. (7) Organization is flexible. Such churches were not formally organized. (8) Probation of inquirers is not less than six months, and prompt discipline is observed. (9) Contributions are sought for benevolent purposes. (10) These churches are aggressive in spreading the gospel and advancing Christian knowledge. See John L. Nevius, "Mission Work in Central Shantung," in *Sources of Korean Christianity,* ed. Sung-deuk Oak (Seoul: Institute for Korean Church History, 2004), 113.

11. Ibid.

12. Ung Kyu Pak, *Millennialism in the Korean Protestant Church* (New York: Peter Lang, 2005), 96.

13. Ibid.

14. In 1907, a single presbytery formed in Korea, in which the self-support system was further codified. See Clark, *Nevius Plan,* 87–95, 292–301; and Harry A. Rhodes, *A History of the Korea Mission Presbyterian Church U.S.A. 1884–1934* (Seoul: Chosen Mission Presbyterian Church, 1934), 397.

15. Clark, *Nevius Plan,* 300.

16. Alex A. Pieters, "Church Finance," *The Korea Mission Field,* September 1915, 251.

17. Clark, *Nevius Plan,* statistics.

18. Rhodes, *Korean Mission Presbyterian Church,* 398–400; Horace G. Underwood, "An Object Lesson in Self-Support," *Missionary Review of the World,* June 1900, 443–449.

19. Underwood, "Object Lesson," 446.

20. "General Missionary Intelligence," *Missionary Review of the World,* October 1910, 787.

21. Rhodes, *Korean Mission Presbyterian Church,* 399.

22. C. C. Vinton, "To-day in Korean Missions," *Missionary Review of the World,* August 1906, 572.

23. "News from Many Lands—How Korean Women Give," *Missionary Review of the World,* December 1917, 950–951.

24. T. H. Yun, "What Shall We Eat," *The Korean Mission Field,* January 1918, 11.

25. W. L. Swallen, "Types of Korean Christian Character," *Missionary Review of the World,* March 1902, 192–193.

26. Clark, *Nevius Plan,* 111.

27. "How Mr. Kim Became a Christian," *The Korea Review,* December 1905, 457–467.

28. Marx insisted that "capital should be defined as a process rather than a thing." David Harvey, *The Limits to Capital* (Oxford: Basil Blackwell Publishing, 1982), 20.

29. Jean Comaroff and John L. Comaroff, *Of Revelation and Revolution,* vol. 2 (Chicago: University of Chicago Press, 1997), 168.

30. Ibid., 171.

31. Yun Kyung-ro, *Han'guk kŭndaesa ŭi Kidokkyo sajak ihae* (Seoul: Yukminsa, 1992), 126.

32. Kim Sang-tae, "Kŭnhyŏndae P'yŏngyangdo ch'ulsin sahoe chidoch'ŭng yŏn'gu" (Ph.D. diss., Seoul National University, 2002).

33. Michael D. Shin, "The Spectre of Yi Kwang-su" (unpublished manuscript, 2009), 13.

34. Ibid., 31.

35. Chang, *Ilche ha Han'guk kidokkyo minjokjuŭi yŏn'gu,* 269.

36. Yun Kyung-ro, *Han'guk kŭndaesa ŭi Kidokkyo sajak ihae,* 339–382.

37. Tetsuo Najita, *Visions of Virtue in Tokugawa Japan* (Chicago: University of Chicago Press, 1987).

38. Daniel T. Rodgers, *The Work Ethic in Industrial America, 1850–1920* (Chicago: University of Chicago Press, 1978), 22.

39. Robert T. Handy, *A Christian America: Protestant Hopes and Historical Realities* (New York: Oxford University Press, 1984), 95–100.

40. For a good sample of articles that encouraged industrializing Korea, see the January 1918 issue of *The Korea Mission Field.*

41. A. E. Lucas, "Industrial Work: The Importance and Opportunities for Industrial Work in Missionary School in Chosen," *The Korean Mission Field,* October 1918, 205.

42. Ibid.

43. T. H. Yun, "What Shall We Eat," 11–12.

44. A. F. Robb, "Letter to A. E. Armstrong D.D." (photocopy, United Church Archives, Toronto), 2.

45. Ibid., 2.

46. Ibid., 3.

47. T. H. Yun, "What Shall We Eat," 11–12.

48. Horace H. Underwood, *Modern Education in Korea* (New York: International Press, 1926), 111.

49. Horace H. Underwood, "Industrial Training in the Far East," *Missionary Review of the World,* September 1918, 679.

50. H. H. Underwood, "Industrial Training," 678.

51. H. H. Underwood, *Modern Education,* 115.

52. H. H. Underwood, "Industrial Training," 680.

53. Frank M. Brockman, "Some of the Problems of Industrial Education in Korea, *The Korea Mission Field,* July 1910, 173.

54. George A. Gregg, "Educating Hand and Brain," *The Korea Mission Field,* June 1912, 171–175; H. H. Underwood, *Modern Education,* 112–119.

55. H. H. Underwood, "Industrial Training," 679.

56. T. H. Yun, "A Plea for Industrial Training," *The Korea Mission Field,* July 1911, 187.

57. Lois Hawks Swinehart, "Industrial Work among the Women and Girls of Korea," *The Korea Mission Field,* January 1918, 13.

58. H. H. Underwood, *Modern Education,* 116.

59. Ibid., 117.

60. Gregg, "Hand and Brain," 173.

61. H. H. Underwood, "Industrial Training," 678.

62. Robert Grierson, "Korean Industrial Characteristics," *The Korea Mission Field,* January 1918, 5–7.

63. Swallen, "Korean Christian Character," 192.

64. C. H. Deal, "Self-Help for Students in Mission Schools," *The Korea Mission Field,* October 1914, 314.

65. Gregg, "Hand and Brain," 172; H. H. Underwood, "Industrial Training," 680.

66. Underwood, *Modern Education,* 117.

67. IEDs expected students to pay for their education partly through their earned income.

68. Sewell argues that the most important aspect of capitalism is "conversion of use value into exchange value or the commodification of thing." See William H. Sewell, *Logics of History* (Chicago: University of Chicago Press, 2005), 150–151.

69. Taylor, "Modern Social Imaginaries," 105.

70. Clark, *Nevius Plan,* 224; Gregg, "Hand and Brain," 174.

71. Clark, *Nevius Plan,* 224.

72. Comaroff and Comaroff, "Millennial Capitalism," 1–56.

73. Ibid., 25.

74. Dilip Parameshwa Gaonkar, "On Alternative Modernities," in *Alternative Modernities,* ed. Dilip Parameshwar Gaonkar (Durham, NC: Duke University Press, 2001), 18.

75. Sewell, *Logics of History,* 369.

2

Taking Jesus Public

The Neoliberal Transformation of Korean Megachurches

EUN YOUNG LEE EASLEY

THE CHRISTIAN POPULATION of Korea witnessed a dramatic growth in the 1960s and 1970s, when the number of believers soared from six hundred thousand to three million. The growth rate somewhat slowed thereafter, but the absolute number still managed to more than double in the 1980s to seven million.[1] In marked contrast, however, the size of Protestant congregations started to decline in the 1990s. From 1995 to 2005, the Protestant population declined for the first time (by 1.6 percent), whereas other religions such as Buddhism and Catholicism showed growth during the same period.[2] This demographic shift in itself represents an interesting change in the history of Protestant Christianity in Korea. Within this context, there was a little analyzed but arguably more important realignment occurring among Protestant Christian congregations in Korea.

While the population of Protestant Christians was stagnating and even declining, a new breed of megachurch experienced outstanding growth by vast traffic among already converted Christians. One church, for example, split into four and then into seven branch churches while experiencing congregational growth in the thousands. Another church announced blueprints for building a brand new complex at an estimated cost of almost

200 million dollars, arguing that they needed enough space for their fast-growing congregation. A third church in the meantime made contracts for eight different satellites to beam back the church's broadcasting station to 170 countries, twenty-four hours a day, every day.

Why have some churches prospered so dramatically while other churches have suffered stagnated growth or even decline since the 1990s? Besides achieving expansive growth, these emerging megachurches have also proven to be increasingly influential within the broader Korean Protestant Christian community, often regarded as models for other churches to follow.[3] This issue has drawn attention from churches and religious scholars and has generated two new terms among the Christian population and scholarly groups: "established megachurches" (*sŏnbal taehyŏng kyohoe*) and "starter megachurches" (*hubal taehyŏng kyohoe*). The established megachurch group includes Yŏngnak Church, Yŏŭido Sunbogŭm Church, and Ch'unghyŏn Church, while the relatively newly established Sarang-ui Church, Somang Church, Kwanglim Church, Onnuri Community Church, and God's Will Church belong to the latter category.[4]

This chapter investigates the growth of starter megachurches in relation to the social upheavals and financial crisis of the late 1990s. In particular, the chapter seeks to answer several interrelated questions: (1) what kind of socioeconomic transformation was Korean society facing in the late 1990s? (2) how did the starter megachurches interpret the global and local socioeconomic changes? and (3) how did the adaptation of starter megachurches to these shifts allow them to expand relative to other churches? In answering these questions, this chapter presents new research conducted by the author on two megachurch case studies: Onnuri Community Church (Onnuri Kyohoe) and God's Will Church (Nop'ŭn Ttŭt Sungŭi Kyohoe).[5] For the purposes of this study, megachurches are defined as churches with congregations numbering over five thousand, with sermons given by a celebrity pastor, and which establish branch churches in addition to growth of the main church. Onnuri Community Church and God's Will Church not only meet these conditions, but are also regarded as leading examples of Protestant churches among the community and provide representative cases of starter megachurches in Korea since the late 1990s. The findings of this essay are based on discourse analysis via close readings of sermons, program contents, books, and website postings produced by the churches and their head pastors. Findings also rely on author interviews with pastors, church members, participants in worship services, and small group meetings.

The Reinvention of Korean Megachurches

Megachurches are far from a new phenomenon in the history of the Protestant Church in Korea. Established and starter megachurches share many common characteristics, but starter megachurches have adapted some of the characteristics and developed them further. Broadly speaking, these characteristics fall into two categories: (1) the diversification and customization of worship services and small group meetings, and (2) application of market mechanisms to expand the organization. Established in 1985, Onnuri Community Church showed modest growth in its first ten years. In the late 1990s, however, Onnuri Community Church experienced dramatic growth. The turning point came when Onnuri Community Church changed its format for worship services to an "open worship service" (*yŏllin yeŭbae*). The term "open," or *yŏllin,* describes worship services that are technically sophisticated in a style friendlier to newcomers. This new kind of worship service originated with a few churches in America, which faced the challenge of declining populations similar to Korean Protestant churches in the 1990s.[6] By introducing a new format for worship services to Korea, Onnuri Community Church began to attract more and more followers from other churches.[7]

The open worship services often start with welcoming and relaxing music and video that previews the theme of that day's sermon. Videos sometimes contain views of the magnificence of nature, innocent faces of children, and Bible verses written in colloquial language. Whereas traditional worship services are usually led by pastors, open worship services are carefully scripted with the help of mixed media. While choir music, sermon, and prayer are proceeding, video clips or PowerPoint slides are projected on a jumbo screen signaling smooth flow of the program, and relaxing contemporary Christian music is provided by bands playing contemporary musical instruments at a professional level. Worship is an hour and a half long performance carefully prepared and coordinated for the congregation.

The overarching theme of open worship services varies according to the age, gender, and personal preferences of the congregation. For example, there are worship services that are modified to the interests of people in their forties and fifties, to teenagers struggling with identity issues, and to those who have just converted, who like music, and who are soon to be parents. The time and locations of worship services also differ from those of established megachurches. Onnuri Community Church provides about eight different themed services on Sundays. There are also services on weekdays at various locations for the convenience of the congregation. Even Starbuck coffee shops and a nightclub turn into worship service venues on certain days for Onnuri Community Church. The established megachurches also have multiple worship services on Sundays, but most of them conduct a traditional form of worship service with the head pastors repeating the same sermon during each service throughout the day. Those services are held in the same building, and they are only differentiated by the order of "first," "second," and so forth. Established megachurches tend not to tailor the theme, time, and location of worship services to the needs of the congregation, whereas starter megachurches delicately cater to the diverse interests of the congregation.

One of the contributing factors behind the fast-paced growth of Korean Protestant churches, including the established megachurches, has been small group meetings. The traditional form of these small group meetings, often called *kuyŏkmoim* or *sokhoe,* is usually organized based on the gender, residential locations, and age of participants.[8] Unless a member moves to a different neighborhood or to another church, the membership of a small group will remain fixed and provide a relatively lasting community. These small group meetings conduct weekly Bible study and provide general support and a new type of community for people experiencing the process of urbanization and industrialization. The starter megachurches also organize small group meetings, but starter churches provide a more diverse range of groups reflecting different needs and interests of the congregation.

According to its sophisticated church web page, small group meetings of Onnuri Community Church can be categorized into four themes: community building, worship, mission, and ministry.[9] Each category includes many different options. For example, the forms of ministry section is divided into eight different subsections, including family consultation, worship service, education, fostering fellow Christians, and recovery. Under the recovery subdivision, there are small groups including groups for people with anger management problems, with alcohol addiction, and who want to overcome financial mismanagement. The lists go a long way to cover detailed interests and concerns of congregations.[10] God's Will Church, another exemplary starter megachurch, offers similar kinds of programs to present functional solutions to its congregation's practical questions of everyday life. The pastor in charge of small group programs said in an interview with the author that God's Will Church focuses especially on troubles within the nuclear family and that their programs include workshops on relationships of married couples based on personality tests, smoother communication with children, and even troubles in sexual relations. By some counts, Onnuri Community Church has about six hundred different meetings of these kinds, and observers say that these focused small group meetings have made starter megachurches more successful than others.

Alongside the diverse and customized nature of worship service and small groups, another defining characteristic of starter megachurches is the establishment of branch churches. Established megachurches have built branch churches for members who live far away from the main church. This trend, however, has declined over the years among established megachurches. The starter megachurches, in contrast, seem to be more active in pursuing growth through the establishment of branch churches. God's Will Church split into four different branch churches in 2009, later adding two more branch churches in and around Seoul and finally one in Japan. Onnuri Community Church has undertaken a sophisticated expansion of its branch churches since its Act 29 campaign in 2003, with great support from the congregation, though it created some controversy among Protestant Christians in Korea. Act 29 symbolizes the Onnuri Community Church's claim that it is supposed to write the last chapter of *Acts of the Apostles* in the New Testament, which has twenty-eight chapters. Under this campaign, the church is to build thirty "vision churches," or branch churches in Korea, and to send two thousand missionaries around the world while securing ten thousand supporters for their missionaries. In creating its branch churches, Onnuri Community Church sends pastors to the locations, sets up the general programs, provides financial support, and regulates the administration of the churches. As of 2010, nine branch churches were established in Korean cities such as Taejŏn, P'yŏngtaek, Suwŏn, and Puch'ŏn, and twenty-five churches in cities around the world including Tokyo, Los Angeles, and Sydney. Pastors of Onnuri Community Church explain that the purpose of establishing branch churches is to share their "know-how" on ministry with other less developed churches in order for them to experience growth like Onnuri Community Church's. However, churches close to Onnuri branch churches are losing many members of their congregation to the Onnuri branches. For example, while one branch church in Suwŏn grew into a mid-sized church with a congregation of eight hundred within the first five months, neighboring churches saw the size of their congregations becoming reduced in size. According to National Statistics Bureau demographic data for 2005, there are about 8.6 million Protestant Christians in South Korea and about 58,000 churches. Based on these counts, each church should average around 150 members. More than 60 percent of churches, however, have fewer than fifty members.[11] In order to counter this imbalance between churches, most denominations do not allow churches under the same denomination to build near each other. Onnuri Community Church, however, has not met the regulation of its own denomination and proceeded with its Act 29 expansion project. Naturally, this kind of expansion necessitates a significant financial contribution and broad recognition. Onnuri Community Church not only depends on offerings and tithes from its congregation, but it has also established other mechanisms to assist its expansion campaign. Sermons of Onnuri pastors and seminar materials easily and quickly regenerate as books, CDs, and DVDs through a publishing company established by Onnuri Community Church. The products are available to purchase through an online shopping mall affiliated with Onnuri Community Church, which targets the larger Korean Protestant Christian population in addition to its own congregation.[12] In 2005, Onnuri Community Church expanded into the realm of broadcasting, launching a cable channel, CGN TV, which broadcasts to areas throughout the world.[13] This satellite broadcasting, which is available in six different languages, has helped to build the popularity of Onnuri Community Church as a brand, inside and outside of Korea.

Since the starter megachurches and their branch churches have grown mainly by attracting people from other churches, they have implemented several methods for getting recently moved parishioners to stay longer. First, starter megachurches are sensitive to the needs of the communicants, the ultimate consumers of the churches' religious products. Illustrative of this approach is the following quote from a pastor of Onnuri Community Church:

> Sales are not about persuading consumers with what you have already made. It is about making what potential consumers will want to buy. Therefore, it is important to know whom you are approaching. In our church, we had festivals specially oriented to newcomers. We decorated the church like a hotel. We interviewed the children of newcomers. We sought the help of professional consultants. Pastor Ha's sermon was tailored to survey results about what people in their fifties would like to know. The outcome was three thousand people coming back to God.

It is important to note that concepts such as collecting surveys from customers, asking for professional consultation, and quantitatively measuring outcomes (e.g., the number of newcomers and their level of satisfaction) are a new phenomenon among starter megachurches that has an obvious resemblance to the practices of business marketing. Another method for retaining communicants is inculcating a sense of membership via *saesinja-kyoyuk* (newcomer education). This too is a comparatively new phenomenon among churches in Korea. The main goal of the program, according to the churches, is to introduce basic doctrines of Christianity. However, since many of the newcomers are already converted Christians, the content of the program is more geared to introducing the philosophy and direction of the church and generating a sense of belonging and pride as a member of the church. Through this kind of membership program, newcomers are encouraged to embody the credos of the churches and to develop loyalty to their new churches. In order to help generate a sense of membership, these megachurches have also created their own logos and mottos that reflect church characteristics, similar to brand marketing by companies.

It is notable that starter megachurches are so open to the idea of growth and that their growth flows beyond denominational and national boundaries, and their religious institutional category. But what are the contents of the services and small group meetings that are so attractive to the Christian population that enable these churches to grow rapidly and distinguish themselves from other types of churches? How does the attractiveness of starter megachurches relate to the larger socioeconomic context in Korea under globalization? The following sections discuss the social context for these changes and help explain the path of starter megachurches in Korea.

Neoliberalism as the Backdrop

Christian churches, like any other institution, do not operate in a vacuum. Thus, it is important to consider the national and global contexts in which Korean Protestant churches are adapting to social transformation. The most significant change that has defined the period since the 1990s in Korea may be the permeation of neoliberalism into Korean society.[14] Defining neoliberalism is no easy task since it refers not only to an economic ideology, but also to a philosophy behind political, social, and cultural changes that are still being developed and applied in the contemporary world. For the purposes of this chapter, the main characteristics of neoliberalism are market-based economics, reduced roles for government, and increased flexibility in labor and cultural practices.

First, neoliberalism prioritizes the unrestrained flow of capital, which ultimately expands the force of the market. Neoliberalism is not a new socioeconomic ideology but one of many philosophies of capitalism that envision a society that runs according to market forces.[15] Neoliberalism emphasizes minimum regulations and restrictions, and champions market forces. The market freedom that neoliberalism pursues, however, is not limited to deregulation within each domestic market. The free flow of capital also requires lowering barriers on trade between nation-states. For that purpose, international organizations such as the WTO (World Trade Organization), the IBRD (International Bank for Reconstruction and Development), and the IMF (International Monetary Fund) encourage countries around the world to support economic policies favorable to free trade and the unrestricted flow of capital.

South Korea was an exemplary case of this global transformation. During the period of the 1960s to the 1980s, the Korean economy achieved rapid development under strict government control, based on close coordination and connection with banks and *chaebŏl* (conglomerates).[16] The government provided the blueprint for the national economy and monitored its implementation; banks adopted finance policy nurturing industries and supporting business, and conglomerates grew as national champions. The 1997 Asian Financial Crisis and its dramatic effects on the Korean economy, however, created the popular opinion that state-business collusion (*chŏngkyŏng yuch'ak*) and the *chaebŏl*-dominated economy were the main reasons for the crisis and thus necessary to dismantle.[17] Financial sectors had to change their rules to adapt to the free flow of international capital, and companies had to transform their organizations for survival within a competitive landscape with international companies.

Second, under the influence of neoliberalism, not only the role of government in leading economic development, but also its role in providing social welfare is reduced. Emphasis on market freedom and deregulation eventually requires limitation and reduction of government's role as a regulator of the market. In a society subscribing to neoliberal principles, it is believed that the overall progress of a nation is determined by free competition between individuals and merit-based rewarding of products and outcomes. Social welfare is understood as discouraging natural competition among individuals and thus disrupting market forces through unfair compensation. Such public services as welfare payment, social insurance, public medical care, and public housing are thus considered undesirable; rather, these functions are recommended for privatization when neoliberalism becomes the dominant philosophy of a society. The government of Kim Dae-jung took steps to privatize welfare programs after the 1997 Asian Financial Crisis, and these policies effectively reduced the social safety net, contributing to the shrinking of the middle classes in South Korea and a widening gap between the rich and the poor.[18]

Instead of redistributing wealth by government intervention, neoliberalism recommends the "trickle down" of wealth from the center to the peripheries. Supporters of neoliberalism believe that the overall growth of the economy will allow the rich to voluntarily help the poor or at least allow their wealth to flow to create opportunities for the less wealthy.[19] In the end, neoliberalists trust that economic growth will solve the problem of poverty and inequality. Son Ho-ch'ŏl notes that in the late 1990s the South Korean government implemented discourses on "two types of citizens" [*tu kungmin chŏllyak*]: one who works hard and pays high tax to support the lazy and independent one who only expects the benefits of social welfare. The criteria distinguishing good citizens (*choŭn kungmin*) and bad citizens (*nappŭn kungmin*) were conservative notions such as diligence, honesty, and happy families.[20] This conception aimed not only to urge everyone to become better citizens, but also to encourage the "good citizen" class to perform their noblesse oblige in donations and contributions at their will in place of a government-provided social safety net or welfare.

Third, the flexible labor principle of neoliberal economics induces psychological uncertainty and fosters a culture of self-discipline and monitoring. Companies influenced by neoliberalism reconstruct their organization to most profitably meet market demand, often resulting in employee layoffs and turning regular jobs into more flexible and less secure ones. From 1997 to 2000, the Korean National Statistics Bureau reported that employees without job security for over two years, such as temporary workers and short-term contractors, increased by 13.4 percent, and in 2005 irregular employees made up 56.1 percent of all employees.[21] In the absence of a social safety net in the face of economic volatility, many people feel anxious and uncertain not only about their jobs, but also about their lives and identities. Sociologist Richard Sennett argues that in an environment where people's jobs and responsibilities change frequently without any expectation of what is coming next, people have a hard time acknowledging self-worth, sometimes resulting in self-denial.[22] In other words, when their jobs change spontaneously, people feel that their lives are a random series of unrelated happenings, and they get nervous about the lack of consistency and coherence in their lives.

To cope with sudden and often dramatic social changes and problems of self-acknowledgment, people seek guidance for their lives that will attenuate their fears and provide confidence. A popular remedy is the so-called self-empowerment discourse, which provides advice for specific situations, almost like an instruction manual for a consumer electronic device. In Korea, especially since 1997—the year of what many Koreans recall as the "IMF Crisis"—self-disciplinary books such as *Seven Habits for Highly Effective People* and programs such as leadership training became pervasive. These self-disciplinary books and various related programs share several essential points. First, they share a consensus that an irresistible change in society has occurred. Because such changes are irreversible, one needs to adjust oneself to the changes as soon as possible. In order to do so, individuals should first objectively diagnose their strengths and weaknesses and make specific steps to improve their strengths and eliminate weaknesses. Second, based on this analysis of one's strengths and weaknesses, popular self-empowerment discourses encourage individuals to train themselves for excellence by constantly monitoring and measuring their ability. Focusing on individuals' responsibility to change themselves according to external circumstances and train themselves to excel in the changed society, the self-empowerment rhetoric embodies the essence of neoliberal philosophy: that one's success or failure should be one's own responsibility. Many educational programs, language courses, and even meditation and diet programs were advertised as tools for self-discipline. The almost obsessive public zeal about self-discipline witnessed in the late 1990s and early 2000s reflected people's fear and anxiety that they might free fall without the help of a social safety net in the turmoil of intensive changes in their socioeconomic environment.

Neoliberalism and the Success of Starter Megachurches

In a recent survey among the Protestant Christian population, 68.7 percent responded that pastors' preaching or teaching is the realization of God's words, and 98 percent said that sermon content is a very important factor in a church's growth.[23] In interviews with communicants who switched churches, the present research also confirms that sermons were important to their decision to move. One characteristic frequently argued as defining megachurches in Korea before the 1990s is their *kiboksinang* (prosperity gospel). *Kiboksinang* offers the theological orientation that you and your family will be better off in health and wealth because of your faith.[24] Sermons acknowledging and even encouraging individuals and nuclear families to accumulate wealth provided a frame to interpret sudden changes caused by fast-paced industrialization. The prosperity gospel offered comfort and motivation to many who were distressed by the instability that intensive social change caused.[25] It has been understood as an important factor in why megachurches in Korea have grown so fast and large. Sermons and messages delivered through starter megachurches in Korea share characteristics of the prosperity gospel in the sense that they also talk positively about one's economic success and happiness. Yet, they are different from the prosperity gospel of established megachurches in several ways, which help explain the success of starter megachurches.

First, starter megachurches' messages emphasize the legitimacy of the current economic system. This is in contrast to established megachurches, which largely remained quiet about economic changes or the financial system, preferring to focus on spiritual aspects of individuals and their economic success as the result. The messages that prevail in the starter megachurches, however, offer direct approval of the current socioeconomic system—departing from the established megachurches' passive consent. Starter megachurches, for example, affirm economic inequality between classes and see the inequality as an opportunity for the flow of the wealth between classes, which resembles the philosophy promoted by neoliberalism. Pastor of God's Will Church Kim Dong-Ho's book *The Clean Rich* (*Kkaekkŭthan puja*), which has been popular and controversial among Protestant populations in Korea ever since it was published in 2001, is a perfect example of this philosophy on current economic systems prevailing among starter megachurches. Based on the popularity he gained through his first book, Pastor Kim has published a series of books contending that Christianity and wealth should exist in harmony, such as *Five Principles to Become Happily Rich* (*Haengbokhan pujarŭl wihan tasŏt kaji wŏnch'ik*) and *The Honest Will Prosper* (*Nanŭn chŏngjik'an chaŭi hyŏngt'ongŭl minnŭnda*). In his books, he refers to biblical stories to justify economic inequality within the current capitalist society, arguing that it is the undeniable planning of God.

> God distributed lands to the Israelites. However, while they were living on the allowed lands over fifty years, the land of some people became enlarged while others' shrunk. There were even people who ended up having no piece of land under their ownership, and some of them became slaves of others. However, God approved all of this. Seeing this example in the Bible, I believe that God is not a socialist. He is not a Communist. . . . Thus, it is right for people to live unequal lives. Otherwise, there will be no progress.[26]

In the above quote, Pastor Kim regards competition and inequality as a natural progression of human history. Pastor Kim insists that competition among people and its effects are a process that God approves and that criticizing inequality is akin to the ideology of communism, which God dislikes. The following quote reaffirms this view: "Of course, I do not believe that there will be any poor people in God's nation, but until we go there, in this world, there always be the rich and the poor."[27] This view is similar to the idea of neoliberalism, which encourages competition among people and believes that what results should be accepted.

In established megachurches, sermons were oriented to comfort people struggling with their unstable economic status and feeling of deprivation resulting from economic inequality during Korea's rapid industrialization process. A common theme in sermons was that the poor will become rich, although discussion of existing inequality was left out. Sermons in established megachurches described God as a generous and benevolent giver of blessings. Starter megachurches, however, tend to stress that it is God's providence that some stay poor while others become rich. So it is more important to pursue the overall progress of a society than to focus on the problem of inequality. They argue against solving problems of inequality because any human intervention will disrupt the flow that God has designed. This view comports well with the philosophy of neoliberalism in the sense that neoliberalism only acknowledges the flow that markets generate in spite of human interventions in that flow.

Second, starter megachurches teach that followers should actively pursue wealth and success. Starter megachurches' pastors preach that people have the choice to become rich or poor. As discussed above, since the current economic system is not to blame for a person's socioeconomic condition and status, being rich or poor is only a matter of people's choice based on their performance. Pastor Kim is critical of the Christian culture that prefers a life of honest poverty (*ch'ŏngbin*), insisting repeatedly in his sermons and books that it is not natural or right to admire poverty.[28]

Pastor Kim preaches that as we are given the choice, it is better to become rich to flow the wealth, instead of trying to challenge the current system in order to correct its structure. He recognizes that differences between the high and the low, and the strong and the weak are designed so by God to yield flow of wealth and power.

> The high and the low, and the strong and the weak, they represent obvious inequality. However, that inequality creates flow. From that flow, there comes life. . . . It is the same with money. There is flow in the life of money. . . . It flows from high to low, from strong to weak. Through that order, genuine equality and fairness can be achieved. Life

will be created finally. However, humans have interrupted this genuine flow. This interruption is the root of every social problem.[29]

With reasoning similar to that of Pastor Kim, many starter megachurches emphasize that it is problematic when people try to address economic disparity by artificial intervention. Good Christians rather should seek to be rich and successful so that they can help the poor in need. This logic resonates closely with the neoliberal belief that interrupting the flow of capital should be avoided; in order to attenuate the tension between the rich and the poor, society should depend on market forces determining the flow of wealth. Pastors from starter megachurches emphasize that Christians should become the leading class in society, elites or successful businesspeople. They should be influential people who "feed at least five thousand people." The symbolic number of five thousand people comes from the New Testament, where Jesus fed five thousand people who did not have food to eat when they gathered to hear him preach.[30] Pastors of the starter megachurches say that this is a model for what Christians should pursue and that they should support many people by their excellence in their jobs or through their economic prosperity.

The philanthropic work of churches has been an important part of megachurches in Korea, but philanthropic activities are calculated and quantified in the starter megachurches. For example, Pastor Kim provides examples of different forms of offerings from the Bible and says that one who offers a minimum of 34.8 percent of one's income can be titled "clean rich" and should be free to enjoy the rest of his or her earnings at will. The number 34.8 percent consists of tithe (10 percent), a yearly portion of a special tithe every three years (3.33 percent), and 21.45 percent of one's earnings, which was induced from the tradition in the Old Testament that people leave the four corners of their farming beds free from harvesting so that poor people in the neighborhood can take. Quantifying the amount of what one should do to help others and granting permission to enjoy assets without feeling guilty is a new characteristic that distinguishes the discourse on Christian ethics of starter megachurches from established churches.[31] This discourse resonates with characteristics of neoliberalism that say everything can be valued in monetary, tradable, or market terms, not to mention the concept that distribution of wealth should be done through voluntary acts of individuals.

Third, starter megachurches argue that, in order to become successful enough to flow their wealth, individuals are to discipline themselves and achieve personal excellence by becoming self-reliant and wealthy. In established megachurches, the way to ask for God's earthly blessing relates more to presenting one's faith to God, as by attending worship services without fail, reading the Bible regularly, and participating in dawn prayer meetings.[32] Strong faith is regarded as the condition necessary to receive the blessing of prosperity, but it is not a sufficient condition, since it is God's decision to endow blessings. In the starter megachurches, however, there is an element in addition to strong faith or God's grace required to achieve God's blessing. People have to pursue God's blessings actively by preparing themselves to be eligible for those blessings. This is a very important factor that differentiates starter megachurches' religious rhetoric from that of established megachurches. Sample churches in this study were found to provide worship services and diverse programs specifically oriented to help people become better workers, better family members, and better citizens, and the religious discourses surrounding these programs are similar to the self-empowerment rhetoric prevailing in neoliberal society.

Not only are these worship services conveniently offered early in the morning or during lunch breaks for people with regular work hours, Onnuri Community Church and God's Will Church have programs specifically addressing Christians' work ethics and attitude toward their occupations. God's Will Church outsources these programs to an organization called Chigŏp Somyŏng Hakkyo (Academy of Vocation as God's Calling) that specializes in providing lessons related to work ethics and attitudes from a Christian perspective. Close readings of sermons and content offered by these programs reveal a reoccurring set of concepts: vision, planning, monitoring, failure, risk, and success. These concepts are used to build the narrative that (1) one should find one's vision and work hard to achieve it, (2) but there are always risks and failures in the process, and (3) in order to overcome those obstacles, one should discipline oneself and monitor one's performance all the time.[33]

I participated in a program offered by the Onnuri Community Church to give guidance to people in finding their vocations from God. The program featured several speakers, including pastors, professionals, psychological therapists, and alumni of the program. At the first meeting, a pastor gave an introduction: "I welcome all of you who come here. I know that you feel like pieces of your life are floating here and there. We know that makes you feel helpless. But we will help you through this program to draw the outline and to find the embedded rules to solve the puzzles."[34]

The first meeting started with people sharing their frustrations about their current lives and their expectations of the program. Interestingly, many of the members of my group were from other churches, some of them from popular established megachurches, who complained that their churches failed to give any practical advice on life even though they liked their churches' worship services. The homework for the week required responding to 137 specific questions regarding your personality on a scale of 1 to 5; the total score for each section was supposed to indicate one's characteristics and personal skills. The same form also had to be filled out by someone who knew the participant well in order to cross-check his or her assessments. The next two sessions were designed to figure out one's strengths and weaknesses in order to determine what one ultimately should do. The last week of the program was devoted to presenting one's vision for one's job, one's family, and one's church in front of all the other participants. Everyone then was given a certificate for completing the program and finding one's own vision. "This was the very basic step," the pastor said at the end as he introduced other programs that people could pursue in further detail. The whole process was similar to what popular self-discipline books and programs do: problematize one's current status, recognize one's strengths and weaknesses, plan out how to achieve excellence, and proclaim it in front of others.[35] Moreover, the process involved constant measuring of oneself by different quantifiable methods. Similar formats are applied in other programs such as the "school for fathers" (*abŏji hakkyo*), the "school for mothers" (*ŏmŏni hakkyo*), and the "school for soon-to-be-married couples" (*yebi pubu hakkyo*). These programs catered to the practical needs of individuals and contributed to making the Onnuri Community Church so popular. Many programs are oriented to improving one's role as a healthy member of the family, an employee, and finally a patriotic citizen.

Anthony Giddens and Ulrich Beck rightly point out that in the postmodern world, where traditions give way to uncertainty and risk, individuals are expected to develop their own system of self-reflection, which helps build the ground and principles for how individuals see their identities and lives.[36] Instead of trying to find a hobby, people look for a self-discipline program or a new religion from which they can find a source of self-reflection or a consistent narrative for their lives. Since the 1990s, these sample starter megachurches have observed this need among potential church members and provided materials that people can use for developing their self-reflection and personal narratives. Many Christian-related books and programs became prevalent for providing itemized guidance for practical needs in life. The starter megachurches and the established generation of megachurches in Korea both grew by providing comfort during a time of uncertain transformation of society. Yet the social instability that Korean society has faced since the Asian Financial Crisis in 1997 was different from that of the established megachurch generation, and the kind of comfort that starter megachurches offered represents an important departure from the older generation of established megachurches.

During the industrialization period from the 1960s to 1980s, Protestant churches in Korea provided comfort to people by proclaiming that a belief in Jesus would lead to blessing and economic prosperity. By avoiding issues regarding the economic system or social changes, many established megachurches indirectly and passively acknowledged the then-current socioeconomic ideology. Since the 1990s—in the postindustrialization period of Korea—several churches have moved a step further by arguing that it is Christians' responsibility to become prosperous and flow their wealth to the poor. When proactively acknowledging the current socioeconomic system and aspiring for blessings from heaven became no longer sufficient in the starter megachurches' religious credo, individuals were charged with achieving earthly prosperity. Starter megachurches in Korea gave followers detailed steps to take in order to become successful and set a quantifiable goal in practicing charity as a good Christian while exhorting those followers to accept economic and social inequality. Starter megachurches succeed in incorporating these teachings into religious discourses and marketed them through diversified services that catered to the demand of followers who looked to the gospel for direction and guidance in the new era of neoliberalism.

Starter megachurches expanded their influence through branch churches and businesses that sold religious-themed products. During the process of expansion, starter megachurches commodified their worship services and other religious products with advertising and using new forms of social media, such as cable television and Internet shopping malls. In turn, the sale of religious products provided resources for further expansion. The astounding number of communicants these churches have drawn and the monetary resources they have amassed are viewed as admirable successes among much of the Christian population in Korea.

This research suggests that the stage of a society's economic development in large part determines which churches will thrive and succeed. The megachurches that most efficiently and effectively adapted to prevailing economic ideologies and social needs were able to expand their congregations and their influence within Korean Christianity. They did so by promptly applying competitive business models and innovations in technology, and interpreting the forces of globalization into their religious doctrines. However, starter megachurches' growth and success highlight serious challenges to traditional church organization and the values and roles of the Christian community in Korea. These challenges include growing imbalances among churches and refocused social participation of congregations on monetary charitable contributions rather than activist support of democracy, labor, and social equality. Such changes merit greater attention, especially given the declining overall Christian population and the ongoing socioeconomic transformation under way in Korea.

Notes

1. Ch'oe Hyŏn-Chong, *Han'guk chonggyo in'gu pyŏndonge kwanhan yŏn'gu* [Study on Religious Demographic Change in Korea] (Puch'ŏn: Hyŏndae kidokkyo yŏksa yŏn'guso, 2011), 30.

2. National Statistics Office, *In'gu chut'aek ch'ongchosa* [Population and Housing Census Report (2005)], last modified January 1, 2006, http://www.kostat.go.kr, accessed April 1, 2009.

3. Onnuri Community Church was ranked as the best church for its cultural activities in a survey conducted among scholars and pastors. The head pastor of God's Will Church was selected as the top future leader in Korean churches. Sŏ Chŏng-Bo et al., "P'ŭrotŭri sŏnjŏnghan uri punya ch'oego Kidokkyo" [The Best Player in Field Christianity], *Donga ilbo,* April 13, 2003.

4. See Ro Ch'i-Jun, *Han'guk kaesin'gyo sahoehak* [Sociology of the Protestant Church in Korea]. (Seoul: Hanul, 1998); Kim Sŏng-Gŏn, *Han'guk sahoewa kaesin'gyo: chonggyo sahoehak chŏk yŏn'gu* [Korean Society and Its Protestant

Christianity: A Religious Sociology Study] (Seoul: Sŏwŏn Taehakkyo Ch'ulp'anbu, 2005); Han Mi Jun and Han'guk Gallup, *Han'guk kyohoe mirae rip'ot'ŭ* [A Report on the Future of the Korean Church] (Seoul: Duranno, 2005); Hong Yŏng-Ki, *Kyohoe sŏnt'aek ŭi chokŏn* [Conditions for Choosing a Church] (Seoul: Kyohoe Sŏngjang Yŏnguso, 2004).

5. This essay is based on the master's thesis of the author. Lee Eun Young, "Sinchayujuŭiwa 1990-yŏndae ihu Han'guk taehyŏng kyohoeŭi pyŏnhwa" [Neoliberalism and a New Protestant Ethic: The Transformation of Korean Megachurches since the 1990s] (M.A. thesis, Yonsei University, 2007).

6. In America, Willow Creek Community Church is considered one of the pioneers that introduced open worship services. In 1998, when Onnuri Community Church was still in an earlier stage of growth, it held a series of seminars over several weeks to study the "growth techniques" of successful churches in America. They inquired into the structures of church organization, traits of sermons, and small group activities that were implemented by growing churches. The next year, Onnuri Community Church invited Bill Hybels and other pastors from Willow Creek Community Church to Korea. From this meeting, Onnuri Community Church learned and adapted traits of Willow Creek Community Church that made it so popular compared with declining churches in the States. That year, Onnuri Community Church started "open worship service." Since 1998, Onnuri Community Church growth rates have soared. Until at least 2006, Bill Hybels has been invited to Onnuri Community Church almost every year for meetings and seminars regarding the example of ministry at Willow Creek Community Church.

7. Yi Wŏn-Kyu, *Kidokkyo ŭi wigiwa hŭimang* [Crisis and Hope of Protestantism] (Seoul: Taehan Kidokkyosŏhoe, 2003); Kim Se-Gwang, *Yebaewa hyŏndae munhwa* [Worship Service and Modern Culture] (Seoul: Taehan Kidokkyosŏhoe, 2005).

8. For further information regarding the small groups of established megachurches, see Ro Bong-Rin and Marlin L. Nelson, *Korean Church Growth Explosion* (Taichung: Asia Theological Association, 1983).

9. See the following link from Onnuri Community Church's web page: http://www.onnuri.or.kr/sub.asp?gubun=31, accessed December 16, 2010.

10. Hwang Il-Do, "Han'guk kidokkyo taep'yo chuja Onnuri kyohoe" [Leading Representative of Korean Christianity: Onnuri Community Church], *Sindonga* 577 (2007): 152–165.

11. National Statistics Office, *In'gu chut'aek ch'ongchosa* [Population and Housing Census Report (2005)], accessed April 1, 2009.

12. See the web pages of Duranno Mall, http://mall.duranno.com/, and Duranno Sŏwŏn, http://www.duranno.com/books/.

13. Ryu Chae-Kwang, "Sŏn'gyosadŭl wihan wisŏng pangsong CGNTV kaeguk 1 chunyŏn" [First Year Anniversary of the Satellite Broadcasting for Missionaries: CGN TV], *Christianity Today*, last modified April 3, 2006, http://www.christiantoday.co.kr/view_eli.html?id=173446, accessed December 16, 2010.

14. Ahn Pyŏng-Yŏng and Im Hyuk-Baek, eds., *Segyehwawa sinchayujuŭi: sasang, hyŏnsil, kŭrigo taeŭng* [Globalization and Neoliberalism: Idea, Reality, and Responses] (Seoul: Nanam, 2000).

15. Neoliberalism could be also understood as the revival of liberalism after the prevalence of Keynesianism during the period of the 1930s to 1960s in America and Britain. Stagflation in the 1970s, however, produced skepticism regarding government regulation of the market. Classical liberalism allowing for freer market mechanisms gained public and political support as an alternative. The Margaret Thatcher and Ronald Reagan governments marked the turn to neoliberalism in Britain and America in the early 1980s. In defining the fundamental philosophy of neoliberalism, this essay draws on Friedrich von Hayek's works. Even though he did not call himself a neoliberalist, his ideas offered a foundation for the revival of classical liberalism and influenced the followers of neoliberalism. Friedrich A. von Hayek, *The Road to Serfdom* (London: George Routledge, 1944); *Law, Legislation and Liberty*, vol. 1: *Rules and Order* (Chicago: University of Chicago Press, 1978).

16. Shin Jang-Sup and Jang Ha-Joon, *Restructuring Korea Inc.* (New York: RoutledgeCurzon, 2003).

17. Lim Hyun-Chin and Jang Jin-Ho, "Neo-Liberalism in Post-Crisis South Korea: Social Conditions and Outcomes," *Journal of Contemporary Asia* 36, no. 4 (2006): 443–445.

18. Chŏng Mu-Kwon, "Kungminŭi chŏngbu'ŭi sahoe chŏngch'aek: Sinjayujuŭiroŭi hwaktae? Sahoe t'onghapŭroŭi chŏnhwan?" [Policies of the Kookmin Government: Expansion of Neoliberalism or a Turn toward the Integration of Society?], in Ahn Pyŏng-Yŏng and Im Hyuk-Baek, *Segyehwawa sinchayujuŭi: sasang, hyŏnsil, kŭrigo taeŭng*, 335.

19. Hayek, *Law, Legislation and Liberty*, 31.

20. Son Ho-Ch'ŏl, "Han'guk ŭi sinchayujuŭiwa minjujuŭi" [Democracy in Korea and Neoliberalism], in Ahn Pyŏng-Yŏng and Im Hyŏk-Baek, *Segyehwawa sinchayujuŭi: sasang, hyŏnsil, kŭrigo taeŭng*, 391.

21. "Pichŏnggyujik pŏbani chŏnggyujik naetchotnŭnda" [Legislation on Contracted Laborer Evacuates Permanent Jobs], *Ecumenian*, December 23, 2006.

22. Richard Sennett, *The Corrosion of Character: The Personal Consequences of Work in the New Capitalism* (New York: W. W. Norton and Company, 2001).

23. Chŏng In-Kyo, "Han'guk kyohoewa sŏlkyo pip'yŏng: isanggwa hyŏnsil

kŭrigo mirae" [Korean Protestant Churches and the Critical Essays on Their Sermons—Ideal, Reality and Future], *Kidokkyo sasang*, no. 588 (2007): 147.

24. Kim Se-Gwang, "Sambakcha guwŏn ochung pogŭme mutcheobeorin yŏksa—Yonggi Cho moksa" [History Hidden by the Prosperity Gospel], *Kidokkyo sasang* 10, no. 48 (2004): 44–57.

25. Yi, *Kidokkyo ŭi wigiwa hŭimang*, 195.

26. Kim Dong-Ho, *Haengbokhan pujarŭl wihan tasŏt kaji wŏnch'ik* [Five Principles to Becoming Happily Rich] (Seoul: Ch'ŏngnim, 2005), 187, 211.

27. Ibid., 30.

28. Kim Dong-Ho, *Kkaekkŭthan puja* [The Clean Rich] (Seoul: Kyujang, 2001), 46.

29. Ibid., 83.

30. This fable appears often in the starter testament of the Bible. See Matthew, chapter 14; Mark, chapter 6; Luke, chapter 9; and John, chapter 6.

31. Yu Kyŏng-Jae, ed., *Han'guk kyohoe 16inŭi sŏlkyorŭl marhanda* [Sermons of Sixteen Korean Protestant Pastors] (Seoul: The Christian Literature Society of Korea, 2004), 216.

32. The morning prayer meeting is one of the practices that is special to Korean churches. Almost every morning, as early as five in the morning, some church members gather and pray for thirty minutes to an hour. The practice is regarded as one of the hallmarks of the believers' faith. For further explanation, see Robert E. Buswell, ed., *Christianity in Korea* (Honolulu: University of Hawai'i Press, 2007).

33. The term "vision," which is the starting point of this narrative, became popular among Korean Christian communities in the late 1990s. Vision in its literal meaning indicates one's ability to see things ahead. It has been used to refer to a particular vocation overarching one's career and life that is a sacred calling from God.

34. Welcoming remarks by one pastor to the program on November 6, 2006, at Onnuri Community Church Sŏbinggo campus.

35. Sŏ Tong-Chin, *Chayu ŭi ŭiji chagiŭi kyebal ŭi ŭiji* [Will to Self-Empowerment, the Will to Freedom] (Seoul: Tol Pegae, 2009).

36. Ulrich Beck, Anthony Giddens, and Scott Lash, *Reflexive Modernization. Politics, Tradition and Aesthetics in the Modern Social Order* (Cambridge, UK: Polity, 1994).

PART II

Religion and Social Relations

3

Guanxi and Gospel

Mapping Christian Networks in South China

Joseph Tse-Hei Lee

Founded in 1849, the Yanzao church was the oldest Presbyterian congregation in the Chaozhou-speaking "Swatow (Shantou) mission" of South China. On October 17, 1999, the church held a thanksgiving service to celebrate its 150th anniversary. The newly opened chapel was the tallest building in the village, and its walls were decorated with beautiful scrolls of Bible verses sent by the Yanzao natives from Hong Kong, Southeast Asia, Europe, and North America. Local church leaders, government officials, and a British delegation led by George A. Hood, a former Presbyterian missionary in Shantou from 1945 to 1950, attended the celebration. The Yanzao Christians are determined to show that they have not only survived turbulent decades of political and social conflicts during the Maoist era (1949–1976), but also rebuilt their networks with overseas Chinese and British churches.[1] The growth of this congregation represents a wider pattern of Christian revival in China today.[2]

The latest scholarship on China acknowledges that social networks and relationships (*guanxi*) are major building blocks of Chinese society, shaping its politics, economy, and culture.[3] Western missionary enterprises and native Chinese churches have greatly relied on *guanxi* for expansion.[4] But little is written about how different forms of *guanxi* have affected the transmission of Christianity in specific temporal and spatial contexts. The

Chinese term for networks, *guanxi,* embodies a complex web of relationships used for instrumental and affective purposes. The strongest relationships exist among immediate and extended family members, but networks also form among people sharing a common and meaningful experience. Using Chinese testimonies and Western missionaries' reports, this chapter examines the formation of Christian *guanxi* (networks) in early-twentieth-century South China by looking at the Presbyterian congregation in Yanzao. These Presbyterians lived under the weak rule of a failed state in modern China. Because state authorities failed to penetrate all the villages in China's vast landscape, conditions were favorable for the spread of Protestant Christianity. The countryside became the center of the Christian movement, and a typical Chinese believer was a man or woman living in a densely populated village. Christianity was integrated into the preexisting kinship and lineage structures and grew as a grassroots movement in which Chinese Christians succeeded in recruiting converts, building churches, accommodating their faith with traditional customs, and developing social and religious bonds. This networking effect contributed to the process of Christianization, as the gospel passed from individual to individual, family to family, and village to village.

The analysis of *guanxi* and gospel offers insights into the transformation of Christianity from a Euro-American religion into an indigenous movement, challenging us to address the related issues of contact and conflict, network and identity, collective rituals and individual belief. This chapter explores the evangelistic, cosmological, and moral modes of Christian *guanxi* in the Yanzao Presbyterian movement. The evangelistic mode refers to the cultivation of social relationships, patronage connections, and interchurch alliances. On conversion, Chinese Christians identified themselves with a particular denomination and their own lineage and village. This overlap of religious, kinship, and territorial identities provided a powerful mechanism for church establishment. The cosmological mode of *guanxi* shaped local Christians' understanding of the sacred and how they ought to relate to it. This spirituality reveals the determinant role of religious faith and the impact of preexisting cultures and norms on the conversionary process. The Chaozhou-speaking Protestants identified themselves in their dialect as "worshippers of Jesus Christ" (*bai yesu*) or "worshippers of the Supreme God" (*bai shangdi*). The Chinese word for worship, *bai,* refers to collective religious practices such as envisioning the supernatural world, appeasing ancestral spirits, and living virtuously. The act of worshipping together first defined the identity of Chinese Christians. This ritualistic element resembles what Richard Madsen calls a "socially embedded religion," in which believers worship together and perform rituals to gain protection for their families here and now.[5] The moral mode emphasizes one's attachment to a larger Christian body beyond immediate kinship and territorial boundaries. When Christians understood the basic tenets of their faith and were socialized as denominational members, they recognized their obligation to safeguard the welfare of others within the church networks. These various networks remained part of the repertoire of survival strategies for local Christians to rise out of uncertainty and turmoil in modern China.

This chapter discusses how the Yanzao Presbyterians combined the denominational structure with Chinese kinship practices to build churches, how they Christianized family genealogies according to their preexisting worldviews, how they formed and maintained a dynamic and flexible web of Christian networks adaptive to external changes, and how they used these networks to engage in disaster relief efforts after the destructive typhoon on August 2, 1922.

Building Churches: The Evangelistic Mode of Christian *Guanxi*

The village of Yanzao (Salt Pan) looks like an isolated fishing and salt-making community on the map (Map 3.1). Located along the border of Chenghai and Raoping districts, it is 35 kilometers northeast of the treaty port of Shantou. To the east are the sea and the islands of Jingzhou and Haishan, to the west is Lotus Hill, and to the north and south are two subsidiaries of the Han River. Before the construction of modern highways, Yanzao was accessible by boat along the inland rivers from Shantou. The journey took almost a day, and one needed to cross three rivers at the market towns of Waisha, Nanyang, and Dongli. Nowadays, it takes thirty minutes to drive along the four-lane highway from Shantou to Yanzao. The village is Chaozhou-speaking, with a current population of 18,500.[6] Yanzao and its neighboring settlements were the homes of emigrants from Hong Kong and Southeast Asia. Because of its close linkages with the outside world, Yanzao was a highly mobile society, one deeply integrated into maritime

Map 3.1. Yanzao in Chaozhou Prefecture. Copyright unknown, and publisher is no longer in business.

networks across the South China Sea, and the people were exposed to the influx of new ideas and newcomers from the outside world, be they Christian missionaries or foreign merchants from the West.

As a multilineage community, Yanzao has four territorial settlements, namely Shangshe (Upper Shrine), Shangcuo (Upper Village), Zhongshe (Middle Shrine), and Gangtou (Sea Port). Whereas Shangshe and Zhongshe were settled by the Liu, Cai, and Li lineages, Shangcuo and Gangtou were the strongholds of the senior and junior segments of the Lin lineage, respectively. The villagers specialized in salt-making, fishing, and maritime trade. Fresh seafood and river fish were abundant, and many oyster farms were built along the shore. Because of the shortage of rice land, they planted fruit trees and vegetables everywhere. Today the four settlements merge into an industrial township. Stores and factories are everywhere. Unless accompanied by local residents, it is impossible for outsiders to identify the locations of the four settlements (Figure 3.1).[7]

The Presbyterian missionary movement in Yanzao reflected the changing relations between China and the West and the rise of the junior Lin segment in Gangtou. Rudolf Lechler of the German Basel Mission came to

Figure 3.1. A view of Yanzao from the top of the church, August 2009. Photo taken by the author.

the British colony of Hong Kong in 1847. His mission field was the Chaozhou region. Lechler traveled to Shantou with several Chaozhou-speaking members of Karl Gützlaff's Chinese Union.[8] One of the helpful assistants was a returning Christian from Southeast Asia named Du, known as A Ai in the missionary literature. Because of the lack of government control, Lechler and evangelist Du stayed on Haishan Island and preached among fishermen and salt makers. On one occasion, Lin Chongyan became fascinated by Lechler's sermon and invited him to Gangtou. On arrival, Lechler converted several members of the junior Lin segment. Lin Lian and Zhang Zhuiru of Gangtou arranged for Rudolf Lechler and evangelist Du to rent an abandoned village school as a mission station. During the five years of his stay in Chaozhou, from 1848 to 1852, Lechler founded a Christian school in Gangtou. His students were teased by non-Christians as "children of the barbarian school" (*fanshuzhai zai*), but several of them later became Presbyterian ministers, including Lin Muzhi, Lin Fang, and Lin Chong-san.[9] Because most people remained indifferent to Christianity, Lechler left for Hong Kong in 1852 to join his colleague, Theodore Hamberg, in more promising missionary work among the Hakka minority newly immigrated to the colony.[10] One of Lechler's converts was Lin Qi from Gangtou, who temporarily gave up his faith because of hostility from relatives and neighbors. When he confessed his faith publicly and refused to participate in ancestral worship, he was compelled by the elders to withdraw from lineage affairs. As a result, he rejected his ritual and social obligations to his lineage. This undermined communal cohesion and provoked much anger from the lineage. In 1856, William Chalmers Burns of the English Presbyterian Mission stopped over at Shantou with James Hudson Taylor, founder of the China Inland Mission, and contemplated opening a new mission field there. It was Lin Qi who then asked William C. Burns to visit Yanzao in 1861. Seeing the potential to expand into Yanzao, Burns accepted Lin Qi's invitation to take up these scattered Christians instructed by Lechler a decade earlier.[11] The Presbyterian arrival was followed by an increase of conversions, with nineteen baptisms in 1862 and thirteen baptisms in 1863.[12] This marked the beginning of the use of lineage networks for evangelization. When a core group of Chinese Christians had formed, they recruited the second generation to the church. They proselytized among close relatives and lineage members.[13] By 1884, 87 people were baptized with 34 men (39 percent) and 53 women (61 percent). More women were incorporated into the congregation than men even before there were many female missionaries working in the field. The women were of all ages and followed their family patriarchs to the church. The male members were young and elderly people.[14] The young people saw conversion as their filial duty toward their Christian parents, and the elderly joined the church because they found Christianity to be useful in overcoming their fear of death.[15]

The congregational rolls suggest that kinship provided an important mechanism for group conversion in Yanzao. Three general principles can be discerned from this pattern of conversion. First, the Protestant missionaries deliberately converted the whole family, partly because they believed in the model of Christianized families and partly because the family structure helped to consolidate faith communities. The 1907 edition of *The Public Regulations of the Chaozhou-Huizhou Presbyterian Church* required baptism applicants to profess their faith at home. Second, many cases of family conversion followed the long-standing generation-age-and-gender hierarchy. The right to spread the gospel was acquired through age and social seniority. Either the patriarchs converted the entire family or the senior family members converted the junior ones. This reflected the traditional respect paid by the younger family members to their seniors. Third, the pattern of female conversion differed from that of male conversion. Many women joined the church because of their Christian parent-in-laws. In this patriarchal society, the family provided security and support for its members in exchange for their loyalty and submission. In the proselytizing process, the Christian parents exerted as much influence over adult children as over teenage sons and daughters, especially before the children divided the family property to set up their own households (*fengjia*). The missionaries fully understood the patriarchal structure of Chinese society and were quick to use parental authority for evangelization. Christian patriarchs saw conversion, baptism, and church affiliation as essential filial duties for their children, and families remained active church members for generations. Thus, one intriguing feature was the lack of individual consciousness. Because the Christian family was a collective unit, individual choice was limited so that all family members could remain cohesive.

After the founding of the Presbyterian congregation in Yanzao, Lin Qi became the church leader, and he received much help from the missionaries to administer the chapel. He sent all his children to the Presbyterian mission schools in Shantou. Lin Wenzhi, his eldest son, later became a deacon and elder of the Yanzao church. Lin Fang, the second son, initially studied the doctrines under Rudolf Lechler. Then he became a Presbyterian evangelist and was ordained a minister.[16] He often mediated conflicts between Christians and non-Christians and appealed to English missionaries and diplomats for help in cases of anti-Christian violence. Lin Qi's third son, named Lin Qi, written with a different character (1857–1944), was trained by William Gauld to be a medical practitioner. William Lin, the fourth son, was named after William C. Burns and went into business after receiving his mission education in Shantou. Phoebe Lin, the eldest daughter, graduated from the Shunde Girls' School in Shantou. At seventeen, she became an instructor at the Bible Women's House, founded in 1881 and known as the "Old Women's School." She taught many elderly, illiterate women to read biblical texts and hymns in the romanized script. After four months' instruction, these women could answer questions on Genesis and translate the Gospel of Mark and hymns into the vernacular. When they returned home, they reached out to over seventy villages not yet visited by the missionaries.[17] Phoebe later married a Presbyterian medical practitioner from Huanggang market in Raoping district. But because of anti-Christian sentiment, her family relocated to Yanzao, where she founded the Peide Girls' School to teach local women to read the Bible in the vernacular. Their close association with the Presbyterian Mission transformed the family of Lin Qi into one of the most well-established Christian elites in early-twentieth-century Shantou.[18]

Lin Qi's conversion was motivated as much by material incentives as by a new vision of cultural and social empowerment. In late imperial China, the only way for ambitious young men to climb the social ladder was to become degree holders through the civil service examination. But this career option was not available to Lin Qi's children because Yanzao was located far away from the center of Confucian orthodoxy in the district and prefectural cities. When Lin Qi reconfessed his faith to William C. Burns, he rejected his inherited religious traditions and shifted his loyalty to the Presbyterian Mission. He was frustrated with the futility of worshipping ancestral spirits and village deities. When he sent his children to Presbyterian schools, he was determined to raise their literacy level and provide them with the necessary knowledge, skills, and networks to compete in the emerging treaty port economy. This decision was of great significance because his family embraced the modernizing elements of Christianity long before China espoused Westernization in the early twentieth century.

Christian women exercised as much influence over the conversion of their children as did family patriarchs. After listening to Rudolf Lechler's sermons, both Zhang Zhuiru and Lai Cunxin converted their sons and daughters-in-law. Lin Jikuan, the son of Lai Cunxin, used to be the treasurer of the powerful Lin lineage. After he was converted by his mother, he was expelled from the lineage. Then he resolved to use his administrative and financial skills to serve the Yanzao church. Madam An was baptized at a very old age. When she died, the Christians organized her funeral, and her son, Lin Guangyu, was so moved by the communal support that he joined the church.[19] Madam Yan, the maternal grandmother of Lin Zhanghan in Gangtou, brought all her relatives to the church and was trained by the English Presbyterians to be a Bible woman. According to Oi-King Ling, Bible women were full-time evangelistic workers "on the lowest hierarchical ladder of their mission churches," and "only those who were tough, modest, conscientious, and relatively free from family obligations" were suitable for such a demanding job. Other women could do itinerant preaching and serve as role models for female faith seekers.[20]

The capacity of Christianity to merge with local cultures and kinship networks strengthened the foundation of the Yanzao church. Many members of the junior Lin segment worked as Presbyterian schoolteachers and evangelists. The family of Lin Zhangzao was another pillar of the congregation. He and Lin Shoutian, the eldest son, were ordained ministers. Lin Xingdao, the second son, graduated from the Shantou Gospel Hospital and ran a successful pharmacy in the Chaozhou prefectural city. Lin Shoutian's eldest son was also a well-known medical practitioner, and the second son became a successful merchant, overseeing business activities in Shantou, Hong Kong, and Australia. His eldest daughter, Lin Zhenhua, was educated at the Presbyterian girls' school in Shantou and later married Wang Chaoying, a minister from Jieyang district.[21] The Presbyterian movement not only provided new career options for the junior Lin segment, but also enabled them to acquire literacy skills and move upward on the social ladder, which otherwise they would have had no opportunity to do. It also transformed Yanzao from an unknown coastal village into a major Christian center in northeastern Guangdong Province.

During the 1860s, three Presbyterian stations in Fushan, Xianzhou, and Huanggang markets developed out of the Yanzao chapel. The church expansion proved beneficial to Lin Qi, giving him the opportunity to preach at and administer these new stations. By 1873, Lin Qi was a full-time preacher in Yanzao. He cultivated peer networks with fellow church leaders and expanded social ties with other Christians through marriages. His sons found their wives from other Presbyterian families. Lin Zhangchong, one of Lin Qi's grandsons, married Guan Jipu, the daughter of a famous Hakka-speaking minister in Jieyang district. The marriages consolidated the kinship and emotional ties among the Presbyterians. When these connections merged with the interchurch networks, they ensured mutual support in a predominantly non-Christian environment.

In rural China, people had very active social lives outside the family sphere. Interpersonal, intervillage, business, occupational, and temple networks permeated local society. Given its strategic location and high concentration of Christians, the Yanzao church was able to reach out to the vast landscape of Chenghai and Raoping districts and converted many outsiders. Coinciding with the Taiping Uprising (1851–1864) in central China, a series of peasant uprisings broke out in Chaozhou. Though Yanzao was not directly affected, the interior became a hotbed of collective violence.[22] Faced with this unprecedented level of chaos and upheaval, the Liu family of Fushan (Floating Mountain) market sought refuge in Huizhai (Ash Village), a walled village west of Yanzao. During their sojourn, Liu Siyi and Liu Siren, brothers and merchants, were converted by the Yanzao Christians. After the imperial government crushed the rebels and restored law and order, the church backed Liu Siyi and Liu Siren to found a mission station in Fushan market. Since then, the Liu family became closely identified with Yanzao through marriages and joint religious and business activities. Liu Siyi's son married Lin Chunshang, the eldest daughter of Lin Lian. Lin Chunshang attended the Shunde Girls' School in Shantou with Phoebe Lin and mastered the romanized Chaozhou script. When her husband defended the Fushan congregation at Raoping district court, she wrote a petition in the vernacular and sent it to the magistrate.[23]

The Xie family in Yihu village shared ties with Yanzao. Yihu is 48 kilometers northwest of Yanzao. A stream flows past the village's northeast. The village is located in the lowlands, and the rain still falls in a vast expanse of whiteness and floods the fields. The people called the settlement White Water Lake (Peh-Tsui-Ou) in the local dialect. In the nineteenth century, the dominant Xie lineage specialized in the sugar trade. Sugarcane refinery facilities and warehouses dotted the landscape. Xie Youpeng was the local church founder. In 1888, his elderly father, Xie Naihuo, had an eye disease and went to the Shantou Gospel Hospital for treatment, accompanied by his grandson, Xie Zehong. Xie Naihuo was healed by Philip B. Cousland. He and his grandson then participated in morning and evening services. They were taught to denounce popular religious practices and to memorize "the ten commandments, Lord's prayer, and hymn book."[24] When they returned home, Xie Youpeng was impressed by the transformation of his own son, Xie Zehong. As "a devout idol-worshipper" himself, Xie Youpeng was curious about the gospel. He pretended to be sick in order to take time off from his business and visit the hospital. His illness was a pretense because "it was not his body but his mind that wanted treatment."[25] He spent weeks in Shantou studying the doctrine with the medical assistant Lin Qi, another Yanzao native. When he returned home, he and his son attended the Yanzao church every Sunday. However, his brothers and uncles criticized him for not helping with the family business. This became a problem during the spring harvest, when the community was busy "cutting down the cane, stripping off the outer covering, and carrying [it] to the crushing place" for refining. The Xie family usually stored the refined brown sugar in their shared warehouses, but when the brothers' objections became serious, they denied Xie Youpeng access to the warehouses.[26]

Meanwhile, Xie Naihuo, the old father of Xie Youpeng, was ridiculed by relatives for his conversion. He gave up his faith and justified the decision by referring to a popular Chaozhou saying: "When one enters a village, one must follow the customs [*ruxiang suisu*]. When one enters a sea port, one must sail along the bay [*rugang suiwan*]."[27] After Xie Naihuo passed away, his relatives proposed a traditional funeral. But Xie Youpeng insisted on a Christian funeral for his father and asked the Yanzao Christians for help. Afterwards, he broke away from the family business and set up his own warehouse. He initially organized family worship at his small warehouse every week. He then planned to use his own share of the family capital to build a chapel, but his brothers opposed the plan and refused to lend him any money. He refused to back down. Accompanied by Yanzao Christians, he went to Shantou to ask the Presbyterian missionaries for a mortgage of $150 to build his business operation and church properties. The missionaries lent him the money, and within a year he had made much profit and was able to pay back the loan. After the buildings were erected, the missionaries sent a preacher to proselytize among members of the Xie lineage. Xie Youpeng never redeemed the buildings as his own properties. He once told his daughter-in-law to seek the preacher's permission before drying clothes in the compound. Before his death, he instructed his children to pay the English Mission a total of $400 if they intended to redeem the buildings. When the local congregation decided to build a new chapel in 1921, his children paid $400 to redeem the buildings and contributed to the chapel's construction fund. As with the Liu family of Fushan, Xie Youpeng arranged for his sons to attend mission schools and marry Yanzao Christians. Once Christianity merged into long-standing social webs in China, it absorbed and redirected existing human bonds for evangelistic purposes. These networks placed early converts like Lin Qi, the Liu brothers, and Xie Youpeng in leadership positions and fostered a distinctive Christian identity and subculture among them.

It is worth emphasizing that the Presbyterian movement comprised clergy and laity. From the start, it relied on both clerical and lay leadership. Congregational life and practice was the purview of Chinese themselves, but the denominational structure introduced by the missionaries added a layer of supervision. The Yanzao church and its subsidiaries in Fushan and Yihu were organized along local lineage or sublineage networks. By definition, *lineage* means groups of people who trace their descent from a common ancestor, and *sublineage* refers to members of the same lineage who identify with different sons of the common ancestor. In a lineage or sublineage church, affiliation was not entirely voluntary because it usually included most members of a particular lineage or lineage segment. When Christianity became a lineage identity, it was a social obligation for its members to join the church. Conversion meant a closer identification with the new Christian lineage. The chapel was primarily funded by the Christian lineage members and became their common religious property. As a form of rural space, the church allowed people to witness their faith, to study the doctrines, to network with others, and to exchange information about their common concerns. The church was as important as an ancestral hall was to the non-Christians.

The internal distribution of power was organized vertically, and church leaders were usually the dominant figures in the Christian lineage. Church leadership was concentrated in a few well-connected individuals. Social prestige, biblical knowledge, wealth, and senior positions in a web of relationships defined their authority. One implication of this hierarchy was that Christian patriarchs could monopolize local church affairs and even turn the church into their new power bases. In tackling this structural problem, the English Presbyterians adopted the plan of a limited tenure for the church elders and deacons. The elders and deacons were to be elected every five years in order to remove inefficient leaders who held the office for too long and to prevent certain factions from monopolizing the church.[28] The regulation separated the control and management of local churches and provided a layer of check and balance. This administrative division paralleled the split between control and management of common resources in traditional lineages. John Campbell Gibson once commented that Chinese became Presbyterians before they became Christians. Evidently Chinese Christians were quick to combine the Presbyterian denominational structure with the traditional practices of lineage management to run the churches.[29]

To avoid the problem of nepotism, the Presbyterian movement was built around presbyteries and synods, and around many ad hoc committees of missionaries, ministers, lay leaders, and supporters. The multiple layers of support and supervision ensured the inclusive nature of the movement. Even though the Lin lineage exerted dominant control in the Yanzao congregation, they admitted Christians of other surnames and evangelists appointed by the missionaries into the church's inner circle. Because Yanzao was far away from the center of Confucian orthodoxy, the congregation allowed women to participate in church management as deaconesses and elders. These mechanisms checked the corrosive influence of territorially based kinship relations and gave local church leaders access to information, resources, and aids greater than those of a traditional lineage.

The Yanzao Christians benefited considerably from conversion. The first generation of converts obtained secure employment opportunities in the mission institutions. Their children attended the mission schools and became medical practitioners, nurses, evangelists, and schoolteachers. The second generation grew up in closely knit Christian families. They socialized among themselves and relied on the Christian resources to pursue their careers. The participation in congregational activities was central to their collective identity. Their shared rituals and beliefs distinguished them from other lineage and temple communities.

Commemorating Ancestors: The Cosmological Mode of Christian *Guanxi*

The Chinese forged their understanding of the gospel within the context of traditional lineage. They organized family worship, studied the Bible themselves, and directed the everyday practices of congregational life. They found much comfort in biblical references to worshipping God as the God of Abraham, Isaac, and Jacob. Even though the Chinese were taught by the missionaries to reject ancestral worship, they argued that God was the God of one's ancestors, families, and lineages.[30] They imitated Abraham, Isaac, and Jacob to break away from traditional lineages and create Christian genealogies. This reflects the different understanding of human life in East and West. The missionaries proclaimed human lives to be created in God's own image. Individuals should be responsible to God for all their acts in this world, and they should answer to God on judgment day. But the Chinese conception of human existence was that of the ancestral lineage. Individuals were exemplars of their lineage throughout their lifetimes. They were responsible to their ancestors and descendants. The feeling between ancestors and descendants correlated with the emotional love between parents and children. People passed down their virtue to their descendants, and their good deeds glorified them and their ancestors.[31] In line with this tradition, Chinese Christians upheld their ancestors' reputations in order to inspire future generations with their religious commitment. They drew relevant moral lessons from the biblical accounts of Abraham, Isaac, and Jacob. When they embraced these biblical narratives, they "performed the scriptural teachings" (*hangdao*) in their own context.[32] They incorporated into the Christian movement the ritual of ancestral worship that had been promoted by the imperial state to all classes of Chinese society since the early sixteenth century.[33] The Yanzao Christians referred to their first converts as new ancestors and evangelistic pioneers, putting them on equal footing with foreign missionaries in the local church history. The congregation maintained a Christian cemetery on Lotus Hill, assuring church members that their tombs would be surrounded by those of their relatives and friends. They revered their ancestors by holding special church services and visiting their graves every spring. The tombstones referred to the first converts as "disciples of Christ" (*Jidu mentu*), expressing the religious identity and pride of the deceased. Early Christian women were hailed as new ancestors too. This commemorative practice subverted the patriarchy in Chinese family structure.

As part of the conversionary process, Chinese Christians were taught to ignore geomantic practice (*fengshui*), a technique used to locate specific points where telluric energies would come to the surface and where humans could tap into the flow of energies for building houses, graves, and temples.[34] If a building was thought to obstruct the free flow of energies, it would upset the cosmological balance with nature and cause misfortune to the family. When Lin Qi died, he was buried on a hillside deemed as unlucky. The Lin family built the Christian cemetery against geomantic principles. When Lin Qi's children became local business and church leaders, non-Christians thought that the Presbyterians had mastered the geomantic technique to access the flow of telluric energies. The non-Christians used to call the burial site "the place where the ghost fell." After seeing the success of Lin Qi's descendants, they renamed it "the site where the ghost discovered gold." By calling Lin Qi a "ghost" metaphorically, they were still expressing antagonism with him for breaking away from the lineage.[35]

The most effective way of maintaining an ancestral lineage was to compile genealogies. The Christian genealogies were works in progress because each generation liked to update the scale of the growing family networks. They differed from traditional genealogies in three areas. First, the Christian genealogies included the names of female descendants and women married into the families, treating them as equal to male members. Second, they included the names and biographies of all male and female descendants. This challenged the Chinese generational hierarchy of keeping the names of the eldest sons only. Third, the genealogies interpreted the history of family conversion as part of their living memories, creating a collective Christian identity that transcended time and space.[36] When Christianity became a family religion, Jesus Christ became the focus of worship and fostered a new religious and social identity to hold different generations of the families together. Therefore, Christian identity was a collective one. These findings confirm Richard Madsen's argument that strong kinship ties held the different generations of Christians together and prevented them from falling apart.[37]

Managing Disaster: The Moral Mode of Christian *Guanxi*

The Yanzao church was the largest congregation along the borders of Chenghai and Raoping districts and a major landmark in the Shantou mission field. It bore witness to the perfect compatibility between Christianity and Chinese culture. The Christian faith, ritual practices, and institutional networks profoundly shaped the church members' encounters with the outside world. The resilience of such Christian networks is best shown in the aftermath of the destructive typhoon on August 2, 1922, the greatest crisis facing the Yanzao community in the early twentieth century. The "typhoon of August 2" (*baer fengzai*) lifted a vast mass of seawater and hurled it on low-lying villages along the entire coastal region, sweeping away hundreds of people, animals, and fishing boats. Farther inland, strong winds flattened buildings and huts, and caused many more casualties. There was utter devastation across the coast: entire villages washed away, paddy fields strewn with corpses and dead animals, survivors sleeping in the rough outdoors. The typhoon was a terrifying experience for survivors. The plight of the villages was the worst. "The houses were flimsy structures or built only of mud. The strong wind and the tidal wave together demolished whole villages and washed away miles of embankment. There were many stories of survivors who lost most of their family members."[38] The coast of Chenghai and Raoping districts was badly hit. According to Fannie Northcott of the American Baptist Mission,

> The most acute suffering from the typhoon was on the great Theng Hai [Chenghai] plain. Before the typhoon, this plain was more or less densely populated by fishermen and a few farmers, who lived in groups of villages. . . . Because the land was level, large numbers of villages were exposed to the tidal wave. When it washed in over the plain, it carried on its course, houses and humans across the plain inland, in some instances 5, 7, or 9 miles. . . . When the wave receded, it carried out to sea, hundreds of bodies, the exact number will never be known. . . . Their fields are soaked with salt water and their houses down; boats washed away, women and children drowned, and the survivors go away from the fearful sorrow of all.[39]

When the agricultural fields were soaked with seawater, farmers lost a season of crops and needed to spend several months using fresh water to flush the salt out of the fields.[40] When the boats were gone, many fishermen had to go elsewhere to look for work. With such losses came a dehumanizing process that deeply affected the male survivors and produced social and cultural scars. One aspect was survivor's guilt as they felt alone and hopeless without their family members around. They blamed themselves for their failure to rescue relatives from the wave. Among the ruins, they found themselves trapped in a vanishing world. The typhoon took away their social and moral orientation, the source of their livelihoods, and their attachment to long-standing social and emotional identities. The survivors were reluctant to accept the shock of family and community breakup, the loss of farmlands, orchards, and fishing boats, the destruction of ancestral tombs, and the difficulty of living alone.

In Yanzao and nearby villages, the mud houses with lime walls could not withstand the typhoon and tidal wave. G. W. Lewis of the American Baptists reported the scale of damage:

> I passed the Iam-tsau [Yanzao] and saw Chia-chiu and other badly damaged villages up there. It also still seems to me like a nightmare. Many of the houses on the seafront whose walls were fully above the average of pounded walls as indicated by the broken parts,–fully up to proportion in lime–yet these walls lay flat. . . . The water marks indicated on the seafront that the water must have been upwards of twenty feet deep, and must have been driven in with great violence. . . . People were drowned in twenty feet deep water and then crushed into the crumbling walls of the houses.[41]

Because of the violent wind and the tidal wave, fishing boats became uncontrolled weapons of destruction that crushed houses and killed many people. Wang Chaoying, a Presbyterian evangelist, saw drowned pigs as large as water buffalo.[42] The coast had become a living hell, and the typhoon totally shattered the fishing economy. Although the Christians were little prepared for it, the mission headquarters in Shantou and the numerous native churches found themselves as the only viable institutions after the disaster and, as such, bore the burden of relief work. Government officials had to rely on the churches to reach out to the devastated villages. Missionaries, preachers, Bible women, medical staff, mission schoolteachers, and students became relief workers on the spot.

The typhoon became an important component of the Yanzao Christians' collective memory. On August 2, 1922, the Yanzao congregation lost 119 members, one-fourth of the total of 476 deaths in the village. Deacons Lin Junjie, Lin Xingyong, and Liao Yuna were killed. Church elder Chen Shunsheng, who lived in a tall three-story house around the fish pond outside the church, lost eighteen family members. The tidal wave also left sixty orphans and large numbers of injured church members.[43] The spirits of the surviving Christians were not defeated, however. Church elder Chen Shunsheng and Guo Jingyun, the ordained minister, "devoted themselves to organization and oversight of the relief and did invaluable and untiring work."[44] Lin Zhangchong organized the survivors and village defense forces to rescue people and survey the damage. Many Yanzao sojourners assisted with the relief operation. Lin Zhangzao, Lin Fang, and Lin Chong-shan, who administrated churches elsewhere, mobilized their congregations to support the suffering brethren and sisters in Yanzao. Lin Shoutian, Lin Wenhe, and Chen Yiting, merchants and elders of the Bethel Church in Shantou, channeled resources to their home village. There was a strong religious component in the disaster relief efforts. Liu Zerong, an ordained minister, "spent weekend after weekend in visiting the area, making careful investigation, and seizing the extraordinary opportunity which he discovered for preaching."[45] He visited victims' families in Yanzao and nearby villages. The disaster eliminated preexisting intervillage tensions and created a social bonding between Christians and non-Christians. As T. W. Douglas James observed, "Just as at Iam-tsau [Yanzao] ancient village feuds which had long separated that village from its neighbor and reacted unfavorably on Christian preaching were swept away and so many new hearers came to Church as to fill up in numbers the gap which the disaster had caused in membership."[46] With the support of the English Presbyterians, Liu Zerong eventually founded a new church in the neighboring village of Nanshengbu.

In the summer of 1923, a year after the typhoon catastrophe, Patrick J. Maclagan visited "the stricken congregation" of Yanzao on behalf of the Foreign Mission Committee of the Presbyterian Church of England. That visit was of high symbolic significance because "the Church at home in the person of the Convener should stand at the salute before those heaps of stones that had been Christian homes, and where Christian families had perished." In China, where ancestry was so much honored, "there could have been no more significant act than the visit to the grave on the slopes of the Lotus Hill of the first Christian of the Hoklo Church."[47] This high-profile visit renewed the historic ties between Chinese Christians and their missionary patrons, and conveyed a clear message that the English Presbyterians would always stand by the "Hoklo Church" in good and bad times. The transnational Christian networks stood the test of time and remained unbreakable. Historian Chen Chunsheng asserts that after the typhoon many emigrant villages in Chenghai district turned to their relatives in Southeast Asia for help. The wealthy emigrants of Zhanglin market paid for all the local relief efforts and set up the Biansheng Hospital to cater to the sick.[48] Li Longqian points out that the Chaozhou Eight Districts' Chambers of Commerce in Hong Kong sent large amounts of rice to Shantou.[49] These examples of institutionally based relief efforts operated within the traditional structure of Chinese society. But what distinguished the Yanzao church from these organizations was their faith-based relief work. Through their extensive networks, the congregation called for financial assistance not only from their missionary patrons in Shantou and fellow Christians in unaffected areas, but also from overseas Chinese churches in Southeast Asia and from the Presbyterians in England and Scotland. The Yanzao migrants in Hong Kong, Siam, and British Malaya helped build an orphanage to discourage the kidnapping and sale of children by starving refugees. The orphans were taught vocational skills and studied with other children at the Presbyterian Zhishang Elementary School.[50] Concerned with long-term community reconstruction, the church leaders worked with the representatives of nearby villages to clear the debris and bury the dead. They employed a large number of workers to reconstruct a dike in Yanzao and offered grants and loans to survivors to rebuild their homes and boats.[51] These capacity building measures helped survivors acquire the necessary skills and resources for community survival. The transnational church networks constituted an invisible maritime highway that channeled resources for the Yanzao Presbyterians to reconstruct and keep alive their Christian homeland.

As a global religion, Christianity is intrinsically translatable, whether to Asia, Africa, or Latin America. But its indigenous forms of expression are shaped by preexisting cultural norms and practices. Ever since the English Presbyterians arrived at the Chaozhou-speaking region of South China, they adopted an innovative strategy of empowering native Christians to interpret the gospel themselves. Religious conversion seldom took place in a social and cultural vacuum. It drew on native institutional resources and was expressed through local cultures and kinship networks. In a society heavily regulated by human relationships, personal dynamics and various networks sometimes took precedence over doctrinal and institutional positions. Long-standing lineage structures and preexisting religious sensibilities overrode strict doctrinal teachings. These features operated naturally together and enabled the Christianizing process to evolve over time.

This essay has highlighted the instrumental, moral, and cosmological dimensions of Christian *guanxi,* and explained why Protestantism made significant inroads into Chinese society. The arrival of the English

Presbyterians coincided with the Western imperialistic intrusions into nineteenth-century China. Although the gospel was rejected by Confucian scholars and imperial officials, it reached the village population, who gained access to mission education and social mobility and created extensive church networks. On the surface, the Christian networks might have been instrumental in helping the Christians secure material resources and political advantages from missionary enterprises. But the Presbyterian movement integrated many preexisting norms and practices into Chinese Christendom and reinforced new emotional attachments and moral obligations among members within the networks. The patron-client relations with foreign missionaries, the Christians' marriage and occupational links, and the interchurch networks ensured trust, emotional ties, and mutual stability in the movement. These networks served as an important avenue of resource allocation for the Christians to empower themselves.

In short, the Chinese expressions of Christianity surpassed the imported ones. One remarkable feature was the ability of rural Christians to manage and finance complicated undertakings on their own. When they embraced the gospel, they were in control of the process of religious transmission. They used their prior knowledge, organizational skills, and personal networks to carve a new social and religious space for themselves. They formed Christian lineages and genealogies to maintain solidarity in a non-Christian environment. Instead of running the church according to rigid regulations imposed by the missionaries, they combined the Western denominational structure with local kinship, village, and lineage networks. This fascinating process of cross-cultural interaction demonstrates the frequent crossover of new and old identities in the lives of Chinese Christians. Only by studying the diversified linkages between *guanxi* and gospel can we appreciate the dynamics of Christianity in modern China.

Notes

I want to thank the Center for Christian Studies of Shantou University for fully supporting this research project through a generous grant (Project Code: CCSRF1112-A).

1. *Chenghai shi Jidujiaohui Yanzao chuangli 150 zhounian jinian (1849–1999)* [Commemorating the 150th Anniversary of the Founding of the Christian Church in Yanzao in Chenghai Municipality (1849–1999)] (Yanzao, Guangdong Province,

1999); *Yanzao Jidujiaohui chuangli 160 zhounian (1849–2009)* [Commemorating the 160th Anniversary of the Founding of the Yanzao Christian Church (1849–2009)] (Yanzao, Guangdong Province, 2009).

2. Joseph Tse-Hei Lee, "Christianity in Contemporary China: An Update," *Journal of Church and State* 49, no. 2 (2007): 277–304.

3. Mayfair Mei-Hui Yang, *Gifts, Favors, and Banquets: The Art of Social Relationships in China* (Ithaca, NY: Cornell University Press, 1994); Thomas Gold, Doug Guthrie, and David Wank, eds., *Social Connections in China: Institutions, Culture, and the Changing Nature of Guanxi* (Cambridge, UK: Cambridge University Press, 2002); Nara Dillon and Jean C. Oi, eds., *At the Crossroads of Empires: Middlemen, Social Networks, and State-Building in Republican Shanghai* (Stanford, CA: Stanford University Press, 2008); Zhao Ma, "Down the Alleyway: Courtyard Tenements and Women's Networks in Early Twentieth-Century Beijing," *Journal of Urban History* 36, no. 2 (2010): 151–172; Xuezhi Guo, "Dimensions of *Guanxi* in Chinese Elite Politics," *The China Journal* 46 (2001): 69–90.

4. Jean-Paul Wiest, "Lineage and Patterns of Conversion in Guangdong," *Ch'ing-shih wen-t'i* 4, no. 7 (1982): 1–32; Joseph Tse-Hei Lee, "The Overseas Chinese Networks and Early Baptist Missionary Movement across the South China Sea," *The Historian* 63, no. 4 (2001): 752–768.

5. Richard Madsen, "Secularism, Religious Renaissance, and Social Conflict in Asia" (2008), Religion and Culture Web Forum, Martin Marty Center for the Advanced Study of Religion, Chicago Divinity School, http://divinity.uchicago.edu/martycenter/publications/webforum/092008/index.shtml.

6. This is based on my fieldwork observation in Yanzao in August 2009.

7. *Shantou shi dimingzhi* [A Dictionary of Place Names in Shantou] (Shantou: Xinhua Chubanshe, 1996), 113.

8. Ellen Xiangyu Cai, "The Itinerant Preaching of Three Hoklo Evangelists in Mid-Nineteenth Century Hong Kong," *Itinerario* 33, no. 3 (2009): 113–134.

9. Lin Zhang and Lin Liangshan, comps., *Liliji mushi yu Yanzao jiaohui* [Rudolf Lechler and the Yanzao Church] (Yanzao, Guangdong Province, 2007): 6–7.

10. John Campbell Gibson, *Mission Problems and Mission Methods in South China* (New York: Revell, 1901), 144–149; Jessie G. Lutz and Rolland Ray Lutz, *Hakka Chinese Confront Protestant Christianity 1850–1900* (Armonk, NY: M. E. Sharpe, 1998), 4–5.

11. George A. Hood, *Mission Accomplished? The English Presbyterian Mission in Lingtung, South China: A Study of Interplay between Mission Methods and Their Historical Contexts* (Frankfurt, Germany: Peter Lang, 1986), 28; Murray A. Rubinstein, "Actors: Protestant Missionaries," in *Handbook of Christianity in China,* vol. 2: *1800 to the Present,* ed. R. G. Tiedemann (Leiden: E. J. Brill, 2010), 162–163.

12. "6. Iam-Tsau (Yanzao)," in Mission Council, comp., *The Congregational Rolls for Use in the Swatow Mission* (Shantou: Mission Press, 1885).

13. Jessie G. Lutz, "Early Chinese Protestants," in Tiedemann, *Handbook of Christianity in China,* vol. 2: *1800 to the Present,* 254.

14. "6. Iam-Tsau (Yanzao)," in Mission Council, comp., *The Congregational Rolls.*

15. Joseph Tse-Hei Lee, *The Bible and the Gun: Christianity in South China, 1860–1911* (New York and London: Routledge, 2003), 73.

16. "Wei Zhonghua Jidujiaohui Lingdong dahui: youguan jiushilu ming mushi chuanlue" [The Lingdong Convention of the Church of Christ in China: Biographical Sketches of Ninety-Six Protestant Ministers] (1948), Shantou Shi Dang'an Guan [Shantou Municipal Archive], Jiuzhengquan Dang'an [The Archives of the Republican Regime], call no. 12/11/16.

17. C. Mann, *Catherine Maria Ricketts of Brighton and China* (London: Women's Missionary Association of the Presbyterian Church of England, 1924), 27–28.

18. Lin Xingcun, interviewed by author, Hong Kong, September 16, 1997. Lin Xingcun was a church elder at the Hong Kong Shantou Christian Church Mission. A native of Yanzao, he is one of the great grandsons of Lin Qi.

19. "Wei Zhonghua Jidujiaohui Lingdong dahui: youguan jiushilu ming mushi chuanlue" (1948); Lin Zhang and Lin Liangshan, comps., *Liliji mushi yu Yanzao jiaohui,* 6–7.

20. Oi-Ki Ling, "Bible Women," in *Pioneer Chinese Christian Women: Gender, Christianity, and Social Mobility,* ed. Jessie G. Lutz (Bethlehem, PA: Lehigh University Press, 2010), 249 and 260.

21. Wang Ruifang and Wang Jianyuan, interviewed by author at Sun-Yat Sen University in Guangzhou, China, August 1 and 2, 2009. They are the children of Rev. Wang Chaoying, who served the Yanzao congregation from 1937 to 1951.

22. Joseph Lee, *The Bible and the Gun,* 10–16.

23. Liu Yihui, "*Liu shi jiapu* jiaodian: Chaoshan Jidujiao bentuhua shiliao juyu" [Commentaries on *The Liu Family Genealogy:* Historical Sources on the Localization of Christianity in Chaoshan], *Shantou Daxue xuebao* [Journal of Shantou University] 19 (2003): 115–117.

24. Joseph Lee, *The Bible and the Gun,* 58.

25. T. W. Douglas James, "The Peh-tsui-ou Congregation," February 1922, Presbyterian Church of England (PCE) Archives, Foreign Mission Committee (FMC), Library of the School of Oriental and African Studies, University of London, UK (SOAS), microfiche no. 874.

26. Ibid.

27. Xie Yufang, "Xie shi jiapu" [The Xie family genealogy] (unpublished manuscript, 1983, author's possession).

28. *The China Mission: Draft of Handbook,* 1920, 4, series 1, box 15, PCE, FMC, SOAS.

29. John Campbell Gibson, *Mission Problems,* 198.

30. Jacob Speicher, *The Conquest of the Cross in China* (New York: Fleming H. Revell, 1907), 252–254.

31. Sarah Allan, *The Way of Water and Sprouts of Virtue* (Albany: State University of New York Press, 1997), 100–101.

32. David S. Cunningham, *Christian Ethics: The End of the Law* (London: Routledge, 2008), 96–99.

33. David Faure, *Emperor and Ancestor: State and Lineage in South China* (Stanford, CA: Stanford University Press, 2007), 13–14.

34. John Lagerwey, *China: A Religious State* (Hong Kong: Hong Kong University Press, 2010), 15.

35. Lin Xingcun, interviewed by author, Hong Kong, September 16, 1997.

36. Liu Yihui, "*Liu shi jiapu* jiaodian"; Xie Yufang, "Xie shi jiapu."

37. Richard Madsen, *China's Catholics: Tragedy and Hope in an Emerging Civil Society* (Berkeley: University of California Press, 1998).

38. Our Sisters in Other Lands, "The Swatow Typhoon," microfiche no. 995, PCE, FMC, SOAS.

39. Fannie Northcott, Shantou, 1922, in RG 8, Box 8, the Hildreth papers, China Records Project, Miscellaneous Personal Papers Collections, Yale Divinity School Library, Yale University.

40. Wang Ruifang and Wang Jianyuan, interviewed by author, Guangzhou, August 1 and 2, 2009.

41. G. W. Lewis, Shantou, to Ben L. Baker, Chaozhoufu, August 19, 1922, RG 8, Box 7, the Hildreth papers, Yale University.

42. Wang Ruifang and Wang Jianyuan, interviewed by author, Guangzhou, August 1 and 2, 2009.

43. Wei Zhiyuan, "Yanzao tanghui bainian shiluo" [An Overview of the History of Yanzao Church], in *Yanzao tanghui bainian jiniankan* [A Special Issue on the Hundredth Anniversary of Yanzao Church] (Yanzao, Guangdong Province, 1949), 5–6.

44. T. W. Douglas James, Chaozhoufu, to Patrick J. Maclagan, London, October 2, 1923, microfiche no. 656, PCE, FMC, SOAS.

45. Ibid.

46. Ibid.

47. Ibid.

48. Chen Chunsheng, "Baer fengzai suojian zhi Mingguo chunian Chaoshan qiaoxiang: yi Zhanglin weili" [Emigrant Villages during the August 2 Typhoon

Disaster in Republican Chaoshan: A Case Study of Zhanglin], *Chaoxue yanjiu* [Chaozhou-Shantou Cultural Research] 6 (1997): 369–395.

49. Li Longqian, *Ming Qing Guangdong shehui jingji yanjiu* [Studies on Guangdong Society and Economy in the Ming and Qing Eras] (Shanghai: Guji Chubanshe, 2006), 313.

50. Wang Ruifang and Wang Jianyuan, interviewed by author, Guangzhou, August 1 and 2, 2009.

51. T. W. Douglas James, Chaozhoufu, to Patrick J. Maclagan, London, October 2, 1923, microfiche no. 656, PCE, FMC, SOAS.

4

Accidental Pilgrims

Modernity, Migration, and Christian Conversion among Contemporary Taiwanese Americans

Carolyn Chen

One of the most striking qualities of East Asian immigrant communities in the United States is the remarkable growth of Christianity among Koreans and Chinese. The place of the Protestant church in Korean immigrant communities is already legendary. A total of 89 percent of Korean Americans claim a Christian identity in the United States.[1] Less well known is Christianity among Chinese immigrants. About half claim no religious identity. But among those who are religiously affiliated, Christians are the majority. Among Taiwanese Americans specifically, Christians comprise between 20 and 25 percent of the population.[2] Taiwan is unlike other East Asian countries, such as China and Korea, where the contemporary growth of Christianity in their respective diasporas is mirrored in the home country. Christians are a mere 2.9 percent of the population in Taiwan. The majority of Taiwanese American Christians convert after migrating to the United States.

The signs of Taiwanese American Christianity are ubiquitous in Southern California's San Gabriel Valley—a region that holds the largest Taiwanese population outside of Taiwan. Churches occupy a good one-third of the advertisements in the local Chinese newspaper. Taiwanese Christians unabashedly display Christian bumper stickers and the Christian fish symbol on their automobiles. And churches that were once occupied by white mainline Protestants are now supplanted by more fervent Chinese and Taiwanese congregations. Even though Buddhism assumes the public face of religion in Taiwan and among Taiwanese Americans, Chinese Protestant churches actually outnumber Buddhist or Taoist organizations four to one in Southern California.[3] Every Taiwanese immigrant has at least one family member who has converted to Christianity, and most Taiwanese Americans have attended church at least once. When the former Taiwanese president, a Buddhist, campaigned for his presidency in Southern California, he spoke of his mission as "carrying the cross," an explicitly Christian reference. This allusion makes little sense to most in Taiwan, where Christians are such a small minority of the population. But Taiwanese change in the process of migration to the United States, most notably in their faith traditions.

Because of the Protestant Christian prohibition of ancestral veneration, conversion to Christianity is unimaginable and considered highly offensive and disloyal to one's ancestors and family in Taiwan. Why, then, is Christianity so appealing to Taiwanese in the United States? Increased religiosity among immigrants to the United States is a commonly observed pattern, both among earlier immigrant groups like the Irish and among more contemporary immigrant groups like Indians.[4] Scholars have made various arguments about why this is the case—to retain ethnic traditions, to create community, and to assimilate into the US religious landscape. These arguments explain why Taiwanese Americans may become more religious in the United States, but they cannot explain why they convert to Christianity. After all, most immigrant groups become more religious but remain in their inherited traditions. Taiwanese Americans, in contrast, break with their inherited traditions to convert to Christianity. And they do so at great cost to their relationships with their families.

Understanding why Taiwanese Americans convert to Christianity requires an examination into both the historical contexts that produced large-scale Taiwanese emigration and the contemporary experiences of Taiwanese migration that influence religious choices. In this essay, I argue that the post–World War II modernization of Taiwan set the stage for the large-scale displacement, or migration, of educated Taiwanese to the United States. Specifically, postwar modernization displaced a certain type of Taiwanese—nonreligious Taiwanese—and encouraged a certain type of immigration—individual or nuclear migration—that created particularly favorable conditions for eventual Christian conversion among Taiwanese immigrants. Based on my contemporary ethnographic fieldwork at a Taiwanese immigrant church and Buddhist temple in Southern California as well as fifty in-depth interviews with Taiwanese immigrant Christians and Buddhists, I further suggest that the experiences of displacement and diaspora elicit religious seeking because they disrupt critical familial networks on which traditional Taiwanese religion is based. The search for community and belonging underlies the immigrant religious quest. Taiwanese immigrants, I argue, convert to Christianity because it fulfills the need for community and belonging in the United States best.

The Modernization of Postwar Taiwan and the Creation of Highly Skilled Emigrants

To understand why Taiwanese immigrants become Christian in the United States, one must first understand who among Taiwanese came, why they came, and how they came to the United States. The particular political, social, and economic events that occurred in postwar East Asia created the conditions for a distinct Taiwanese American immigration—one that I argue has been favorable toward Christian conversion.

The story of contemporary Taiwanese immigration to the United States must begin with an accounting of how the United States first came to Taiwan. As Yen Le Espiritu suggests, the American narrative of the immigrant story valorizes the United States as a land that offers unending opportunity to migrants yet ignores the larger political context of how American imperialism and violence abroad uproots populations in the first place. Linking Filipino immigration to the history of American occupation of the Philippines, she says, "We came to the U.S. because the U.S. first came to us."[5] Her perspective destabilizes the traditional immigration narrative and focuses on how American imperialism unleashes an unstoppable movement to migration. Similarly, Saskia Sassen has observed how American involvement in developing the Third World is often accompanied by its bedfellow, mass migration to the United States.[6]

This perspective is helpful in understanding the role of the United States in creating mass Taiwanese immigration, and for that matter Korean migration as well, to the United States. Taiwanese first came to the United

States on a noticeable scale in the mid-1960s. Having been a Japanese colony for nearly fifty years beginning in 1895, Taiwan was returned to Chinese control after the Japanese were defeated in World War II. At the time, China was embroiled in a civil war between the Nationalists, or the Kuomintang, led by Chiang Kai Shek, and the Communists under Mao Zedong. In defeat, Chiang Kai Shek and roughly two million mainland Chinese retreated to the island of Taiwan in 1949.

With the onset of the Korean War in 1951, Taiwan and the survival of "Free China" became central to American political interests. The United States offered Taiwan more than 4 billion dollars in aid from 1951 to 1965. The US Navy was sent to patrol the Taiwan Strait. The Kuomintang used American aid to build an impressive economic infrastructure. In the 1950s, the Kuomintang instituted major land reform, leading to increased agricultural productivity.[7] Agricultural profits generated the capital to finance labor-intensive manufacturing industries beginning in the 1960s. As Western industrialized nations were beginning to outsource manufacturing, Taiwan was perfectly poised to meet their demands. By the 1970s, Taiwan had transformed into an export economy specializing in labor-intensive and service-oriented industries.[8] With the development of an industrial economy, Taiwanese society exhibited the typical transformations that accompany development and modernization—the shifting of jobs from the agricultural to industrial sphere, rural to urban migration, and the increased participation of women in the labor force.[9]

Aid from the United States allowed Taiwan to focus its own resources on building a solid education system. Starting in the 1950s, Taiwan began investing in basic and vocational education at a rate that outperformed nations with comparable resources. Its vocational educational program filled the need for its increasingly semi-skilled labor force.[10] Taiwan's concentrated investment in basic and vocational education, however, left those seeking higher education to go elsewhere. The emergence of a middle class and the rising affluence of Taiwan created a growing number of Taiwanese seeking higher education, which outgrew the local supply of universities. Starting from the 1960s until today, the majority of Taiwanese who seek education abroad have come to the United States. And many decide to stay. Among my own subjects, over 70 percent of the men came to the United States for higher education. In fact, only recently has Taiwan seriously invested in building up its universities, having preferred all along to outsource its higher education to the West and Japan. Sending the Taiwanese elite to study in universities abroad, and particularly the United States, served the dual purpose of relieving Taiwan of the cost of supporting an extensive higher education system, while simultaneously promoting Taiwan's cause for international diplomatic status.

The first wave of Taiwanese immigrants in the 1960s and 1970s was largely students, whose objectives were not to settle in the United States but to receive a degree and return home. But these highly educated émigrés were not so easily absorbed into Taiwan's manufacturing export economy. And highly skilled professionals could command ten times their salary in Taiwan if they stayed in the United States. On top of that, the United States' own immigration policies had shifted dramatically in 1965 with the Hart Cellar Act, removing earlier race-based quotas barring Asians and establishing a preference policy that prioritized highly skilled immigrants and the family members of existing citizens. This turn in immigration policy, which was largely due to American Cold War concerns of building up US scientific armor against the Soviet Union, was favorable to the very Taiwanese who wanted to leave Taiwan—educated, highly skilled professionals. The percentage of Taiwanese immigrants who have entered the United States through an occupational preference category is quite high—ranging from 30 to 45 percent. Taiwan is a classic case of the brain drain. Since the 1950s, over 100,000 Taiwanese have pursued higher education in the United States, and only 20 percent have returned to Taiwan.[11] Ironically, the United States had to rely on an educated immigrant labor force to fight its Cold War—one that it had a hand in creating and displacing abroad.

Taiwan's contentious relationship with China and its lack of international recognition as a nation-state have also been important issues motivating many Taiwanese to migrate, or at least to establish residency in a foreign country, since the 1970s. Before 1971, the United States, along with the United Nations, recognized the Kuomintang in Taiwan as the legitimate government of China. In the early 1970s, when the United States and the United Nations switched and recognized Mao's People's Republic of China, and not Chiang's Kuomintang, as the legitimate state of China, this sudden drop in diplomatic status created a sense of political uncertainty that has motivated large-scale emigration from Taiwan ever since. From the 1970s onward, the majority of Taiwanese immigrants have entered the

United States through family reunification and have been motivated by Taiwan's political instability.

Class, Migration, and Religion in the United States

Postwar political and economic transformations in Taiwan created the critical push factors that initiated large-scale emigration from Taiwan to the United States. These postwar events also determined who could migrate to the United States—a class of Taiwanese who, I argue, are more favorably disposed to Christian conversion than the average Taiwanese. Taiwanese immigration draws largely from the educated and highly skilled, even among those who immigrated through family reunification. For example, in Southern California, over 70 percent of Taiwanese adults have a college degree. In the Taiwanese population, the educated are also the least likely to be religious.[12] In my own study, this was particularly the case among men, the majority of whom come from science and engineering backgrounds. As scientists, they find traditional Taiwanese religion to be "superstitious" and "supernatural." Although they do not "believe" in these native rituals, they participate in them for the sake of family tradition. They do so, however, only when they are in Taiwan. In the United States, away from their extended families, they have little personal investment in these traditions. Taiwanese Americans draw from a larger Taiwanese population that is religiously unattached and therefore, theoretically at least, more open to new religious traditions such as Christianity than those invested in other religions.

Other Taiwanese immigrants become more open to Christianity, a religion that most would never imagine converting to in Taiwan, because of the challenges they face in maintaining their religion in the United States. Most Taiwanese practice a syncretic form of popular religion that combines Confucianism, Buddhism, Taoism, and folk religion.[13] Practiced by 90 percent of the population, Taiwanese popular religion is so deeply embedded in the fabric and culture of Taiwanese society that it does not even have a name.[14] Much of Taiwanese traditional religion is centered on ancestral veneration and is located in the home. There is a public dimension to Taiwanese religion as well. Temples are plentiful in Taiwan, and Taiwanese go to temples to worship particular deities, pray, and light incense, especially on the first and fifteenth of every month. Commercial spaces like stores and offices frequently house shrines, and store owners burn paper money outside of their stores as offerings to gods in hopes of improving their business.

In the United States, popular Taiwanese religious practices are difficult to maintain. The lack of temples makes religion difficult or at the least inconvenient to practice. For many Taiwanese immigrants, there simply is no temple to worship at. This was especially the case before the 1990s. Today, there are temples (which are mostly Buddhist) in areas like Southern California with a sizable Taiwanese population.[15] But they are hardly plentiful and convenient as in Taiwan. For example, in Southern California, most Taiwanese immigrants must drive anywhere from thirty minutes to an hour to reach a temple, whereas in Taiwan most people live within walking distance of a temple. Partly owing to the inconvenience, the majority of Southern California Taiwanese limit their temple visits to special holidays like the Lunar New Year. Other public religious practices, such as the burning of paper money outside of businesses, are outright illegal in the United States. And important Taiwanese religious holidays simply do not coincide with holidays in the American Judeo-Christian calendar.

A minority of immigrants today come to the United States as practicing Buddhists. Most of the non-Christian religious outlets for Taiwanese are Buddhist, as a direct consequence of the recent development of modern Chinese Buddhism in Taiwan, particularly among the middle class who can migrate to the United States. Approximately 20 to 25 percent of Taiwanese Americans claim a Buddhist identity, although the majority are nominal and not practicing Buddhists. Taiwanese Buddhist organizations like Fo Guang Shan and Tzu Chi are now household names and have vast transnational media empires reaching into the lives of Taiwanese around the world. As Taiwanese have migrated to the United States, so too have these Buddhist organizations, building temples and communities. Perhaps the best known of these is the Hsi Lai Temple—a vast and stunning Ming dynasty–style temple jutting out of the hills in Hacienda Heights. The largest temple in North America, it is also the site of the notorious 1992 Clinton-Gore campaign finance scandal.

Largely because of stereotypes and the fact that Taiwanese Buddhist organizations are media savvy, the public face of Taiwanese American religion continues to be Buddhist.[16] Yet despite appearances, there are 195 Chinese Protestant churches compared to only 45 Buddhist and Taoist temples and organizations in Southern California. Furthermore, churches exert a powerful influence over the moral, cultural, political, and social life of the Taiwanese American community.

The disproportionate number of churches as compared to temples reflects the particular historical circumstances of Taiwanese immigration and the early advantage that Taiwanese Christians had in establishing churches. Christians were disproportionately represented among the early wave of Taiwanese immigration because they tended to be more educated than the general Taiwanese population. For example, in 1971, 32 percent of Christians had a college education compared to 9 percent of the general Taiwanese population.[17] These early Christian Taiwanese immigrants, who were predominantly graduate students, set up Bible studies and Christian fellowships in the 1960s.[18] Furthermore, Protestant Christianity has an institutional advantage in propagating lay organizations over Chinese Buddhism. As a lay congregational religion, Protestant Christianity can establish lay religious communities and scriptural study groups far more easily than Chinese Buddhism, a more hierarchical and monastic-based religion.[19] In fact, Taiwanese American Buddhists often remark on having attended Taiwanese American Christian events. Taiwanese American Christians in the 1960s and 1970s were critical in establishing Taiwanese churches as the central Taiwanese American ethnic institution early on. Other Taiwanese American associations, such as political clubs, hometown associations, or alumni associations, were and still are dependent on Taiwanese American churches to publicize their events and to provide space for meetings. Churches established their centrality to Taiwanese American community life very early on and have continued to maintain that importance. For this reason, the common wisdom among Taiwanese Americans is that the best place to go to makes friends is a Chinese/Taiwanese church.

The draw of the church as a social outlet is particularly attractive to many Taiwanese because of the way they migrate to the United States. A significant number of Taiwanese immigrate through the skilled preference categories or migrate through temporary visas such as student or H-1B visas and then choose to stay. These students and highly skilled workers who migrate for school or work tend to come alone, or sometimes as nuclear families, and often do not have family close by in the United States. Migration is already a lonely process. Being separated from kinship networks, these Taiwanese immigrants are especially drawn to the church to seek community and support, as I will discuss. Taiwanese immigrants without family close by are also more likely to convert to Christianity than immigrants who have family in the United States. Three factors taken together—the nonreligiousness of most Taiwanese immigrants, that many immigrate alone, and the general difficulty in maintaining traditional Taiwanese practices—make Taiwanese immigrants a ripe "mission field," so to speak, for Christianity in the United States.

Religion as Kinship and Community

Perhaps the most important reason that Taiwanese immigrants convert to Christianity is the absence of the extended family. The family stands at the center of traditional Taiwanese religious practices. The absence of the extended family not only makes continuing traditions more difficult, but it also makes religion less real. Rituals of ancestral veneration bind the living and the dead into an ongoing relationship of social and material interdependence. Rituals to the dead, such as the offering of food and the burning of paper money and incense, assure the happiness and well-being of those family members who are deceased. As the beneficiary of their ancestors' merits, the living present these offerings to symbolize their reverence and indebtedness to them. Taiwanese religion morally binds the extended family together and makes this evident through ritual and symbol.

The prohibition against ancestral veneration among Protestant Christians is a very real obstacle to Taiwanese who may consider converting. Refusing to participate in rituals of ancestral veneration is tantamount to rejecting one's family and one's obligations to the family. For this reason, many of my respondents claimed that they would never even have imagined becoming Christian in Taiwan. So integral is ancestral veneration to one's identification with and membership in the family that one respondent remarked, "All your family and friends in Taiwan worship idols. You cannot change. You change and they see you as a stranger." In Taiwan, one cannot afford to be estranged from one's family. As this respondent emphasized, "you cannot change." The calculation for considering Christianity, however, looks very different in the United States, where people are already separated from their families.

The sentiment that immigrants in Southern California expressed to me time and time again regarding their experience in the United States is a feeling of insecurity, even among educated and skilled immigrants who are seemingly financially secure. One respondent, Mr. Hou, a forty-two-year-old immigrant, described it most vividly. He told me, "The first thing you have to realize is that when you come to America you no longer have a safety net. You're all on your own now." The safety net that Mr. Hou referred to is the security of having someone or something to turn to in a time of need. In Taiwan, that safety net is obvious—the family. But in the United States, things are different. Taiwanese who immigrate through skill-based or investment visas often do not have local family members, unlike those who immigrate through family reunification. Eighteen of the fifty respondents in my sample had no extended family in the area. Half of the Christian converts had no extended family nearby compared to 20 percent of Buddhists.

But even among those immigrants who do have family, I was struck by the reluctance of my respondents to "bother" their relatives for help. Some of my respondents lived with an extended family member briefly on first arriving in the United States but quickly attempted to establish independence. Immigrants also complained that the traffic in Southern California prevented them from seeing their relatives, and relying on them, as often as they liked.

With their own extended families geographically dispersed, Grace Church members rely on one another as they would rely upon family in Taiwan for emotional, material, social, and spiritual support. Grace and other immigrant churches take pride in being not merely a community but indeed a family. The church becomes the new family, replacing the extended kinship networks and friendship circles that immigrants had in Taiwan. Grace cultivates this familial culture as members of the congregation refer to each other as "sister" and "brother," and children refer to adults as "uncle" and "aunty."

Belonging to a church yields similar benefits to belonging to a large kinship network. The expanded social network is particularly useful for the newly arrived who may be looking for employment. In new immigrant communities that lack the presence of established families and reputations, a person's association with a particular church can vouch for his or her reputation in the larger Taiwanese American community. Church networks also share the work of caring for dependents, both children and the elderly. Some churches have day-care facilities. Informally, church members help each other out with child care. The church is furthermore a draw for immigrants because it offers a "Taiwanese public," an alternative civic space to the American mainstream that reproduces Taiwanese traditions, culture, and values for the second generation. It is commonly felt within the Taiwanese American community that if you do not want your children to go astray, meaning to become too Americanized, you should send them to church.[20]

Finally, the church takes special interest in taking care of the immigrant elderly, who are among the most vulnerable in the Taiwanese American population. Churches create elderly meeting groups and education programs. Some churches sponsor elderly day-care programs. Informally, many elderly will rely on younger church members for transportation or shopping, things that they would otherwise depend on their younger kin for in Taiwan.

For diasporic peoples, religious decisions are never merely spiritual choices but social and material choices that are wrapped up in larger concerns about kinship and community.[21] Religion is so attractive to immigrants precisely because it offers the social, material, and spiritual support they need in the absence of their families. These factors do not downplay the sincerity or legitimacy of their religious choices but highlight the complex ways that religion is negotiated in individual lives.

This sociological reality is strikingly illustrated in the practical considerations that one family made when deciding to become Christian. Mr. and Mrs. Hsiao and their two young sons immigrated to the United States in 1995 and settled in the San Gabriel Valley. Having no family and very few friends in Southern California, the Hsiaos were eager to make connections with other Taiwanese Americans. They were instructed, like most immigrants, to find a Taiwanese church.

The Hsiaos started attending Grace Church soon after immigrating to the United States. Nearly all of their friends were from the church community, and the family's social life was largely organized around the church. Mrs. Hsiao in particular loved going to church. Away from the comfort of her friends and family in Taiwan, she felt happiest and most loved at Grace Church. She also enjoyed singing and had joined the choir, and she said she learned a lot from the sermons.

After attending Grace Church for over a year, Mrs. Hsiao wanted to get baptized. Her husband, however, was not ready. He offered no religious or philosophical grounds for his hesitation. Instead, he asked Mrs. Hsiao to postpone her decision until they decided whether they were going to settle permanently in the United States. If they stayed, he had no objection to her getting baptized, but if they were going to return to Taiwan he felt that she should not become Christian. He pointed out that, as the only Christian in an entirely Buddhist family, she would lead a difficult existence. When they lived in Taiwan, Mrs. Hsiao helped her mother-in-law to prepare offerings of fruit and incense every day at the ancestral altar that was housed in Mr. Hsiao's parents' home. As a Christian, she would no longer be able to fulfill these obligations. Being a Christian in Taiwan would not only be an extremely uncomfortable position for her, it would be disrespectful toward the Hsiao family. As it turns out, they remained in the United States, and Mrs. Hsiao got baptized. Her husband soon followed. Why? Something Mr. Hsiao told me early in our interview was very instructive. I asked him if he had any relatives in the United States, and he responded, "Our family is the church." In the end, practical matters such as belonging and family obligations determined the Hsiaos' religious decisions. Depending on where the Hsiaos lived, in the United States or in Taiwan, their "family" was the church or their blood kin. Indeed, those without family in Southern California were more likely to convert and converted much more quickly than those who had family.

Christian Conversion as Reconstructing Community and Kinship

Converting to Christianity is a way that Taiwanese immigrants reconstruct community and kinship in the United States. From its very beginnings, Christianity posed a challenge to the "traditional family" because it offered an alternative kind of communal or kinship system based on choice and faith rather than inheritance. In the Gospel of Luke, Christ preaches that the costs of discipleship are steep: "If anyone comes to Me, and does not hate his own father and mother and wife and children and brothers and sisters, yes, and even his own life, he cannot be My disciple" (14:26).[22] And Matthew, in announcing his discipleship to Christ, says, "Behold, we have left our homes and followed you" (Luke 18:21). To its faithful, Christianity offers the institution of the church as the new family and an ethic of brotherhood that is based on love rather than blood. The church is a voluntary kinship whose precarious bonds are based on choice rather than inheritance. In the United States, the church has been considered the bedrock of American community.[23] Largely owing to the Protestant religious heritage of the United States, the notion that religion is a voluntary community is deeply embedded in American understandings of what constitutes religion.[24] Taiwanese immigrants are following the well-established traditions of Christianity and American religious tradition by constructing new bonds of kinship and community through religion.

But clearly, the challenges in creating a voluntary family are different from those where kinship is based on blood. Unlike one's inherited family, the church must take deliberate steps to build trust, accountability, shared identity, and affection among its members. And as it is a voluntary association, rather than an inherited group, the church's foundation is based on the ongoing, willful choice of its members to continue identifying with and sharing with the church community. For an institution, these mechanisms are not random but strategic and planned. One could say that the immigrant church is in the business of building community. For immigrants especially, community is the linchpin for conversion.

Recruiting

Like the Hsiaos, most Taiwanese immigrants are initially attracted to the church to make friends. Church leaders are quite conscious that the draw of the church is friendship and community. Regular religious gatherings, such as Bible study, prayer meetings, cell group meetings, Sunday worship, and so on, are typically followed by fellowship and food. The time devoted to fellowship may actually be more lengthy than that devoted to the religious event itself. For example, Sunday worship can be an all-day affair. One might attend the early-morning prayer meeting, then Sunday worship, followed by Sunday school, lunch, committee meetings, and softball. Outside of the regular religious gatherings are various social events like concerts, sporting events, and classes teaching English, painting, or dance.

The church holds nonreligious social events that are "seeker-friendly" to attract newcomers. Friday night church meetings will frequently feature talks on topics such as health, diet, parenting, and so on, that are not overtly Christian but of general interest. Church leaders are constantly encouraging members to invite their friends. The church takes welcoming and including visitors very seriously. It has a "caring group" committee with elaborate and personalized procedures for welcoming visitors and making sure that they continue attending. For example, one of the church leaders described the welcoming procedure as follows: "There's a caring group and there's a caring group leader. We have people assigned to care for that person. Of course when we assign we try not to make the person feel like it's just a formality. That person will call the newcomer. We try to make friends with that person. That's the right intention to have when you try to care for somebody . . . everybody has to be in a caring group at some point and you take turns."

Leadership Roles—Building Accountability

Perhaps what makes a church like Grace so successful in converting Taiwanese is not merely that it attracts visitors through its programs and network but that the church quickly incorporates them and makes them indispensable to the community. As the above quote suggests, members take turns with church responsibilities. Once newcomers attend the church, they are encouraged to "get involved." New and old members alike are given responsibilities in the church community that serve as "mechanisms of commitment."[25] For example, Mr. Kau, an immigrant of nine years, told me: "We started going to church because we wanted to know more people and we felt that Christians were good for us. I joined a fellowship and they assigned events at my house—like taking care of a group of kids. I was never against it. I always participated even though I was not a Christian." These leadership roles have an additional draw of conferring status on immigrants, especially men, who may have experienced downward mobility in their professional lives.[26]

Running the church requires an endless number of rotating responsibilities among members. Cell groups rotate serving lunch on Sundays. People rotate setting up chairs for services, teaching Sunday school, making tea, directing traffic, and the like. Leadership positions in the church are plentiful. At Grace Church, making people feel a part of the community means making them feel responsible for the community. The more invested they are in the community, the more likely they will become Christian.

Building Trust and Intimacy

To become a family, the church needs to cultivate more than accountability among its members but true trust and intimacy. The church does this most explicitly through cell group meetings. The cell group, a small Bible study group, is important for cultivating fraternity and trust among Grace Church members. Cell groups comprise anywhere from five to ten families and include people of similar age or professional interests. Meetings include singing, Bible study, sharing, and prayer. Members feel accountable to one another because they take turns hosting and leading meetings in their homes each Friday night.

The cell groups are organized around what I call intentional practices of intimacy. For example, during meetings members break into groups of two and three to share with one another the events in the week that they wish to praise God for or bring to God in concern. Burdens like the health of elderly parents or problems raising teenage children are collectively shared. These meetings create a safe and distinct space for people to share details of their personal lives that they might otherwise reserve for their family and close friends. Through this intentional practice of intimacy, churchgoers, who were once strangers, become a community and indeed a family.

Identity and Boundaries

Grace Church and other churches like it create tight-knit, high commitment, and highly interdependent communities. The social lives of most members revolve around the church. Once one is involved, church commitments can occupy each and every evening. Respondents told me that, after becoming involved in Grace Church, they have fewer non-Christian friends and that most of their friends are from the church. In between balancing family, work, and church responsibilities, few have time to join other organizations or make friends outside of the church. Some even told me that their non-Christian relatives feared that religious activities would take them away from time spent with them.

The level of commitment that church requires functions to create strong boundaries of community and identity among its members. For those involved in the church, it is difficult to extricate themselves from the web of responsibilities and relationships that they have developed. Members have come to depend on one another for support and stability. When a member misses a Sunday service or a weekend meeting, his or her absence is noticed and felt. As church members come to depend on one another, they identify with one another as members of the same community. These social commitments to the community reinforce an ideological commitment to a Christian symbolic universe by preventing them from seeking other alternatives.

Church members start to think of themselves as Christians and others as non-Christians, who are potential members that can be brought into the fold. More pointedly, Christians define themselves in contrast to Buddhists, people who ignorantly follow Chinese traditions without truly knowing who or what they worship. Buddhists, in particular, are in dire need of being saved. Taiwanese American Buddhists, for their part, perceive coethnic Christians as being cliquish, exclusive, and self-righteous.[27] Because many Taiwanese American extended families include members who are Buddhist and Christian, Christians, with their strong religious identification, make religion a potential source of familial tension and division. Similarly, because of the strong boundaries that Christians draw, religion is a source of cleavage in the larger Taiwanese American community.

Like the family, the church is a demanding, but generous, institution. Because of the demands of the church, the majority of Christians in my sample converted within five years of moving to Southern California, when they were relatively new to the area and had fewer ties and obligations to competing organizations. That Christians are also less likely to have local extended family obligations than Buddhists suggests that Christian converts tend to be more unattached and have more freedom, both ideologically and socially, and can afford to make new commitments and assume new identities that are potentially controversial.

Why the Christians Are Not Buddhists

The question might still persist, why do Taiwanese immigrants convert to Christianity? Why not stay Buddhist? After all, Buddhism is less offensive to one's family, and temples offer similar resources as churches. The answer, I believe, comes back to community. Christianity creates stronger and more vibrant communities than Buddhism does. First of all, the notion of community differs widely between Buddhism and Christianity. In Chinese Buddhism, on the one hand, the community, or *sangha,* refers to the community of monastics. Laypeople help the *sangha* survive through almsgiving and volunteering, and in turn earn merits to improve their chances of a higher rebirth. On the other hand, in Protestant Christianity, the congregation is the community of believers. Believers are accountable to one another and not the clergy. Protestant clergy are hired professionals that may stay or go, but the community remains intact.

These different understandings of religious community deeply affect the ways that Buddhists and Christians form and practice community. Buddhists have a different sense of obligation to and ownership over the religious community than Christians. When Buddhists volunteer at the temple, they tell me that they do so in order to help the monastics. Buddhists in Southern California worship at multiple temples and do not feel beholden to any particular one. Furthermore, the majority do not attend the temple regularly, whereas the majority of Christians I interviewed attend church regularly. In fact, the most pious Buddhists told me that they actively avoid the temples because the crowds and socializing distract them from their religious practice. Buddhists do not see the temple community as integral to their spiritual development. Even the dharma master of the temple compared the temple to a gas station, where devotees should come and "fill up" when they are in need of spiritual fuel. Nor do Buddhists regard the temple as integral to their social lives. In comparison to the Christians, Buddhists rarely linger to socialize after religious ceremonies and events. In fact, Buddhists are deeply critical of Christians for operating like a "social club." A minority of temple leaders actively avoid developing social activities because they do not want their temples to become places associated with socializing rather than serious Buddhist practice.

Christians, in contrast, feel a strong sense of personal identification with and belonging to their churches. In my sample, Christians faithfully attend one church regularly. Because of the leadership roles they are given, Christians quickly develop a sense of indispensability to and accountability to the community. In contrast to the Buddhists, religious attendance is considered absolutely critical to one's spiritual development. And service to the church is considered a badge of piety and spiritual maturity. The church adopts a very different attitude toward socializing and social activities than the temple. No dichotomy is drawn between the "social" and "religious." Socializing is considered "fellowship" and integral to the development of one's personal spirituality and the health of the larger congregation. Protestant Christians take community so seriously because it is a religious virtue of the highest order.

Taiwanese immigrants who convert to Christianity are accidental pilgrims. The majority of Taiwanese come to the United States seeking the security of this world—particularly economic and political security. But along the way, some find security of another world—religious salvation. Most of the people I studied would not have converted to Christianity had they remained in Taiwan. As one respondent told me, his life in Taiwan was one of decadence and indulgence, where he would have "wined, dined, partied and probably died of liver disease" at a young age. Pilgrimage is one kind of migration. It is the act of leaving the comforts and familiarity of home to become spiritually transformed. To those Taiwanese immigrants who become Christian, migration to the United States has become a form of spiritual pilgrimage.

For immigrants, the spiritual is inextricably connected to the material and social conditions of existence in diaspora. Taiwanese who convert to Christianity are those who, in a sense, can afford to or, perhaps, cannot afford not to. Postwar modern development in Taiwan created a highly educated class of émigrés who were both more Christian and more nonreligious than the general Taiwanese population. The nonreligious, who were not ideologically and spiritually committed to a religion, could be more open to new religious traditions. The early Christian immigrants established Christian churches and organizations that would become the foundations of Taiwanese American community life.

The Taiwanese American Christian church offers something that few immigrants can refuse—the opportunity to build new kinship and community ties that have been weakened through migration. The price for Christian conversion can be steep—sometimes costing Taiwanese immigrants their own blood family ties. But the benefits are certainly numerous and, for some, even life-saving. The need for community and belonging among immigrants runs deep, even deeper than the need to maintain inherited traditions. For this reason, many Taiwanese immigrants in the United States do what would be inconceivable in Taiwan—they convert to Christianity.

Notes

1. Pei-te Lien and Tony Carnes, "The Religious Demography of Asian American Boundary Crossing," in *Asian American Religions: The Making and Remaking*

of Borders and Boundaries, ed. Fenggang Yang (New York and London: New York University Press, 2004).

2. "Taiwanese" refers to all persons from Taiwan and includes both pre-1949 and post-1949 Han Chinese who migrated from China. "Chinese" refers to all Han Chinese regardless of national origin. Southern California Taiwanese have their own ethnically exclusive organizations but also participate in organizations that include other Chinese.

3. These churches are, for the most part, theologically conservative and evangelical. They are networked into the larger international Chinese evangelical and American evangelical subcultures.

4. Jay P. Dolan, *The Immigrant Church: New York's Irish and German Catholics, 1815–1865* (Baltimore: Johns Hopkins University Press, 1975); Jay P. Dolan, *The American Catholic Experience: A History from Colonial Times to the Present* (Garden City, NY: Doubleday, 1985); Prema Kurien, "'We Are Better Hindus Here': Religion and Ethnicity among Indian Americans," in *Religions in Asian America*, ed. Pyong Gap Min and Jung Ha Kim (Walnut Creek, CA: Altamira Press, 2002), 99–120.

5. Yen Le Espiritu, *Home Bound: Filipino American Lives across Cultures, Communities, and Countries* (Berkeley: University of California Press, 2003).

6. Saskia Sassen, "America's Immigration Problem," in *Globalization and Its Discontents* (New York: The New Press, 1998), 31–54.

7. Murray A. Rubinstein, *The Other Taiwan: 1945 to the Present* (Armonk, NY: M. E. Sharpe, 1994).

8. Christian Aspalter, "The Taiwanese Economic Miracle: From Sugarcane to High-Technology," in *Understanding Modern Taiwan: Essays in Economics, Politics, and Social Policy*, ed. Christian Aspalter (Aldershot, England: Ashgate Publishing Limited, 2001), 1–32.

9. Rubinstein, *Other Taiwan;* Arland Thornton and Hui-Shen Lin, *Social Change and the Family in Taiwan* (Chicago: University of Chicago Press, 1994).

10. Kevin O'Neil, "Brain Drain and the Gain: The Case of Taiwan," Migration Policy Institute, 2003, http://www.migrationinformation.org/Feature/display.cfm?ID=155.

11. Shirley L. Chang, *Taiwan's Brain Drain and Its Reversal* (Taipei: Lucky Bookstore, 1998); O'Neil, "Brain Drain and the Gain."

12. Li-Shou Yang, Arland Thornton, and Thomas Fricke, "Religion and Family Formation in Taiwan: The Decline of Ancestral Authority," in *Family, Religion, and Social Change in Diverse Societies*, ed. Sharon K. Houseknecht and Jerry G. Pankhurst (New York: Oxford University Press, 2000), 121–146.

13. Note that although many Taiwanese Americans will nominally call themselves "Buddhist," traditional Taiwanese religion is not Buddhism. And Buddhists

are eager to disassociate themselves from popular religious practices that they perceive to be superstitious.

14. Yang et al., "Religion and Family Formation"; Robert P. Weller, "Identity and Social Change in Taiwanese Religion," in *Taiwan: A New History,* ed. Murray A. Rubinstein (Armonk, NY: M. E. Sharpe, 1994), 339–365.

15. Class plays a large factor in the Taiwanese American religious landscape in Southern California. Most Taiwanese American religious outlets are either Protestant Christian or Buddhist (orthodox Buddhist). This is not the case in Taiwan, where popular religious temples abound in far greater numbers than churches or Buddhist temples. Because Taiwanese Americans, who are largely educated and professional, do not tend to hold popular religious beliefs, they have not imported these institutions to the United States. In contrast, popular religion temples are far more likely to exist among working-class Chinese immigrant groups. See Kenneth J. Guest, *God in Chinatown: Religion and Survival in New York's Evolving Immigrant Community* (New York: New York University Press, 2003).

16. Carolyn Chen, "The Religious Varieties of Ethnic Presence: A Comparison between a Taiwanese Immigrant Buddhist Temple and an Evangelical Christian Church," *Sociology of Religion* 63 (2002): 215–238.

17. Allen J. Swanson, *The Church in Taiwan: Profile 1980: A Review of the Past and a Projection for the Future* (Pasadena, CA: William Carey Library, 1981).

18. Hsing-Huang Chao, "Mobilizing to Grow: The Persistence and Transformation of the Evangelical Formosan Church of Los Angeles" (Ph.D. diss., Purdue University, 1995).

19. With modern reforms in Chinese Buddhism, far more emphasis and power is given to the laity. Still, monastics have an overwhelming authority over the laity in the temple community.

20. Carolyn Chen, "From Filial Piety to Religious Piety: Evangelical Christianity Reconstructing Taiwanese Immigrant Families in the United States," *International Migration Review* 40, no. 3 (2006): 573–602.

21. Thomas J. Douglas, "The Cross and the Lotus: Changing Religious Practices among Cambodian Immigrants in Seattle," in *Revealing the Sacred,* ed. Jane N. Iwamura and Paul Spickard (New York: Routledge, 2003), 159–176; Pyong Gap Min, "Religion and the Maintenance of Ethnicity among Immigrants: A Comparison of Indian Hindus and Korean Protestants," in *Immigrant Faiths: Transforming Religious Life in America,* ed. Karen I. Leonard et al. (Walnut Creek, CA: Altamira Press, 2005), 99–122; Karen Richman, "The Protestant Ethnic and the Dis-Spirit of Vodou," in *Immigrant Faiths: Transforming Religious Life in America,* 165–188.

22. New American Standard translation.

23. Alexis de Tocqueville, *Democracy in America* (New York: HarperCollins,

2000); Robert N. Bellah, Richard Madsen, William Sullivan, Ann Swidler, and Stephen Tipton, *Habits of the Heart* (Berkeley: University of California Press, 1985).

24. Stephen R. Warner, "The Place of the Congregation in American Religious Configuration," in *New Perspectives in the Study of Congregations*, ed. James P. Wind and James W. Lewis (Chicago: University of Chicago Press, 1994), 54–99.

25. Rosabeth Moss Kanter, "Commitment and Social Organization: A Study of Commitment Mechanisms in Utopian Communities," *American Sociological Review* 33 (1968): 499–517; Donald E. Miller, *Reinventing American Protestantism* (Berkeley: University of California Press, 1997).

26. Carolyn Chen, *Getting Saved in America: Taiwanese Immigration and Religious Experience* (Princeton, NJ: Princeton University Press, 2008), 131–140.

27. Ibid., 94–98.

PART III

The Sacred and Social Activism

5

Christianity and Civil Society in Colonial Korea

The Civil Society Movement of Cho Man-sik and the P'yŏngyang YMCA against Japanese Colonialism

KYUSIK CHANG

PROTESTANTISM, along with Marxism, was a foreign idea that had a profound influence on Korean society in the twentieth century. In the early modern period, Korean intellectuals accepted Christianity not as a religion but as a driving force behind the country's push toward a modern society. Rhee Syngman, who, along with Ahn Chang-ho, was one of the most prominent leaders of the Christian nationalist movement, defined modern Western civilization as Christian civilization. He emphasized the need for achieving the same freedom and happiness that the United States had by making Christianity the basis of political, moral, and social reforms in Korea.[1] Lee Dong-hui, who, with Rhee Syngman and Ahn Chang-ho, was one of the three main leaders of the Daehan Min'guk Imsi Chŏngbu (Provisional Government of the Republic of Korea), also insisted that Koreans preserve national freedom and independence by fostering brotherhood, patriotism, and independence through Christianity as Western nations did.[2]

Ahn Chang-ho accused American missionaries in Korea of trying to spread their religion while neglecting the cultural movement.[3] However, instead of criticizing Christianity itself, he criticized their mission policy, which reflected the views of conservative Presbyterian missionaries such as Samuel Moffett, who emphasized direct evangelism rather than educational or medical missions. Ahn Chang-ho's criticism represented Korean intellectuals' understanding of Christianity at the time; that is, they recognized Christianity and modern Western culture as two sides of the same coin. In fact, the international network of Christianity was a primary pathway leading to the adoption of Western culture, particularly the American culture of civil society within Korean society.[4]

Historical studies on Christianity in Korea have focused on the development of local churches and their roles in the nationalist movement.[5] The rapid proliferation of Korean churches was exceptional in the history of modern Protestant missions. Further, Christian groups played a key role in the Korean national movement, as the three main leaders of the Provisional Government of the Republic of Korea had a Christian background. The lack of attention given to the Korean national leaders' acceptance of Christianity as a symbol of modernity in the context of Western civilization, rather than merely as a religion, is noteworthy; that is, studies have focused on church growth or the Christian national movement.

This essay traces the relationship between Christianity and modernity by focusing on P'yŏng-an, a province that had accounted for almost half of all Korean Christians during the first half of the twentieth century. It reconstructs the early history of Christianity in Korea by incorporating the modernity factor into the study of church growth and the national movement.

One way Christianity contributed significantly to forming modernity in Korea was by its nourishment of the public sphere in the private realm through organizing debate clubs. In this regard, Jürgen Habermas' theory of the public sphere provides a useful tool in the analysis of the Christian social movement in Korea. Habermas presented a blueprint illustrating the bourgeois public sphere in eighteenth-century Europe with his concept of the private realm and the public authority sphere, that is, the state. Within the private realm, he distinguished the public sphere from civil society as the realm of commodity exchanges and social labor.[6] According to his analysis, the public had long since grown out of early institutions such as coffeehouses, salons, and banquets and was held together through the medium of the press and its professional criticism. The press and its public formed the public sphere of a rational-critical debate in the world of letters. The public sphere in the political realm evolved from the public sphere in the world of letters. The state-governed public sphere was appropriated by the public of private people making use of their reason and was established as a sphere of criticism of public authority.[7] The public sphere in the political realm became institutionalized within the European bourgeois constitutional states of the nineteenth century.

Although the historical context of capitalist development in Korean society was different from the Western society context in Habermas' study, Korean Christian intellectuals examined Korea's civil society and public sphere by following the Western model. These intellectuals attempted to foster the public as modern individuals by encouraging thoughts and customs based on Protestant ethics. To that purpose, they built a cultural movement in the YMCA, the Epworth League, the Christian Endeavor Society, and the Hŭngsadan (Young Korean Academy) on the border of church and secular society. These associations were equivalent to the public sphere in the world of letters that Habermas conceptualized. At the same time, the Christian intellectuals tried to enhance the infrastructure of civil society by promoting education and industry. They also tried to form a public sphere in the political realm, which brought the state in touch with the needs of society through public opinion.[8] The Christian social movement in P'yŏngyang, the center of P'yŏng-an Province in the northwest region of Korea, was a typical case.

Based on the above discussion, this essay explores how Protestantism was adopted by the leading class of the local society in P'yŏng-an Province in the context of the affinity between the new social order of civil society and commoners' traditional self-government in the region. It then analyzes the nation-building project of Ahn Chang-ho, P'yŏng-an Province's prominent national leader, by considering Habermas' public sphere theory. Further, the essay narrates how Ahn's project was practiced by Cho Man-sik and the P'yŏngyang YMCA during the 1920s and 1930s in the context of building up the infrastructure of civil society and the public sphere. Lastly, it considers the relationship between civil society in colonial Korea and the pressure of Japanese colonialism. The cultural space in colonial Korea competed with Western modernity represented by Protestant missionaries and colonial modernity transplanted by Japanese imperialism.[9] P'yŏngyang in particular was the place where the two sides were in bitter conflict over the hegemony of modernity. In the midst of such contention, the P'yŏngyang YMCA under Cho Man-sik's guidance led Korean's public opinion and took a long-term position against the public authority of Japanese colonialism. This essay traces the process through which Cho Man-sik attempted to establish a political public sphere critical of Japanese authority, which he later used as the basis for the independent nation-state. In addition, this essay illustrates the form of civil society and the public sphere in colonial Korea by investigating the depoliticization of the indigenous bourgeois under the pressure of Japanese colonialism.

Acceptance of Protestantism and the Nation-Building Project of the Independent Middle Class in P'yŏng-an Province

P'yŏng-an Province, a region of commoners who had suffered from political alienation throughout the five hundred years of the Chosŏn dynasty, emerged as the center of Christianity in modern Korea. As a result of long-term discrimination, Yangban aristocrats, who were the traditional power elite of the Chosŏn dynasty, could not establish a firm foothold in P'yŏng-an Province; nor did Neo-Confucian social order and culture take root properly. However, as differences in social status were not large, P'yŏng-an Province was able to institute widespread commoners' self-governance by establishing a sense of unity among its residents. In addition, there was a tendency to regard ability as more important than social status; competition for elevating social status was more acute and widespread than in other regions.

The vitality of commoner society in P'yŏng-an Province was reflected in its economic growth. Located in the northwest region of the Korean Peninsula, P'yŏng-an Province was a region where natural conditions were not ideal for agriculture, but through trade with China and active domestic commercial activities, the province accumulated remarkable wealth. As a result, the region was considered the most prosperous province in the eighteenth century.

Thanks to this economic development, members of the independent middle class, such as small business owners, small landowners, and independent farmers, became a newly emerging social group in P'yŏng-an Province. They managed their own businesses by using knowledge gained through *sŏdang* (common educational facilities in traditional villages). They were also a dominant force in the province's commoner-based self-government. As William Baird, a missionary of the Presbyterian Church U.S.A. and the founder of the Soongsil Academy in P'yŏngyang, stated, these individuals represented a modern-oriented social class "who have to work for their own living, and as a result have more muscle and more brains."[10]

In the nineteenth century, the independent middle class of P'yŏng-an Province, which had faced more than its share of discrimination, began to demand political rights that would correspond to its social and economic abilities. The armed uprising of 1812, led by Hong Kyŏng-rae, signaled the beginning of such activities. Although the Rebellion of Hong Gyong-rae, a primitive bourgeois revolution, was unsuccessful, the independent middle class of P'yŏng-an Province never ceased its pursuit of civil liberties. It sought alternatives to the rule established by Neo-Confucianism and the Yangban caste system. This was the sociohistorical context in which middle-class people took the initiative toward adopting Protestant Christianity.[11]

After the acceptance of Christianity, the members of the independent middle class of P'yŏng-an Province operated churches by themselves without relying on missionaries, driving the rapid proliferation of churches.[12] They also established modern educational institutions and began social movements. As a result, they competed with the Yangban, the ruling class, of Seoul. They actively absorbed Christianity and modern civilization because they sympathized with the Protestant ethics and liberal values propagated by Protestant missionaries of the time, such as just implementation of laws; emphasis on freethinking; and ability, diligence, faithfulness, and the sacredness of labor.[13] In this regard, the independent middle class of P'yŏng-an Province could accept liberalism more easily because it experienced political alienation and economic exploitation under the dynasty state. Its members prized personal achievement through fair competition, not through inherited status or property. To them, the loving sprit of Christianity, which preached equality for all, was an alternative to Neo-Confucianism based on the caste system. Thus, they pursued a new order of civil society through the modernization of the commoner self-government that sprang up under the rule of the Yangban elite.

Ahn Chang-ho was a leader representative of those who extended the social interests of the independent middle class in their nation-building efforts based on civil society. He highlighted the virtues of the modern public, such as *musil* and *yŏkhaeng,*[14] by combining Protestant ethics and the commoner culture of P'yŏng-an Province. He tried to organize a new society and a new nation based on these virtues. The nation-building plan in the "Sinminhoe t'ong'yong changchŏng" (Regulations of the New People's Association), which he drafted, was a representative case.[15]

In "Regulations," he presented his methodology for nation-building as follows: "renew the Korean people by eliminating corrupt ideas and practices, establish a new foundation of society by reforming deteriorated education and industry, and build a civilized free nation by achieving the solidarity of new people."[16] He, then, consistently pushed to actualize his nation-building plan by forming a trinity of the cultural, educational and industrial, and political movements in each sector of society.

He organized the Ch'ŏngnyŏn Hakuhoe (Young Korean Association) and the Hŭngsadan (Young Korean Academy) to cultivate the public as modern individuals through the cultural movement, which he referred to as the fundamental movement for all movements. At the same time, he pushed the educational and industrial movement to strengthen the infrastructure of civil society, resulting in the establishment of Daesŏng Middle School and the Ceramics Company in P'yŏngyang. He also tried to establish a public sphere in the political realm for nation-building through national unity based on public consensus. He wanted to build an independent nation through the principle of opinion-based politics and the cooperation of various nationalist sectors formed since the movement of the New People's Association.[17] Ahn Chang-ho's nation-building plan and practice are presented according to Habermas' scheme in Table 5.1.

Ahn Chang-ho's nation-building project based on creating a civil society was not widely supported in regions outside P'yŏng-an Province, however. The main criticism was that Ahn's project could result in the dispersal among many sectors of the energy that should be integrated in the struggle for national independence. For its part, the independent middle class of P'yŏng-an Province welcomed Ahn's project. Having experienced long-term political alienation during the Chosŏn dynasty, its members considered the establishment of modernized individuals and civil society infrastructure as important as national independence in terms of achieving their political and social interests.

Table 5.1 Ahn Chang-ho's Nation-Building Project and Practice

	Private Realm			Sphere of Public Authority
	Civil Society	Public Sphere		
		World of Letters	Political Realm	State
Main issues	Promotion of education and industry ←	Cultivation of the public as modern individuals through spiritual, mental, physical, and social training →	National unity based on public consensus	Nation-building based on democracy and liberty
	Daesŏng Middle School, Ceramics Company in P'yŏngyang	Chŏngnyŏn Hakuhoe (Young Korean Association)	Sinminhoe (New People's Association)	National Movement for Recovering Sovereignty
Activities	Korean Students Center in Claremont, Korean Business Company of North America	Hŭngsadan (Young Korean Academy)	Daehan'in Kukminhoe (Korean National Association)	National Independence Movement
	Dongmyŏng Academy in Nanjing, Farmers' Cooperative in Manchuria, Ideal Village Movement	Far East Branch of Hŭngsadan	Provisional Government of the Republic of Korea, Kukmin Daepyohoe (Conference of National Representatives), Minjok Yuildang Undong (Promotion Movement of the United National Party)	National Independence Movement

Ahn Chang-ho's nation-building project was adopted and executed by Cho Man-sik, who emerged as a national leader in the northwest of Korea after Ahn was exiled. As the secretary-general of the P'yŏngyang YMCA, Cho Man-sik positioned the YMCA as the foundation of a public sphere in the cultural realm. He led the public opinion of the local community through the network of YMCAs and tried to establish the infrastructure of a civil society. In addition, he experimented with the political public sphere to bring Korea a step closer to national independence from the public authority of Japanese imperialism.

Strengthening Civil Society Infrastructure by the P'yŏngyang YMCA

During the first decade of Japanese colonial rule, freedom of speech, the press, assembly, and association were categorically restricted in Korea. After the March First Independence Movement in 1919, Saito Makoto, the new governor-general of Korea, replaced terror and coercion with a more subtle policy called the Munhwa Chŏngch'i (Cultural Policy). As a result, political and social activities were allowed on a restricted basis in Korea, and Ahn Chang-ho's nation-building project was also implemented in P'yŏng-an Province. The promotion of the Chosŏn Mulsan Changryŏhoe (Society for the Promotion of Korean Production) in P'yŏngyang in August 1920 marked its beginning.

The Society for the Promotion of Korean Production aimed at countering the inflow of Japanese capital and products, which dramatically increased after World War I because of the wartime boom and the economic growth Japan was experiencing at the time. The promoters of the movement, including Cho Man-sik, declared that "we do not have protective trade laws or policies because of the loss of sovereignty; thus, we have no choice but to rely on the people's movement for economic self-defense and the public interest."[18] They defined the Korean Production Movement as the movement for protective trade at the nongovernmental level.

It is noteworthy that the argument for securing economic sovereignty by exercising the public's right of self-defense against the Japanese colonial administration at the nongovernmental level was not found in the prospectus of the Society for the Promotion of Korean Production that was established in Seoul in January 1923. The founders of the Seoul society declared simply that they would promote Korean industrial production and the development of the nation's livelihood and social evolution by consuming Korean-made products.[19] The difference between the prospectus of P'yŏngyang and that of Seoul reflected the level of understanding regarding civil society at the time. In this regard, the local characteristics of P'yŏng-an Province and the fact that the promoters of P'yŏngyang society were Christian leaders should be considered.

The promotion of the Society for the Promotion of Korean Production in 1920, however, did not automatically result in the establishment of the organization because Japanese merchants defined the movement as a boycott of Japanese products and placed pressure on colonial authorities to restrict the movement. The Society for the Promotion of Korean Production in P'yŏngyang was formally founded in June 1922. Meanwhile, Christian leaders in P'yŏngyang founded the YMCA as the basis for social movements in northwest Korea.

The P'yŏngyang YMCA was established in March 1921. Its leaders claimed that they would build the Kingdom of God on earth, full of humanity and justice by the gospel of Jesus Christ and the spiritual, mental, and physical training of young men.[20] Most of the board members were promoters of the Society for the Promotion of Korean Production in 1920. All of the YMCA's 150 members were powerful Christian leaders who wielded considerable power over the economy and culture of P'yŏngyang, the second largest city of Korea. As a result, the P'yŏngyang YMCA emerged as the center of social movements in the region.

From its foundation, the P'yŏngyang YMCA networked extensively with local social organizations, strengthened civil society infrastructure, and led public opinion. The Korean Production Movement was its key social effort. The Society for the Promotion of Korean Production and the P'yŏngyang YMCA were practically one and the same group. Cho Mansik, the secretary-general of the P'yŏngyang YMCA, was also the president of the Society for the Promotion of Korean Production, and nine of the twelve members of the society's board of directors were also officers of the P'yŏngyang YMCA. The society's office was also located in the P'yŏngyang YMCA. The practical strategy to form a secular organization reflecting the YMCA's agenda in civil society was generally adopted by the Christian social movement at the time.[21]

The main activities of the Society for the Promotion of Korean Production were enlightening lectures and propaganda campaigns. In particular, a street parade promoting Korean products became one of P'yŏngyang's major events. The parade was held on Lunar New Year's Day every year from 1923; it started from the P'yŏngyang YMCA hall and made its way downtown. The parade was sponsored by Korean stores and factories. In 1928, thirty member companies, consisting of factories making rubber and socks, and stores in P'yŏngyang, participated in the parade with their products proudly displayed on carts. From 1930, the Society for the Promotion of Korean Production hosted the parade with the Alliance for Temperance and Antismoking (Kŭmchu Tanyŏn Tongmaeng) and the Alliance of Tenants (Ch'aga-in Tongmaeng). In the process, the Society for the Promotion of Korean Production strengthened its solidarity with movements advocating improved living conditions.

In its movement, the society did not establish executive institutions, such as a consumers' association or a producers' association, but it allowed Korean stores and factories in P'yŏngyang to join and control the quality and price of their products. The society also promoted civilians' observance by mobilizing church groups composed of young men and women as well as secular social organizations. In P'yŏngyang the society continued its activities with the support of local residents, whereas the society in Seoul nearly collapsed after a year in the face of criticism from socialists that it was a selfish movement of the Korean bourgeoisie.[22]

With the active participation of merchants and industrialists, the Society for the Promotion of Korean Production in P'yŏngyang was able to exert an influence consistent with the reputation of Korea's premier commercial and industrial city. The tradition of commoner self-government and public consensus on civil society's values based on Protestantism also contributed to the society's influence. However, the society would not have succeeded if President Cho Man-sik, often called the Gandhi of Korea, had not led the movement effectively and pushed the use of local products.

While managing the Korean Production Movement, Cho Man-sik categorized the civil economic movement as having three areas: the consumption of Korean products, the promotion of domestic commerce and industry, and the improvement of living conditions. This movement was supported by Christian groups, commercial and industrial groups, and local groups. Cho Man-sik tried to promote newly emerging domestic industries by promoting campaigns pushing the use of domestic products. Factories producing socks and rubber in P'yŏngyang had actually entered the stage of mechanical automation in the mid-1920s when the Korean Production Movement began in earnest. These industries became the dominant force in the local economy, despite their disadvantages in terms of capital, technology, and the support of the Government General of Korea (Chosŏn Ch'ongdokpu) compared to current Japanese companies.[23] Remarkably, the majority of businessmen producing socks and rubber were Christians. In this regard, the potential influx of Japanese capital might have been successfully prevented through general cooperation among Christians and the economic ethics of Protestantism, which highlighted credibility, thrift, and the frontier spirit, as well as P'yŏng-an Province's efficient financial structure.[24] A large portion of sock factories were small businesses with less than 10,000 won in capital. The owners were mostly self-made individuals who started as store clerks or self-employed businessmen; they succeeded by diligence and credit. In terms of the rubber industry, church organizations frequently facilitated the pooling of capital for business purposes, often coming up with 50,000 won in capital for business start-ups.

These industries were able to ensure competitiveness through the assistance of the Korean Production Movement and the economic practices of Christian churches, even though most industries in P'yŏngyang were under the control of Japanese businessmen. From the late Tachan empire, new companies based on thrift and savings fraternities were steadily formed in P'yŏngyang, often through the support of church organizations. Cho Man-sik also established the Savings Association for the Promotion of Industry in P'yŏngyang (P'yŏngyang Silŏp Chŏkŭm Chohap) with YMCA members in December 1921. As a result, each of the Savings Association's hundred members saved five won on a monthly basis, and the association was able to manufacture and sell ink under the brand name Taedong Kang (Taedong River) the following summer.[25]

In this way, Cho Man-sik broadened the scope of self-sufficiency by encouraging small and domestic industries to produce goods for daily use with minimum capital. In addition, he proposed the development of large-scale industries through the pooling of capital and the industrial capitalization of venture capital firms to fight against the inflow of large-scale Japanese capital. In the process, joint-stock companies or corporations manufacturing socks and rubber were established in P'yŏngyang.

Subsequently, YMCA leaders including Cho Man-sik, Oh Yun-seon, and Kim Dong-won founded the Association of Commerce and Industry in P'yŏngyang (P'yŏngyang Sangkong Hyŏphoe) in December 1928. The Chamber of Commerce already existed in P'yŏngyang , but it was an organization more or less serving Japanese businessmen. Therefore, YMCA leaders founded the Association of Commerce and Industry to support the development of Korean businessmen. They also tried to establish Korean local banks for smooth flow of capital.[26] In addition, Cho Man-sik reorganized Soong-in Middle School as a commercial school dedicated to producing outstanding business minds and tried to establish an apprentice school providing technology education for the manufacturing industry.

In sum, Cho Man-sik promoted indigenous commerce and industry at the civil society level by establishing companies through savings associations and pooling capital, founding the Association of Commerce and Industry, and establishing commercial schools, among other measures. According to a reporter in P'yŏngyang, these efforts were the catalyst that resulted in the Korean-led economic revival movement and set Korean standards.[27]

Cho Man-sik also wanted to improve people's living conditions and reform their consciousness through the Korean Production Movement. To him, the use of Korean products meant the rationalization of consumption suitable for the level of Korean production. He insisted on securing minimum living conditions and achieving economic independence by patronizing locally made products and balancing the household budget, claiming that this would minimize opportunities for exploitation by Japanese businessmen. He also proposed the practical reform of traditional clothing, the simplification of the four ceremonies (i.e., coming-of-age, wedding, funeral, and ancestral rites), temperance, and antismoking as guidelines for improved living conditions.

Through the civil economic movement comprising the above-mentioned three categories, Cho Man-sik and the P'yŏngyang YMCA tried to establish the material basis of a civil society that would be free from Japanese colonial authorities. In addition, they expanded the autonomous space of civil society into social institutions for public interest while establishing the P'yŏngyang Orphanage as a private orphanage, Paek Seonhaeng Memorial Hall as a public hall, and Injeong Memorial Library as a public library through civic fund-raising and donations.

Because of his efforts, Cho Man-sik was referred to as a pioneer of Korea's civil society. In fact, he reigned as the uncrowned king in P'yŏngyang and managed all of the region's social events after he was appointed as secretary-general of the P'yŏngyang YMCA in 1921. He took office as the president of the Society for the Promotion of Korean Production in 1922 and led P'yŏngyang's Christian community (together with Kim Dongwŏn and Oh Yun-seon) as an elder of Sanchŏnghyŏn Presbyterian Church. When the Society for the Establishment of the Korean People's University (Chosŏn Minrip Taehak Kisŏnghoe) was founded in 1923, Cho Man-sik held promotional lectures and fund-raisers, touring P'yŏng-an Province as a member of the central executive committee and the itinerant commissioner of the society. He was also appointed as the principal of Soong-in Middle School when the school experienced financial difficulties in 1927; he transformed it into a commercial school. In addition, he was elected president of the Sports Association of Northwest Korea (Kwansŏ Ch'eyukhoe) in 1931; he used the opportunity to promote physical fitness in the region. As a result, P'yŏngyang was able to maintain its vitality as the "P'yŏngyang of the Korean people," even though it was under Japanese colonial rule.[28]

Public Sphere in the Political Realm at the Local Level and Japanese Colonialism

Efforts to strengthen civil society infrastructure through movements such as the Korean Production Movement required situating Protestantism in its social context. P'yŏngyang YMCA leaders, then, sought to expand the movement toward the political public sphere while leading public opinion in the local community. In the process, they tried to construct an independent nation-state based on civil society and the public sphere. As the P'yŏngyang YMCA advocated, they made national independence the first step toward the Kingdom of God on earth.

However, implementation of the project was difficult under Japanese colonial rule. It was almost impossible to secure the autonomy of civil society and the public sphere because colonial public authorities monitored Korean society closely using a carrot and stick policy. As a result, there was stiff tension between colonial public authorities and Korean society. In the process, colonial administrators induced a class division within Korean society by a series of appeasement policies presented as cultural policies, which led to agitation among local businessmen who formed mainstream Christian society in P'yŏngyang.

The rescinding of the Hoesa Ryŏng (Company Act) in 1920 marked the beginning of the divide and rule policy in colonial Korea. The measure guaranteed freedom of business activities. As a result, Korean businessmen were torn between the great cause of national independence and their class interests (i.e., the pursuit of profits within the colonial system). Moreover, they called on colonial police to help resolve labor issues when strikes occurred frequently in the mid-1920s.[29]

Under this situation, Yi kwang-su, a key member of the Young Korean Academy's domestic branch, the Brotherhood for Self-Discipline (Suyang Tonguhoe), proposed the depoliticization of civil society to avoid the Korean bourgeois dilemma. In his article "Minjok kaejoron" (A Treatise on National Reconstruction), he argued that "because the political independence of Korea will be approved by international procedures when we have the ability to become independent and the situation is friendly, political independence cannot be achieved by movements alone."[30] In addition, he insisted on separating the cultural movement from the political movement. He emphasized that the only way to save Korea would be to strengthen the activities of the cultural movement, such as the National Reconstruction Movement, through self-discipline.

Meanwhile, in the article "Minjokchŏk kyŏngryun" (National Administration), he suggested the deployment of a nationwide political movement by setting up a political association within the Japanese imperial system.[31] He wanted to protect the interests of the Korean bourgeoisie and to cultivate political skills by establishing a colonial self-governing body. This argument contradicted his earlier proposal to separate the cultural movement from the political movement. His opinions reflected the Korean bourgeoisie's approach to the colonial authorities based on their class interests in the mid-1920s.

Although some Korean bourgeois members were politically indifferent or had reached a compromise with the colonial authorities as a result of the divide and rule policy, Ahn Chang-ho and Cho Man-sik steadfastly promoted the need to combine the cultural, industrial, and political movements. Cho Man-sik maintained an uncompromising attitude regarding the Japanese colonial authorities, emphasizing the leading role of civil society in the construction of the national economy through the Korean

Production Movement. In addition, when the Singanhoe (New Korea Society) was organized as the national united front between the uncompromising nationalists and socialists, he participated in that society as one of its twenty-seven founding promoters. He also tried to establish a P'yŏngyang branch of the Singanhoe to experiment with the political public sphere at the local level.

This did not prove easy; the P'yŏngyang branch had to wait ten months after the Singanhoe's headquarters were established. The difficulty came primarily from conflicts within the Suyang Tonguhoe, a line organization of Ahn Chang-ho. At that time, many P'yŏngyang YMCA leaders were also members of the Suyang Tong'uhoe, including Kim Dong-wŏn. The internal conflict started when Cho Byong-ok and Chu Yo-han criticized the compromising nationalism of Yi kwang-su. They opposed Lee Gwang-su's theory of an apolitical cultural movement and insisted on the transformation of the Suyang Tonguhoe to a political organization.

The Suyang Tonguhoe's internal troubles were finally resolved through the arbitration of Ahn Chang-ho, who was in exile in China. He proposed that the Suyang Tonguhoe convert itself and train revolutionaries, suggesting that political organizations put forth a united front by including a wide variety of nationalist groups. As a result of Ahn's arbitration, Suyang Tonguhoe members started to participate in Singanhoe, and the P'yŏngyang branch was also established in December 1927.[32] However, Kim Dong-won did not participate in the Sinkanhoe.

Cho Man-sik was elected the president of the P'yŏngyang branch of the Singanhoe, which formed the political public sphere of a coalition between the left- and right-wing factions by combining Christian leaders, Suyang Tonguhoe members, and socialists. When the P'yŏngyang YMCA relocated in February 1930, the P'yŏngyang branch of the Singanhoe also moved to the same location.[33] This indicates that the P'yŏngyang branch of the Singanhoe was under the influence of the P'yŏngyang YMCA. The P'yŏngyang branch organized the Association of South P'yŏng-an Province of the Singanhoe and proposed that a council be formed to seek to reduce rents for housing by people power.[34] P'yŏngyang's housing problems were serious during its urbanization; thus, the P'yŏngyang branch of the Singanhoe experimented with community politics at the local level. However, the Singanhoe was unable to meet its goals because the majority of indigenous capitalists, the community's mainstream, took compromising attitudes toward the Japanese colonial authorities and excused themselves from the front lines of the nationalist movement.

Cho Man-sik tried to reconstruct the agents of the civil society movement centering on the young men's groups and the urban populace with the breakaway of local capitalists and the impoverishment of the populace brought about by the Great Depression. The cosponsored campaign to promote Korean production by the Alliance for Temperance and Antismoking and the Alliance of Tenants in 1930 is one example. The strategy of the Korean Production Movement also moved toward the center: from fostering indigenous commerce and industry by creating demand for Korean products to improving stability and promoting improved living conditions for the urban populace and small farmers through rational consumption.

Cho Man-sik's political experiment based on civil society failed when a bill to dissolve the P'yŏngyang branch of the Singanhoe was passed with a majority vote during the fourth periodic meeting in December 1930.[35] Cho Man-sik opposed the dissolution, proposing an internal reform as an alternative;[36] however, the bourgeoisie, the majority, were not interested. They did not attend the meeting; thus, the decision was irreversible. This outcome illustrates the limit of the bourgeois public sphere under Japanese colonialism. Afterward, Cho Man-sik focused on Christian socialism and sought new breakthroughs through rural movements.[37]

Christianity was accepted as a symbol of modernity in Korea. To modernize Korea, Korean Christian leaders paid close attention to Western culture and public spheres. The independent middle class in the northwest region of Korea was the most earnest in this endeavor. Under the continuing political discrimination from the dynasty state, it accepted Protestantism to replace rule by Neo-Confucianism and the Yangban caste system. This group sympathized with Protestant ethics preaching love, equality for all, and the sacredness of labor. It went a step further and tried to foster new modern individuals and an autonomous civil society free from state interference based on traditional commoner self-governance in P'yŏng-an Province. As a result, P'yŏng-an Province emerged as the center of Christianity and modern culture in Korea.

Ahn Chang-ho sublimated the social orientation of the northwestern independent middle class to reflect the principle of new individuals, a new society, and a new state. He proposed a nation-building project that comprised the fostering of the public as modern individuals, the establishment of a foundation for civil society, and the organization of a public sphere in the political realm based on public opinion.

To achieve his objectives, Ahn advocated a cultural movement fostering modern individuals by combining Protestantism and traditional commoner culture. For this purpose, he organized an association that promoted self-discipline by benchmarking the Fourfold Program of the North American YMCA, including spiritual, mental, physical, and social training. At the same time, he advocated the importance of education and industry in the establishment of civil society infrastructure that would serve as a foundation for the development of a capitalist economy. He also tried to create a public sphere in the political realm for democratic nation-building through national unity that was based on public consensus.

In sum, Ahn Chang-ho's project presented a road map for the establishment of civil society infrastructure and a political public sphere, starting from the cultural movement equivalent to the public sphere in the world of letters that Habermas conceptualized. Ahn's nation-building project, based on civil society and the public sphere, was welcomed by the independent middle class of P'yŏng-an Province. Having experienced political discrimination during the Chosŏn dynasty, they also believed that modern individuals and civil society would be helpful to achieving their social interests as well as national independence. After Ahn Chang-ho was exiled in 1910, his project was taken over and put into practice by Cho Man-sik, the secretary-general of the P'yŏngyang YMCA.

With members of the Brotherhood for Self-Discipline, who were directly under the influence of Ahn Chang-ho, Cho Man-sik established the P'yŏngyang YMCA as the center of the public sphere in the cultural area in 1921. P'yŏngyang was Korea's second largest city and the center of northwest Korea. Using the P'yŏngyang YMCA as his social base, Cho Man-sik began building the civil society infrastructure with P'yŏngyang as the center. As a part of their efforts, the leaders of the P'yŏngyang YMCA, including Cho Man-sik, founded the Society for the Promotion of Korean Production. The society began a campaign encouraging the purchase and use of domestic products at the nongovernmental level to promote Korean industries and to improve people's living conditions. In the process, Cho Man-sik, the president of the society, established a material basis for a civil society that would be free from the influence of the Japanese colonial authorities by mobilizing Christian groups, merchant and industrialist groups, young men's groups, and women's groups in P'yŏngyang. He also expanded the autonomous space of civil society into social institutions for the public interest while establishing, through civic fund-raising and donations, a private orphanage, a public hall, and a public library. Through such social activities, Cho Man-sik came to be known as the Gandhi of Korea or the president of Korean society in P'yŏngyang.

In the political area, Cho Man-sik tried to create a public sphere as a foundation for the establishment of an independent nation-state. As advocated by the P'yŏngyang YMCA, he considered it the first step toward the Kingdom of God on earth. The P'yŏngyang branch of the Singanhoe was the fruit of that effort. Composed of YMCA leaders and socialists in P'yŏngyang, it was a national united front at the local level. Cho Man-sik, who was elected as the president of the P'yŏngyang branch of Sinkanhoe, sought an uncompromising political struggle against Japanese imperialism by networking local community social groups and experimented with community politics, such as the tenant issue at the local level. However, his political experiment was unsuccessful because the local Korean bourgeoisie, the mainstream of Korean society in P'yŏngyang, abandoned the nationalist movement, compromising with Japanese colonial authorities. This illustrates the limits of the bourgeois public sphere under Japanese colonialism at the time and raises the fundamental question of whether it would have been possible to secure political autonomy in the public sphere under the colonial state.

However, in the cultural realm of P'yŏngyang, a Korean version of Western modernity, which was formed through the naturalization of Protestant ethics, was engaged in a long-term war of position against Japan's attempts to secure cultural hegemony in Korea by implanting colonial modernity. The civil society movement of the P'yŏngyang YMCA reflected typical movements in the 1920s and 1930s. The P'yŏngyang YMCA, under the leadership of Cho Man-sik, attempted to create a modern, Protestant ethics–based civil society that would be free from the control of the Japanese authorities. In light of the above discussion, the history of Christianity in Korea should be examined in the context of modernity as well as church growth and national movements.

Notes

1. Rhee Syngman, "Yesukyo ka Daehan changrae ŭi kich'o" [Christianity Is the Foundation of Korea in the Future], *Sinhak wŏlpo* [Monthly Theological Review] 3, no. 8 (1903): 332–333.

2. Lee Dong-hui, "Yuko ich'ŏnman tongp'o hyŏngche sŏ" (A Letter to the Korean Nation), 1905; Yun Byeong-seog, ed., *The Complete Works of Lee Dong-hui* (Cheonan: The Independence Hall of Korea, 1998), 1:8–9. Later, Lee Dong-hui converted to socialism and organized the Hanin Sahoedang (Korean Socialist Party), which was the first Korean socialist party, in 1918.

3. Ahn Chang-ho, "Nakkwan kwa pikwan" [Optimism and Pessimism], *Tong-kwang* [The East Light] 12 (1927): 3–4.

4. Yi Man-yŏl, *Han'guk Kidokkyo munhwa undong sa* [The History of the Christian Cultural Movement in Korea] (Seoul: The Christian Literature Society, 1987), 47–54.

5. The Institute of Korean Church History Studies, *Han'guk Kidokkyo ŭi yŏksa* [A History of the Korean Church] (Seoul: The Christian Literature Press, 1989), 1:2–10.

6. Jürgen Habermas, *The Structural Transformation of the Public Sphere* (Cambridge, MA: The MIT Press, 1989), 30.

7. Ibid., 51.

8. Chang Kyusik, *Ilcheha Han'guk Kidokkyo minjokjuŭi yŏn'gu* [Christian Nationalism in Modern Korea] (Seoul: Hyean Press, 2001), 97–100.

9. Kim Jin-gyun and Jung Keun-sik, eds., *Kŭndae chuch'e wa sikminji kyuyul kwŏnryŏk* [Modern Subjects and Colonial Disciplinary Power] (Seoul: Munhwa Gwa Haksa, 1997), 19.

10. William M. Baird, "Notes on a Trip into Northern Korea," *The Independent,* May 20, 1897; Lee Kwang-in, "Kaehwaki kwansŏ chipang kwa Kaesinkyo" [Northwest Korea and Protestant Christianity in the Later Chosŏn Dynasty], in *Han'guk Kaehwa sasang yŏn'gu* [Studies on Ideas of Enlightenment in the Later Chosŏn Dynasty] (Seoul: Iljogak, 1979), 244–249.

11. Chang Kyusik, "Dosan Ahn Chang-ho ŭi minjokjuŭi wa simin sahoeron" [Ahn Chang-ho's View of Nationalism and the Theory of Civil Society], *Dosan sasang yŏn'gu* [Journal of Dosan Ahn Chang-ho Studies] 6 (2000): 49–52.

12. Homer B. Hulbert, *The History of Korea* (Seoul: Methodist Publishing House, 1905), 2:325–326.

13. Chang Kyusik, *Ilcheha Han'guk Kidokkyo minjokchŭi yŏn'gu,* 39–40.

14. *Musil* and *yŏkhaeng* were Ahn Chang-ho's version of work ethic and pragmatism. *Musil* means "to raise the virtues of honesty and faithfulness against

the Neo-Confucian formalism of vanity." It was linked with economic ethics that emphasized diligence and the capital of credibility. *Yŏkhaeng* means "real practice rather than empty words." It also entailed economic ethics that emphasized the sacredness of labor and pragmatism. See Chang Kyusik, "Dosan Ahn Chang-ho," 74–78.

15. The Sinminhoe (New People's Association) was formed secretly in 1907. Most of its members were Protestant Christians from northwest Korea, including Ahn Chang-ho, Yang Ki-tak, and Lee Seung-hun. The leaders of The New People's Association took the initiative in organizing the Provisional Government of the Republic of Korea in Shanghai, China, after the March First movement in 1919.

16. "Taehan Sinminhoe tongyong changchŏng" [The Regulations of the New People's Association], in *Han'guk tongnip undongsa* [The History of Korean Independent Movement] (Seoul: The National Institute of Korean History, 1968), 1:1028.

17. Chang Kyusik, "Dosan Ahn Chang-ho," 48.

18. "Chosŏn Mulsan Changryŏhoe ch'uijisŏ" [The Prospectus of the Society for the Promotion of Korean Production in P'yŏngyang], *Dong-a ilbo* [Dong-a Daily News], August 23, 1920.

19. "Chosŏn Mulsan Changryŏhoe ch'uijisŏ" [The Prospectus of the Society for the Promotion of Korean Production in Seoul], *Sanŏpkye* [Industrial World] 1 (1923): 55–56.

20. "P'yŏngyang Kidokkyo Ch'ŏngnyŏnhoe ŭi sŏlrip" [The Establishment of the P'yŏngyang YMCA], *Ch'ŏngnyŏn* [The Young Man] 1, no. 2 (1921): 38.

21. Chang Kyusik, *Ilcheha Han'guk Kidokkyo minjokjuŭi yŏn'gu*, 259–262.

22. Chang Kyusik, "Ilcheha Kidokkyo kyeyŏl ŭi minjok kyŏngje kŏnsŏlron" [The National Economic Development Theory of Christian Nationalists under Japanese Colonial Rule: The Case of the P'yŏngyang YMCA], *Han'guk sasang sahak* [The Study of the History of Korean Thought] 15 (2000): 260–262.

23. Ibid., 263.

24. Cho Ki-joon, *Han'guk chaponjuŭi sŏngrip saron* [Historical Essay on the Establishment of Capitalism in Korea] (Seoul: Daewangsa, 1977), 507–512.

25. Kyusik Chang, "Ilcheha Kidokkyo Kyeyŏl ŭi minjok kyŏngje kŏnsŏlron," 267.

26. Ibid., 268–269.

27. P'yŏngyang Il Kija, "Puk Kŭmyung Chohap isa insŏn munje" [Problems of the Appointment of Directors in the North Finance Cooperative, P'yŏngyang], *Dong-a ilbo,* April 5, 1928.

28. Chang Kyusik, "Chosŏn ŭi Gandhi Kodang Cho Man-sik" [Kodang Cho Man-sik Called the Gandhi of Korea], *Naeil ŭl yŏnŭn yŏksa* [History to Open the Future] 26 (2006): 92–93.

29. Chang Kyusik, *Ilcheha Han'guk Kidokkyo minjokjuŭi yŏn'gu,* 234–235.

30. Yi Kwang-su, "Minjok kaejoron" [A Treatise on National Reconstruction], *Kaebyŏk* [Creation of the World] 23 (1922): 47.

31. Yi Kwang-su, "Minjokchŏk kyŏngryun 2" [National Administration], *Dong-a ilbo,* January 3, 1924.

32. Chang Kyusik, *Ilcheha Han'guk Kidokkyo minjokjuŭi yŏn'gu,* 188–189.

33. "P'yŏngyang Kidok Chŏngnyŏn hoekwan ichŏn" [Relocation of the P'yŏngyang YMCA], *Dong-a ilbo,* February 14, 1930.

34. "P'yŏngyang Singanhoe" [P'yŏngyang Branch of the New Korea Society], *Dong-a ilbo,* December 3, 1929; Oh Giyoung, "P'yŏngyang sahoe danch'e gkaekwan" [Overview of NGOs in P'yŏngyang], *Pyŏlkŏnko* [Another World] 32 (1930): 43–44.

35. "Singanhoe P'yŏngyang chihoe" [P'yŏngyang Branch of the New Korea Society], *Dong-a ilbo,* December 29, 1930.

36. Cho Man-sik, "Ŏin e i rŭl chum ŭn taekŭmmul" [Internal Division Is Our Greatest Enemy], *Samch'ŏlli* [Korean Peninsula] 12 (1931): 7–8.

37. Chang Kyusik, "1920 nyŏndae kaejoron ŭi hwaksan kwa Kidokkyo sahoechuŭi ŭi suyong chŏngch'ak" [Spreading the Reconstruction Argument in the 1920s and the Establishment of Christian Socialism], *Yŏksa munje yŏn'gu* [Critical Studies on Modern Korean History] 21 (2009): 127–128.

6

Between Mission and Medicine

The Early History of Severance Hospital

Yunjae Park

In 1994 Severance Hospital, one of the leading hospitals in Korea, proclaimed its mission to, "with the love of God, free humankind from disease and suffering." It also manifested its vision "to be the most reliable medical institution, following in the footsteps of Missionaries, Allen, Avison, and donor philanthropist Severance."[1] As its mission and vision show, Severance Hospital has introduced itself as a Christian hospital and, to realize its vision, it established in 2001 a Center for Medical Mission that aims to support activities of Korean medical missionaries. It is clear that Christianity is the guiding spirit of the hospital. It was not, however, a Christian hospital from the beginning although it was established in 1885 by Horace Allen, an American medical missionary. As Korea then prohibited missionary work, even after opening itself to foreign countries in 1876, a missionary like Allen had to disguise himself as a medical doctor. In the process of founding Jejungwon, a predecessor of Severance Hospital, he had to stress that he was planning to establish a new Western-style hospital rather than a missionary one. Formally, it was a government or royal hospital, but it was a missionary hospital and a base for missionary work to Allen.

The main theme of the history of Severance Hospital until 1894 was the struggle to transform the hospital into a purely missionary hospital. Even after a successful change, the job was not complete. It had to deal with the Japanese colonial government, which had a mixed attitude toward missionaries. As Japan was not a Christian country, missionaries were required to cooperate with the government to achieve their goals. Severance Hospital had to adjust to this changing environment. Balancing between mission and medicine was the fate of a missionary hospital like Severance Hospital in order to survive in a non-Christian country. Investigating the case of Severance Hospital, this chapter shows how it was transformed into a Christian hospital from a governmental one and how the medical missionary negotiated with government authorities in a non-Christian land. In conducting this investigation, this chapter highlights the ways in which Christianity emerged and grew with the help of medical work in Korea.

Even after Korea opened itself to Western powers, the government prohibited the spread of Christianity because the Korean ruling elite, who were Sinocentric, believed that Christianity collided with traditional Confucian belief.[2] It was a natural reaction for a country like Korea that had been accustomed to Confucian thought for more than five hundred years. The reaction and response by Koreans toward Western science and technology was different. The idea spread rapidly among Koreans that Western science and technology could be effective in making Korea a wealthy and mighty country. Indeed, Western medicine was regarded as a crucial component of Western science and technology. Koreans thought it could cure wounded soldiers more successfully than Eastern medicine. They also thought it could contribute to the protection of people's lives by preventing the spread of contagious diseases.[3] As early as 1884, a Korean newspaper printed an article demanding the establishment of Western medical schools at major ports.[4]

The question was how to teach Western medicine to Koreans. At the time, there were no Koreans who were skilled enough to give instruction in Western medicine. Hiring a foreign medical doctor was a practical way to overcome this problem. The opportunity to hire a foreigner to teach Western medicine came from an unexpected direction with the arrival of Horace N. Allen as the first Protestant missionary in Korea in 1884. In addition to being a missionary, Allen was a medical doctor. He had stayed in Shanghai for his first field mission and wanted to move farther north, where the environment would be more comfortable for his wife, who was about to give birth. Fortunately for Allen, an American Presbyterian mission had launched a plan to expand its mission base to Korea, which had once been regarded as one of the lands most hostile to Christianity, and decided to send Allen as its first missionary.[5]

On his arrival in Korea, Allen had to conceal his true purpose, pretending to be a medical doctor affiliated with the American legation. In less than four months, he was fortunate enough to have a chance to treat a high-ranking official and cousin of the queen, Min Young-ik, who was wounded during a coup d'état against the government. Allen devoted more than three months to treating him, using Western surgical skills. The unprecedented quick recovery from stab wounds must have impressed the royal family, including the queen, because she, according to Allen, "assur[ed] me of her confidence in me and her desire to have me alone attend to her royal cousin."[6] King Kojong was also impressed with Allen's work and invited him to start a Western-style hospital in Korea. The king had already showed an interest in Western civilization. Before Allen arrived in Korea, King Kojong had permitted the establishment of a Western school and hospital after having met Robert S. McClay, a Methodist missionary in Japan.[7] He had wanted to make Korea a strong and wealthy country by adopting aspects of Western civilization, such as Western medicine. Hence, it seemed to Allen that "the King was earnest in desiring a modern hospital and it had to be fitted up."[8]

After receiving the invitation, Allen submitted a proposal offering to establish a Western hospital and work without a salary if the government granted a proper site and a house. He also expressed a desire to teach Korean students. The new hospital "would be the means of instructing young men in Western Medical and Sanitary Science."[9] While the proposal most certainly impressed the king, foreign diplomats opposed this proposal because of Allen's missionary background. Having lived in China, German consul Hermann Budler, for example, disliked missionaries and spoke out against the proposed hospital, declaring it to be a "hotbed of trouble" and a "proselytizing scheme."[10] Along with Budler, other influential foreign officials voiced their concerns to the Korean government that patients would not be treated unless they promised to believe in Christ.[11] To dispel the rumor that the new hospital would be mission-oriented, Allen purposely mentioned China and Li Hung Chang in his proposal. In China, there were hospitals in several cities, such as Peking, Tientsin, Shanghai, and Canton, started and operated by Western missionaries. Two of these hospitals, in fact, were supported by Li Hung Chang, a Chinese figure well known in Korea.[12] In the end, throughout his proposal, Allen made sure to emphasize that the proposed hospital would be open to all and would have no relation to missionary work.

To help him achieve his goal of building a new hospital, Allen was clever enough to attract King Kojong's attention by mentioning that the new hospital would be called "His Corean Majesty's Hospital." Being benevolent was a traditional duty for the Confucian nobility in Korea, especially for the king, who was expected never to neglect his duty of caring for the people.[13] Founding a hospital where people would be treated and receive medicine without charge would be an exemplary action of the king. Allen thus recognized that King Kojong would be able to show that he cared for the overall well-being of his people.[14] Despite his various efforts such as emphasizing the connection of the hospital to Korean royalty, it appears that Allen hardly needed to convince King Kojong to start a hospital. Indeed, the royal family's trust in Allen was unshakable. Both the king and the queen had employed him to treat them for various ailments, and the king himself told Allen several times that he should not hesitate in asking for whatever he wanted.[15]

King Kojong ultimately allowed Allen to build a new Western-style hospital. By most accounts, the construction of the hospital happened very fast, although Allen wrote in a diary that "everything is in such a muddle that nothing can be hurried."[16] On April 10, 1885, Jejungwon, the predecessor of Severance Hospital, was established. Jejungwon began by serving as an "emigration company" that provided Western missionaries with official positions in Korea. For instance, Horace G. Underwood, the first Presbyterian pastor, worked as a medical assistant and later as a teacher at Jejungwon.[17] Missionaries working at the hospital, however, soon became dissatisfied with their position because they wanted to also conduct religious activities, like evangelizing Koreans. Many missionaries complained about the hospital's designation as a government institution rather than as a religious institution. William B. Scranton, the first Methodist missionary doctor, who helped Allen run the hospital, resigned from the hospital, saying that the Methodist Board would not sanction his work at Jejungwon because it was not a religious institution.[18] The Methodists even sneered at the Presbyterians for running a hospital financed by a pagan government.[19]

Presbyterians themselves complained about the nonreligious nature of the hospital. For example, John W. Heron, the second Presbyterian medical doctor to work at Jejungwon, criticized Allen and declared that he longed to tell Koreans about Jesus Christ, who had died for them.[20] Lillias S. Horton, another Presbyterian medical doctor, was also uncomfortable with the restrictive atmosphere of Jejungwon. On reaching Jejungwon, she was disappointed to find that she could only conduct religious work indirectly.[21] She later gave up working at the hospital, mentioning that she was highly dissatisfied with the rules forbidding religious-related work.[22] Allen responded to his critics and their complaints by emphasizing that the hospital was the first step toward helping Koreans learn about Western civilization. He added that there was nothing that could prevent the hospital from conducting missionary work. Hence, he asked his colleagues to be patient and said, "We will be doing aggressive work in the hospital by the time we are ready for it."[23]

As these debates between missionaries continued at the hospital, the Korean government began to loosen its restrictions on foreigners conducting religious activities. For example, when Roman Catholics wanted to construct a building that overlooked an ancient royal temple, the Korean government permitted construction. In the dispatch that authorized the construction of the building, the government essentially acknowledged the presence of Christianity.[24] It further mentioned that it was well known that American teachers were teaching Christianity. Though treaties with foreign powers and laws in Korea forbade the spreading of Christianity, the dispatch stated that missionary work would be tolerated as long as it never interfered with government activities and national issues. Under this changing environment, therefore, Jejungwon slowly became more religiously oriented. An event in 1889 highlighted this transformation. After a student in the hospital school saw a Christian student talk about Christ with his fellow classmate, he ran to the president of school to say that he could not study with someone who was associated with missionary work. The president's response was unexpected. "What of it? Is he any worse for it? Your teacher is a missionary. If you do not care to study with him, you can leave."[25] By the end of the 1880s, missionary work was no longer a taboo in Jejungwon. Gradually and slowly, Jejungwon was transforming from a government hospital operated in the name of the king into a Christian hospital.

Conservative missionaries still were unsatisfied with the gradual pace of this transformation. They wanted fundamental change and believed that the hospital's designation as a "government hospital" prevented it from becoming a Christian hospital that would spread Christianity. Heron again was one of those conservative missionaries who complained about the situation. He declared that "the fact that the hospital is a government one will prevent us from ever doing much in the way of teaching Christianity."[26] He longed to have a Presbyterian hospital where medical doctors could serve in the name of Christianity and teach Christian principles.[27] Heron, who was in charge of Jejungwon after Allen left for America in 1887, died of dysentery in 1890. His death prompted Presbyterian missionaries to discuss the future of the hospital. Over a series of meetings, missionaries including Allen, who returned to Korea in 1889, agreed that the hospital would be best served if people were introduced to both Christianity and Western medicine. Everyone, apparently including Allen, thought it would be good plan for Christian missions to take over the hospital from the government, if it allowed it, and make it into a missionary hospital.[28]

As missionaries sought to gain full control of the hospital and change its identity, Allen, who had plans to move away from being a missionary and become a diplomat, was reappointed the chairman of the hospital.[29] During his second term, Allen not only had to run the hospital, but he also had to fight off attempts by various missionary groups, particularly the English Society of the Propagation of the Gospel and Catholics, to take control of the hospital.[30] At the time, the Korean government considered giving the hospital to any mission group. Allen, however, fought for Presbyterian control of the hospital. With the support of the American legation, Allen prevented the government from handing the hospital to another missionary group. If he had not been in Seoul, according to his writings, the handover might have happened.[31]

Oliver R. Avison, who arrived in 1893 as a Presbyterian medical missionary, helped in preventing the government from handing over the hospital to various foreigners and transforming the hospital into a Christian institution. After he started working at Jejungwon, Avison took over most of the administrative duties at the hospital. As its administrative leader, Avison allowed more religious work at the hospital. Allen thus wrote that "if we want to try it, no objections would be made to the opening of a preaching service everyday to the waiting patients."[32] The restriction of religious work, if there was any, existed only in the minds of a few. Despite this permissive environment, Avison wanted to increase religious activities and make the hospital into a mission institution, which he believed could only be achieved through raising enough funds to allow the hospital to become independent from the government.[33] Securing money from groups in America would be challenging, so Avison first proposed that the Korean government send officials (*jusa*) who would reside at the hospital but would not interfere with the way the hospital operated.[34] The government refused to send officials in this capacity and simply handed over the hospital to the Presbyterian mission.[35] There was no clear reason why the government transferred control over the hospital to the missionaries. It is possible that the government recognized that it was impossible to prevent the expansion of religions activities by missionaries. Although the Korean government never officially gave missionaries permission to evangelize, missionaries traveled throughout Korea to spread Christianity. The government may have understood the inevitability that the hospital would become a religious institution and therefore transferred ownership to the missionaries. A more plausible reason for the transfer may have been the inability of the Korean government to support the hospital financially. In an official document on Jejungwon, the American minister stated that, if the Korean government let Avison and the missionaries take sole control of the hospital, "the trouble you have had regarding funds will be obviated."[36] Financial difficulties experienced by the government had long prevented the hospital from performing many activities. As Allen pointed out, it had been impossible to do anything with Jejungwon in spite of promises made by the king himself. To Allen, the government seemed to be on "its last legs."[37]

In 1894, the shift of management to the American Presbyterian mission transformed Jejungwon into a Christian hospital. The official catalogue of Severance Hospital stated that, "in 1894, the hospital was taken over from the Government by the Presbyterian mission (north), and since then has been a distinctly missionary institution."[38] It was a victory for the missionaries who had wanted a purely Christian hospital where missionaries could preach Christianity without restriction since its founding.

Avison felt that more work was needed at the hospital in order for it to become an effective missionary institution. As a way to strengthen the hospital and increase its resources, Avison called for the various missionary groups in Korea to pool their manpower and resources. Instead of the seven doctors in Korea, who were assigned by various mission boards, each running a small and poorly equipped hospital in Seoul, Avison argued that the doctors and the mission boards should devote their energy and resources to one hospital, like Jejungwon, and create a super institution that made a significant impact on society. He believed that this super hospital would be far more effective and influential than seven smaller hospitals. Moreover, since three or four doctors would only be necessary at this super hospital, it was thought that the remaining three doctors could work in other parts of Korea and extend missionary influence.[39]

Avison left Korea in 1899 for a furlough with hopes of raising funds to achieve his vision of improving and strengthening Jejungwon. To Avison, obtaining money was crucial because Jejungwon was in a poor state. It was mostly a complex of traditional buildings that lacked essential equipment, such as a Western-style heating, water, and drainage systems. What allowed Avison to obtain the necessary funds to remodel and strengthen the hospital was a simple speech he made in New York. While staying in Canada for his furlough, he was invited to attend the Ecumenical Conference of Foreign Missions in New York. While participating in the conference, Avison was asked to make a speech for the conference on the subject of "Comity in Medical Missions." In his speech to conference participants, he emphasized the importance of cooperation in missionary hospitals and the need for developing new, modern hospitals.[40] Louis H. Severance attended the conference and heard Avison's speech. Severance was a well-known Cleveland businessman who had made his fortune through oil and mineral exploration. Severance was well known for donating large sums of money to support churches in the Cleveland area, YMCAs, and missionary efforts throughout the world. After hearing Avison's speech, Severance decided to donate ten thousand dollars to Avison's cause of improving Jejungwon.

Despite this large sum of money, which would have immediately solved all of the problems at Jejungwon, Severance's large donation became embroiled in controversy. Conservative Presbyterian missionaries in P'yŏngyang opposed the use of the entire sum toward remodeling and expanding Jejungwon. These conservative missionaries worried that building a large and notable hospital would give Koreans the wrong ideas about

Christianity. They feared that, in seeing the hospital, Koreans would gain the impression that Christianity emphasized philanthropic enterprise over spiritual refinement and cultivation. Consequently, these missionaries in P'yŏngyang, which was already gaining a strong reputation as a bastion for fundamentalist theology, thought the donation and a new hospital would be an obstacle to the preaching of the "real gospel." Avison thought their concerns were unfounded, which led the conservative missionaries to write to the Presbyterian Board in New York and ask them to divide Severance's donation between the hospital and evangelical activities.[41] This division reflected the different ideas missionaries held regarding how to preach the gospel and expose Koreans to Christianity and served as a potential threat to the expansion of the hospital. In the end, however, this division failed to derail Avison's plans because the mission board in New York rejected the request by the conservative missionaries—mostly because Severance himself rejected the proposal. In addition, Severance gave another fifteen thousand dollars to buy a new site for the hospital and offered to provide more money for the rising cost of construction. With Severance's generous support, a newly modernized Jejungwon emerged as Severance Hospital in 1904.

Despite achieving the goal of building a missionary hospital, Avison realized that he still needed to persuade missionaries, like the conservative Presbyterian missionaries in P'yŏngyang, that medical work was more than just offering medical help, but also a way of exposing Christianity to Korea.[42] Indeed, Avison stated that "the medical work is in no way behind the other missionary methods of presenting the gospel of Christ to the people."[43] Avison and his supporters were convinced that curing patients was a way of realizing the love of God.[44] To them, a medical mission was the means to restoring and strengthening both the physical and spiritual sides of Koreans. Certain evangelical missionaries came around to supporting this view, arguing that medical work was the work of carrying out the Lord's command "as ye go heal the sick."[45]

In order to advance the mission of offering medical help and spreading the gospel, Avison stressed the importance of training Koreans to become Christian doctors. As Koreans, these doctors would have better access to the people and would be able to express the Christian spirit and Jesus' love. Korean doctors, according to Avison, would be able to maintain medical and missionary roles.[46] Under this mission to train Korean doctors, Koreans would first become medical assistants, and medical missionaries would teach clinics where young Koreans would learn about medical technology. Missionaries hoped that the beginning stage of medical training would be an ideal way of showing them the value of medical missions and transforming young Koreans into disciplined Christians. This hope came from seeing that some of the most influential Christians in Korea were former students at Jejungwon.[47] After returning from his furlough in 1900, Avison reorganized the teaching system, giving proper grades to students and providing scholarships. Full-time medical students in Jejungwon matriculated for the first time in September 1900.[48] Avison emphasized the importance of training Koreans to become doctors in a medical school because failure to train them to become doctors would result in a lost opportunity to build an influential student body. He stressed that medical instruction was a matter of great importance to the future task of building a strong native Christian community.[49]

After the opening of Severance Hospital in 1904, the Presbyterian mission dispatched Jesse W. Hirst to Korea so Avison could spend more time teaching. In 1908, seven Koreans became the first graduates from the medical school at Severance Hospital to become doctors. The Korean government rewarded the work of the medical missionaries by presenting government certificates to the graduates, the first of their kind issued in Korea. Missionaries were sure that "this act gives the doctors a recognized standing in the country."[50] Avison was encouraged by all that had happened and grew more ardent about the need for cooperation among missionaries to educate Koreans. He declared that medical education for Christian doctors had to be carried out as a joint undertaking of all missions, which he believed would ensure that enough medical teachers, nurses, and funds were available.[51] Since there was great respect for the work at Severance and its ability to produce highly educated graduates who were strong Christians that sacrificed self-interest, calls grew for missionaries to work together to build up the medical school at Severance.[52] Indeed, a missionary raised the question: "What is the reason the missionary bodies in Korea cannot unite on this one thing and lend support to the first establishment of this Christian Medical College[?]"[53] In 1909, the Medical Missionary Association in Korea resolved that there would be a single medical college in Seoul in which doctors from all missionary groups would teach and provide help.[54] It was decided that Severance Hospital would be the site of this new medical college that was named Union Medical College of the Christian Churches of Korea.[55]

Besides the practicality of pooling resources to create and operate a medical school at Severance, the establishment of Jike Hospital, a charity hospital, by the Japanese colonial government was another reason for missionaries to establish a unified medical school and advocate closer ties in 1913. Before the establishment of Jike Hospital, missionary hospitals had no serious rivals, at least in rural areas. The situation changed with the establishment of Jike Hospital. Competition grew.[56] In this environment, a missionary doctor complained that "even the ignorant Korean coolie coming to our dispensaries will compare us and our work with that he sees in the Government hospital across the town and will make demands of us which will call for our very best effort."[57] Japanese military doctors took positions at Jike and worked together to create a substantial hospital. Jike still had problems because the hospital was not equipped with in-patient wards. Military doctors were not accustomed to treating children and women since they had mostly treated male soldiers in their careers. With these limitations, Jike Hospital failed to meet all of the people's medical needs.[58]

However, Jike Hospital still appeared to be a superior institution to any missionary-operated hospital. The government hospital had more medical practitioners, well-equipped facilities, and a secure financial base, while missionary hospitals lacked vital equipment and had poorly constructed buildings. Many missionary hospitals had to close temporarily because of the absence of a system to handle missionary furloughs. Missionary hospitals also had a weak financial base that left them without sufficient funds.[59] In 1913, thirteen out of eighteen stations were in need of at least one more medical doctor. Without the help of Korean assistants, they could hardly undertake necessary activities. The practical way to overcome this situation was to merge smaller hospitals since medical missionaries believed that one institution thoroughly staffed and equipped would do more for the cause of Christ than forty scattered, smaller institutions.

Against this backdrop, missionaries and missionary doctors increased their collaborative efforts to strengthen the medical school at Severance. Representatives from various missionary groups, such as the Southern Presbyterian Mission, the Southern Methodist Mission, the Methodist Episcopal Mission, and the Australian Presbyterian Mission, decided to pour more resources into the medical college and created a new unified board made up of members from six missionary groups that would operate and oversee the hospital and medical school at Severance. In order to reflect the changes at Severance, the board decided to rename the medical school Severance Union Medical College in 1913.[60] At this new medical school, the board and all teachers were active Christians. However, the school admitted non-Christians to its medical school.[61]

After 1910, Avison turned his attention toward making sure the new medical school ran smoothly and efficiently under colonial rule. With the rise of Japan as a colonial power, Avison took steps to ensure that the medical school was in line with new educational rules and requirements outlined under the colonial educational system. In 1908, Avison visited the Resident-General and asked the government to recognize the medical school officially. The Resident-General agreed to Avison's request and even attended a graduation ceremony for medical students, where he handed out medical certificates that allowed the new Korean doctors to practice in Korea.[62]

Overall, Avison never relied on a single way to determine how medicine would be taught to Koreans. He structured the curriculum based on practicality. When he first arrived at Jejungwon, he translated medical textbooks from English into Korean. In the process of translation, Avison discovered that some words and terminology could not be adequately translated into Korean,[63] so he created Korean medical terms in Chinese characters with the help of assistants and continued to use some English words.[64] With this sense of practicality, Avison reorganized the new medical school based on the changing education reforms issued by the colonial government. In 1915, for example, the colonial government excluded all religious subjects and ceremonies from private school curricula, emphasizing the importance of "national" education. Despite reforms that interfered with the mission of the hospital and medical school, Avison realized that it was important to negotiate with the colonial government and adapt to colonial government regulations. Avison wrote that the school had made "a constant effort to keep in touch with all the governmental changes concerning educational and medical work." The school favorably responded to colonial government requests that it teach modern medical knowledge and construct modern buildings that housed the latest equipment for medical work.[65] Moreover, Severance hired a secretary to supply the latest translations of educational and medical papers coming from the government.[66] The school even agreed to allow one-third of its board members to be made up of Japanese Christians.[67] To help the hospital and school deal with all of these regulations and its negotiations with the government, Severance Hospital hired a Japanese advisor.[68]

The exhaustive effort by Avison and his staff ultimately paid off because the government recognized Severance Union Medical College as an official school in 1917. This designation was important on many levels, including allowing graduates from Severance Medical College to receive licenses to practice medicine in Korea without a government examination.[69] When the Ministry of Education in Japan also designated Severance as an official school in 1934, graduates of the medical school were finally able to practice medicine throughout the Japanese Empire. This designation from the colonial government and the Japanese Ministry of Education reflected how well Severance followed government rules and regulations and how much government authorities trusted its students to practice medicine in Korea.[70] Following graduation, a number of students went on to become well-known doctors who made large contributions to the medical field, especially by opening private hospitals.[71] To an extent, the colonial government and the Severance medical school were partners in providing medical services and establishing a Westernized medical system in Korea and the Japanese Empire.

Yet the appearance of a happy partnership between the colonial government and Severance masked some feelings of dissatisfaction on the part of Avison. Needing to obey all of the detailed rules on education issued by the colonial government frustrated him, for example. He was particularly annoyed when the colonial government established Keijo Imperial University in Seoul, which derailed his plan for creating a new national university for Koreans by combining Severance Union Medical College and Chosen Christian College.[72]

Despite these frustrations, officials at Severance and the colonial government often shared similar viewpoints on medicine that brought them together in treating Koreans. For example, both sides opposed the practice of traditional Eastern medicine. In 1913, the colonial government essentially outlawed the practice of Eastern medicine by issuing a medical law that only authorized doctors who studied Western medicine to practice medicine. The colonial government attacked Eastern medical practices based on the theories of Yinyang and the Five Elements. Whereas Western medicine was "modern," the colonial government regarded Eastern medicine as nothing more than an accumulation of experiences dating back several thousand years and therefore traditional.[73] Some Westerners showed an interest in Eastern medicine, especially trying to understand the effectiveness of ginseng in treating people with ailments. However, like the colonial government, most Westerners, especially doctors, criticized the theories of Eastern medicine and gave strict warning against the use of acupuncture.[74] According to medical missionaries, Eastern medicine lacked anatomical and physiological studies that were essential for the investigation of the causes of diseases and chemical research that was important for drug discovery.[75] In the words of one Westerner: "From time immemorial the practice of medicine by the native doctor has not changed; this practice is ignorant of the human body, ignorant as to disease, and cannot but be inadequate; to say nothing of the criminal and other malpractice that sometimes accrues. The native old style medicine man cannot meet the needs of Korea's suffering millions."[76] Sharing a negative view of Eastern medicine and a positive view of Western medicine with the colonial government, medical missionaries unsurprisingly held favorable views of Japanese doctors. They argued that a number of Japanese physicians employed modern Western knowledge to design effective sanitary reforms and relieve the physical pain experienced by Koreans.[77] They also praised the medical policies of the colonial government.

With shared viewpoints on medical practice and similar views on modernity and how to transform Koreans into modern subjects, the colonial government and missionary hospitals partnered in delivering Western medicine and trying to transform Korea into a modern country based on Western reforms. Some missionaries, however, were concerned that missionaries and the colonial government were cooperating at a level that could compromise the identity of the Christian institution. They criticized the staff at Severance Hospital for its strict obedience to colonial rule. According to critics, the more closely Severance followed the rules of the colonial government, the more likely it was to lose its goal of evangelism. E. W. Demaree was one sharp critic:

> In Severance Medical College, we find the school launched on a program looking toward recognition for its graduates in any part of the

> Japanese Empire. In order to accomplish this most of the departments must be headed by a doctor with a Hakase degree. This practically eliminates the missionary doctor. Already he has been practically eliminated from any teaching. The result has been that the present graduates from Severance Medical College are filled with the Japanese system of medical treatment, empirical remedies, shot-gun prescriptions, and intra-cutaneous, intra-muscular, intra-venous, and intra-anything injections. It certainly seems to me that there is a far cry between the two methods. I find them quite incompatible.[78]

According to Demaree, peaceful coexistence between the Western and Japanese medical systems was impossible. To him, Severance was losing its autonomy and identity as a Christian institution as it tried to adapt to the changing educational system. For example, the medical school was forced to hire at least one professor who held a Hakase degree, a degree issued by the Japanese government, in order to maintain its designation as an official school.[79] Demaree was convinced that the Japanese system interfered with Severance's mission of exposing Koreans to Christianity. He likened Severance's policy of cooperating with the government to "seeking gold." The lust for gold, he believed, should be replaced with the call to service.[80]

From the 1920s onward, doubts were cast on the justification of hospital work and medical missions. As funds from abroad were shrinking and nonreligious medical schools of Japan and Korea were producing a growing number of doctors, missionaries faced the question of whether medical work and training were still relevant and needed.[81] Critics of medical missions in Korea also said that evangelicalism had taken a backseat to medical work. They added that the missionary medical school was no different from government medical schools since they followed the same curriculum that taught anatomy, physiology, and pathology. Medical education without Christ in the foreground was considered a waste of money and effort and a betrayal of the highest aim of the medical missionary.[82]

Most of the criticism was directed at Severance Union Medical College. Among the changes and sacrifices made by the school in order to comply with educational laws, people were most critical of the medical school for not teaching religion or Christianity. Before colonial rule, the school offered a class on medical evangelicalism.[83] However, from 1910 to 1922, the school restricted the teaching of Christianity owing to colonial rules.

Even though new government educational regulations removed all restriction of religious teaching in 1922,[84] the school could only teach religion outside of the curriculum.[85] Bible studies at the school began in 1924, but the curriculum still did not include the subject of Christianity.[86] As these developments undoubtedly troubled conservative missionaries, teachers at Severance defended themselves, stressing again that their work was to realize the goal of mission, and they had no real interest in simply training doctors. "We are vitally interested in training Christian doctors."[87] Avison emphasized that he always remembered that God, his Father and Friend, was interested in what he was doing, assuring his colleagues that they could succeed if they leaned on God and expected His help.[88] Evangelism was constantly stressed as an important factor for the growth of Severance.

As Avison stressed the importance of evangelical work in medical missions, he also defended his stance on closely cooperating with the colonial government. He recognized it was difficult to deal with colonial rule and to change the nature of the school in response to government reforms. He argued, however, that it would be virtually impossible for the school not to work with the colonial government and to act autonomously if it wanted to work in Korea and achieve its goal of medical mission. He posed the following question to missionaries: "By what stretch of imagination can we suppose the government of this country or any other would now permit an independent system of medical schools or nursing schools or hospitals to be set up?"[89] He also believed that it was important to work with the colonial government on medical issues since both the government and missionaries shared the mission of spreading Western-based knowledge among Koreans. Both sides believed that Western medicine was rational and achieved progress.[90] To Avison, Japanese and missionary medical practices were the same since they were derived from Western medicine. He believed therefore that both sides shared the same goals in medicine and could cooperate.

Until the late 1930s, Severance Union Medical School remained extremely popular even though many Koreans entered government schools, which provided a diploma that automatically meant a certificate for a certain job and entry into an institute of higher education.[91] For instance, 265 students took an entrance examination for Severance Medical College in 1930. Only 40 of them could matriculate.[92] The ratio of total applicants to those matriculated was close to 7:1. Recognition by the colonial government must have contributed to the popularity of Severance. After the outbreak of the Sino-Japan War in 1937 and the Pacific War in 1941, Japan cut ties with Western missions. From late 1930s onward, missionaries had to leave Korea. Though missionary hospitals were less of a threat to the rule of the colonial government than mission schools or churches, missionary doctors were also forced to leave. After the Western missionaries left, the medical school continued to be pragmatic and to change its policies and orientation in response to government regulations. Koreans who worked at Severance during the Pacific War visited a Shinto shrine and vowed that they would follow the policies of the Japanese Greater East Asia Co-Prosperity Sphere and fight against the "evil West." In 1941, the name of the school was changed to Asahi to distance it from its American ties.[93] Avison continued to believe that the colonial regime was inescapable and that the only way to survive was for the school to obey colonial rule. In many ways, Korean administrators of Severance followed Avison's philosophy throughout World War II.

Western missionaries used medicine as a way to enter and work in Korea. Once in Korea, missionaries at Jejungwon/Severance Hospital experienced a turbulent process in negotiating the role and place of the hospital in the mission field and in society. This unruly process stemmed from hospital officials needing to maneuver and navigate in between two poles. On one side, the colonial state, which shared missionary views on Western medicine and modernity, required the hospital to carry out various reforms in order to be recognized as a legal institution that could not only offer an education in medicine, but also provide medical care. Carrying out these requirements, the hospital came to be accused by missionaries of collaborating with the colonial state and losing its religious identity. On the other side, conservative missionaries continually attacked Severance officials for running a religious institution that appeared to do little in spreading the message of Christianity. Questioning the motives of missionary doctors and whether medical missions represented the most effective method to spread Christianity, these conservative missionaries emphasized traditional means of evangelism and called for curtailing the activities of social institutions like Severance.

From its beginning, Severance Hospital walked a fine line between mission and medicine. What allowed it to become a preeminent institution was the realistic attitude adopted by officials like Avison that led to certain positive results. Collaborating with the government, for example, enabled Severance to obtain designation as an official school, which caused it to become popular among Koreans. In the end, the experiences of Severance Hospital illustrated the complications of the relationship between mission and medicine and the politics of missionary work.

Notes

1. http://www.yuhs.or.kr/en/about_yuhs/yuhs/Mission_vision/.
2. Chung-shin Park, *Protestantism and Politics in Korea* (Seattle and London: University of Washington Press, 2003), 18–19.
3. Park Yunjae, *Han'guk kŭndaeŭihak ŭi kiwŏn* [The Origin of the Modern Korean Medical System] (Seoul: Hyean, 2005), 25–37.
4. *Hansŏngsunpo* [A Ten-Day Report in Seoul], March 27, 1884.
5. Fred Harvey Harrington, *God, Mammon, and the Japanese* (Madison, Milwaukee, and London: The University of Wisconsin Press, 1966), 6–8.
6. Kim Wŏn-mo, trans., *Alrenŭi ilki* [Allen's Diary] (Seoul: Kunkuk University Press, 1991), 428.
7. *Han'guk Kidokkyo ŭi yŏksa 1* [A History of the Korean Church 1] (Seoul: The Christian Literature Press, 1989), 177–180.
8. Horace N. Allen, "Medical Work in Korea," *The Foreign Missionary* 44 (1885): 76.
9. *Miwŏnan* [Materials on America], Seoul National University Kyujanggak No. 18046–1.
10. Kim Wŏn-mo, *Allen's Diary,* 458.
11. Allen, "Medical Work in Korea," 74.
12. *Miwŏnan,* Seoul National University Kyujanggak No. 18046–1.
13. Shin Dong-wŏn, "Han'guk ŭiryoyulriŭi yŏksajŏk kochal" [History of Medical Ethics in Korea], *Ŭisahak* [Korean Journal of Medical History] 9, no. 2 (2000): 171.
14. Ibid., 171.
15. Allen, "Medical Work in Korea," 75–76.
16. Kim Wŏn-mo, *Allen's Diary,* 441.
17. Park Hyŏng-woo, *Chejungwŏn* (Seoul: Mom Kwa Maŭm, 2002), 142.
18. Kim Wŏn-mo, *Allen's Diary,* 475.
19. Harrington, *God, Mammon and the Japanese,* 77.
20. Kim In-soo, trans., *Heronŭisaŭi sŏngyopyŏnchi* [John W. Heron, M.D.'s Missionary Letters] (Seoul: Institute of Studies of the Korean Church History Presbyterian College and Theological Seminary, 2007), 171.

21. Yi Man-yŏl and Oak Sung-Deuk, trans., *Ŏndŏudu charyochip 1* [Horace G. Underwood Papers 1] (Seoul: Yonsei University Press, 2005), 465–466.

22. Ibid., 566.

23. Kim In-soo, trans., *Alrenŭisaŭi sŏngyo oekyopyŏnchi* [Horace H. Allen, M.D.'s Missionary and Diplomatic Letters] (Seoul: Institute of Studies of the Korean Church History Presbyterian College and Theological Seminary, 2007), 549.

24. Kim In-soo, *Heron's Letters,* 279.

25. Yi and Oak, *Underwood Papers 1,* 530.

26. Kim In-soo, *Heron's Letters,* 188.

27. Ibid., 323.

28. Yi and Oak, *Underwood Papers 1,* 604–605.

29. Harrington, *God, Mammon, and the Japanese,* 87.

30. Kim In-soo, *Allen's Letters,* 894.

31. Harrington, *God, Mammon, and the Japanese,* 94.

32. Yi Man-yŏl and Oak Sung-Deuk, trans., *Ŏndŏudŭ charyochip 2* [Horace G. Underwood Papers 2] (Seoul: Yonsei University Press, 2006), 363.

33. "Graduate Exercises," *Korea Mission Field* (hereafter *KMF*) 4–8 (1908): 123.

34. *Miwŏnan,* Seoul National University Kyuchangkak No. 18046–1.

35. Park Hyŏng-woo, *Chejungwŏn,* 219–227.

36. *Miwŏnan,* Seoul National University Kyuchangkak No. 18046–1.

37. Kim In-soo, *Allen's Letters,* 932. When submitting his proposal to establish the hospital in 1884, Allen mentioned that the new hospital would not be a financial burden for the Korean government. He wrote, "Your Excellency's gov'mt will secure a first class hospital for nothing." In addition, "he [Allen] will secure the necessary foreign assistants and give his and their labor and time free of charge in conducting the Hospital providing he be placed in entire charge." *Miwonan,* Seoul National University Kyujanggak No. 18046–1.

38. *Catalogue Severance Union Medical College* (Seoul), 1917, 6.

39. Oliver R. Avison, *The Land of the Morning Calm: Reminiscence of Oliver R. Avison, M.D.* (Daegu: Taegu University Press, 1988), 479.

40. Ibid., 474–485.

41. Ibid., 489–490.

42. W. E. Reid, "The Annual Meeting of the Korea Medical Missionary Association," *KMF* 9–12 (1913): 318.

43. Oliver R. Avison, "Some High Spots in Medical Mission Work in Korea," *KMF* 35–7 (1939): 148.

44. Yi Man-yŏl, *Han'guk Kidokkyo ŭiryŏsa* [A History of Christian Medical Work in Korea] (Seoul: Acanet, 2003), 294–302. Yi points out that, as mission-

ary doctors realized that medicine was the realization of God's love, their works expanded into promoting the welfare of patients, spreading preventive medicine, improving the sanitary environment, and so forth.

45. Yi Man-yŏl and Oak Sung-Deuk, trans., *Ŏndŏudŭcharyochip 3* [Horace G. Underwood Papers 3] (Seoul: Yonsei University Press, 2007), 312.

46. J. D. Van Buskirk, "Christian Medical Education, Its Place and Opportunity," *KMF* 10–7 (1914): 213.

47. Yi and Oak, *Underwood Papers 2,* 416.

48. *Catalogue Severance Union Medical College* (Seoul), 1917, 7.

49. Oliver R. Avison, *Annual Report of the Imperial Korean Hospital* (Seoul: Methodist Publishing, 1901), 16.

50. *The Seventy-Second Annual Report of the Board of Foreign Missions of the Presbyterian Church in the United States of America* (New York: Mission House, 1909), 281.

51. Oliver R. Avison, "Some High Spots in Medical Mission Work in Korea," *KMF* 35–7 (1939): 147.

52. "A Christian Korean Celebration," *KMF* 5–12 (1909): 208.

53. "Editorial," *KMF* 4–8 (1908): 121–122.

54. "A Christian Korean Celebration," *KMF* 5–12 (1909): 207.

55. E. W. Anderson, "Early Days of the Korea Medical Missionary Association," *KMF* 35–5 (1939): 96.

56. R. K. Smith, "Medical Practice in Chosen," *KMF* 13–5 (1917): 120.

57. *Korea Medical Missionary Association Branch of the China Medical Association Third Annual Report* (Yokohama, Kobe, and Tokyo: The Fukuin Printing Company, 1913), 31.

58. Park Yunjae, *Han'guk kŭndaeŭihak ŭi kiwŏn,* 254–255.

59. R. K. Smith, "Medical Practice in Chosen," *KMF* 13–5 (1917): 120.

60. *Catalogue Severance Union Medical College* (Seoul), 1917, 8.

61. Ibid., 9.

62. Avison, *The Land of the Morning Calm,* 382.

63. Oliver R. Avison, "Some Spots in Medical Mission Work in Korea," *KMF* 35–7 (1939): 146.

64. *Kidok sinbo* [Christian Newspaper], July 13, 1932.

65. Oliver R. Avison, "Some Spots in Medical Mission Work in Korea," *KMF* 35–7 (1939): 147.

66. Annual personal report of Dr. O. R. Avison, April 1, 1918, to March 31, 1919.

67. *Catalogue Severance Union Medical College* (Seoul), 1917, 12.

68. "Extracts from Report of Severance Union Medical College and Nurses' Training School," *KMF* 18–7 (1922): 162.

69. *Catalogue Severance Union Medical College* (Seoul), 1917, 9.

70. *Sepŭransi kyouhoepo* [The Severance Bulletin] 21 (1934), 12.

71. Ibid., 16.

72. Sato Gozo, *Chosen iikusi* [The History of Medical Education in Korea] (Ibaraki: Sato Sensekijusyukugakai, 1956), 78–79.

73. Yunjae Park, "Early Colonial Laws on Medical Practitioners and the Japanese Colonial Rule," in *Japanese Studies around the World 2002* (Kyoto: International Research Center for Japanese Studies, 2002), 338–345.

74. Yeo In-sok, "Hanmalkwa ilchesiki sŏngyoŭisadŭlŭi chŏntongŭihak insikgwa yŏn'gu" [The Gaze of the Other: How Western Medical Missionaries Viewed Traditional Korean Medicine], *Ŭisahak* [Korean Journal of Medical History] 15, no. 1 (2006): 1–21.

75. "Severance Hospital Medical College," *KMF* 4–7 (1908): 102.

76. J. D. Van Buskirk, "Christian Medical Education, Its Place and Opportunity," *KMF* 10–7 (1914): 213.

77. Ibid.

78. E.W. Demaree, "The Future of Medical Missions in Korea," *KMF* 30–4 (1934): 74.

79. *Sebranshi rengo igaku senmongakko ichiran* [Severance Union Medical College Catalogue] (Seoul: Severance Union Medical College, 1934), 17.

80. E. W. Demaree, "The Future of Medical Missions in Korea," *KMF* 30–4 (1934): 75.

81. John D. Bigger, The Mission Hospital and Evangelism, *KMF* 24–4 (1928): 74.

82. Z. Bercovitz, "The Position and Scope of the Mission Hospital in Korea Today," *KMF* 24–5 (1928): 91.

83. "A Christian Korean Celebration," *KMF* 5–12 (1909): 208.

84. Oliver R. Avison, "Recognition of the Severance Union Medical College's Examinations by the Governor-General," *KMF* 19–5 (1923): 105.

85. Yi Yi Man-yŏl and Oak Sung-Deuk, trans., *Ŏndŏudŭ charyochip 5* [Horace G. Underwood and Lillias Horton Underwood Papers 5] (Seoul: Yonsei University Press, 2010), 534.

86. *Severance Union Medical College Catalogue 1925–6* (Seoul), 21–23. Before 1923, only a voluntary Bible class for students was conducted by a Western missionary professor.

87. J. D. Van Buskirk, "Present Problems," *KMF* 21–10 (1925): 206.

88. *Sepŭransi kyouhoepo* [The Severance Bulletin] 25 (1936): 4.

89. Oliver R. Avison, "The Future of Medical Missions," *KMF* 30–36 (1934): 115–116.

90. Cho Hyŏng-gŭn, "Ilcheŭi kongsikŭiryowa kaesingyo seonkyoŭiryokan

hegemoni kyŏngchaengkwa kŭ sahoechŏk hyokwa" [Hegemonic Competition and Its Social Effects: Focusing on Japanese Colonial Medicine and Protestant Missionary Medicine], *Sahoe wa yŏksa* [Society and History] 82 (2009): 149.

91. Lee Seongjeon, *Mikuk sŏnkyosawa Han'guk kŭntae kyoyuk* [American Missionaries and Modern Education in Korea], trans. Seo Jeongmin and Kamiyama Minako (Seoul: Han'guk Kidokkyoyŏksa Yŏn'guso, 2007), 216–225.

92. J. W. Hirst, "Severance Union Medical College Graduation Exercise 1930," *KMF* 26-5 (1930): 101.

93. *Insul, pŏngsa kŭriko kaecheokgwa tochŏnŭi 120nyŏn* [120 Years' History of Benevolent Art, Service, Cultivation, and Challenge] (Seoul: Yŏnsei Ŭiryowŏn, 2005), 313–327.

7

Kagawa Toyohiko (1888–1960) and the Japanese Christian Impact on American Society

MARK R. MULLINS

STUDIES OF CHRISTIANITY for most of the past century were dominated by a Euro-American "master narrative" and largely focused on the history and impact of the Western missionary enterprise. It has become increasingly clear that this approach is no longer viable given the emergence of new centers of Christianity in Asia, Africa, and Latin America. Many non-Western and independent expressions of Christianity emerged in a critical response to the modern missionary movement from the West. We can no longer ignore the fact that many dynamic forms of Asian and African Christianity (or "Christianities," as Peter Phan recently reminded us) are spreading across the globe through transnational religious networks and reshaping the religious landscape of Europe and North America.[1] These recent developments are clear evidence that globalization is not a unidirectional process facilitating only the export of Western Christianity and culture but a more complicated process that includes significant "reverse influences" from non-Western countries.

Although Christianity in Japan remains a minority religion and is not a major player in these more recent developments, Japanese have also been significant actors who reshaped received traditions from the West through the formation of new independent movements and institutions. Studies of

Christianity in relation to Japan and Japanese Americans often highlight the role of churches as "carriers" of Western culture or as agents of assimilation in American society. Conversion to Christianity and participation in a Protestant denomination, in fact, has often been seen as an abandonment of Japanese identity and as a sign of assimilation. The image of Japanese that sometimes emerges from these studies is that of a passive recipient of an alien religious tradition.[2] A more careful examination reveals that a number of Japanese who embraced Christianity over the past century have shown considerable independence from American missionaries and institutions. The formation of minority churches or Japanese ethnic congregations and conferences within established denominations represents one concrete example of this within the history of religion in America.[3] In short, adoption of the new religion—evangelical Protestantism—did not bring with it a unilinear pattern of Japanese assimilation into American society.[4]

Christianity in Japan has also been reshaped by various independent and indigenous initiatives. Early on in missionary circles there were serious discussions on developing indigenous churches, but this was understood primarily in terms of the "three-selfs": self-support, self-control, and self-propagation. The idea that Japanese Christians might have their own insights and ways of organizing and practicing the faith was not generally entertained. Transmission of the missionary culture without corruption or addition was the primary concern. After Japanese converts were introduced to the scriptures and went on to pursue serious theological studies, many realized that it was possible to distinguish the Christian faith and biblical traditions from the theology, church polity, and cultural values that were embedded in the transplanted American and European mission churches. The fact that numerous denominations were competing for converts on Japanese soil (each with its own doctrinal peculiarities and forms of government) indicated to many leaders that there might be room for Japanese interpretations and cultural expressions of Christianity. In fact, many independent and indigenous Christian movements were organized in Japan over the past century, beginning with the formation of the Nonchurch movement (Mukyōkai) by Uchimura Kanzō in 1901. Uchimura's version of Christianity was a Confucian one, grafted onto *bushidō,* and had particular appeal to the educated members of Japanese society.[5]

The successive appearance of numerous other charismatic leaders and indigenous movements revealed many other ways to be both Japanese and Christian.[6] These Japanese leaders accepted the Christian faith (on their own terms), but often rejected the missionary carriers and their individualistic and denominational understanding of religion. The religious experiences of these leaders and their unique combination of foreign and native religious and cultural elements produced a number of alternative Japanese Christian traditions. Alongside a variety of transplanted denominations and sects of Western origins, a variety of indigenous Christian groups—Confucian, shamanistic, Pentecostal, evangelical, and so on—have become a part of the religious landscape of modern Japan. These movements provide clear evidence that Japanese were not passive recipients of transplanted Christianity but active agents who reinterpreted and reconstructed the faith in terms that made sense to them.

Most of these founders and new movements were largely preoccupied with "being Japanese" (over against the "Western" church) and almost exclusively focused on concerns within Japan. There was one important exception to this generalization: Kagawa Toyohiko (1888–1960), a Protestant leader whose interpretation and practice of Christianity evolved into a transnational social movement that had a significant effect on American society decades before globalization became a concern. Although few people recognize Kagawa's name today, he was widely known internationally from the 1920s to the 1950s as a visionary religious leader, author, social reformer, and leader of cooperatives and labor unions. While many came to regard him as the "Saint Francis of Japan" for his identification with the poor and for his compassionate work in the slums, others viewed him as a dangerous social activist and rabble-rouser for his leadership in the labor movement and organization of unions for struggling workers in developing industries and tenant farmers in rural areas.

Kagawa was an ordained minister in the Presbyterian Church, but he was disillusioned with the established churches and their individualistic interpretation of the faith. In 1919, he published *Seishin undō to shakai undō* (Spiritual and Social Movements), a title that captured his concern for both individual and social transformation. Kagawa was extremely critical of a church that failed to practice what he termed "redemptive love" (*shokuzai ai no jissen*), which for him meant moving outside the walls of the church to live and work with those in greatest need. The member-

Figure 7.1. Kagawa in the Shinkawa slums of Kobe, Japan, circa 1910–1913. Courtesy of the Matsuzawa Shiryōkan Kagawa Toyohiko Archives and Resource Center, Tokyo.

ship composition of established churches tended to be dominated by the educated and white-collar classes, and people who were in most critical need—the "underside of modern Japan"—were largely missing. Kagawa reasoned that clergy were failing to cultivate lay leaders and mobilize them for ministry to the poor and to be involved with movements for social transformation.[7]

To address this failure, Kagawa launched the Friends of Jesus movement (Iesu no Tomo Kai) in 1921, modeling his organization after the third order of the Franciscans. While personal piety and purity were central concerns, membership also involved a commitment to live fully in the "world" and work for the transformation of society. By 1928, there were some 1,300 members mobilized for social transformation through the organization of labor unions, cooperatives, and educational programs. All of these numerous activities and initiatives coalesced in the Kingdom of God movement in Japan. By the late 1930s, thirty-five institutions and over one hundred projects dedicated to relief work, social reform, and Christian education were under Kagawa's supervision.

One important feature of Kagawa's movement that distinguishes it from other Japanese independent movements (such as Uchimura Kanzō's Nonchurch movement) is that he did not advocate a complete break from the missionaries and their churches but maintained both an ecumenical and an international orientation. Kagawa had such a compelling presence and vision that many missionaries were attracted to his movement and supported his work. By 1929, some forty-three missionaries were contributing financially to Kagawa's work. Over the next several years, denominations in the United States and Canada began to provide direct financial

Figure 7.2. Kagawa with Dr. Harry Myers at the tenth Friends of Jesus summer retreat, July 1932. Courtesy of the Matsuzawa Shiryōkan Kagawa Toyohiko Archives and Resource Center, Tokyo.[8]

support to Kagawa's movement and even assigned missionaries to work under his direction.[9] International recognition and support for Kagawa's wide-ranging programs in Japan were cultivated by these missionary supporters through their network of churches and Christian publications in the United States.

Because of his reputation as a social activist, it is sometimes forgotten that Kagawa was also a prolific author. Over the course of his career, he wrote over 150 books and translated a number of books into Japanese.[10] It was the appearance of his autobiographical novel *Crossing the Death Line* (*Shisen o koete,* 1920) that made Kagawa a household name. Although the literary establishment was rather critical of the novel, very positive reviews appeared in the major newspapers of the time, which encouraged a wide readership (it went through over two hundred printings in a year and a half). The success of this novel is one reason Kagawa was thereafter able to attract large audiences to his lectures and evangelistic meetings when he traveled throughout the country. The royalties from this publication, likewise, provided Kagawa the financial means to launch his various social projects and religious activities. According to one recent estimate, the royalties Kagawa received for this one novel would be equivalent to over 11 million US dollars today.[11]

Over a period of five decades, Kagawa traveled extensively outside of Japan, including trips to Taiwan, China, Manchuria, Korea, the Philippines, India, Australia, England, Norway, Sweden, Denmark, Brazil, Canada, and the United States. His version of the Kingdom of God movement spread to the United States over the course of a number of speaking tours (1924, 1931, 1935, 1941, 1950), which were extensively covered by newspapers across the country, including the *New York Times,* as well as numerous magazines and religious periodicals, such as *Time,* the *Christian Century,* and the mass market *Reader's Digest.* In addition, twenty-three of his books were published in English translation (some of which were also published in various European languages), which also contributed to his international reputation. Although his movement attracted many supporters in the United States, particularly among Japanese Americans and mainline Protestant leaders, his version of Christianity provoked numerous critical reactions as well since it challenged some taken-for-granted American views on race relations, denominationalism, and capitalism.

Kagawa in America: 1914–1916

Kagawa's relationship with America began before he became a Christian "celebrity" from the mid-1920s. After graduation from Kobe Seminary and five years of work in the Shinkawa slums, Kagawa was given an opportunity to continue his education at Princeton University and Theological Seminary. The two years and nine months in the United States was a formative period for Kagawa. He completed an M.A. in experimental psychology in 1915, and a Bachelor of Divinity degree in 1916. More important than his studies, however, was exposure to the labor movement in New York and his realization that labor unions and collective action represented important means for improving the living conditions of the working poor.

He also gained some initial experience organizing laborers in the United States. In order to earn funds for his passage home, he moved to Ogden, Utah, and worked as a secretary for the Japanese Association for some eight months before returning to Japan. During his stay in Ogden, he helped Japanese and Mormon tenant farmers organize a union, an experience that would be put to good use in the years ahead. On his return to Japan in 1917, he resumed his work in Shinkawa but added methods and strategies for the prevention of poverty to his earlier programs of evangelism and relief work. This meant involvement in the labor movement and the organization of cooperatives. It was this larger vision of individual and social transformation that he carried back to the United States over the course of several lecture tours.

Kagawa in America: 1924–1925

Kagawa returned to the United States to attend the Pan Pacific Student Convention and participate in a speaking tour from late 1924 to early 1925. On his way to the mainland, Kagawa first stopped in Hawai'i, where he spoke to various Christian groups. He also met with Japanese and Filipino plantation workers who were on strike to encourage them in their cause. A branch of the Friends of Jesus was organized in Honolulu after this visit. From there Kagawa went on to speak to Japanese American communities on the West Coast and lectured in cities across the United States.

Japanese American communities in Southern California welcomed Kagawa, and enthusiastic supporters quickly organized another chapter of the Friends of Jesus in Los Angeles. This was the beginning of a long and close association between Kagawa and Japanese Americans. Records show that Kagawa always included Japanese communities and congregations in his subsequent speaking tours of the United States, and the Friends of Jesus group in Southern California continued to support his activities financially well into the 1950s.[12]

In addition to the organization of the Friends of Jesus branch in Los Angeles, a Kagawa Cooperators group was also organized in Berkeley, California. Both groups sought to keep Kagawa's vision alive in America and to provide financial support for his religious and social activities in Japan. Two years later, the Kagawa Cooperators and Fellowship group in Berkeley sent Helen Topping to Japan, where she served as Kagawa's personal secretary and assisted with English correspondence and translations. Topping was the child of American Baptist missionaries in Japan who had also become staunch supporters of Kagawa. She became the editor of the English publication *Friends of Jesus,* which was published from 1928 to 1937, assisted with the translation of many of Kagawa's books into English, and helped organize his international trips and speaking engagements.

Although many American Christians welcomed Kagawa and regarded him as living proof of the success of Christian mission in Asia, some were not prepared for his critical messages to America. He did not hesitate to point out the contradictions he saw between churches' claims about a gospel of love and their actual practices with regard to people of color. During his sojourn in the United States, one year after the Exclusion Act (1924) was passed, Kagawa pointed out that many of his fellow citizens in Japan were "alarmed" to see that the United States was enacting laws to exclude Japanese and distressed to realize that the spirit of Abraham Lincoln was not shared by American citizens. "America today is only a land of liberty for the White race," Kagawa explained. "It is no more a land of liberty for the Yellow race. America has closed her doors absolutely to the Oriental nations." His words only got harsher: "Though the white races believe in Christianity, they are not believing in true Christianity. Their Christianity is only in words."[13]

Kagawa in America: 1931

By the time of Kagawa's next speaking tour in 1931, the United States was in the midst of the Great Depression and his social vision of Christian brotherhood and cooperatives found an even greater resonance among many more Americans. In addition to the difficult economic circumstances, there was considerable disillusionment with the state of religion in America. Churches were divided by both denominationalism and the fundamentalist-modernist controversy.

Kagawa sought to transcend "creedal" Christianity and these divisions by focusing on a practical faith that reconciled people and created communities and cooperatives of mutual support and care. This was a breath of fresh air to many Americans who were disillusioned by the excessive individualism and sectarianism that appeared to be the most obvious fruits of the Christian churches. His message also had the ring of authenticity—he had actually lived in the slums and shared his life with the underside

Figure 7.3. Kagawa with supporters ("Kagawa Cooperators") in Berkeley, California, September 1931. Courtesy of the Matsuzawa Shiryōkan Kagawa Toyohiko Archives and Resource Center, Tokyo.

of Japanese society.[14] This image was captured and promoted by Kenneth Saunders, the vice-chair of the Berkeley Kagawa Cooperators group and professor at the Pacific School of Religion, who wrote an article presenting Kagawa as "the St. Francis of Japan" just before his 1931 visit.[15]

During the whirlwind three-month tour of the United States and Canada, Kagawa traveled some 30,000 miles and spoke at 185 meetings and addressed a total audience of over 120,000. In addition, he gave lectures at sixteen colleges and universities, including Yale, Chicago, Oberlin, and the Pacific School of Religion. Fifty-nine of these speaking engagements were in Japanese, which reveals the close connection he maintained with Japanese American communities. It is not surprising that Kagawa's activities in the United States received regular coverage in the newspapers published by the Japanese American community. The *Nichibei shinbun* contains scores of articles about Kagawa's lectures and speaking engagements. In 1931, for example, there were some seventy-six articles about his lectures and speaking engagements as well as announcements about the screening of *Grain of Wheat,* a movie based on Kagawa's book by that title.

Kagawa in America: 1935–1936

It was Kagawa's next tour that generated the most excitement and controversy. The Federal Council of Churches, representing mainline Protestants, was the key sponsor and organized the speaking engagements through a National Kagawa Coordinating Committee. The press coverage given to Kagawa's speaking events—as well as events organized by his critics and detractors—was remarkable. Helen Topping reported that in 1935 and 1936 she "was getting from 80–100 clippings a day" about Kagawa's "messages and travels in America."[16] A review of *The Christian Century* for 1936 reveals that in almost every issue there were articles, interviews, or reports about Kagawa's lecture tour in the United States.[17] The report on his visit to Baltimore on January 29 is typical of the coverage given in many other cities: "In two days here last week he spoke in two college chapels, to two luncheons (one with more than 1,100 women present), to the ministerial union, the Youth Council, the Johns Hopkins Supper Club, and finally to a public mass meeting in the Lyric, the city's largest auditorium. In all, more than 7,000 people heard him speak."[18] It is estimated that, by the end of the six-month tour, Kagawa's speaking engagements in 150 cities across forty-

Figure 7.4. Kagawa speaking to an audience of seven thousand in Iowa City, Iowa, February 26, 1936. Courtesy of the Matsuzawa Shiryōkan Kagawa Toyohiko Archives and Resource Center, Tokyo.

four states attracted a total audience of some 750,000, which far exceeded his 1931 visit.[19]

Following Kagawa's return to Japan, there was a flurry of activity and meetings to organize groups and publish materials that would contribute to the implementation of his vision for the Kingdom of God movement in America. A confidential report titled "Tentative Proposal for a Continuing Movement following the American Itinerary of Dr. Toyohiko Kagawa" was considered by the National Kagawa Coordinating Committee and developed for presentation at the June 1936 international conference at Lake Geneva, Wisconsin. It contained the following assessment:

> Everywhere, in scores of communities across America, there are great numbers of people who have heard one or more messages of Kagawa and who are eager to go further and to learn more of the nature of his challenge to American Christianity and what they can do about

it. Here is a great resource, a providential impetus to the beginnings already noted, of a real Kingdom of God Movement in America. Here, too, is a possible linkage with a world movement of similar character, which, under the leadership of Kagawa, may grow into the Cooperative International Fellowship so deeply needed for the future life of mankind on this planet.[20]

The document goes on to outline a proposal for the Kingdom of God movement in America that would attempt to "translate the ideals of Kagawa into American life."

In the months to follow, numerous publications promoting Kagawa's vision were widely disseminated. Dr. Eugene C. Carder of Riverside Church, New York, for example, prepared a pamphlet titled *Discovery: A Manual of Prayer for the Kingdom of God,* which encouraged individuals to "start a prayer group or Kingdom of God Fellowship" and to study and develop various cooperatives.[21] Victor Marriott, another leader of these efforts, also published two booklets that explained Kagawa's vision and how it was being implemented in America.[22] As a result of Kagawa's visit and these follow-up efforts, a number of nonsectarian and interracial fellowship groups and cooperatives were organized in various cities, such as Minneapolis, Kansas City, and Chicago.

The impact of Kagawa's lecture tour on the development of student cooperatives has been widely noted. Many students from across the nation heard Kagawa speak at a Student Christian Conference in Indianapolis and returned to their own campuses to start student-housing cooperatives. The Michigan State University Campus Cooperative records that "the co-op activist and religious leader Toyohiko Kagawa provided the nation's students with a renewed vision of social and economic cooperation. With the spark of Kagawa's enthusiasm, the 1930s saw the establishment of such long-standing co-op systems as those in Berkeley, California, Ann Arbor, Michigan, and Toronto, Ontario."[23] Even today the Cooperative Development Foundation in Washington, DC, manages a Kagawa Fund for Student Cooperative Development to address "the need for democratically-controlled, affordably-priced cooperative housing in campuses across North America."[24]

Kagawa's influence extended beyond Japanese Americans, the Federal Council of Churches, and the cooperative movement. African Americans also embraced him for his progressive stance on race relations during this period.[25] Records reveal that Kagawa was holding biracial meetings in the southern United States on his 1936 lecture tour—hardly a common practice at the time. Alva W. Taylor, a Vanderbilt University professor, explains how Kagawa was able to transcend the race divide on his trip through the south: "All the meetings were interracial without any segregation in the seating but not many colored folk came to any but the special meetings at their own college auditoriums. In Atlanta the program was bi-racial and the Negro meetings were attended with the same crowds and enthusiasm as the white."[26] The southern cities visited by Kagawa on this tour included Memphis, Nashville, Birmingham, Atlanta, Chattanooga, Knoxville, Durham, and Richmond.

This wider impact of Kagawa outside of Japanese American and white Protestant circles is revealed most clearly in the writings of Francis J. Grimké (1850–1937), a well-known African American leader who became one of Kagawa's staunch supporters.[27] Born in 1850 as the son of a slave mother and white slave owner in Charleston, South Carolina, Grimké pursued a higher education in the north after the Civil War. He graduated from Lincoln University (1870) and Princeton Theological Seminary (1878), and he served as a pastor of 15th Street Presbyterian Church in Washington, DC, until his retirement in 1923. Correspondence between Kagawa, Grimké, and Rev. Henry Topping, one of Kagawa's key missionary supporters in Japan, reveals that Grimké closely followed Kagawa's career and even contributed financially to his work in Japan. A year before his death in 1937, Grimké wrote a tribute to Kagawa that included the following words:

> While I am speaking of this great and good man, may I not also say that *I thank God that he is not of this great white race, that thinks that it alone is the favorite of heaven, and that everything of value is to be traced to it. Here is a man of another race that, in the qualities that go to make up greatness of the highest order, is without a superior anywhere. A man doesn't have to be white, doesn't have to have Caucasian blood flowing in his veins in order to be worthy of consideration. . . .*
>
> On this highest plane of noble character and life this man, a Japanese, stands and challenges the attention of the world. . . . As this man moves about; as he lives his simple, beautiful, self-sacrificing life of love, *he is a standing rebuke to race prejudice, and all narrowness and*

bigotry based on race or color everywhere. . . . I thank God, I say, among other things, that this illustrious visitor is not of the white race, lest its sense of superiority, already too great, be still more inflated.[28]

It is important to place Grimké's remarks about Kagawa within the larger context of African American appreciation for the Japanese race. Decades earlier there was already a developing consciousness of solidarity with other people of color and pride in the success of Japanese in their struggle for a place in a world dominated by European (white) nations. Grimke's own brother, Archibald, a Harvard-trained lawyer, for example, celebrated Japan's victory over Russia in a 1905 essay. In short, many African Americans looked upon Japan as a "champion of the darker races" in the decades before World War II and the attack on Pearl Harbor.[29]

Kagawa's Critics on the Right and the Left

Although Kagawa had a wide circle of supporters, he also attracted his share of harsh critics—whom Schildgen bluntly refers to as "the bigots, right-wing fundamentalists, superpatriots and paranoid nativists, who pestered Kagawa and assailed his sponsors throughout the tour."[30] A number were alarmed by Kagawa's social agenda and emphasis on the formation of cooperatives, which was regarded as something that would undermine free-market American capitalism.

Some amusing correspondence related to this concern has been preserved in archives. In a collection of correspondence related to Kagawa's visit to Chicago, I discovered a letter from H. A. Yung, the Honorary General Manager of the American Vigilant Intelligence Federation, addressed to Mr. Charles Walgreen, a businessman who owned a chain of several hundred drugstores by the 1930s. In the letter, Yung notes that Mrs. Walgreen's name appears in the list of "sponsors" of Kagawa and his "so-called Christian Cooperative Movement" and warns him: "if that Movement succeeds there will be no more Walgreen stores." The letter goes on to mention the "communistic record" of Kagawa and encourages Mr. Walgreen to attend the upcoming Fuel Merchants' Association meeting and hear Dr. J. Frank Norris, the fundamentalist Baptist minister from Fort Worth, Texas, "speak the truth about Kagawa and his dangerous movement."[31]

Dr. Norris was one of Kagawa's harshest critics and devoted most of

1936 to following his speaking tour and exposing him as a "dangerous radical" and a "communist," who "has designs to overthrow the American government and should be banished from this country." These are just a few of the wild claims gleaned from a series of articles in *The Fundamentalist,* a newspaper published by Norris, which appeared during the months of April and May.[32] Other newspapers included Kagawa's reactions to the kind of charges expressed by Norris, which had been circulating widely in fundamentalist Christian circles for some time. "Dr. Kagawa is only amused at tales he is Communist," notes one headline in the *Post-Standard* (Syracuse, NY). "In his own country," the article explains, "he is regarded as the chief bulwark against communism."[33] An incident in 1931 reported in the Japanese American newspaper *Nichibei shinbun* provides additional support for this claim. Communists in Japan had clearly disowned Kagawa because of his Christian views and criticisms of the labor movement, and an "antireligion" group within the Japanese American community expressed opposition to him and his message at one of his speaking engagements in Los Angeles during his 1931 trip to the United States. The September 15, 1931, *Nichibei shinbun* ran a story titled "Communists Start Row at Kagawa L.A. Lecture," which reported that, "on September 14, Japanese communists disturbed Dr. Toyohiko Kagawa's lecture here last night. One red rushed to the stage and attempted to give a speech but was pulled down by Rev. Ogawa. A group started to sing the Internationale and were evicted."[34] Although this indicates that communists themselves did not recognize Kagawa as a comrade, Norris and other fundamentalist critics did not recognize any difference between Kagawa's vision and that of his communist opponents.

Norris went so far as to organize alternative meetings at the Convention Hall in Rochester to coincide with and protest against the Colgate-Rochester Theological Seminary's sponsorship of Kagawa's Rauschenbusch lectures. *The Fundamentalist* reported that 100,000 copies of his Convention Hall address, titled "Sovietizing America through Churches, Colleges, and Cooperatives," were issued to warn the public about Kagawa and his "communist sponsor" (the president of Colgate-Rochester Seminary).[35] Norris made it clear that Japanese were not needed "to tell us how to run our business, our homes, our churches."[36]

Norris was not yet finished with Kagawa. He went on to introduce a resolution to the Southern Baptist Convention to cancel Kagawa's invitation to speak since he denied the fundamental doctrines of the Baptist faith and "advocates un-American, unsound 'consumer's cooperatives.'" He is also to be censored, Norris concluded, because he "denies the preaching of the gospel of individual salvation as the only mission of the church, and attempts to substitute in the church a program of economics."[37]

Although the most strident opposition to Kagawa came from the far right, he also attracted criticism from the other end of the theological and political spectrum. The well-known theologian and ethicist Reinhold Niebuhr, who had given the Rauschenbusch Lectures two years before Kagawa, expressed admiration for his character and "sacrificial life" but was unconvinced by his vision of cooperatives as a cure-all for the economic troubles in American society. In an editorial titled "The Political Confusion of Dr. Kagawa," Niebuhr argued that Kagawa was overly optimistic about the potential of cooperatives. Niebuhr expressed great relief that the leadership of the American cooperative movement had not swallowed his naive idealism and continued to recognize that "the development of cooperatives cannot, without the aid of the economic organizations of workers and a political struggle for the socialization of economic processes, achieve a genuine socialism or any other kind of healthy society."[38] In sum, the building of cooperatives based on brotherly love cannot achieve a new social order unless accompanied by political methods and engagement.[39]

Niebuhr further argued that Kagawa's idealistic vision was powerless before the brutal political realities of Japanese militarism and empire building.

> There is no evidence that Dr. Kagawa's movement has the slightest effect upon Japanese imperialism even though he prays that "some day Japan may cast away sword and gun and awaken to the love of the cross." We do not criticize him because he has failed to have that impact upon Japanese imperialism. We criticize him rather for an interpretation of the Christian gospel that allows him to live under the illusion that such a day will come. The forces of evil in the world are really greater than either Dr. Kagawa or his liberal followers believe. And history is a more tragic process than they know. (p. 7)

Although Kagawa was able to see many inconsistencies in American Christianity with regard to matters of race and economics, Niebuhr is correct to note that he sometimes failed to see matters as critically within the Japanese Empire. After the Japanese invasion of Manchuria in 1931, for example, Kagawa offered an apology to the Chinese on behalf of Japanese Christians. Only a few years later, however, on a speaking tour of Manchuria in 1938, he warmed up to Matsuoka Yosuke, a political figure who was also head of the South Manchurian Railway (and who was indicted as a war criminal during the Occupation) and a key advocate for Japan's war of liberation in Asia. He later wrote fondly about Matsuoka and his "love of the Chinese people." "It was somewhat alarming," Schildgen writes, "that Kagawa could be sold on the imperialist Matsuoka's 'love' and paternalistic rationalization for invading the mainland under the guise of protecting Asia."[40] Kagawa's naive idealism and failure to recognize (or admit) the power of the militarists was also revealed in a statement he made at the beginning of his lecture tour in 1935: "Talk of a war between Japan and America is a foolish thing. The Japanese people as a whole have never thought of such a conflict. What profit would we get if we should make a conquest of America? We would lose our best market—we would be bankrupt."[41] These words would come back to haunt him when Japan launched its attack on the United States some six years later.

Kagawa in America: 1941

Over the course of his many trips and speaking engagements in the United States, Kagawa had been a strong voice for Christian pacifism and gave the impression that many Japanese were not inclined to join in support of their government's increasingly militaristic tone and policies in Asia. Given Japan's record of imperial expansion over several decades, Kagawa was losing credibility. In 1941, however, he made another trip to the United States as a part of a five-member Japanese delegation sent by the National Christian Council in Japan. The purpose of the trip was to meet with American Christian leaders and pursue ways to improve the strained relations and avert a war between the two nations. Although it was billed as a "peace mission," there were only two conferences planned for the delegation from Japan. It quickly became clear that a small and powerless group of Japanese Christians visiting America could do little to slow down Japan's war machine. The only impact of the visit was a renewal of the bonds of friendship between a few Protestant Christians from two different sides of the Pacific.

In the end, the "peace mission" turned out to be primarily a fund-raising trip for Kagawa. For many years Kagawa had provided much of the financial support for his work in Japan from his own earnings, but it became increasingly difficult from the late 1930s. Given his political situation and the difficult economic conditions in wartime Japan, the royalty income from his publications had declined considerably, and he was rather desperate for funds to support the work in Japan. Kagawa remained in the United States for several more months, and his American friends arranged speaking engagements in churches across the country, which made it possible for him to raise considerable funds for his work before returning to Japan in August 1941.

Although the "peace mission" was clearly a failure, the ever-idealistic Kagawa continued to pray and make his appeals for peace. As late as September 4, he even sent a telegram to President Roosevelt, imploring him "to try to avert the impending crisis of the Pacific."[42] His own government, however, was already making other plans and three months later bombed Pearl Harbor on December 7, 1941. This finally put to rest any illusions about the possibilities for peace.

The circumstances of Japanese Americans and Kagawa's standing were about to change dramatically. On February 19, 1942, Franklin Roosevelt issued the executive order that authorized the military to detain and expel individuals and groups from designated zones on the West Coast. This allowed some 110,000 Japanese nationals and Japanese Americans to be removed from coastal areas into relocation centers and internment camps. The vast majority of Americans supported this policy, but there was strong opposition among a number of former missionaries to Japan and Kagawa Cooperators in the United States.[43] One prominent example is Galen Fisher, who had served with the YMCA in Japan and later worked closely with Japanese American students at the YMCA in Berkeley. Fisher was a key member of the Kagawa Cooperators in the United States and became an outspoken critic of the government's treatment of Japanese Americans. He also was a leader of the Pacific Coast Committee for American Principles and Fair Play, which was organized to address the issues of discrimination and unfair treatment of Japanese throughout the war and early postwar period.

Kagawa's reputation as an advocate for peace and justice was quickly overshadowed by serious allegations that the actual purpose of his 1941 "peace mission" had been "espionage and propaganda."[44] A letter addressed to the United States Attorney at Los Angeles precipitated an extensive FBI investigation of Kagawa. The letter was from an individual who signed his name as Tom F. Yamada and was mailed from the evacuation assembly center in Fresno, California (September 23, 1942). The letter, forwarded to the FBI Field Division in Los Angeles, claimed that Kagawa was acting as a spy for the Axis during his last trip to the United States. It also stated that he had received assistance from two Japanese Christian pastors in California, the Rev. Kunikichi Inori in Hanford and Rev. Totsuo Sakaguchi in Fresno, who supplied him maps and photographs of factories, dams, and oil fields, which Kagawa then took back to Japan.[45]

Another letter obtained by the FBI—also forwarded from the United States Attorney at Los Angeles (October 11, 1942)—added to the suspicions about Kagawa. The letter (in Japanese) dated January 4, 1941, was sent by Mataro Nakayama, who "was with the Central China Expeditionary Forces in Shanghai, China." The antiwar Kagawa, it explains, had a change of heart and was now fully behind Japan's national ambitions and willing to serve the cause on a special mission to the United States:

> One matter for rejoicing is that during last year Toyohiko Kagawa also decided to add his strength to the Axis. As you know, for a long time Kagawa opposed the military party in Japan, but former Foreign Minister Matsuoka and I acting as intermediaries to the result that he decided to turn over and assist the nation. While it is not known just when the war between Japan and America will open, if everything can be kept secret till it actually opens, Rev. Kagawa, as the messenger of the Japanese people, will go to America and try to become an international roving power. (p. 2)

The letter goes on to indicate that a group of Japanese was also working in collaboration with Kagawa:

> On the outside, Rev. Kagawa's purpose in going to America will be to cooperate with the church of Americans for peace, however, on the inside, really, it will be to collect material for war tricks. For example,

> his purpose is to collect maps, and data, with respect to oil pipelines, gas pipelines, water works, dam establishments and electric generating plants and electric lines. I request that all you Fresno Crisis Committee gather all the material you can and pass it over to Rev. Kagawa. (p. 3)

Given such letters in a time of war, it is not surprising that the FBI began a serious investigation of Kagawa and his colleagues. The inquiry lasted several years and involved numerous interviews with both Japanese Americans in internment camps and former Japan missionaries who were knowledgeable about Kagawa and Japanese pastors on the West Coast.[46]

Two key individuals consulted by the FBI were Rev. Gordon K. Chapman, executive secretary of the Protestant Church Commission for Japanese Service, and Dr. Harry Myers. Both had known Kagawa since he had been their student at Kobe Theological Seminary several decades earlier. Neither could believe that Kagawa had been working for the Japanese government. "As we know his life and character, and as it is reflected in his books and speeches," they explained, "it seems incredible to us that he should become a tool of the military clique in Japan. In fact, he has suffered in the past because of his opposition to this clique."[47] They also testified to the "trustworthiness" of both Inori and Sakaguchi, the two Japanese pastors implicated in the letters.[48] Of particular interest is Chapman's statement about the possible identity of the person who made the initial charges:

> The Japanese name which is signed to the charge is unknown to any of the Christian ministers, although there was a man with the same family name who was a pastor at Fresno, California. There are some who feel that the real author of the letter, which implicated Sakaguchi and Inori as well as Kagawa, is Mr. Kamakichi Sekiguchi, who is now in the Jerome Relocation [Center] at Denson, Arkansas. He was originally a Christian pastor, but has for years been inactive, and has of late been leading the Seicho-no-Ie cult, which as you know claims to take the good things from all religions but is quite nationalistic. This man has been most critical of Christian pastors in the things he has written and said, and thus the Japanese pastors have suggested

> that his name should be dropped from the list of his denomination as a Christian pastor. Sekiguchi is fully cognizant of this opposition to his critical ways, and it is well within possibility that he might have written the letter. I might add that he has also been opposed to Kagawa for some time because of an alleged slight some years ago.[49]

This speculation—that Sekiguchi, a Seicho-no-Ie leader, may have been the one who framed Kagawa—was never substantiated, nor did it appear in any other reports.

Not all of those consulted by the FBI were so favorable in their assessment of Kagawa. For example, Dr. Dirk Van H. Labberton (1874–1961), a Dutch theosophist and scholar residing in Los Angeles—identified as the translator of a Japanese booklet titled *Tōhō no hikari* (Light from the East)—seemed confident that Kagawa had in fact been involved in espionage activities. "I do not doubt that he finally went over to the service of his country, and came on his last trip to the United States for espionage purposes," Labberton writes, "because, for being a Christian, *Kagawa is a Japanese*" (emphasis mine). No evidence was offered, however, to support his claim. His assessment appears to be based largely on his anti-Japanese sentiments and a cynical view of Kagawa as "the one Japanese who has made a successful racket of Christianity. Princeton gave him a degree, all congregations and women's clubs in this country fell over him and he has many friends and admirers, also on account of his truly great social and cooperative work. He certainly is a 'key-man' in whichever direction he chooses to apply his talents."[50]

In spite of an extensive investigation and numerous interviews, the FBI were never able to confirm the identity of those who authored the incriminating letters and discovered no hard evidence to support the charge that Kagawa had been involved in espionage activity with his Japanese colleagues on the West Coast. At the end of the war, nevertheless, J. Edgar Hoover sent an FBI report with the allegations to the Occupation authorities in Tokyo. This meant that a dark cloud of suspicion hung over Kagawa in the early postwar period.[51] The records reveal that Kagawa was still under investigation by SCAP's Counter Intelligence Section in August 1946, and the authorities were still trying to locate "Nakayama," the alleged author of the letter that incriminated Kagawa.[52]

The Postwar Period

Kagawa faced considerable challenges in rehabilitating his public image in the United States after the war. The allegations of espionage and reports of his "anti-American" radio broadcasts during the war were widely disseminated in a *Stars and Stripes* article by Barnard Rubin titled "Under Christian Guise, This Jap Fostered War" (December 20, 1945). Again, some five years later, James R. Young, associate editor of the *Anderson Independent Tribune,* Anderson, South Carolina, used the reports and allegations when he launched a protest against Dr. Kagawa's planned five-month speaking tour to the United States and appealed to the US government not to give him an entry visa in 1950.[53]

Supporters of Kagawa, however, did not remain silent. In 1951, for example, Clarence Hall defended Kagawa against the charges in the *Stars and Stripes* article and suggested that his radio broadcasts were done out of a sense of desperation after American bombs killed thousands of civilians and destroyed the settlements and mission projects under his direction. "The militarists persuaded him, 'in humanity's name,'" Hall explained, "to broadcast protests against American obliteration bombing. They made recordings of his broadcasts, adroitly tacked on inflammatory propaganda, and beamed them to America."[54] First published in the *Christian Advocate,* a Methodist magazine, Hall's essay was reprinted in condensed form by *Reader's Digest* in February 1951. A newsletter issued by "Friends of Kagawa" in America concluded that the "*Reader's Digest* reprint ends forever the cruel assault made on him by some unprincipled reporters."

In the midst of the destruction and devastation of postwar Japan, it is not surprising that Kagawa appealed again to his friends and supporters overseas to assist with the relief work and recovery efforts. After the controversy surrounding his wartime activity subsided, Kagawa was again able to inspire many Christians outside of Japan to give generously to the rebuilding efforts, social welfare activities, and expanding evangelistic outreach programs. The records reveal that, even in the 1950s, the Kagawa National Committee was contributing $1,000 monthly, and the Friends of Jesus Branch in Los Angeles was contributing another $350 monthly to Kagawa's work. By this time, Kagawa had some forty-six staff workers to support and thirty-nine different projects, including farmer gospel schools, orphanages, slum centers, day nurseries, and a number of evangelistic centers. In addition to this regular monthly support, major fund-raising campaigns were undertaken for various new projects and reconstruction in the postwar period. These were particularly effective when combined with Kagawa's visits and tours of the United States. The Kagawa National Committee coordinated these lecture tours and speaking engagements for Kagawa. In 1950, for example, Kagawa's American tour included four hundred speaking engagements in 150 cities, which attracted some 300,000 people and raised $60,000 (above expenses) to support his work in Japan. Similarly, Kagawa's lecture tour in 1954 raised a total of over $161,000 in honorariums and contributions, and over $100,000 was transferred to Japan for mission projects under Kagawa's direction. In spite of his early calls for "self-support" among Japanese Christians in the early 1920s, Kagawa found it necessary to rely on his international supporters until his death in 1960.

Some Concluding Observations

Japanese Christians have always been only a small minority in both Japan and the United States, but they have not simply been a passive flock under the direction of an American church. This study of Kagawa reveals that Japanese Christians have also taken the initiative and played a significant role in shaping their own lives and the societies in which they live. His alternative version of Christianity combined strategies for individual and social transformation that attracted followers both within and outside of Japan. Whereas the founders of other Japanese Christian movements largely severed relations with established churches and foreign missionaries, Kagawa nurtured cooperative relationships that were transdenominational and international. Although some observers feared he would follow a sectarian impulse and break with the Protestant establishment, the Friends of Jesus remained within the established churches as a "reform" or "revitalization" movement (*ecclesiola in ecclesia*) that effectively mobilized its members for social engagement and cultivated both ecumenical and international relationships and support. Although other Japanese leaders similarly created new religious communities and movements, they were largely focused on personal spirituality and cultivation and did not seriously address the many problems faced by Japan during the difficult early stages of modernization.[55]

Since 2009 Kagawa's legacy has been the focus of renewed attention in Japan. A number of special events were organized to commemorate the hundredth year since Kagawa began to live and work among the poor. It was on Christmas Eve in 1909—when he was still a young theological student of twenty-one—that he moved out of his dormitory room at the Kobe Seminary and carried his few belongings into an old rented shack in the Shinkawa slums.[56] Given the global economic crisis of the past several years, Kagawa's writings and work on cooperatives are seen to be particularly relevant again.[57] This case study has shown that many American Protestants also found Kagawa's vision compelling and sought to apply it to the disparities and contradictions that had emerged in their own society. This largely forgotten story surely deserves reconsideration and a place in the history of American religion and society.

Notes

I would like to express appreciation to a number of institutions and individuals that made this study possible. First, I am grateful for a generous research grant from the Tokyo Club that allowed me to gather materials from a number of archives in the United States from 2005 to 2008. During this time period, I was also a visiting researcher at the Matsuzawa Shiryōkan Kagawa Toyohiko Resource Center, Tokyo. I would like to express appreciation to Dr. Hisao Kayama, executive director of the center, for many hours of helpful conversations and for arranging my affiliation as a research associate of the center. I was also fortunate to have the able assistance of Hidenori Sugiura, curator of the center, who kindly opened the archives to me and shared photographs from the collection. A special thanks also to Ruth Tonkiss Cameron, archivist at the Burke Library at Union Theological Seminary and Columbia University, who on two different occasions guided me through their special collection of the "Kagawa Toyohiko Papers, 1929–1968," which is undoubtedly the most extensive collection related to Kagawa and his supporters in the United States and an important resource for this study.

1. See Peter Phan, ed., *Christianities in Asia* (Chichester: Wiley-Blackwell, 2011).

2. Although Christian missionaries were active among Japanese immigrants and their children, it is important to remember that most were Buddhist (at least nominally) and only 15 to 20 percent of Issei and their children were affiliated with Christianity by the 1930s; see Paul R. Spickard, *Japanese Americans: The For-*

mation and Transformations of an Ethnic Group (New York: Twayne Publishers, 1996), 54–56.

3. One volume that celebrates this dimension of the Japanese American experience is Rev. Sumio Koga, comp., *"A Centennial Legacy": History of the Japanese Christian Missions in North America 1877–1977,* vol. 1 (Chicago: Nobart, Inc., 1977).

4. In his study of prewar Japanese Protestants in the United States, for example, Brian Masaru Hayashi discovered that many converts to evangelical Christianity remained "highly nationalistic in their sentiments toward Japan and far less positive about American culture than had been assumed." *For the Sake of Our Japanese Brethen: Assimilation, Nationalism, and Protestantism among the Japanese of Los Angeles, 1895–1942* (Stanford, CA: Stanford University Press, 1995), 6–7.

5. See Mark R. Mullins, *Christianity Made in Japan: A Study of Indigenous Movements* (Honolulu: University of Hawai'i Press, 1998), 61–65.

6. In an earlier study *Christianity Made in Japan,* I attempted to provide basic documentation of these "missing persons and movements," which had been largely ignored by representative historical and sociological studies.

7. On Kagawa's dissatisfaction with the tendency of churches in Japan to be passive and to interpret Christianity simply as a "spiritual movement," see Sumiya Michio's study *Kagawa Toyohiko* (Tokyo: Iwanami Shoten, 1995), 168. Kagawa's vision of Christianity as a "social movement" of emancipation can be found in many of his writings and sermons. For one example in English, see "Following in His Steps," *Friends of Jesus,* vol. 4, no. 1 (January 1931): 6.

8. Myers was one of Kagawa's mentors in the Christian faith. Kagawa was baptized by Myers in Tokushima in 1904 at the age of fifteen and was later his student at Kobe Theological Seminary (from 1908). In the 1930s, Meyers was assigned to work with Kagawa and assist with evangelistic efforts in the Kingdom of God movement. When Kagawa was under investigation for espionage during World War II, Meyers vouched for his character in a letter addressed to Gordon K. Chapman, Executive Secretary of the Protestant Commission for Japanese Service, which was included in an FBI report dated November 29, 1943. See FBI File No. 65–3558.

9. Whereas in the postwar period it became common for missionaries to be invited to Japan to work cooperatively and under the authority of the Japanese Church (mainline Protestant missionaries have been assigned to the United Church of Christ in Japan, for example), this was an unusual pattern for missionary assignment in the prewar period.

10. Tabulating the books and number of pages of Kagawa's publications listed in Haruichi Yokoyama, *Toyohiko Kagawa and His Works* (Tokyo: Friends of Jesus, 1961)—and this does not include his magazine and newspaper articles—the total

number of pages in print comes to 50,348. His publications can be divided into the following categories: 62 religious books (13,334 pages); 40 books/pamphlets dealing with economics, poverty, labor, and cooperatives (8,917 pages); and 58 books of fiction, including novels, poetry, and children's stories (17,825 pages). In addition to his own writing, Kagawa was also involved in translation work. In 1929 alone, for example, the following translations by Kagawa appeared: *John Wesley's Journal* (575 pages), J. R. Smith, *The World's Food Resources* (664 pages), and F. A. Lange, *History of Materialism* (949 pages).

11. See the article "Kagawa Toyohiko o debyū saseta zasshi *Kaizō* de no rensai *Yorozu banpō,*" May 7, 2003, http://www.yorozubp.com/0305/030507.htm.

12. See the reports on Kagawa's trips (1924, 1931, 1941) and his role in Japanese American communities in Koga, "*A Centennial Legacy,*" 16–17, 113, 188. Additional information on the relationship between Kagawa and the Japanese American communities can be gleaned from various archive collections, including the West Adams Christian Church Archives in the Japanese American National Museum, Los Angeles, and the Special Collections at the University of California, Los Angeles. Files contain various newspaper clippings as well as Friends of Jesus newsletters in Japanese. Of particular interest in the Japanese American Museum collection is an oral history interview of the Reverend John and Mrs. Miyoko Mizuki, by Paul Tsuneishi, April 15, 2002. Mizuki was encouraged by Kagawa to become a missionary to Brazil and later became Kagawa's interpreter for 110 days when he was on a tour of Brazil. That intense experience, Mizuki explains, "changed his theology from *only* winning persons to Jesus Christ to a broader inclusive social gospel that called him to minister to every person . . . including the very poor of every society." Mizuki interview, 1.

13. Toyohiko Kagawa, "Christianity and Race Prejudice: A Japanese Plea," *The Friend* 65 (1925): 281. Quoted in Robert D. Schildgen, *Toyohiko Kagawa: An Apostle of Love and Social Justice* (Berkeley, CA: Centenary Books, 1988), 150. Many observers have noted that Kagawa was not entirely consistent in his views on race. Since his death in 1960, for example, there has been a movement within the United Church of Christ in Japan to critically reassess the man and his life in light of the "discriminatory" language and attitudes toward *burakumin*—the outcastes of Japan—that permeated his first book, *Hinmin shinri no kenkyū* (A Study of the Psychology of the Poor). This book was first published in 1915, when Kagawa was still in his late twenties and a student at Princeton. The inclusion of this book as volume 8 in the publication of Kagawa's collected works in 1962—in spite of the widely recognized discriminatory language—became the precipitating event that led to a critical reevaluation of Kagawa and the problem of discrimination within Japanese Protestant churches as a whole.

14. Protestants in Canada were struggling with the same problems and were

similarly enamored with Kagawa as well as Mahatma Gandhi, another "holy man" from the East. See J. K Unsworth, "Gandhi and Kagawa: Two Spiritual Forces of the East," *The Churchman* 1926: 10–11; and Robert Wright, *A World Mission: Canadian Protestantism and the Quest for a New International Order, 1918–1939* (Montreal and Kingston: McGill-Queen's University Press, 1991), especially chapter 6.

15. "Toyohiko Kagawa: The St. Francis of Japan," *Pacific Affairs* 4, no. 4 (1931): 308–317.

16. Letter from Helen F. Topping to Dr. Toyohiko Kagawa, January 16, 1950; Matsuzawa Shiryōkan Kagawa Toyohiko Archives, English Correspondence, A330E00321. Interesting "insider" accounts of these trips and speaking tours include *Friends of Jesus,* vol. 8, no. 1 (February 1936), which focuses on "Kagawa in Australia, New Zealand, and Hawaii," and includes a note on "Rauschenbusch and Kagawa"; and *Friends of Jesus,* vol. 8, no. 3 (July 1936), which is titled "Kagawa in Lincoln's Land," compiled and edited by Emerson O. Bradshaw, Charles E. Shike, and Helen F. Topping, and published by the National Kagawa Coordinating Committee, New York.

17. This tour was also given extensive coverage by the Japanese American newspapers (over seventy articles about Kagawa's activities appeared in the *Nichibei shinbun* during 1935–1936). In addition to the announcements of Kagawa's various speaking engagements, many articles expressed pride that Japan had produced such a great religious leader—referring to him as the St. Francis of Japan and an equal of Mahatma Gandhi and Albert Schweitzer. The newspaper also gave some attention to the "suffering" Kagawa experienced on this lecture tour owing to serious opposition. For example, the December 26, 1935, edition of the *Nichibei shinbun* reported that "the American Coalition," represented by John B. Trevor, protested the entry of Kagawa to the United States and had sent a telegram to President Roosevelt that claimed Kagawa was "an alien propagandist seeing to tour the country for an organization closely associated with groups carrying on a campaign to undermine all our agencies of national defense."

18. "Baltimore Hears Kagawa Speak," *The Christian Century,* February 12, 1936, 273.

19. "Kagawa Completes Lecture Tour," *The Christian Century,* July 15, 1936, 994.

20. The report and pamphlet of the International Conference, Lake Geneva, Wisconsin (June 27–30, 1936), are contained in the Missionary Research Library (MRL) archives of Burke Library at Union Theological Seminary and Columbia University. MRL 7: Japan, Toyohiko Kagawa Papers, American Tour, 1936 Papers, Kingdom of God Fellowship, box 2, folder 14.

21. This was published by the National Kagawa Coordinating Committee and

is on file in the Burke Library, MRL 7: Japan, Toyohiko Kagawa Papers, American Tour, 1936 Papers, box 2, folder 4.

22. See Marriott's *Kagawa and Cooperatives* (Chicago: Kingdom of God Fellowship, 1936) and his *Kagawa and the Kingdom of God* (Chicago: Kingdom of God Fellowship, 1936), in which he explains: "The Kingdom of God Fellowship in Chicago was formed with the idea of translating the ideals of Kagawa into American life. The name was chosen with the idea of relating the movement in this country to the Kingdom of God enterprise in Japan. Kagawa defines his purpose in the Kingdom of God Movement to carry forward these three objectives in unity and harmony—evangelism, education and work for a better social order. That is just the thing we have never been able to do in America. We have had an evangelism, which laid stress on saving the individual but forgot about the Kingdom of God. We have had a great emphasis on religious education, which gave itself to its technique and lost the flame of the evangel. We have had our Social Gospel that some way became estranged from the other two objectives and even from the church in many instances. But we have not succeeded in uniting all three objectives in one grand movement as has Kagawa in his Kingdom of God movement in Japan" (p. 12).

23. Another report similarly explains: "Student housing cooperatives expanded during the 1930s, partly because the Depression meant that minimizing living costs was essential to those trying to keep college places and partly for ideological reasons. A Japanese cleric, Toyohiko Kagawa, believed that co-operatives were the foundation of world peace and inspired many students during his speaking tours in North America. . . . In Canada, the first student housing co-operative was set up at the University of Toronto in 1936, inspired by a visit from Kagawa" (see *A Co-operative Future for Student Housing*, Urban Economic Development Group, First Stage Report, June 2004, 12).

24. For helpful treatments of the relationships between Kagawa and the cooperative movement in the United States, see M. A. Dawber, "The Cooperative Movement and the Church," *Annals of the American Academy of Political and Social Science* 191 (1937): 70–75, and chapter 8, "The Cooperator's Message to America," in Schildgen, *Toyohiko Kagawa*, 164–196.

25. Although African Americans may have regarded him as progressive at this time, Kagawa became the focus of sharp criticism in postwar Japan (after his death in 1960) because of the discriminatory language used with reference to the Eta or *burakumin* outcaste group in his early book on poverty, *Hinmin shinri no kenkyū*. While understandably criticized today, it was the first serious study of poverty (based on his life in the slums), sold some eight thousand copies, and prompted the government to provide a substantial budget for slum reconstruction.

26. "Southern Cities Greet Kagawa," *The Christian Century* 53, no. 36 (1936).

27. See Carter G. Woodson, *The Works of Francis J. Grimké* (Washington, DC: The Associated Publishers, 1942) (4 volumes). Woodson observes: "Kagawa had some followers among the Negroes in the United States. Dr. Grimké was an ardent admirer of this Oriental Christian" (1:553).

28. Emphasis mine. The tribute to "Dr. Toyohiko Kagawa" (Washington, DC, 1936) has been preserved in the Francis J. Grimké (1850–1937) Papers, Howard University, Washington, DC, Founders Library (40–48, F 377).

29. On this point, see the helpful essay on Grimké's tribute to Kagawa "'Thank God That He Is Not of This Great White Race . . .': Francis Grimké Praises Toyohiko Kagawa (1936)," available as a working draft at http://www3.amherst.edu/~aardoc/Grimke_Kagawa_1936.html; see also Reginald Kearney, *African American Views of the Japanese: Solidarity or Sedition* (Albany: State University of New York Press, 1998); and Ernest Allen, Jr., "When Japan Was 'Champion of the Darker Races': Satokata Takahashi and the Flowering of Black Messianic Nationalism," *The Black Scholar* 240, no. 1 (2001).

30. Schildgen, *Toyohiko Kagawa,* 183.

31. Letter from H. A. Yung, Honorary General Manager, American Vigilant Intelligence Federation, Chicago, Illinois, to Mr. Charles R. Walgreen, Chicago, May 11, 1936, contained in MRL 7: Kagawa, American Tour, 1936 Papers, Correspondence, box 2, folder 1. The American Vigilant Intelligence Federation, which Yung represented, was known in the 1930s as an anti-Semitic lobbying group that was also opposed to Franklin D. Roosevelt's New Deal policies.

32. *The Fundamentalist,* April 24, 1936, 4. See also April 17, and May 1, 8, 15, 22, and 29, 1936. Materials on the fundamentalist response to Kagawa and *The Fundamentalist* are available in the Garman Collection, Bob Jones University Library.

33. *Post-Standard* (Syracuse, NY), April 4, 1936.

34. *Nichibei shinbun,* English edition, September 15, 1931, 1.

35. *The Fundamentalist,* May 8, 1936, 2.

36. Schildgen, *Toyohiko Kagawa,* 191.

37. *The Fundamentalist,* May 1, 1936, 7. An article in the *Rochester Journal* (April 15, 1936) notes that Norris also tried to get a movement going among American Baptists to have Dr. Albert W. Beavens "ousted" as president of Colgate-Rochester Divinity School.

38. *Radical Religion* 1, no. 2 (1936): 6–7 (published by the Fellowship of Socialist Christians).

39. It should be noted that Kagawa would agree with Niebuhr's statement here. He did not depend entirely on cooperatives for his social agenda and was involved in the development of the Socialist Party in Japan. His lectures in the United States, however, focused largely on the role of cooperatives.

40. Schildgen, *Toyohiko Kagawa,* 208.

41. Reported in the *Nichibei shinbun,* December 24, 1935.

42. "Telegram from Kagawa to the President, The White House, September 4, 1941," in RG 59, State Department Records, the National Archives and Records Administration (NARA) of the United States.

43. See the detailed analysis by Robert Shaffer, "Opposition to Internment: Defending Japanese American Rights during World War II," *The Historian* 61, no. 3 (1999): 597–620.

44. In what follows I am drawing on over two hundred pages of correspondence and reports preserved in the Federal Bureau of Investigation Records (RG 65) and Department of Justice Records (RG 60).

45. These letters are contained in the FBI File No. 65–3558, Title: Toyohiko Kagawa, Rev. Kunikichi Inori, Rev. Totsuo Sakaguchi, Report by William J. McCormick, Los Angeles, November 27, 1942, Character of case: Espionage-J.

46. It is worth noting that the FBI had already been following Kagawa in 1941, over a year before these letters appeared and allegations were ever made. *Monthly Intelligence Summary #8, dated July 3, 1941,* received from the Military Intelligence Division contains a report dated June 30, 1941, with the heading "Suspected Propagandist." It reported that "Dr. Toyohiko Kagawa, Christian and Cooperative leader, lectured at Market Square Presbyterian Church, Harrisburg, on June 20, 1941," and indicated that the FBI was following his movement and next flight to Seattle. J. Edgar Hoover, the director of the FBI, also took an interest in Kagawa and his "Peace Delegation," and instructed agents to find out about their itinerary and ascertain if they are actually "disseminating propaganda or are engaged in legitimate activities." Kagawa sailed for Japan on August 4, 1941, so the agents were too late to follow up on Hoover's request (see FBI 100–21138–2, Letter from John Edgar Hoover, Director, to Special Agent in Charge, with Five Copies of a Summary Memorandum concerning Kagawa and Five Copies of a Summary Memorandum Regarding Yoshimune Abe, New York, New York, Re: Toyohiko Kagawa; Yoshimune Abe; October 23, 1941).

47. The views of Chapman and Myers are recorded in FBI File No. 65–3558, Title: "Toyohiko Kagawa, Reverend Kunikichi Inori, with alias: Kunishichi Inori, Rev. Totsuo Sakakuchi, with alias Tatsuo Sakaguchi, Report made by Special Agent Charles C. Shaw, Los Angeles, California, November 29, 1943, Character of case: Espionage-J.

48. In another report, Chapman refers to being interviewed earlier in Jerome, Arkansas, at which time he also presented letters he had received from both pastors in which they deny any involvement in espionage activities with Kagawa (see FBI File No. 65–3245, Title: Toyohiko Kagawa; Reverend Kunikichi Inori; Rever-

end Totsuo Sakaguchi, January 22, 1944, Report by Agent Robert Barrows Hawley, San Francisco, California, Character of case: Espionage–J, 8 pages).

49. This explanation appears in FBI File No. 65–3558, p. 3.

50. Labberton's comments are included in FBI File No. 65–3558, Title: Toyohiko Kagawa; Reverend Kunikichi Inori; Reverend Totsuo Sakaguchi, Feb. 8, 1944, Report made by J. Richardson Jones, Los Angeles, Character of case: Espionage-J, 6 pages (4–5).

51. See the letter from J. Edgar Hoover, Director, FBI, to Frederick G. Tillman, Tokyo, Japan, Re: Toyohiko Kagawa, November 13, 1945, which was accompanied by a seven-page summary of information about Kagawa in the FBI files.

52. See the letter from F. G. Tillman, Liaison Officer in Charge, to the Director of the FBI, August 9, 1946, Re: Toyohiko Kagawa, Foreign Political. The letter raises concerns regarding Kagawa's qualification for leadership in postwar Japan: "Kagawa was appointed to the House of Peers on March 12, 1946, to please the Americans under the misapprehension that because of his influence among religious groups in the United States and England he would be acceptable to General Headquarters in Tokyo. The military authorities feel that Kagawa is an opportunist and would contribute nothing to U.S. aims in Japan. This phase of his character is evidenced by his acceptance of the seat in the House of Peers after a lifetime of working against class distinctions and by his acceptance, during and before the war, of the militaristic aims of the Japanese government."

53. See the letter (file 100–41138–33) from James R. Young, Associate Editor of the *Anderson Independent Tribune,* Anderson, South Carolina, to the Chief, Visa Division, Department of State, Washington, DC, May 30, 1950.

54. Clarence W. Hall, "Unconquerable Kagawa," *The Christian Advocate*, January 4, 1951, 23.

55. See Amemiya Eiichi, "Nihon kindaishi ni okeru Kagawa Toyohiko to Uchimura Kanzō," *Kagawa kenkyū*, no. 14 (1988), for a helpful comparison of Kagawa and Uchimura Kanzō. Amemiya points out that both Uchimura and Kagawa were critical of churches and denominationalism. In the case of Uchimura, the primary criticisms were related to accumulated Western church traditions, sacraments, and clericalism (priesthood), which were regarded as unnecessary for biblical faith. Kagawa, by contrast, was concerned that the theology in churches was too conceptual or abstract and lacked an adequate expression of love (*ai no jissen*). Amemiya also notes that the "stance" of these two minor founders was fundamentally different. Uchimura's standpoint was that of the elite, whereas Kagawa saw things from below, from the standpoint of those in positions of weakness and vulnerability.

56. A Japanese translation of his English book *Brotherhood Economics*, based on the Rauschenbusch lectures on "Christian Brotherhood and Economic Recon-

struction," which he delivered at Colgate-Rochester Divinity School in 1936, was also prepared for publication to coincide with this celebration. The Japanese version is titled *Yūai no seiji keizai gaku.* For an overview of these events and a reassessment of Kagawa by Japanese scholars, see the special edition of *AT* [Alternative], 15 (2009).

57. Another recent boost to Kagawa studies came when it was revealed recently that Kagawa had been nominated for the Nobel Prize for Literature from the Swedish Academy two years in a row (1947 and 1948). It was already well known that he had been nominated for the Nobel Peace Prize for three years from 1954, but his nomination for the prize in literature was made public for the first time. Only two Japanese have ever received this award (Kawabata in 1968 and Oe Kenzaburō in 1994), so the news that another Japanese had been seriously considered for this award was a pleasant surprise for many Japanese—especially Kagawa admirers (*Mainichi shinbun*, September 9, 2009).

PART IV

Religion and National Identity

8

Preaching Modern Japan

National Imaginaries and Protestant Sermons in Meiji and Taishō Tokyo

GARRETT L. WASHINGTON

BEGINNING IN THE MID-NINETEENTH CENTURY, Japan embarked on a feverish quest to reach the promised land of modernity. To more fully understand this objective and the means of achieving it, the country's most sociopolitically active men and women looked to the advanced nations of Europe and the United States. Through encounters with Westerners and Western sources, they sought and found formulas and models for dramatically improving the condition of the Japanese people and their systems of governance. Taken together, several of the most frequently repeated elements of this blueprint emphasized that the teleological destiny, and pinnacle, of humankind was the sovereign nation-state. The ideal modern nation would be led by civilized individuals, strengthened by heavy industry and expansion, and peopled by loyal citizens.[1]

Although the new national government continuously strove to make the populace aware of their membership in the Japanese nation and to instruct them of their duties to that entity, questions about the nature of the nation persisted and even multiplied for the citizenry. The modernizing people of Meiji Japan were increasingly literate, versant in the recently standardized national language, formally educated, linked by a growing national mass media, and connected by the expanding national network of railway lines.[2] So armed, they often dealt with this challenge by adding their own interpretations to government rhetoric. Struggling to make sense of their national community and their respective places within it, many Japanese reacted by creating and tuning in to a multiplicity of discourses on the nation.

More than ever before, being Japanese became a challenge for all classes, and an array of ideologues quickly appeared in the late nineteenth century offering explanations and guidance. Through the strong language of decrees and pronouncements and the softer language of advertising campaigns and imperial visits, the Meiji government aimed to foster and instill in the public an appropriate Japanese national identity and pride.[3] Government-affiliated ideologues and publicists were not alone, however, and complementing their efforts were popular (*minkan*) ideologues who made themselves increasingly available to the Japanese public. They surfaced "all around, plying different interpretive trades in different social places."[4] Making use of a variety of old and new gathering spaces, from urban temple precincts to the floor of the new Imperial Diet to lecture halls at the Imperial University, nation-minded activists and orators enhanced, reinterpreted, reduced, and refuted the views promulgated by the state.[5] The new religious gathering space of the Japanese Protestant church figured among these forums, providing thousands of attendees with new meeting spaces and discursive tools for imagining and coming to terms with the new nation.

Urban Protestant churches were particularly attractive to the cosmopolitan new middle class as its members worked to define and embody Japaneseness. Converging in large numbers on the new national capital in the 1880s and 1890s, they often discovered within Tokyo's largest Protestant churches words and interactions that addressed their dilemmas. The nation's intellectual elite possessed superior education, broad travel experiences, proficiency in one or more Western language, and ambitions to shape Japan's future. Yet these very characteristics made the task and process of constructing a workable nation-view all the more complex for these individuals. The country's new intelligentsia could not but be troubled by the difficulty of navigating between the moral hierarchies of loyalty and status of the Tokugawa period, the new national morality espoused by the imperial government, love and respect for Japan in general, and Western forms of knowledge and culture. The *shūkaidō* (meeting hall) or *reihaidō* (worship hall) of Tokyo's most influential Protestant churches played host to ideologues and rhetoric that spoke directly to the concerns of those searching for a solid sense of national belonging and individual purpose within the nation.

Protestant church meeting halls in the capital offered well-read, well-traveled, multilingual Japanese a highly qualified popular ideologue in the person of the Protestant pastor. Themselves well educated, often familiar with English or German, experienced in studying and living abroad, mentored by Western experts, and preoccupied with the essence and fate of the nation, Tokyo's Protestant pastorate was particularly well positioned to respond to the questions and anxieties of nationally aware and concerned attendees.[6] In addition to their weekly and monthly articles in Christian and secular periodicals, pastors' Sunday sermons could appeal to men and women caught between universal ideals, Western learning, and Japanese national identity. The appeal was strongest in the social, economic, and political center of the nation, where the need for and visibility of such cultural interpreters remained high until the 1930s. For those grappling with the increasingly complex set of topics surrounding the definition of Japan and national citizenship, spoken pastoral discourse presented a supplemental and highly relevant set of national imaginaries. For those concerned with the relationship between the nation and religion, pastoral discourse situated Protestant religiomoral guidance in a distinctly Japanese cultural context.

This chapter sheds new light on the types of nation that Tokyo's most popular Protestant pastors helped their listeners to imagine from the pulpit. The following paragraphs will examine sermons by the well-known pastors of Tokyo's two largest Protestant churches, Congregationalist Ebina Danjō (1856–1937) of Hongō Church and Presbyterian pastor Uemura Masahisa (1857–1925) of Fujimichō Church, and by the seldom-mentioned pastor of another of Tokyo's most famous churches, Congregationalist Tsunajima Kakichi (1860–1936) of Banchō Church. These three very different pastors are representative of a sociopolitically conscious Tokyo pastorate sensitive and responsive to those walking the line between the world of Western ideas and traditions and a Japan rapidly becoming aware and proud of itself. Their special "nationalisms"[7] diverged significantly in direction and depth from the forms of nationalism most prevalent in Meiji and Taishō Japan, and their sermons went to the heart of the pressing nation-related questions of the day.[8]

From the nature of national identity to the individual's responsibility to and love for the nation to the proper composition and boundaries of the national body (*kokutai*) to the glorious national past and future, these pastors consciously blurred the line between religious and secular discourse each week. Prominent pastors such as Ebina, Tsunajima, and Uemura selected elements from within their personal reflections on Japan to project a specific image of the nation to their middle-class audiences. This chapter analyzes the national community that each pastor verbally constructed and describes the context and ideological ramifications of these creations. In doing so, the essay also aims to add new color to a monochromatic depiction of Meiji and Taishō era Japanese Protestant Christian nationalism that often ignores the existence and diversity of coexisting nation-views among Christian leaders.

Since the 1890s, the nationalistic tendencies of certain turn-of-the-twentieth-century Japanese Protestant pastors have drawn considerable attention and even criticism from foreign missionaries, fellow Japanese Christians, and subsequent religious scholars. The fervent patriotism of Ebina Danjō in particular has come to represent the most extreme form of Japanese Protestant nationalism, leaving the impression that more moderate Christian leaders were not nationalists. In reality, war-supporting Protestants and jingoistic Christians held no monopoly on nationalist sentiment, and there was more than one kind of Christian nationalism at work in prewar Japan. Prasenjit Duara has demonstrated that, although the modern nation unites the affections, worries, and ambitions of its citizens, the shapes and shades of "nationalism" among the members of any modern nation can be varied and multiplicitous. While the object of nationalism, the nation, is constant and shared, "nationalism" is in fact the "site where different representations of the nation contest and negotiate with each other."[9]

This definition makes it possible to see that Protestant churches in Tokyo, including but not limited to those led by nation-focused pastors such as Ebina, acted as loci for the formation and transformation of Japanese nationalisms. The moderate Tsunajima and even the allegedly apolitical Uemura were also busy building and propagating specific nationalisms. For all three, the Japanese nation comprehended a set of meanings and responsibilities that went above and beyond official nationalisms and government dicta. They each firmly believed that their audience could only truly make sense of the problems and potential of the Japanese nation through the prism of Protestant belief and action. Each Sunday, these pastors and others like them negated the claims of Christianity's many detractors that the religion was not nationalist by offering the Japanese educated elite unprecedented, pertinent, empowering ways of seeing their nation and actively contributing to its present and future.

The Nation, Obvious and Elusive

The nation and its destiny were at the heart of many Tokyo pastors' sermons. Listeners at each of Tokyo's largest Protestant churches were exposed, on a weekly basis, to variants on this theme. As one might expect, the nation played a decisive role in the vast majority of sermons that Ebina gave at Hongō. He made frequent and clear reference to the Japanese nation in the titles of his sermons, often using the suggestive diction of "our nation" (*wagakuni, wagakokumin,* or *wagakokutai*). Ebina's tendency to focus on the nation continues to interest many different types of religious scholars, and sermon titles such as "The New Way of the Warrior" (Shin bushidō), "Gentry Religion" (Shi no shūkyō), and "The Meaning of a Virtuous Country" (Kunshikoku no igi) offer evidence as to why he has been singled out so prominently by scholars such as Shuma Iwai and Dohi Akio.[10] From making criticisms and suggestions about Japan as a whole to outlining strategies for Japanese Christians to act as catalysts for national change to locating the Japanese national past in Western rubrics of race, sovereignty, progress, and expansion, Ebina consistently and directly engaged the nation in ways that many of his colleagues did not.

In contrast to Ebina's overt references and emphases, the nation is often only present at a more subtle level in the sermons of the much less sensational Tsunajima Kakichi and the outspoken, popular, and more theologically focused pastor Uemura Masashisa. Only two of Uemura's several hundred extant sermons, "The Christian Family and the State" (Kirisutokyō no ie to kuni) from March 1898 and "Christianity and the Way of the Warrior" (Kirisutokyō to bushidō) from July 1897, testify to his interest in nation-related themes and topics. In the case of Tsunajima, it would appear from a distance that none of his twenty surviving sermons appears to deal with the "nation" directly. An analysis of the content of these pastors' sermons reveals, however, that both aimed to affect the shape of the Japanese nation imagined by their listeners through their mention and use of nation-related rhetoric. They drew upon images, symbols, figures, events, and ideologies linked to the national past of Japan and other countries in order to put the messages of Protestant Christianity in terms more familiar to the Japanese audience. At a deeper level, Uemura and Tsunajima used these discursive tools to lift out elements within the Japanese national imaginary that they considered most compatible with Christianity and to suppress others, valorizing ideals that they judged as crucial for the creation of a new and better Japan and avoiding or discarding others.

Despite their substantial dissimilarities, Tokyo's Protestant pastors shared a strong interest in the fate of the Japanese nation-state and its people. Tsunajima, Uemura, and Ebina were all, regardless of their differences in theological or political orientation, self-aware members of and advocates for the Japanese national community. As such they, like their listeners, were increasingly surrounded on all sides by the national narratives and moral injunctions prescribed by the national government. Ultimately, these religious leaders and their audience members would each have to flesh out government rhetoric with his or her sociopolitical and religiomoral preferences and knowledge. With their sermons, these pastors crafted and propagated specific nationalisms that they considered beneficial to Japan. In these constructions, these men also proposed elements with which listeners could construct their individual nation-views and work to actualize them. The three subsequent sections of this essay will explore the nation in general and the Japanese nation in particular that the three popular Protestant pastors in Tokyo conjured from their pulpits.

The Nation of Tsunajima Kakichi

In his role as pastor of one of Tokyo's four largest Protestant churches, Tsunajima Kakichi spoke to a congregation of more than three hundred each Sunday morning, and he often clothed his rhetoric in the motif of the nation. Speaking directly in his sermons to the citizens of a nation characterized by domestic and international wars during the nineteenth and early twentieth centuries, Tsunajima often borrowed metaphors and paragons from the Japanese military past and present. He singled out the patriotic soldier as a model for Christian behavior. The pastor paid specific attention to military men in Japan and elsewhere who had fought for their national community and demonstrated qualities such as sacrifice, leadership, and self-mastery. Tsunajima considered these ideals translatable to the Christian and his or her task for Japan.

Tsunajima argued that the Christian, like the soldier, was motivated by and responsible for the triumph of the nation. At the root of the soldier's courage lay his conviction that he is fighting "on God's side" for "sincere loyalty and patriotism, truth, a righteous death . . . [and] his fellow countrymen."[11] In particular, Tsunajima pinpointed some Western military leaders who exemplified this combination of patriotism and Christian righteousness, designating them as "the ideal for people who believe in God."[12] He spoke of the English general Oliver Cromwell who chanted "psalms in a loud voice" and "Union Army generals [who] advanced while singing psalms" during the US Civil War.[13] In a sermon titled "The Lord Is My Castle," (Kami wa waga shiro nari) and several other sermons, Tsunajima idealized both literal and figurative Christian soldiers who had exerted themselves for the good of their respective countries. In order to impress upon listeners the type of dedication that would allow the Japanese Christian soldier to fight successfully "for the moralization of his fellow countrymen," he spoke admiringly of British efforts to save their homeland during World War I. Tsunajima praised the young soldiers "in the prime of their lives [who] were sent to the battlefield to serve the nation" and who had "sacrificed everything for the survival of Great Britain; they offered up their whole heart, whole soul, and whole life without looking back." The pastor asked his listeners to develop a similar "resoluteness" as they carried out their roles as "Christian soldiers," since in fact "[o]ur spiritual battle is also like this."[14]

In fact the Japanese Protestant was not akin to just any soldier for Tsunajima, but instead constituted a member of a small elite specifically charged with a mission for the nation. In a sermon on "Gideon's Elite Troops" (Gideon no seihei), the pastor likened his listeners to two groups whose members disregarded their own lives in order to fight for their respective nations: biblical judge Gideon's select, three-hundred-man elite troop (*seihei*) and the Japanese suicide corps (*kesshitai*).[15] The well-known term "suicide corps" had existed for centuries. In the aftermath of a famous and successful *kesshitai* operation in 1905 during the Siege of Port Arthur by a *kesshitai,* however, the term gained new significance and visibility.[16] Tsunajima told his listeners that "we Christians are God's chosen suicide corps" in Japan's spiritual battle and then told the story of one such unit formed bravely and spontaneously to eliminate the threat to the new Japan at any cost.[17] On a train ride from Osaka to Kobe in 1883, a stranger with a "commanding face and powerful physique" told Tsunajima that he had "personally taken the initiative of forming a suicide corps [of] sixteen volunteers" during the Satsuma Rebellion of 1877. The self-selected band of healthy, strong, young soldiers, "vigorous" and "full of life," swooped down upon the "rebels" like an "irresistible force," and "of the seventeen, not even a single one was killed or injured."[18] Tsunajima was confident that his listeners were capable of such a victory for God in Japan.

Like the members of Gideon's elite troop or the Japanese suicide corps, the Japanese Christian was a member of a select, proactive, and well-equipped few who were responsible for positively affecting the nation's destiny. Just as many Japanese students hoped to become influential, wealthy, or famous, many men and women sought to guide Japan's spiritual development. In the spiritual, as in the secular realm, however, only a select group would "take the lead." Tsunajima asked, "Of the countless students who harbor high ambitions . . . how many really attain the success they expect? Every year, among the hundreds and thousands of graduates, how many take the lead in the business world, the political world, the intellectual world? There are truly not many."[19] This small group was composed of individuals who were selected, at least in part, because each of them possessed the necessary qualities for leadership. These ranged from the "dignity [required] of a high-level executive" to the respective appropriate qualities of a "school principal . . . company president . . . prefectural governor . . . [or] cabinet minister."[20] In a similar fashion, Tsunajima encouraged church attendees, many of whom were part of the same socioeconomic group that his sermon no doubt purposefully targeted, to assume their roles of spiritual leadership in the nation just as they had in sociocultural, educational, political, and economic affairs. These members of the new middle class were endowed with the traits and skills to remold Japan.

As with other leadership positions, the responsibility of the Japanese Christian community to the nation required the development and possession of a special set of characteristics.[21] The Japanese Christians' "duty as the chosen" was to "save our fellow countrymen," and for the completion of this task Tsunajima recommended a distinct combination of practical virtues. He looked not only to Western Christian models, but also to some particularly empowering elements in Japanese Neo-Confucian moral teachings. As the "face of the church," the Japanese Christian needed to learn "self-respect, self-appointment, self-confidence," and the quality from which all of these qualities derived, the all-encompassing Neo-Confucian virtue of "self-cultivation."[22] For the sake of the nation, then, Tsunajima's recommendation focused not on those authority-related Neo-Confucian virtues that the Meiji government was advocating most strongly, namely, loyalty and filial piety, but on the personal, reflective virtue of self-cultivation and its capacity to inspire individuals to affect substantial change.[23] Japan needed cultivated leaders more than obedient subjects.

In this small sample of Tsunajima's spoken pastoral discourse, he clearly argues that Japanese Christians were designated to play an important role in the continued existence and amelioration of Japan. Although nation-related themes do not arise with notable frequency in Tsunajima's other seventeen extant sermons, this is most likely owing to the preferences and biases of their collector and republisher, Fukunaga Bunnosuke. Tsunajima's interest in the nation manifested itself in other sermons and speeches that have not survived up to the present. They include, for instance, a lecture to the Banchō youth Sunday school class titled "War Talk" (Sensō no hanashi) in 1906.[24] Furthermore, he addressed issues surrounding Japaneseness and race and entered the realm of the public intellectual entirely with a critical essay on anti-Japanese sentiment and legislation in the United States.[25] Tsunajima Kakichi formulated and expressed a form of nationalism, and these three sermons used Japanese morality, national consciousness, military metaphors, and patriotic Christian models to galvanize his listeners to think about and contribute to the nation.

The Nation of Uemura Masahisa

In his sermons each Sunday at Fujimichō Church, Uemura Masahisa did not feign to be either a critic or a proponent of the prosperity of the Japanese nation. He sought to encourage individual Christians to develop moral strength and apply it in the secular world, whether or not it benefited Japan. On certain occasions, however, fundamental disagreements with particular formulations of the Japanese national polity motivated Uemura to enter the realm of political discourse. By examining two such instances, it becomes clear that Uemura's more doctrine-based religious morality in fact could have direct sociopolitical application. In 1890 in the first issue of his new religiopolitical journal *Nippon hyōron,* Uemura wrote that he thought of his ministry "in terms of Japan." He explained that, like other Japanese, "I have critical opinions about politics, literature, social issues, economics and education."[26] Although scholars have shown that Uemura demonstrated interest in and passion for Japan in his actions and written words, none have remarked that he also spoke aloud on the Japanese nation in his sermons at Fujimichō Church.

In 1897, Uemura challenged one of the theoretical foundations for the Japanese national polity that was beginning to gain popularity during the 1890s with its unprecedented linkages between religious belief and nationalism. Several political ideologues in the nineteenth century told Japanese citizens that, under the guidance and protection of the Japanese emperor, they were a body of brothers and sisters. Japanese Protestant Christians, who were aiming to construct a new society based on the principle of brotherhood for all under Christ, agreed with many elements of this discourse. By the end of the decade, however, some of them had become wary of the type of brotherhood that conservative nationalist Hozumi Yatsuka wrote of in his 1897 work *Kokumin kyōiku: aikokushin* (National Education: Patriotism). While many voices praised the ethnicity-based concept of the Japanese family-state that Hozumi developed, advocated, and placed at the center of a nascent State Shintō ideological constellation, some writers and speakers in Japan, including the least politically active Protestant pastors, encouraged their audiences to reevaluate Hozumi's claims about the true Japan.[27]

Uemura claimed that Hozumi's ideology contained a blurred vision of the nation and its foundational elements. First, the Tokyo Imperial University legal scholar had misunderstood the origins of patriotism. He viewed patriotism as both analogous to and a natural outgrowth of ancestor worship, Uemura explained. According to Hozumi's version of Shintō cosmology, all Japanese were blood relatives of the same race (*minzoku*) practicing simultaneously "reverence for one's mother and father . . . reverence for the family's ancestors . . . [and] reverence for the common ancestors of the Japanese race."[28] By loving one's country, as a collective body of blood relatives (living and deceased), one was showing the ultimate level of "love and respect" for all these individuals.[29] This was how Uemura summarized Hozumi's argument before presenting several reasons for his listeners to refute it.

Uemura argued that the relationship between patriotism, familial love, and supernatural religion constructed by Hozumi was backwards. To begin with, the idea that "if he does not worship and trust in an invisible supreme being, man is unable to govern himself or raise a country" was completely false.[30] Religion and the nation-state did not and should not depend on one another, a contention that echoes the division between church and state found by Takenaka Masao and, more recently, J. Nelson Jennings in Uemura's writings.[31] Second, Uemura contended that it was by loving one's family members that one could be most patriotic and not vice versa. To make this point, Uemura found the poem "Hermann and Dorothea" by Johann Wolfgang van Goethe (1749–1832) to be poignant and pertinent.[32] In this story, set when Napoleon had extended his control over all of Europe in the early 1800s, "German customs and manners were being destroyed, [and] a young married man and woman, Hermann and Dorothea, built a family and from it patriotism sprung forth. . . . Love for the family needs to become . . . love [for] the country."[33] Furthermore, whereas Hozumi equated the family with the country, Uemura imagined an entirely different set of familial relationships.

Uemura also took issue with the delimitation of Hozumi's family-state and the consequences that such definitions would have inside and outside Japan. Whereas the all-inclusive family-state developed by Hozumi and later Meiji ideologues enveloped all Japanese, Uemura expressed concern about the fate of Taiwan's inhabitants as residents of Japan's first colony since 1895. The Taiwanese could have no place in bloodline-based nationalism, leaving the Japanese only two choices of treatment. Given the impossibility of assimilating such people into Hozumi's Japanese race–based family-state, the invading Japanese would have to "completely slaughter this people or if not make them all into slaves."[34] Although Uemura shows no awareness of the inferior treatment afforded the Taiwanese (of Chinese ancestry) and the even more inferior treatment of the territory's aborigines (*seiban*), his dire vision proved prophetic. The hard labor, severe punishment and repression, low and infrequent wages of the aborigines, and other conditions were in many ways similar to slavery. The Musha Incident of 1930, during which 134 Japanese were slain by Taiwanese aborigines testified to the contradictions between Japanese imperialism and the Japanese ethnicity-based family-state. In punitive revenge, the Japanese killed some 500 Taiwanese.[35] As Uemura drew this sermon to a close, he spoke of "confusion" and "pity" as he expressed strong reservations about "Japan's expansion" across the North Sea into the Shandong Peninsula as well.[36]

Within the international and philanthropic constellation of Uemura's nationalism, there remained room, nonetheless, for a strong emphasis on ameliorating the situation of the Japanese people at home. He idealized the "burning patriotic passion" of the "Old Testament prophets" who were deeply saddened by the "immorality and sin of [their] country." "In Japan too," he said, "this [type of] patriotism is desirable."[37] In particular, Uemura lamented the situation among the young men and women coming of age in Japan's urban centers. In the Japan of Uemura's time, love suicides, depression, and other problems among the capital's maladjusted young adults served as daily reminders of the identity issues that this age group faced.[38] Uemura's love for Japan led him to work toward replacing the insufficient ideologies and world-views popular among this age group with the promises and ideals of Protestant Christian morality.

Around the turn of the twentieth century, as Meiji youth sought to identify and understand their lack of cultural certainty and navigate Japan's complex new loyalty structure, *bushidō* or "the way of the warrior," experienced a discernible resurgence.[39] While Confucian scholar, professor, and state-sponsored philosopher Inoue Tetsujirō held up Yamaga Sokō (1622–1685) as the original theorist of this ideology and disseminated his own interpretations of *bushidō* in various forms, Meiji youth were drawn to this ideology by their own needs and priorities.[40] By Uemura's estimation, this was because that ideology drew images that resonated with those youths' emotional state and offered directives that simplified moral dilemmas. In some ways, Uemura sympathized with "the many in today's society [who feel] aloof from the world, like a rootless floating plant, transiently passing through life." He understood how they could read Tokugawa era samurai Daidōji Yūzan's (1639–1730) *Budō shoshinshū* (Initiation into the Warrior Way) and identify with phrases such as "in general man's life is transient, like the evening dew [and] the morning frost."[41] After repeating these lines aloud in his sermon "Christianity and

Bushidō" (Kirisutokyō to bushidō) in 1898, Uemura explained the attraction that the allegedly uncomplicated value system of the samurai, whose "highest aim is to . . . fully accomplish loyalty and filial piety," could have for young wonderers at the turn of the century.[42] Despite this ideology's attractiveness, Uemura urged caution.

Japan's youth could not solve the modern problems that they and their nation faced by simply following *bushidō*'s prescriptions because the ideology overemphasized obedience and disparaged liberty, love, and the individual. According to Uemura, on the one hand, the *bushidō* that pursued the very filial piety and loyalty that the Meiji state preached so diligently viewed all of these elements as greatly inferior to the obligations that all Japanese citizens shared toward their nation and its leaders. On the other hand, religion, while it admittedly "implies obedience to someone with control over oneself," in fact "also implies developing and maintaining oneself." Religion improves upon behavioral codes like *bushidō* by addressing the individual and placing "obedience and love and liberty . . . parallel to one another," Uemura declared. For him, Christianity in particular was the "religion that harmonizes, arranges, and most beautifully fulfills this [set]."[43] Uemura was characterizing Protestant Christianity as a religion that established balance between the Western ideals of love and liberty, the modern category of the individual, and the Meiji era's most touted Neo-Confucian virtues of obedience and duty toward authority. Without Christianity, *bushidō* and the nationalistic ideologies linked to that belief system would inevitably lead Tokyo churchgoers and other Japanese down a dangerous path.

On the opposing side of Uemura's argument were the many Japanese whom, through the language of *bushidō,* were inflating the national pride of Japan beyond its healthy limits, he complained. Worried that *bushidō,* "our nation's bright flower . . . is now gradually losing its loveliness . . . and no longer wields the power it did in the past," these pastors "work hard . . . to maintain [*bushidō*], to promote it."[44] At that time, he remarked, "the Japanese are a people whose heart's blood jumps when they hear the words 'prestige,' 'popularity,' 'acclaim,' 'glory,' and so forth."[45] As evidence, Uemura called listeners' attention to the fact that children sang the stanzas of "At the Foot of Mount Fuji" at the middle school near Fujimichō Church, where he was pastor, promoting the "sense of honor" (*renchi*) valorized by *bushidō* rhetoric.

Gathered at the foot of the mountain,
The towering peak of Mount Fuji,
Looking up in the morning and at night,
Let us lift honor up high.[46]

The situation had become so acute that the preservation and enhanced glory of "the country's national honor" had become the top priority in Japan's foreign diplomacy, he explained.[47] During the late 1890s, as Japan sought diligently to step out from under the heavy financial and emotional burden of its various unequal treaties with Western nations, calls for national dignity reached an unprecedented high.[48] The recent repopularization of *bushidō* was at once a product of and a contributing factor to this trend that sought to rediscover and praise Japan's indigenous past. Even Christians, such as the Quaker Nitobe Inazō (1862–1933), represented the Japanese past and present through the lens of *bushidō*.[49] All of this attention, however, had ignored the fundamental question of the origins and distinctiveness of *bushidō* for the Japanese people.

In response to the rise of national pride surrounding this ideology, Uemura set out to analyze and demystify the long-lived cultural link between *bushidō* and Japan. He criticized outright the glorification of *bushidō* as a specifically Japanese moral system. To demonstrate the errors in such a claim, Uemura highlighted various sightings of the *bushidō*-type ethos in non-Japanese settings. He derided the millions of Japanese

> who chant *Yamato damashii* [the Japanese spirit] . . . and have a habit of being proud that *bushidō* is something that [they] exclusively possess. This is nothing other than favoritism. It cannot be said that *bushidō* is entirely our nation's tradition [alone]. It exists in Turkey; It exists in Tartary; If we think back to the foundation of the Ottoman Empire, that ethos is very similar to that of our nation's *bushidō* spirit. . . . And even perusing Greek [and] Roman history, there are many of their manners and customs that, when considered in comparison with our nation's warriors, would be viewed admirably.[50]

This insight was meant less to insult Japanese tradition than to free Japanese minds from what he considered baseless chauvinism. Rather than focusing on the in fact limited Japanese nature and origins of *bushidō* or seeking to accumulate honor and glory by practicing the old warrior way, Uemura encouraged Japanese to think more carefully about *bushidō* as a moral code.

Despite some apparent hostility toward elements within *bushidō,* Uemura was in fact more of a reformer than an enemy of the ideology. As an advocate of "Baptized Bushidō," the fulfillment of Neo-Confucian morality with Christian elements, Uemura found a great deal of value in many portions of *bushidō* thought.[51] He looked positively on the self-sacrifice, literally and figuratively, adherence to a moral code, respect for truth and honesty, appreciation for teachings and reason over emotion, and development of self-control advocated by *bushidō.* These were the elements worth upholding in *bushidō.* He hoped listeners would see that the best things within *bushidō* could be developed and achieved by "pouring into our nation" the tenets of Christianity. Christianity is, above all, a religion that values "doctrine," "self-sacrifice," and the search for "truth over profit."[52] To make these characteristics clearer, Uemura drew upon an example of *bushidō*-inspired bravery from the recent Japanese past.

In 1877, several men in Kōchi Prefecture, a seaward coastal area on the island of Shikoku, were plotting with Saigō Takamori to "betray the Meiji government," as part of the same rebellion mentioned by Tsunajima above.[53] A young national tax official named Watanabe Kunitake (1846–1919) received and accepted a government commission to come from Tokyo to deal with this situation. Politician Ozaki Yukio recalled that, in 1877, this man was "sent to Tosa [Kōchi Prefecture] as governor, though he must still have been only in his twenties. . . . Watanabe arrived alone to take office in an uncertain land without even a bodyguard."[54] He resolutely declared, as the old story goes, that the Meiji government could not permit the prefectural army to join Saigō's forces, and in obedience the leadership in Kōchi did not fight alongside the so-called rebels in the famous war.

Whereas some claimed that by nature, Watanabe was just a brave man, Uemura insisted that only through training had he developed into man capable of such a task. Uemura, like Ozaki Yukio, demonstrated a certain admiration for Watanabe's thorough training in Zen Buddhism and strict regimen based on *bushidō.* In order to achieve this level of self-mastery, Uemura emphasized, Watanabe had employed the same portions of *bushidō* that resonated with the virtues of Christ and his most successful followers. By "cultivating morality, studying knowledge, and exercising discipline," both Watanabe and numerous courageous Christians had developed the will necessary to overcome the challenges that stood before them. For in *bushidō*, as in Christianity, "genuine bravery can only be reached through the cultivation of character."[55] The other overemphasized elements of *bushidō* paled in comparison, and by replacing the objectives of fame and pride with the empowering imperative to "act with love," Christians could in fact elevate *bushidō* into a world-changing moral code.[56]

Rather than trying to sell his vision of Japan to listeners, it would seem that he sought to encourage them to reflect carefully about their own nation-views before taking action outside the church. As historian Dohi Akio has explained, Uemura aimed to empower free-thinking, responsible Christians to take action for the improvement of the nation.[57] By this understanding, it would ultimately be up to these active, thoughtful Japanese Christians to determine the nature and function of the nation as well as its future. Therefore, by concentrating on definitions of the Japanese national polity and the value systems that would guide and motivate its citizens, Uemura was in fact playing an active role in their sociopolitical preparation. However, there were other pastors in Tokyo that addressed the nation and its destiny much more directly and more often than either Uemura or Tsunajima.

The Nation of Ebina Danjō

Among the Protestant pastors in Tokyo during the Meiji and Taishō periods, none have been treated as "nationalist" or "patriotic" as frequently as Hongō Church pastor Ebina Danjō. Although pastors such as Uemura and Tsunajima evinced concern and excitement for the present and future condition of their nation, Ebina's sermons addressed more often and made bolder statements about the nature and primacy of the Japanese nation and Japanese national identity. From making positive reflections on national heroes to isolating the core qualities of the nation and its citizens, he created a Protestant Christianity that could claim to be both Japanese and patriotic. And yet somehow, Ebina's sermons appealed to a mixed audience that included not only right-wing politicians and conservative thinkers, but also left-wing students and activists. An investigation of the nation that he constructed in his sermons reveals a complex mixture of Christian humanism and nationalism that had attractive elements for various types of listeners and defies simplistic categorizations.

Ebina imagined certain elements of Japanese national identity in terms reminiscent of some of Meiji Japan's most conservative nationalist thinkers. In his 1901 sermon on "Our Moral Cultivation," he explained that each Japanese individual's identity was inevitably derived from that person's lineage and ancestors. Contradicting the old Japanese proverb that "breeding more than birth makes a man," Ebina argued that "birth more than breeding makes a man."[58] To determine our nature, "we must know our lineage; knowing our lineage is, namely, knowing what type of thing we are. What kind of parents do I come from? What sort of character do my parents have?"[59] For Ebina, this road of genealogical inquiry inevitably led back for all Japanese to the "founding ancestors of the [Japanese] nation."[60] Just as Imperial University constitutional law professor Hozumi Yatsuka conceptualized the Japanese state as an ethnic group of "blood relatives of the same womb," Ebina linked all Japanese to the country's legendary founding emperor Jinmu and his descendents.[61] Whereas Hozumi employed this logic to place all Japanese under the hereditary rule of the Japanese emperor, Ebina had a different legacy in mind.

For Ebina, the most important element transmitted to his listeners through their ancestors was the "national historical spirit" (*kokumin rekishiteki seishin*) that touched each and every Japanese and made them members of the Japanese nation.[62] To be Japanese was to be "linked to the flow of the pulsing of that great spirit."[63] At home or abroad, "no matter where we go, we are Japanese; the Japanese nation's spirit is our spirit; our spirit is Japan's spirit," he proclaimed.[64] Japanese men and women would always be possessed of the "national historical spirit" that made them typically Japanese, just as historical figures from other countries remained part of and shaped by their respective original national cultures. "Great men transcend their times, but certainly they cannot escape being the product of their nation's character. Plato, Socrates, Aristotle were born in Greece . . . and they remained children of Greece's [national] character. Cicero [and] Caesar built Rome, but nonetheless they still came to be creatures of Rome's [national] character."[65] Just as Rome and Greece had national characters that produced great men, Ebina was quick to show that Japan did as well.

The national historical character of Japan had laid the foundation for the "great Japanese character" (*daijinkaku*) of the admirable men of Japan's recent and distant past.[66] Although Ebina offers no definition for this term, *daijinkaku* appears to have been a somewhat popular term in prewar Japan.[67] In usage, *daijinkaku* carried a similar connotation to that of "the Japanese spirit" (*Yamato damashii*), the inner force bequeathed to the Japanese people by their long line of powerful ancestors and particularly referenced in times of war.[68] In a sermon on "The Beauty of War" given while Japan was in the midst of the Russo-Japanese War in August of 1904, Ebina recalled certain paragons of military bravery who embodied *daijinkaku.* He called to mind ultraloyalist Satsuma samurai "Saigō Takamori's bronze statue in Ueno Park."[69] He spoke of the monument to the founder of Japan's modern military, "the bronze statue of Ōmura Masajirō [standing] before Yasukuni Shrine" with reverence.[70] Looking back to the Gempei War (1180–1185), Ebina praised the bravery and acumen of Minamoto loyalist samurai Nasu no Yoichi (1169–1232), who so famously "shot down the fan target with just one shot."[71] These men represented the embodiment of the *daijinkaku* that was available to all Japanese since the original founders' first manifestations of this trait. Although anyone could claim to personify *daijinkaku,* Ebina proceeded to explain why these men and many like them in Japan's history had truly come to possess this characteristic.

In an age of increasingly large and damaging wars, Ebina used the examples of these military figures to demonstrate that war, a real crucible of "purification," provided Japanese with an "opportunity to develop the great national character."[72] For both soldiers and civilians, Ebina argued that it was in war and such moments of national crisis that "Japanese patriotism . . . was so strikingly manifested" in those Japanese who exerted themselves for the nation.[73] After all, "war is not just a soldiers' war; the whole nation is fighting. . . . After victory, soldiers cannot be proud of themselves alone."[74] Looking around him, he remarked that in this particular instance, he saw the Russo-Japanese War "beginning to produce the great national character" in the Japanese.[75] Toward the end of his sermon, Ebina proclaimed that "seeing the splendid [national] character now being born within our nation, I truly cannot suppress my happiness."[76] It would take a lot more than patriotic displays of *daijinkaku,* however, for Japan to become one of the world's great powers. Ebina called his listeners' attention to other pertinent inherited elements within the Japanese national historical spirit that would serve Japan as it continued marching forward onto the international stage.

Ebina explained that within that same "national historical character," his audience's ancestors had also passed down a certain expeditionary spirit into which all Japanese were now able and strongly encouraged to tap. In response to the countless Westerners who insisted that "the Japanese are an island race; their spirit does not escape the island country mentality," Ebina's 1901 sermon on "Our Moral Cultivation" offered a very different interpretation of Japan's history and national essence. Japan, though indeed an island nation, had reasserted its connection with the "people of the continent" under the leadership of Toyotomi Hideyoshi and general Date Masamune (1567–1636) when they invaded Korea at the end of the sixteenth century.[77] For Ebina, adventurer and explorer Yamada Nagamasa (1590–1630) was another good example of Japan's noninsularity, and his "departure from the island country [to Thailand] displayed our nation's character."[78] The task of uncovering and employing that expeditionary spirit was especially incumbent on the Japanese people of Ebina's day, and in a 1902 sermon on "The New Way of the Warrior," the pastor outlined motivations and strategies for employing this spirit.

To Ebina, it was very important for Japanese to develop the related quality of "martial spirit" (*bu*) in order to facilitate the realization of their inherited expeditionary spirit. It was by exercising this character trait, he said, that Japanese could work for the betterment of Japan beyond its immediate frontiers. For all classes, Ebina recommended that "we thank God who gave this warrior spirit to the Japanese race" and declared that "with this [spirit], wherever the Japanese race goes, they advance, and [we] must not stop advancing."[79] He went further, specifying the applications of a *bu*-inspired expeditionary ethos for different occupational classes in Japan. "The Japanese scholar," for instance, was for Ebina "a warrior, fighting against the cosmos and the universe, conquering them and enlarging humankind's territory."[80] This extended to the Japanese merchant intending to become "prominent in the world" and even to the "farmer."

Just as so many other voices in the Meiji media were inundating farmers with pro-expansion discourse, Ebina spent a significant portion of his sermon on "The New Way of the Warrior" promoting the expeditionary warrior spirit among Japanese farmers. He wholly endorsed Japan's growth beyond its borders and believed strongly in the Japanese people's mandate to spread prosperity and order to its neighbors. The Meiji Japanese state colonized Hokkaidō and Okinawa in the 1870s and Taiwan and Korea in 1895 and 1910, respectively, in an effort to make economic gains and secure their still-sovereign islands against Western colonization.[81] As the result of a "deliberate colonization policy of the Japanese government," Japanese settlers, of whom the majority were farmers, were arriving in Korea and other colonies by the late Meiji period.[82] Politician Nagai Ryūtarō (1881–1944) and historian and statesman Takekoshi Yosaburō (1865–1950) and other ideologues depicted glowing images of paradisiacal lands in Japan's overseas territories that Japanese farmers could come and cultivate without limit.[83] In agreement, Ebina preached that it was the task of Japan's agriculturalists to subdue the "savage wastelands" of "Hokkaido, Taiwan, Manchuria, and Korea . . . taking up their hoes, with their shovels on their shoulders, conquering nature with [their] hands." If they did not go to these places and "cultivate that warrior spirit and plan expeditions, [then] our national agricultural policy . . . is just useless talk," he explained.[84]

As one might expect, Ebina also had a great deal to say about the recently repopularized ideological constellation of "loyalty" and "filial piety" (*chūkō*) that had become intimately linked with the Meiji revival of *bushidō.* One would also expect that, given his reputation for patriotic Christianity, his pronouncements on these two ideals would coincide with the nationalist discourse of progovernment Meiji ideologues. Indeed, he clearly grasped and supported the conservative ideological understanding of the concept in which "the Japanese people's spirit manifests loyalty to [their] sovereign. . . . Loyalty to the monarch is direct loyalty to the state and love for country." Here and elsewhere, he repeatedly emphasized moral values that the Meiji government had enshrined and propagated in both the 1890 Imperial Rescript on Education and the commentaries and glosses of the text that appeared during the last decades of the Meiji period.[85] In his 1902 sermon on new *bushidō,* Ebina admitted to thinking immediately of loyalty and patriotism when he thought of *bushidō.* In the words that followed these statements, however, the Hongō pastor demonstrated that he had a lot more to say about true patriotism and loyalty than the vague language of the Meiji government's moral directives and that his nation-view was in fact very different from that propagated by the state.

Mixed in with all of his praise and admiration for the Japan of yesterday, today, and tomorrow in this sermon, Ebina built a working definition of loyalty that incorporated elements of his influential Christian humanism and casts his nationalism in a new light. The Hongō pastor signaled an upcoming deviation from the mainstream nationalism promoted in his previous sentences when he told listeners that "we must remember not to narrowly limit loyalty to the monarch and filial piety to parents."[86] Using his expanded understanding of loyalty, Ebina then went on to criticize certain soldiers because "on the one hand they boast of loyalty to the emperor, but on the other they inflict insults on the people; this is not true loyalty. If one love's the emperor, that love must necessarily extend to the people as well. . . . [We must] build the nation, person by person, with love for the people . . . for this is the Christian's heart."[87] As Ebina would explain three years later in an October 1905 sermon on Christianity in wartime, loyalty to the monarch meant more than obedience and respect for the imperial family, and patriotism was more than simply proclaiming love for one's country. If "the people are treated as inconsequential, where is the patriotism?" he pondered. The people of Japan together formed "one body . . . [and] without the individual there is no national polity."[88] Going beyond reformulations of loyalty and patriotism, Ebina also addressed the goals and application of the warrior's moral code itself. "The spirit of the warrior way does not mean simply boasting of strength, but helping the weak. . . . He [the warrior] not only sacrifices himself for noble, strong, and great people, but also lends his life for the sake of the weak, small, and humble."[89]

It is perhaps for this reason that Ebina placed such a marked emphasis on improving the nation for the sake of his "forty million countrymen," in 1901, 1902, and 1903, "fifty million fellow countrymen" in 1905, and "sixty million fellow countrymen" in 1920.[90] Contrary to Inoue Tetsujiō's assertion that for Japan's national success "we can only rely on our 40 million fellow countrymen," Ebina instead believed that it was the responsibility of each Christian to serve those fellow countrymen.[91] In the end, the nationalist rhetoric that Ebina propagated from his pulpit left plenty of space for listeners to interpret, adjust, and select relevant elements into a workable and powerful mandate for Christian social activism in the name of both the Japanese nation and humankind.

If even the nationalism of Ebina Danjō is impossible to confine to a single hue, it stands to reason that Japanese Protestant nationalism in Meiji and Taishō Japan was not a single entity but many. The interplay of the three pastors' understandings of and hopes for the nation provides compelling evidence that nationalism is a body of competing conceptualizations of the meaning of the nation rather than one ideology, a debate more than a speech, a journey more than a place. The undeniably present and powerful

Japanese national community was a constant within all of these shifting definitions, and official and popular ideologues alike strove to influence how the Japanese would perceive and interpret it. Although the national government aimed to create a modern nation-state and a unified and dutiful body of imperial subjects, the questions and concerns of Japan's educated elite became a sea of competing and complementary nationalisms by the 1890s. As these individuals searched for ways to think about and interact with the nation and turned to various types of popular ideologues, Protestant pastors became one important source of inspiration and new paradigms.

Tokyo's Protestant pastors formulated their nationalisms as both religious and secular responses to the sociomoral dilemmas inherent in the rise of the modern nation. In doing so, they filled important roles as cultural interpreters and popular ideologues for the most educated, ambitious, worldly members of Japan's new middle class. Ebina espoused an intense nationalism filtered through Christian humanism, brotherhood, and individualism. Uemura selectively criticized and promoted a *bushidō* ideology supported by but beyond the control of the Meiji government.[92] Tsunajima called his listeners to bravery, sacrifice, and self-discipline in the service of God and nation. Tokyo's Protestant pastors, considered together, offered nation-minded Japanese a set of perspectives and impetuses that they could not find elsewhere. Equipped with original, timely, and applicable fragments of these pastors' alternative nation-views, Christians and other churchgoers set about transforming Protestant national imaginaries into reality.

Notes

1. On the nation-state as the predominant social form produced by the conditions of modernity, see Anthony Giddens, *Modernity and Self-Identity: Self and Society in the Late Modern Age* (Stanford, CA: Stanford University Press, 1991), 15.

2. On the nation as an imagined political community whose members' connections are created and reinforced through the modern phenomenon of mass media, see Benedict Anderson, *Imagined Communities: Reflections on the Origin and Spread of Nationalism* (London: Verso, 1991), 6–7.

3. For brief summaries of government efforts to foster nationalism among Japanese citizens, see Andrew Gordon, *A Modern History of Japan from Tokugawa*

Times to the Present (New York: Oxford University Press, 2003), 111–113; Carol Gluck, *Japan's Modern Myths: Ideology in the Late Meiji Period* (Princeton: Princeton University Press, 1985), 102; and Takeshi Fujitani, *Splendid Monarchy: Power and Pageantry in Modern Japan* (Berkeley: University of California Press, 1998), 42–65.

4. Gluck, *Modern Myths*, 10. Gluck has employed the term *minkan* to distinguish these individuals from ideologues directly affiliated (officially and unofficially) with the national government.

5. See Kenneth Pyle, *The New Generation in Meiji Japan: Problems of Cultural Identity, 1885–1895* (Stanford, CA: Stanford University Press, 1969), 36, 42–43. Pyle provides insightful summaries of sections on national destiny in Tokutomi Sohō's *The Future of Japan.*

6. On the background of some of Tokyo's most famous Protestant pastors in the Meiji and Taishō periods, see Irwin Scheiner, *Christian Converts and Social Protest in Meiji Japan* (Berkeley: University of California, 1970).

7. For an argument for the existence of multiple nationalisms, see Prasenjit Duara, *Rescuing History from the Nation: Questioning Narratives of Modern China* (Chicago: University of Chicago Press, 1997), 8. See Duara, *Rescuing History*, 10, for an introduction to Duara's neologism "nation-view."

8. Aasulv Lande, *Meiji Protestantism in History and Historiography: A Comparative Study of Japanese and Western Interpretation of Early Protestantism in Japan* (New York: Peter Lang, 1989), 92.

9. Duara, *Rescuing History*, 8.

10. See Shuma Iwai, "Japanese Christianity in the Meiji Era: An Analysis of Ebina Danjo's Perspective on Shintoistic Christianity," *Transformation: An International Journal of Holistic Mission Studies* 25, no. 4 (2008): 195–204; Wada Yōichi, ed., *Dōshisha no shisōkatachi* [Dōshisha's Thinkers] (Kyoto: Dōshisha Daigaku Seikyō Shuppanbu, 1965–1973); and Dōshisha Daigaku Jinbun Kagaku Kenkyūjo, ed., *Kumamoto bando kenkyū: Nihon Purotesutantoisumu, genryū to kaiten* [Study of the Kumamoto Band: Japanese Protestantism, Origins and Development] (Tokyo: Misuzu Shogo, 1965). Other works on Ebina's nationalism include Imanaka Kanshi, "Ebina Danjō to sono shisō" [Ebina Danjō and His Thought], *Kirisutokyō shakai mondai kenkyū* 23 (1975): 1–27; Kuniyasu Take, "Ebina Danjō no sensō ron" [Ebina Danjō's Arguments on War], *Kirisutokyō shakai mondai kenkyū* 23 (1975): 44–82; and Sekioka Issei, "Ebina Danjō ni okeru sekaishugi to Nihonshugi" [Ebina Danjō on Internationalism and Japanism], *Kirisutokyō shakai mondai kenkyū* 44 (1995): 26–48.

11. Tsunajima Kakichi, *Gyakkyō no fukuin* [The Gospel of Adversity] (Tokyo: Keiseisha, 1924), 7–8.

12. Ibid., 7–8.

13. Ibid.

14. Ibid., 121–122. Given the details provided in this quote, it is reasonable to infer that this sermon dates from 1916 or 1917.

15. See Judges 7 RSV.

16. On this incident, see Naoko Shimazu, *Japanese Society at War Death, Memory and the Russo-Japanese War* (Cambridge, UK: Cambridge University Press, 2009), 123–124, 202–203.

17. Tsunajima, *Gyakkyō,* 106.

18. Ibid., 105.

19. Ibid., 107.

20. Ibid., 109.

21. Ibid., 111.

22. Ibid., 110.

23. For an illustration of the means by which samurai learned to practice self-cultivation, see Marleen Kassel, *Tokugawa Confucian Education: The Kangien Academy of Hirose Tanso: 1782–1856* (Albany: State University of New York Press, 1996). On the inculcation of loyalty and filial piety in Japanese students during the Meiji period, see Wilbur M. Fridell, "Government Ethics Textbooks in Late Meiji Japan," *Journal of Asian Studies* 29, no. 4 (1970): 823–833.

24. *Kirisutokyō sekai,* no. 1193 (July 12, 1906).

25. See Tsunajima Kakichi, *Hai-Nichi mondai to Kirisutokyō* [The Anti-Japanese Problem and Christianity] (Tokyo: Keiseisha, 1917).

26. J. Nelson Jennings, *Theology in Japan: Takakura Tokutaro, 1885–1934* (New York: University Press of America, 2005), 126.

27. See Walter A. Skya, *Japan's Holy War: The Ideology of Radical Shinto Ultranationalism* (Durham, NC: Duke University Press, 2009); and Richard H. Minear, *Japanese Tradition and Western Law: Emperor, State, and Law in the Thought of Hozumi Yatsuka* (Cambridge, MA: Harvard University Press, 1970).

28. Uemura Masahisa, *Uemura Masahisa Zenshū* [The Collected Works of Uemura Masahisa], vol. 1 (Tokyo: Uemura Zenshū Kankōkai, 1931–1934), 169.

29. Ibid.

30. Ibid., 170.

31. See Jennings, *Theology;* and Masao Takenaka, *Reconciliation and Renewal in Japan* (New York: Student Volunteer Movement for Christian Missions and Friendship Press, 1957).

32. For the original text of this epic poem, see Johann Wolfgang von Goethe, "Hermann and Dorothea," in *The Harvard Classics,* vol. 19, part 4, trans. Ellen Frothingham (New York: P. F. Collier and Son, 1909–1914).

33. Uemura, *Zenshū,* 170.

34. Ibid., 174.

35. Leo T. S. Ching, *Becoming Japanese: Colonial Taiwan and the Politics of Identity Formation* (Berkeley: University of California Press, 2001), 137–143.

36. Ibid., 174.

37. Ibid., 172.

38. On the pervasiveness of the "love suicide" in turn-of-the-century Japan, see the stories of famous Meiji author and pulse-taker Higuchi Ichiyō. See also Timothy J. Van Compernolle, *The Uses of Memory: The Critique of Modernity in the Fiction of Higuchi Ichiyō* (Cambridge, MA: Harvard University Press, 2006).

39. On the popularity of *bushidō* and *bushidō*-related heroes in the Meiji period, see See Cyril H. Powles, "Bushidō: Its Admirers and Its Critics," in *Nitobe Inazō: Japan's Bridge across the Pacific,* ed. John F. Howes (Oxford, UK: Westview Press, 1995), 107–118; John Tucker, "Tokugawa Intellectual History and Prewar Ideology: The Case of Inoue Tetsujirō, Yamaga Sokō, and the Forty-Seven Rōnin," *Sino-Japanese Studies* 14 (2002): 35–70; and G. Cameron Hurst, III, "Death, Honor, and Loyalty: The Bushidō Ideal," *Philosophy East and West* 40, no. 4 (1990): 511–527.

40. Tucker, "Prewar Ideology," 3; Inoue Tetsujirō, *Bushidō sōsho,* 3 vols. (Tokyo: Hakubunkan, 1906–1909).

41. Daidōji Yūzan, *Budō shoshinshū* [Initiation to the Warrior Way], ed. Tetsushi Furukawa (Tokyo: Iwanami Shoten, 1943; original 1720), 161.

42. Uemura, *Zenshū,* 189.

43. Ibid.

44. Ibid., 185.

45. Ibid., 192.

46. Ibid., 191. "Fujimichō," the name of the neighborhood in which the school and Fujimichō Church were located, can be translated literally to mean "the neighborhood that looks at Mount Fuji," making this particular song a logical choice.

47. Uemura, *Zenshū,* 192.

48. See Sandra T. W. Davis, "Treaty Revision," in *Japan in Transition: Thought and Action in the Meiji Era, 1868–1912,* ed. Hilary Conroy, Sandra T. W. Davis, and Wayne Patterson (London: Associated University Presses, 1984), 151–173.

49. See Inazō Nitobe, *Bushido: The Soul of Japan* (Philadelphia: Leeds and Biddle, 1900). Also see Hurst, *Death, Honor, and Loyalty,* 511–514.

50. Uemura, *Zenshū,* 185.

51. Jennings, *Theology,* 121.

52. Uemura, *Zenshū,* 194.

53. Ibid.

54. Yukio Ozaki, *The Autobiography of Ozaki Yukio: The Struggle for Constitutional Government in Japan,* trans. Fujiko Hara and ed. Marius Jansen (Princeton: Princeton University Press, 2001), 136.

55. Uemura, *Zenshū*, 195.

56. Ibid., 197.

57. Akio Dohi, "Christianity and Politics in the Taishō Period of Democracy, Part 1," *Journal of Japanese Religions* 5, no. 4 (1969): 1–24.

58. In Japanese, the phrase reads *uji yori sodachi*. For English translations of this common phrase, see Daniel C. Buchanan, *Japanese Proverbs and Sayings* (Norman: University of Oklahoma Press, 1965), 104; and Basil H. Chamberlain, *Things Japanese: Being Notes on Various Subjects Connected with Japan* (London: J. Murray, 1905), 399.

59. Ebina Danjō, "Gojin no shūyō" [Our Cultivation], *Shinjin* 1, no. 7 (1901).

60. Ibid.

61. Skya, *Holy War*, 56. Skya has translated this phrase from Hozumi Yatsuka, *Kokumin kyōiku: Aikokushin* [National Education: Patriotism] (Tokyo: Yuhikaku, 1897), 16.

62. Ebina, "Gojin no shūyō."

63. Ibid.

64. Ibid.

65. Ibid.

66. Ebina Danjō, "Sensō no bi" [The Beauty of War], *Shinjin* 5, no. 8 (1904).

67. For examples of this term's use, see Maekawa Shinjirō, *Zetsudai naru jinkaku* [Tremendous Character] (Tokyo: Seikokai Shuppan Sha, 1929); and Hiroyoshi Saiga , *Saigō nanshūoū: daijinkan no ikan* [Venerable Man of the South, Saigō: Magnificent Example of the Great Character] (Tokyo: Shizendō Shoten, 1919).

68. On *Yamato damashii* and its wartime popularity, see Gluck, *Modern Myths*, 136.

69. On Saigō see Charles S. Yates, "Saigo Takamori in the Emergence of Meiji Japan," *Modern Asian Studies* 28, no. 3 (1994): 449–474. It is worth noting that Hiroyoshi Saiga, author of one of the few works with *daijinkaku* in its title, used this term to praise Takamori Saigō just as Ebina did.

70. Ebina, "Sensō no bi." For background on the origins and importance of the shrine, see John Nelson, "Social Memory as Ritual Practice: Commemorating Spirits of the Military Dead at Yasukuni Shinto Shrine," *Journal of Asian Studies* 62, no. 2 (2003): 443–467.

71. Ebina, "Sensō no bi." Here Ebina refers to the incident written of in the *Heike monogatari* in which Nasu no Yoichi shot down a red fan, thought to be a trap, hoisted up on a Taira vessel by a lady of the court. See the story in Helen Craig McCullough, *The Tale of the Heike* (Stanford, CA: Stanford University Press, 1988), 367–369.

72. Ebina, "Sensō no bi."

73. Ibid.

74. Ibid.

75. Ibid.

76. Ibid.

77. Ebina, "Gojin no shūyō." Here, Ebina is referring to Hideyoshi's ultimately unsuccessful attempts to invade China through Korea in 1592 and 1598. See Mary Elizabeth Berry, *Hideyoshi* (Cambridge, MA: Harvard University Press, 1982).

78. Ebina, "Gojin no shūyō."

79. Ebina Danjō, "Shin bushidō" [The New Way of the Warrior], *Shinjin* 3, no. 10 (1902); reprinted in *Ebina Danjō no sekkyōshuū* [The Collected Sermons of Ebina Danjō] (Tokyo: Shinkyō Shuppansha, 1973), 86.

80. Ibid.

81. For an overview of Japanese colonization, see Ramon H. Myers and Mark R. Peattie, eds., *The Japanese Colonial Empire, 1895–1945* (Princeton, NJ: Princeton University Press, 1984).

82. Thomas F. Millard, "Japanese Immigration into Korea," *Annals of the American Academy of Political and Social Science* 34, no. 2 (1909): 185.

83. Myers and Peattie, *Japanese Colonial Empire*, 89.

84. Ebina, "Shin bushidō," reprinted in Ebina, *Ebina Danjō no sekkyōshū*, 86.

85. For the translated text of the Imperial Rescript, see Gluck, *Modern Myths*, 121.

86. Ebina, "Shin bushidō," reprinted in Ebina, *Ebina Danjō no sekkyōshū*, 86.

87. Ibid., 87.

88. Ebina Danjō, "Ima wa kitō toki nari" [Now It's Time to Pray], *Shinjin* 6, no. 10 (1905).

89. Ibid.

90. Ebina Danjō, "Kirisutokyō to demokurashii" [Christianity and Democracy], *Shinjin* 21, no. 6 (1920).

91. Gluck, *Modern Myths*, 130.

92. On the explicit links between national education and *bushidō*, as manifested in documents such as the 1890 Imperial Rescript on Education and the Bōshin Rescript of 1908, see Yushi Ito, *Yamaji Aizan and His Time: Nationalism and Debating Japanese History* (Kent, UK: Global Oriental, 2007), 426.

9

"Smelling of Pickled Radish, Not Butter"

The Wartime Search for a Christianity Viable in Japan

Gregory Vanderbilt

The question of what might constitute "Japanese Christianity" came to the surface in the 1930s, at the time that military aggression on the Asian continent and increased political controls and mobilization of the populace, recognizable as fascism, were swept up into ideology that promised the "overcoming of modernity" and the purification of the national body. At that time, the first generation of Protestant Christian leaders, who had been born into samurai families before Christianity's relegalization in 1873 and encountered the long-proscribed "foreign" religion within questions of how Japan might attain the civilization needed to survive in the world, were passing from the scene. The generation that was assuming leadership was one that had been born into the ideology historians and activists have called "the emperor system" and was now looking beyond aspirations to cosmopolitan culture to grounding in their own nation, as it was being defined for them as much as they tried to define it themselves. Despite reverberations in a different key with the struggle that wracked the German churches of the day, theirs was at the same time a conversation about the viability of Christianity itself as it travels to new situations. This essay returns to the efforts and dilemmas experienced by one Christian of that second generation and his circle, moving from the context of participation in religion within the nation to the text of a Christian magazine he edited as the war intensified, the *Voice at the Lakeside.*

Context: Religion and Nation in the Late 1930s

At eight in the morning on August 13, 1937, five weeks after the war in China escalated with the "incident" at the Marco Polo Bridge near Beijing, a scene that was both startling and routine unfolded at the Imperial Shrine at Ise. Leading a delegation of nine, a Japanese Christian named Yoshida Etsuzō (1890–1942) performed the act of worship before the shrine, announcing himself as the representative of the Omi Brotherhood, an independent Christian community started some three decades earlier as the Omi Mission, when a young American teacher had come to teach at a rural commercial school as part of the Student Volunteer Movement and influenced a number of students, including Yoshida, toward declarations of Christian faith and life. In stilted formal language, he read aloud the ritual prayer, or *norito:* "Prosper and favor the reign of the Emperor who rules over the Great Eight Islands as Manifest Kami and make it a majestic reign and a prosperous reign. Grant that the august person of the Emperor be kept in ever increasing health and grace." He declared that the "spiritual, educational, and social work" of the Omi Brotherhood, the name the organization had adopted three years earlier to shed the foreign overtones of "mission," reverberated with the awakening "great Japanese spirit" and sought to bring peace to the people of Omi and to the countries of the world as they were incorporated into the Great Japanese Empire, the land of Japan's deities or *kami no kuni,* a term that, due to nineteenth-century translators and the language's vagueness regarding pluralization also referred to the Kingdom of God. Another member of the group then offered a ritual song: "At the sacred barrier of Ise, everlasting prosperity / Oh shrine that is the foundation of the Imperial Line / Inner Shrine of the Fifty Bells, Shrine of a Thousand Ages, of Eternity / Here we ever come to worship, purifying ourselves." Finally, together they performed the ritual two bows, two claps, and two bows, and then went home to Shiga prefecture.[1]

The episode did not pass unnoticed. Yoshida's guide that day, the pastor-turned-novelist Okino Iwasaburō was exuberant over this "unforgettable" act because, he said, Yoshida had gone to the shrine as a Christian, in "Christian attire" (his silk hat and formal morning suit, apparently), and announced himself to the *kami* (the deities revered at shrines—in this case, Amaterasu, the sun *kami* and imperial ancestress) as a Christian. (Yoshida had not, in fact, mentioned Christianity, but he had given both his own name and that of the Omi Brotherhood.) There was, declared Okino, no precedent of a Buddhist priest going in priestly garb to this "great shrine that surpasses shrine rankings, a shrine where the entire nation of Japan pays reverence [*sūkei*], not as Christians or as Buddhists." According to Okino, going to the shrine as a member of the nation meant that the shrine could not be understood as a site for religion (*shūkyō*), as defined in both law and academia, and that its existence did not infringe on the freedom of religious belief (*shinkyō no jiyū*) protected (but limited and ambiguously defined) by the 1889 Constitution. Nor were Christians in danger of violating the commandment against the worship of false or other gods, because the *kami* were specific to life in Japan: to emphasize this point Okino replaced the single Chinese character for *kami* that nineteenth-century translators had taken to indicate the God of Judeo-Christian monotheism with a compound meaning "hidden body." Okino offered no hint of awareness of the Christians in Korea and Taiwan who had refused to be coerced into shrine worship out of loyalty to both their Christian faith and their own nation.[2]

Having read about the visit in Okino's 1939 book *The Shrine Issue,* the Baptist missionary and Shintō expert Daniel Clarence Holtom criticized this action by "a group of prominent Christians," situating their visit as a stage in the accommodation of Japanese Christian leaders to the demands of the Japanese state, which he saw as having manipulated the primitive religiosity of local shrines into a nationalistic religious system, or what historians would call State Shintō. In the Haskell Lectures in Comparative Religion he gave at the University of Chicago in 1940 and published three years later as *Modern Japan and Shinto Nationalism: A Study of Present-Day Trends in Japanese Religions,* Holtom argued that with the presentation of a *norito* at the shrine to the sun goddess, Yoshida (left unnamed by Holtom) had gone beyond what many Christians were doing in participating in shrine rituals, although not as far as those who were making efforts to "adjust their faith as followers of Jesus to the claims of nationalism . . . in an ethical apologetic which makes the chief moral requirements of Christianity identical with those demanded by the state."[3]

Between Okino's and Holtom's interpretations lay questions. Why and how had Yoshida gone to the shrine? There was an expediency explanation, upheld by the presence of Yuasa Hachirō, who had been embroiled in controversy as the chancellor of Doshisha University as the result of such incidents as the one in which a portrait of the school's founder, Niijima Jō, in its high school's martial arts hall had been replaced by a small shrine containing a talisman representing the Emperor Jinmu. As a Christian university with international and missionary networks, Doshisha was under increasing scrutiny from military authorities at the same time that demands for so-called *kokutai* clarification, routing liberals and others from university faculties around Japan, were threatening its academic integrity.[4] This explanation occurred to Yoshida's mentor and coworker Wm. Merrell Vories (by then naturalized as a Japanese imperial subject named Hitotsuyanagi Mereru) in 1944 as he was reading the manuscript of Okino's biography of Yoshida:

> In the night, last night, I got a definite guidance concerning the incident of *E. V. Y.'s norito* at *Ise,* in 1936–7 (?),—which we were reading of in the biography m.s. yesterday. . . . Because *E. V. Y.* was a *riji* [trustee] of Doshisha and active in its defense *vs. investigation* of alleged disloyalty, he feared *O*[mi] *B*[rotherhood] *would* be next victim and risked trouble for himself to save it. Thus his *motive* was good but the *method questionable.* It broke O.B. regulations: *"Representing it"* officially *without authorization;* fear overbalanced Faith; *not convincing* to a thoughtful investigation; caused internal and external objections. It may have marked the definite turn of O.B. from Faith in GOD's GUIDANCE to dependence upon *political* and *financial* strengths (much as the *ancient church* turned, with Constantine leading).[5]

While Vories' objections showed tensions with Yoshida that had developed as their beliefs and aspirations diverged, he also recognized the problems his fellow Christians had long faced in relation to the state, even comparing the situation to what had happened in the transformation of a faith persecuted within the civic religion of the Roman caesars to a church with the imprimatur of the empire. Fifty years earlier, the complicated place of

Christians in the Japanese state had been made apparent in the controversy that followed the refusal of a Christian teacher at the First Higher School named Uchimura Kanzō to bow before a copy of the then newly promulgated Imperial Rescript on Education, the central text of what historians and critics have called Japan's emperor system, which filled editorial pages with the question of how Christians could be loyal to the nation and its emperor.

Yoshida offered his own answer when he announced the visit to Ise in the editorial of the September issue of the Omi Brotherhood's Japanese-language magazine *Kohan no koe,* referred to hereafter by its English name, *Voice at the Lakeside.* Urging readers that the Omi Brotherhood had a "special calling" in this "time of crisis," he explained that "at the same time as I believe in a religion of Christian lineage, I was born a Japanese and am devoted to the service of Amaterasu and the Imperial Ancestors and to the Total Mobilization of the Nation." Readers could then turn to the facing page, where the large and bold characters "Worship" (*reihai*) were surrounded with photos of Protestant morning services around the Brotherhood—in its Mentholatum factory, architecture office, and tuberculosis sanatorium's chapel—and at the local Hachiman Church, including photos of the pastors, the choir, and children in sundresses at Sunday school.[6] The implied distinction between the performance of ritual reverence at Ise and the worship that went on in church and in daily life paralleled Yoshida's pairing of himself as a Japanese and as a Christian, and made it clear that what had happened at Ise was to be understood as categorically different from Christianity, in no way violating the First Commandment. When Yoshida described himself as believing in "a religion of Christian lineage" (*Kirisuto ryū no shūkyō*), the key term was *shūkyō,* literally "sectarian teaching" and the favored translation for the nineteenth-century concept of religion. In Japan the term had figured in a long-standing discussion of "religion and the state" and, unlike the state churches of Europe and the early United States, it was plural, with a state-recognized place for Christians, notable in Japan more for influence than numbers, following the 1912 Assembly of the Three Religions. Two months before going to Ise, Yoshida had offered his own definition of *shūkyō,* in the pages of *New Omi,* a newspaper the Brotherhood published for local audiences for several years in the 1930s, invoking the key concept of the 1920s *seikatsu,* or daily life, while maintaining the other power of God:

> True religion is the reality of humanity's original *seikatsu* (if you look around the world, you will see there are good ways of living greater than morality). It is power itself. It is unity between us and God. It is unending joy. It is becoming incapable of sin. It is healthy spiritual and physical ways of living. It is like a spring of divine wisdom and spiritual consciousness. It is not enlightenment. It is not a life of quiet sitting with only faith. It is a power that surpasses explanation, unlimited energy and ceaseless turning on the inside revealed in humanitarian and moral life that naturally brings light to the hearts of the world.[7]

But religion could not exist entirely in the private realms of the soul. In its ethical and evangelical imperatives it had to be public, and, as such, it was object of both academic inquiry and government regulation. Okino's *The Shrine Issue* was bound together with *Japan and Christianity* by the educator and journalist Tagawa Daikichirō, who closed his half of the volume this way: "Christianity, as something which aids the development of man's spiritual life, has a future in which it can make a great contribution to the spiritual world of Japan, and we must bear that responsibility."[8] His argument turned on the responsibilities of Japanese Christians in the immediate context of both the war in China and the government's release that March of its curriculum of emperor-system ideology *Kokutai no hongi* (translated as *Fundamentals of Our National Polity*), but the most immediate political context to which Tagawa directed *Japan and Christianity* and his *State and Religion*, published the previous year, was scrutiny of Christians and an inadequate legal standing for religion. Tagawa entered the fray over the definition of religion when he provided a detailed account of a March 1938 incident in which the Osaka Military Police sent a questionnaire to twenty-four Christian leaders, reprinting the questions from the newspaper and offering answers from "one Christian" as well as his own suggestions. The police questions were based on a plural and comparative definition of religion: they raised a series of equivalencies of deity (Emperor and Christ), sacred text (Imperial Rescript on Education and Bible), and education program and then inquired into questions of false images and freedom of belief. To a question (number 3) concerning "the relationship between our Emperor and the Christian God," Tagawa reported the Christian's answer that "our nation has a national polity the axis of which is the

Emperor, who is a direct continuation of an imperial line unbroken for ages and unique in the world, and honors the Emperor as a living *kami.* This is the intuitive conviction of the national people, which supersedes abstraction. This ideal is a historical fact and differs from a theoretical view of the divine." Tagawa's own answer added that the "*kami* of heaven and earth" mentioned in a poem by the Meiji Empress was worshiped as if identical with the God Christians believe in.[9] Yoshida was also following the controversy and reprinted answers proposed by Matsuyama Tsunejirō, a longtime Diet member and leader in Kozaki Hiromichi's Reinanzaka Church, in his Q&A column in *Voice at the Lakeside.* In his answers, Matsuyama sought to maintain the integrity of Christianity and of Japanese life, defined through imperial rescripts (but not the Constitution) and through the ideologies attached to them, including "so-called Imperial Way-ism," a term that had more relevance in Buddhism. Matsuyama's answer to question 3 played with the universal and the particular by first defining the God of Christianity as the creator of the universe and then explaining how God's existence reached the thought and *seikatsu* of each people: in the case of Japan, the three *kami* described by "the ancient historians" as being present in the heavenly realm of Takamagahara at the origin of the universe "correspond" to the Christianity Trinity.[10]

The second political context Tagawa addressed was the passage of the Religious Organizations Law, or Shūkyō Dantai Hō, of 1939. For Tagawa, the law presented a fair and impartial form of regulation of religious organization, as opposed to belief or practice, that was normal in modern nations. It marked progress over two earlier bills, put forth in 1899 and in 1927, which had sought to regulate belief. Indeed, this shift to the regulation of organizations was one reason many Christians welcomed the new law. The law, which named Christian churches alongside Buddhist denominations, Shintō sects, and "others" as its objects, seemed to promise a kind of stability lacking in the regime for religious regulation taking shape in the late 1930s based on the Peace Preservation Law of 1925 and on nebulous prosecutions for lèse-majesté. Christians had commented little on the suppressions of new religions like Ōmoto-kyō and had largely embraced their own place within the recognized religions incorporated into the emperor system in contrast to the suppressed cult. The following year, as celebrations were held of the supposed 2,600th anniversary of the founding of the nation, Japanese Protestant churches were consolidated into one body, the

Nihon Kirisuto Kyōdan, which took the untranslatable new word *kyōdan* from the law for its name, unlike its English version, United Church of Christ in Japan. Yoshida greeted the new body as the beginnings of a new age, for just as seventy years passed between Christianity's arrival and its suppression in the sixteenth and seventeenth centuries, so too had seventy years passed since the ban had been lifted. Now that, under the New Order, Japan had become a leading nation of the world, Western dogmas were unnecessary and inappropriate for "its incomparable *kokutai,*" and Christians should celebrate by flying the rising sun flag and gathering before Amaterasu.[11] Sharing Tagawa's feeling of responsibility for the nation, Yoshida had none of his caution in his enthusiasm for a Christianity that appeared to him to be viable in Japan even as it was "overcoming modernity," even as it was produced in wartime.

Text: Japanese Christianities in *Voice at the Lakeside*

In the March 9, 1934, internal weekly newsletter of the Omi Brotherhood, as the Omi Mission had been reborn the previous month, Yoshida reported that five thousand copies of its magazine *Voice at the Lakeside* had been distributed that month and announced his intention to make it into an "All-Christian *King*" on a par with the popular national mass magazine.[12] Yoshida was aspiring to a mass-market readership extending to factory girls and the "kids" of farming and fishing villages, setting his project against intellectual magazines like Ebina Danjō's *New Man* (*Shinjin*), organizational magazines like the YMCA's *The Pioneer* (*Kaitakusha*), and the Salvation Army's *Voice of the Times* (*Toki no koe*), and magazines tied to individuals like Kagawa Toyohiko's *Pillar of Cloud* (*Kumo no hashira*) and Yanaihara Tadao's newsletter later known as *Good News* (*Kashin*). The 253rd of what Yoshida, Vories, and two coworkers had started in July 1912 as a sixteen-page pamphlet with the manifesto "fervent in our feelings of patriotism, we raise the banner of love for God and love for our neighbor as we seek to do battle with all the darkness in the world" now contained fifty pages and had a photograph of the scenic rocky coast of Lake Biwa, a reminder of the Sea of Galilee, on the cover. On its back cover was an advertisement for Mentholatum, the well-known skin salve the Brotherhood manufactured and sold in Japan and its empire, that had been run in China: alongside a young woman in a *cheongsam* were two captions, one giving the Chinese name for Mentholatum and another celebrating the enthronement of the emperor of the Japanese puppet state of Manchukuo. Inside were an essay in which Vories explained his five ideals for the Omi Brotherhood—united cooperation, demonstration, faith, efficiency, and modeling the Kingdom of God—and the transcript of a lecture titled "Japan and the World" he had given at a Christian university in Tokyo, where he explained that Christianity was the right preparation for a future era of "scientific internationalism." Elsewhere in the issue Shimizu Yasuzō, a Japanese missionary to China, wrote on "the Christian Church in Japan of the Future" and Yanaihara Tadao, the soon-to-be controversial Tokyo Imperial University professor, addressed the question of "Christianity on Japanese terms," a premise he would reverse a few months later as "Japan on Christian terms."

The pages of *Voice at the Lakeside* in this period invite close reading as an entry point into Christianity in the period the historian Dohi Akio called the "manic" consolidation of empire and the emperor-centered state.[13] By using the writings Yoshida assembled as materials for a small intellectual history, I avoid the question of a theological canon and instead look to the conversation he orchestrated as editor of the *Voice at the Lakeside* about how Christianity could be viable in Japan.[14] As the magazine fulfilled Yoshida's ambitions to engage a broad readership with the question of how Christianity could be viable in Japan, most important, however, was "Nihonteki Kirisutokyō," rendered here as "Christianity on Japanese terms." Like other streams, including the theology of Karl Barth as read in Japan, it rejected modernist theology, including experience as touchstone and daily life as the site of demonstration, and put Christianity on the terms of an absolute, the nation. A Christian intellectual historian named Kasahara Yoshimitsu writing in 1974 divided the writings of "Nihonteki Kirisutokyō" into three categories of syncretism—blending, coexistence, and contact—before concluding both that Christianity is never "pure" but that the "Japanese" elements with which it came into contact could be "of the ethnic nation" (*minzoku*) or of the "political power of the state" (*kokka no kenryoku*).[15] More recently the church historian Hara Makoto has not only been careful to situate those writers who called for "Nihonteki Kirisutokyō" in the perilous ground between "orthodox evangelicalism" and the emperor system, but also to note that it might well be, in the words of Kumano Yoshitaka, a theologian of that day, "a healthy desire for the church" to build "relationality" with the other, the neighbor.[16]

In defining this "Nihonteki Kirisutokyō," it is worth pausing over the suffix *-teki,* a grammatical unit and character taken directly from Chinese to assign one noun to another. To emphasize that it has none of the impressionistic quality of the indigenous suffix *-rashii* and instead functions like the conjunction *no,* akin to the English "of," and that it is always preceded by and helps to define another complex noun, I have translated it, particularly in its 1930s usage, as "on the terms of." As with the discussions of *seikatsu* during the 1920s, questioning the *-teki* also implied that the West could be removed from the religion: Christianity in and for Japan need not be Seiyōteki Kirisutokyō (Christianity on Western terms).[17] Two earlier examples of *-teki* modifying Christianity could be found in the pages of *Voice at the Lakeside* in 1929 and 1930, in two series by Shimizu, who followed his 1929 "Advocating Christianity on Oriental Terms," in which he set out to argue that Christianity was already Oriental since Jesus was himself an Oriental (*tōyōjin*) who sat on the floor in the Upper Room and had none of the aggressive traits of the Anglo-Saxon, with another titled "Advocating Society-*teki* Christianity," in which he began with a biography of Karl Marx, whom he identified along with Jesus Christ as "the greatest of the many great Jews in history," and then turned to Walter Rauschenbusch when he called on his readers to overcome the "versus" in the common opposition between the "individual gospel" and the "social gospel."[18]

Both Kasahara and Hara point to the theologian Fujiwara Fujio, who invoked a phrase associated with science in coming up with his definition in his 1941 *Christianity and the Japanese Spirit:* "Christians must not forget that 'Christianity may have no national borders, but Christians have homelands.'" As he argued for removing what was specific to other national cultures from Christianity, Fujiwara Fujio explained that he was neither seeking "Japan-ification" (*Nihonka*) nor trying to locate points of identity or of commonality between the Christian religion and something Japanese. At the extreme, even inquiring into any equivalency between the emperor and Christ or between the Bible and the Imperial Rescript on Education or the *Kojiki* and other ancient texts was to return to the interrogations Christian leaders described by Tagawa had been subjected to by the special police. Instead these theologians were attempting to apply what Okino and others had argued about *shūkyō* and the original spirit of the *kami:* that, rather than serving as a measure of civilization, Christianity had a history in each place it had been and that, like Buddhism, Confucianism, and Shintō, its form in Japan would grow to fit the historical conditions of life there. What Fujiwara's strategy had in common with the three others he pointed to—calling for adaptation or assimilation, looking for collapsibility into sameness, seeking out points of commonality or correspondence—was the historical moment and the centrality of the concept of the Japanese spirit. In the wake of the "clarification of the *kokutai*" movement that pushed university professors and administrators like Yuasa into difficult positions, these Christian writers had before them the Ministry of Education's *Kokutai no hongi.* As a central text of the emperor-system ideology and State Shintō, the booklet implied that Christianity belonged to the West, with its fundamentally different ways of being. For example, it argued that "in our country, 'God' is not a terrible being, but one that extendeth divine help and is fondly esteemed and [toward whom] gratitude is felt." Yet, in a section titled "Ceremonial Rites and Morality," it also made clear that Buddhism—"a faith as well as a rule of morals and at the same time a system of knowledge"—had been introduced from abroad and "hence, its introduction into our country saw its fusion into and sublimation in our national spirit; and it developed in a way befitting the people." Though Buddhism "assimilated in this manner" had more than a thousand-year head start in "permeating the national people's *seikatsu*" and "inspiring the national people's spirit," *Kokutai no hongi* appeared to conclude that Christianity might undergo the same process.[19]

Yanaihara's 1934 essay was, in fact, the first time the words *Nihonteki Kirisutokyō* appeared in *Voice at the Lakeside.* Eulogizing the Nonchurch theologian Ebara Banri, Yanaihara recalled their teacher Uchimura Kanzō's famous statement in English of a decade earlier:

> I love two J's and no third: one is Jesus, and the other is Japan . . . my faith is not a circle with one center; it is an ellipse with two centers. My heart and mind revolve around the two dear names. And I know that one strengthens the other; Jesus strengthens and purifies my love for Japan; and Japan clarifies and objectivises my love for Jesus. Were it not for the two, I would become a mere dreamer, a fanatic, an amorphous universal man.

As early as 1920, Uchimura had written of a "Japanese Christianity" as a way of puncturing American Christians' claims of universality: this Japanese Christianity would be "Christianity received directly from God with no foreign intermediary; no more, no less. . . . Only Japanese Christianity will save Japan and Japanese." Though he wrote, again in both languages, that "the spirit of Japan inspired by the Almighty is Japanese Christianity," Uchimura made it clear he was more interested in national pride than in naming a national spirit.[20] In 1934, Yanaihara had been professor of colonial policy at Tokyo Imperial University for a decade, but three years later he would be forced from his position following his lament for his nation's loss of ideals as a "Kingdom of God" in the wake of its increasing aggression in China. It is not clear how Yanaihara came to publish "Christianity on Japanese Terms," which was first printed in his own newsletter the previous December, and a follow-up titled "Japan on Christian Terms" in *Voice at the Lakeside,* but perhaps he exchanged the prestige of a Tokyo Imperial University professor and Nonchurch movement leader for a broader audience and the Omi Brotherhood's image as an organization independent of mission boards.

In his eulogy for Ebara, Yanaihara introduced two unexpected Japanese thinkers to explain what he meant by "Christianity on Japanese terms." The first thinker was the thirteenth-century Buddhist prophet Nichiren, whose sect could, Yanaihara felt, be understood as "Buddhism on Japanese terms." Nichiren's sect had overcome the "degeneracy" of *nenbutsu* sects (faith sects based on calling out the name of Amida Buddha) and found the higher truths of Buddhism and sought to save the Japanese nation. From Nichiren, who had also been one of Yanaihara's mentor Uchimura's "representative men of Japan," he turned to the materialist philosopher Katō Hiroyuki and his thirty-year-old criticism of Christianity as a "poison to the nation." Christianity on Japanese terms could answer Katō's allegation that Christianity's insistence on one universal God confused individual morality and national morality and thus made Christians incapable of loyalty to the emperor. Instead, "Christianity on Japanese terms" could best develop "true" patriotism and draw out the beautiful parts of the "Japanese spirit." Yanaihara had had to go beyond his mentor and add that "we revere the emperor," but, in a follow-up that September he titled "Japan on Christian Terms," he emphasized that Christianity with its Western components stripped away had much to offer a troubled Japan. (Here he alluded to an age-old complaint when he quoted a friend: "We must cease this Christianity that stinks of butter and establish one that smells of *takuan* [pickled radish].") Yanaihara was careful to distinguish his approach from what he termed secular ethnic nationalism and the irreducible contradictions that would three years later force him from his academic position.[21]

Though Yanaihara used the phrase "Christianity on Japanese terms" to criticize nationalist ideologies, most who used the term were looking for ways to connect them. In an explanatory note inset in an article in the January 1935 *Voice at the Lakeside* called "The Christ of the Japanese," the novelist Katō Kazuo wrote: "My intention . . . is not to reach a compromise between Christianity and Japan but to return Christianity that has compromised with Western civilization to original Christianity and appreciate it with a Japanese heart. . . . What I want to write is a fifth gospel."[22] Such an explanation was necessary because the article itself was a detailed account of the climatic and political situation of the Palestine into which Jesus was born, with its readers intended to make the leap from the Japanese in relation to the West to the Jewish ethnic nation (*minzoku*) in the Roman Empire. While Katō's stated intention of cutting away that which was Western was shared with others like Uchimura, his desire to write a fifth Japanese gospel took form in his *Christ: A Novel,* published two years later. Explaining that his purpose was to make a way for Christ's "blameless character" to be made known to "the Japanese heart, on Japanese terms," Katō, earlier an explicator of Tolstoy and Kropotkin, removed the divine aspects of Christ from his novel. He began with his birth as "lumpen" and ended with his death on the cross.[23] Just as the genre of novelistic lives of Christ was well known in the West, dating back to at least *Ben-Hur* (1880), but new in Japan in the 1930s, the historicized Jesus had special significance in relation to removing the Western standard from daily life in the 1920s and early 1930s.[24] Two years after Katō's *Christ* was published in 1937, Okino would close his *The Shrine Issue* with a description of Katō leading a delegation of the "Japan Church" of the "Imperial Way of Christ League" (Kōkoku Kirisuto-dō Dōmei) to worship at Ise in 1939. Paired with the concepts of "Japan faith" (*Nihon shinkō*) and "emperor faith" (*tennō shinkō*) Katō favored over "Nihonteki Kirisutokyō," his Imperial Way of Christ League had found a different resolution to the question of what constitutes a *shūkyō:* they had changed their name for Christianity from the teaching of Christ (Kirisuto*kyō*) to the way (*dō, michi*) of Christ, like Shintō, the way of the *kami.*[25]

Yoshida's most important contribution to the question of Christianity viable in Japan was *The Story of Jesus as Told by Mark,* serialized then published as a book, which occupied a position between novel and translation and between Christianity and religiosity. During the Kingdom of God evangelism campaign of the early 1930s, Kagawa and Yoshida had discussed a new translation of the Bible and so, prefacing *The Story of Jesus as Told by Mark* with a photo of himself in a gondola in front of St. Mark's Basilica in Venice, Yoshida described how he had spent a decade studying the Greek original and the Japanese, Chinese, French, German, and English translations while carrying the manuscript with him on three trips to America, one to India, and ten to China. Moreover, Yoshida was one of a group of Japanese Christians, also including Kagawa, Okino, and the WCTU's Kubushiro Ochimi, who gathered to discuss their impressions of "the Holy Land" at the YMCA in November 1934 in a roundtable published in the following issue of *Voice at the Lakeside.* They compared their travel experiences in "modernizing Palestine" but also shared interest in Nazareth and wondered how to characterize it. In his translation, Yoshida's only claim to "Japanese terms" was to note how difficult other translations of the Bible were to read, but his translation retold the Gospel of Mark in simple Japanese with phonetic glosses and extensive notes. However, Mark's gospel was an interesting choice: the shortest and sparest of the four, it begins with Jesus' baptism and concludes soon after the Resurrection with one of the two gospel accounts of the so-called Great Commission that missionaries took into the world. Far from trying to reconcile Mark's Jesus to a Japanese spirit, Yoshida tried to make it make sense in a modern world, going so far as to reexplain "unclean spirits" as mental illness (*seishinbyō*) and to add the adjective "religious" (*shūkyōteki*) to "fishers of men."[26]

Unlike the *seishin* of *seishinbyō,* the concept of the Japanese spirit (*Nihon seishin*) was key to articulating a Christianity on Japanese terms. The concept had first appeared in the pages of *Voice at the Lakeside* three years before *Kokutai no hongi* was issued, when the magazine serialized the final writings of Ebina Danjō, a series of essays on the "new Japanese spirit." The contents of said Japanese spirit were not well defined. The only member of the first generation of Japanese Protestants to appear in *Voice at the Lakeside*, Ebina explained that the "new Japanese spirit" had much in common with the old Japanese spirit, which bound together the Japanese (a category he took for granted): it was a spirit of reverence for the *kami* (*keishin no seishin*) that led to the awareness of being descended from the *kami* and called to build the Kingdom of the *Kami* in this world. The "Japanese spirit" both distinguished Japanese Christians as Japanese from, for example, American missionaries as non-Japanese and suggested points of commonality between Christianity and a specifically Japanese way of being. One example Ebina offered was from the opening of the Gospel of John: just as "the Word became flesh and dwelt among us," *kami* inhabit natural forms.[27] Published the same year as Ebina's death, *Kokutai no hongi* used the concept of the "national people's spirit" (*kokumin seishin*) interchangeably with *kokutai* (the national polity or body), thereby mixing body and spirit.

The "national people's spirit" was at the same time the object of the Campaign for the Total Mobilization of the National People's Spirit (Kokumin Seishin Sōdōin) begun in September 1937, following the escalation of aggression in China that July. The contrast is instructive not only because the concept of *kokumin* included colonial subjects in the way *Nihon* could not, but also because, inasmuch as "spiritual mobilization" consisted largely of austerity campaigns that continued the "moral suasion" (*kyōka*) of preceding decades, *seishin* was a continuation of *seikatsu* as the object of individual and national exhortation without the explicit social questions. Two decades earlier, *seishin* had been used in contrast to the "material" of "materialism" and the social philosophies based on a materialist conception of the world, its usages overlapping into the realms of psychology and spiritualism in the hands of writers like Takahashi Usaburō, the pastor of the Hachiman Church and former publisher of the magazine he called *Spiritual Tide.* Now it distinguished the nation, either as the *kokumin* who related to the emperor according to the ideology of the emperor system or as the Japan invoked vaguely as a spirit or, less frequently here, a Volk. Either way, this spirit was no longer part of the Orient as it had been in Shimizu's explanation of a decade earlier, when Christianity was already Oriental and already relevant to Japan. If, however, *kokumin seishin* was an object of exhortation, *Nihon seishin* had to be located with continuity from the Japanese past. It was not only Christians who looked for a definition for this concept, as philosophers like Watsuji Tetsurō showed in the

1930s when they added the concept to their vocabularies, but I will limit my answers to where the writers in *Voice at the Lakeside* found theirs.

Bushidō, the so-called way of the warrior, offered one such source for defining the Japanese spirit., The concept had been popularized four decades earlier through the English-language book first published in 1899 and authored by Uchimura's fellow Sapporo Band member, the Quaker Nitobe Inazō. "The soul of Japan," the subtitle Nitobe had given to his *Bushidō,* was not initially translated, and the book was not connected to the concept of *seishin* until the 1930s. Instead, Nitobe had tried to extrapolate from virtues associated with the warrior and the Christian gentleman to lay out an ethical system that put his nation on a moral par with the supposedly Christian West. As such, his citations had come from such luminaries of late-nineteenth-century Western thought as John Ruskin, Matthew Arnold, and George Muller and culminated with lines from the Quaker poet John Greenleaf Whittier and not from Japanese sources, where the word for the most part did not appear.[28] Soon after Nitobe's book, Inoue Tetsujirō, the Tokyo Imperial University professor of philosophy and ardent opponent of Christian influence in Japanese society, published a *Bushido Anthology,* putting the medieval sources Nitobe had not consulted alongside the 1882 Imperial Rescript for Soldiers and Sailors in order to make clear a different continuity, this time from ideas about warrior ethics to what later historians would call the emperor system.[29] Echoes of Nitobe driven on by Inoue would have informed *Voice at the Lakeside* readers, who encountered a seven-page piece on "Peace and Bushidō" by the Army Minister general Araki Sadao (illustrated in uniform and mustache in a large photograph) in the September 1934 issue. Nitobe's sense of comparability, however, was gone. Araki, known as a central figure among the military officials who formed the so-called Imperial Way Faction (Kōdōha) and called for a non-rational spirit of loyalty to the emperor to drive politics, went to pains to explain the contents of "our" *bushidō.* He emphasized primarily that it was neither militarist nor bloodthirsty, but rather was premised on a consciousness of death and compassion, based on the admonition that "the national people's *seikatsu* is their *seikatsu,* and war is war." Reportedly a transcript of a lecture Araki had given at the mountain resort of Karuizawa, where Vories and Yoshida summered, "Peace and Bushidō" was perhaps part of Yoshida's attempt to reach a broader audience, but it also introduced a rightist argument into the magazine's pages a year and a half before the coup Araki's faction attempted in February 1936 and three years before Yoshida's visit to Ise and the inauguration of the spiritual mobilization campaign.[30] A secondhand apologetic, this use of *bushidō* was as close as "Christianity on Japanese terms" came to ethics.

A series of theological pieces written for consumption by *Voice at the Lakeside* readers related Christianity to the "Japanese spirit." Each invoked a national essence revealed in history and put this idea into the words of the Kokugaku (Tokugawa-era nativist learning) scholars who, during the late eighteenth and early nineteenth centuries, had looked for a Japanese essence in ancient and long unreadable texts like the *Kojiki* and *Manyōshū*. In a 1939 book (serialized first in *Voice at the Lakeside*) subtitled "a way of reading the [two ancient classics] *Kojiki* and *Nihon shoki*," Okino asserted that each nation's myths are integral to the writing of its history. Though he put Japanese myth on a par with Greek and Hebrew mythologies and, by implication, relativized it, Okino escaped difficulties for his views as he asserted that this was just as Confucianism, Buddhism, and Christianity had superseded their Chinese, Indian, and "Jewish" versions and become Japanese. Thus Okino pointed to the possibility of a Japanese Christianity, commenting that it was striking that while the three founders (Confucius, Buddha, Christ) had all come from the "Orient," only Christ had come to Japan via the West. Even so, Christianity came the closest of the three to Japanese conceptions of the *kami*, for Christ had been thought to be dead but had come back to eat and drink before ascending to Heaven (for which Okino used the Shintō name Takamagahara).[31] Nearly two decades earlier, Kagawa had used the Kokugaku figure Motoori Norinaga as a character in a vision at the climax of his best-selling quasi-autobiographical novel *Crossing the Death Line* when particularism gives way to universalism. Motoori pays respect to Immanuel Kant at a shrine and then washes Kant's back in a bath and tells Kant that his book had had more to say about Japan than Norinaga's own. Kagawa's alter ego is inspired by this vision to enter the slums and serve their denizens. But by the 1930s, though he remained the most famous Japanese outside Japan and the most famous Christian inside, Kagawa's story had been brushed aside. Kagawa had little involvement in the question of Christianity on Japanese terms, and Kokugaku and its sentiments could be authoritative.[32]

Unlike Uchimura's and even Ebina's attempts to remove the Western components of Christianity, these moved closer to the strategies Fujiwara had rejected with the *-teki:* calling for adaptation or assimilation, looking for collapsibility into sameness, and looking for points of commonality. In the January 1938 *Voice at the Lakeside,* Sano Katsuya subtitled an article on the "Japanification of Christianity" with the "Fusion of Christianity and the Japanese Spirit." Going beyond Uchimura's criticism of current Western nations, Sano, a philosophy professor trained in the historical theology of Gustav Adolf Deissmann, used his historical higher criticism to argue that, just as Christianity of the era of the New Testament showed the effects of Jewish, Greek, and Roman "culture," so too could it take on a form suitable for the "characteristics of ethnic nations" (*minzokuteki tokusei*). In Western countries, Christianity had instilled a spirit of self-sacrifice for the greater good in spite of those countries' rationalism and individualism.[33] Coming from a similar background in historical theology, Uoki Tadakazu, a Doshisha theology professor, used the nineteenth-century Kokugaku ideologue Hirata Atsutane to argue that Christianity must take the Japanese past into account just as, in Hebrews 11, Paul showed the events of Jewish history to be demonstrations of human faith in God. Moreover, giving credit to Hirata and other Kokugaku scholars who preceded him, Uoki presented the idea that Japanese were truly theist while the Chinese concept of Heaven was in fact a deistic one. It was thus already possible to fuse Christianity and the Japanese spirit and to declare the superiority of Japanese as Christians over other Asians. Although Uoki used the same verb as Sano—*yūgō,* to fuse—he, like Fujiwara, refused the *-teki* and called his project "Japan Christianity" with its parallel in the Christianity of the Anglo-Saxon.[34] In another essay the next year, Yamabe Kyūkichi also turned to Kokugaku to look for commonalities between Christianity and "the Japanese spirit," finding, for example, that not only had the Kokugaku scholars pointed to Amanominakanushi as a creator *kami,* but they had also pointed to two companion *kami,* thus constituting a trinity. Recently retired as pastor of an Episcopal church in Ōtsu, Yamabe had more to say about the apparatus of State Shintō and the levels of shrines that had entered Japanese life. Still, his conclusion was that the Japanese spirit of loyalty and filial piety was the same as in Paul's admonition in Romans 13:1–7 to recognize earthly authority as instituted from above.[35]

At least in retrospect, the most important foil to this "Nihonteki Kirisutokyō" should have been the "dialectical" or "crisis" theology of Karl Barth, which arrived in Japan at the time of the critique of liberalism and receptiveness to the things German that accompanied the shift toward fascism. Barth's theology was known to English readers in Japan, including Vories, who had picked up on the fact that Barth smoked, but the process by which Japanese Christians read the Swiss theologian has led to criticism of an inadequately digested "Japanese Barthianism" that "placed excessive emphasis upon the transcendent sovereignty of God and upon a supra-historical interpretation of Barthian eschatology, [leaving] the interim, mundane area of practical life in the state subject to the delegated power of government authority."[36] Awareness of the German Confessing Church's Barmen Declaration of 1934, which powerfully dissected and rejected the Nazi regime as a false religion, seems to have reached Japan late and incomplete, but *Voice at the Lakeside* did have its own Barthian theologian. Harada Nobuo had become a Christian while a teenage patient in the Omi Mission's tuberculosis sanatorium, went on to study the theology of Barth and Kierkegaard at Doshisha, and then decided to defer the path of study in Germany to return to serve as the sanatorium's chaplain. At Doshisha, he was part of the circle around theology professor Ashida Keiji, who, along with the circle of Takakura Tokutarō at the Presbyterian Tokyo Shingakusha, served as one of the two points of entry for Barth's theology into Japan in the 1920s. His book *Karl Barth's Anthropology,* the first monograph written in Japanese on Barth, was published in 1935 with a salutary letter in German from Barth himself and with a preface by another Doshisha theologian, Ōtsuka Setsuji, who wrote that this young man understood Barth so deeply because he had himself experienced "crossing the death line." His monograph turned on a concept of his own making, *ningen no gimonsei,* or humanity's nature is questioning God, whereas the articles Harada contributed to *Voice at the Lakeside,* such as a March 1937 essay titled "Barth's Theology and the Omi Sanatorium: Narrating Religion and Daily Life," tried to bridge theology and life in the world. He began that essay by poking fun at himself, insisting that he loved Jesus more than Barth, and at the impression that theologians were cut off from ordinary life. Emphasizing that the Bible must be the center of daily life, he called for a theology, not a sociology or philosophy, that taught the consciousness, both as an individual and in the running of a sanatorium, of failing to live up to Christ's own daily life. He reported being moved at the sight of a nurse who, with no mask, dared come within inches of a patient in the ward for serious cases, one whose mother and aunt stayed across the room. The nurse had attended Bible study that morning and felt the calling to make God's love real in her care for the dying patient. Was Harada then "a Japanese Barthian"? Certainly his emphasis was far from Yoshida's, and, aside from a passing reference in his book to Barth "witnessing the emergence of the worst of neo-Protestantism in the *Deutsche Christen* determined to recognize the unity of God's revelation/will and man's judgment/desires," he made no mention of politics.[37]

The extremes of "Christianity on Japanese terms" also reached the pages of *Voice at the Lakeside.*[38] One such statement came from Yoshida himself: "I think that the time has come for Japanese to serve *Amanominakanushi no Mikami,* the Heavenly Father. There is urgency to the emergence of a Christianity containing the faith that is knit together with our *kokutai* of Japan and its theology. . . . The point of accord between faith on Japanese terms and Christianity is belief in One God, the Creator of the Universe."[39] Even here, though, the question is to find a Christianity viable in Japan. Another example was the transcript of a lecture given at the Hachiman YMCA at the end of 1933 by Hiyane Antei, a professor of religious history. Under the title "The Customs of Japanese Folklore and the Biography of Jesus," Hiyane declared the *Nihon shoki* and *Kojiki,* ancient texts that had been codified and given canonical, emperor-centered interpretations by Kokugaku scholars, to be equivalent (or parallel?) to the Old and New Testaments. Just as the Bible and the Christian religion emerged from a Jewish context, these texts came from the Japanese one. Carrying through this way of historicist thinking, Hiyane elaborated this point in his 1938 book *Christianity's Development on Japanese Terms.* At the same time, he distanced himself from what he saw as more extreme and reductive Nihonteki Kirisutokyō taking shape after 1937: its claims to equivalency between the ancient Japanese and Hebrew texts or between Amanominakanushi and Yahweh were "unnecessary."[40] Hiyane's teacher at Tokyo Imperial University, Anesaki Masaharu, was internationally recognized as an academic interpreter of Japan and was not a Christian. Written in English, his 1930 *History of Japanese Religion* was in fact a history of religions, fully formed systems in interaction with each other. It concluded pessimistically that Christianity was "not a solution, but a problem in Japan" and was "not taking the lead in civilization but . . . struggling to accommodate itself to it," though it offered the same evaluation of Buddhism.[41] In contrast, the definition of religion Hiyane used in his first book, his 1925 *History of Religion in Japan,* pointed to a sphere of human existence alongside and touching others he named, including psychology, ethics, literature, and society. His history extended from the periods he called "primitive" and "mythological" through his present, when Kagawa best embodied the relationship between religion and society. Much of Hiyane's subsequent scholarly work centered on the hidden "Kirishitan" of the Tokugawa period and on the history of Christianity in Japan, culminating in two books published in 1938: *History of Christianity in Japan* and *Christianity's Development on Japanese Terms.* These were followed by *History of Christianity in China* in 1940, which he introduced in an imperial voice reminding readers of the need for more knowledge about this place pejoratively called Shina. Hiyane's dispassionate histories were a stark contrast to his contributions to the formulation of Nihonteki Kirisutokyō and to the Nihon Kirisuto Kyōdan. It is equally important to observe the centrality of Hiyane's history as contributing to what one historian has called "Japanese historicism," a line of thinking that posited a vague Hegelian dialectic between Christianity and national character or culture (later called "spirit"), as opposed to "correspondence" or "equivalency."[42]

Hiyane greeted the attack on Pearl Harbor in the February 1942 *Voice at the Lakeside,* joining the fanfare for the expulsion of Anglo-Saxons from East Asia. In "Christianity and the Future of the Orient," he hailed the attack as filling Japan's mission in world history and righting the wrong that had begun with the Opium War a century earlier. However, he insisted Christianity remained essential and that it would take its place alongside Buddhism and Islam as religions of East Asia and the Co-Prosperity Sphere. Hiyane declared that he had felt the superiority of Christianity in Japan to that in the rest of Asia when he reviewed the outcomes of the 1938 meeting of the International Missionary Council, even if Christianity in Japan was still incomplete: more ethical than religious, more practical than spiritual, more applied than speculative. Hiyane buttressed his nationalistic conclusion regarding Madras by commenting that the Imperial Army was now standing where the sixteenth-century *Kirishitan daimyō* had once trod in Malaysia and the Philippines.[43] This essay and one following it by Sano's student Matsumura Katsumi came at the end of the discourse on a Christianity viable in Japan as it appeared in the pages of *Voice at the Lakeside.* The lecturer on Christianity at Kyoto Imperial University and hence the bridge to the school of philosophy based there, Matsumura emphasized the "and" of his title "Our Homeland Japan and Christianity" as necessary for the development of "Japan Christianity" and "Japanese people who are Christians." He went on to define the "Japanese spirit" as "working as the spiritual motivating power for East Asia."[44] Both Hiyane and Matsumura had transferred the significance of Christianity in Japan to the war in Asia, and Matsumura added his hope for the ideal of the "national people's church" realized in the new Kirisuto Kyōdan according to the Religious Organizations Law but recalling the earliest Protestant church in Japan, which called itself a *kōkai,* or "public meeting," rather than the more denominational *kyōkai* (teaching meeting), which became the standard translation for church.[45] They had resolved the question of the viability of Christianity in Japan with outside forces. Within a year of the attack on Pearl Harbor, Yoshida would be dead, and the increased scrutiny and austerity of the Pacific War era would leave much less room for such conversations.

Meaning: Christianity on Japanese Terms

The attempts to define a Christianity viable in Japan to which Yoshida devoted the pages of *Voice at the Lakeside* as the Japanese Army penetrated the Asian continent are not easy to evaluate. It is not enough to accept the quick and shallow repudiation that came in the wake of Japan's defeat less than four years later or to assume that Hiyane and others were mouthing propaganda, though postwar apologies and continuing activism on behalf of the 1947 Constitution's renunciation of war (Article 9) and for the removal of government from religious activity (Article 20) deserve notice. The range of the authors Yoshida included is testament to the difficulty of the central question of how Christianity could be viable in Japan, a question premised not just on the awareness of the foreignness of the religion's concepts and practices but on the problem of defining Japan itself. Between these problems of nation and religion in formation, it was not adequate to point to apostasy of the sort of reverse conversion or *tenkō* leftist intellectuals were undergoing at the same time, though that did entail a recognition of the deficiency in ethics this "Christianity" brought to the world. Although the idea of *Nihon seishin* dropped away following the defeat (until it was revived in a different form in the 1970s), attempts to locate "Christianity on Japanese terms" have continued under the rubric of *dochaku,* or indigenization. When the historian Takeda Kiyoko observes that "throughout the history of modern Japan, it has been extremely difficult to sustain with impunity 'orthodoxy-versus-heterodoxy' battles among Christian groups espousing different interpretations of the gospel truth in a culture which is not only non-Christian but also has a Japanese orthodoxy already firmly entrenched in the form of the emperor ideology," she recognizes the difficulties these writers faces as Christians trying to be viable in Japan and the political nature of the orthodoxy they faced. Although Takeda's dominant metaphor is that of indigenization (being planted in the soil of a place), the writers Yoshida published fall within what she considers "between orthodoxy and heterodoxy," as the questions were open and there were numerous definers of orthodoxy, both in relation to the emperor-centered state and the united church it ordained and to the worldwide networks of Christians.[46]

Hiyane's comment about the December 1938 meeting of the International Missionary Council, which was relocated from Hangzhou to Tambaram, a suburb of Madras, India, as the Japanese invasion of China intensified, offers a clue to two points of significance for this small intellectual history. First, though overshadowed by delegations numbering more than fifty from India and from China, the sixteen men and three women who represented Japan, thirteen Japanese and six missionaries, joined the first such conference at which delegates from Asia comprised the plurality (if not quite the majority) of the 450 attending, and representatives of the missionary "home" countries amounted to fewer than 25 percent. Having just sent his own novel *Christ* to press, Kagawa was there and would go on from Madras to meet Gandhi, with whom he had long been compared.[47] Hiyane was not at Madras, and his assumption that Japanese Christians would take the position of leadership among the nations of Asia would likely have come under question had it been allowed to be broached at all, but the welcoming of the Japanese delegation to Madras stood in contrast to Japan's withdrawal from other internationalist bodies including the League of Nations and the Institute for Pacific Relations. The few scattered mentions of war and empire in East Asia made at Madras were, however, subsumed within the call to build an ecumenical church.

Second, where the Jerusalem conference a decade earlier had devoted considerable attention to the social and political contexts of religious life and had commissioned a great deal of social scientific research from the now closed Institute of Social and Religious Research, the Madras meeting zeroed in on the church and the "authority of the faith." The International Missionary Council commissioned Hendrik Kraemer, a Dutch historian of religions who was himself a former missionary to Indonesia, to lay out the question of "the fundamental position of the Christian church as a witness-bearing body in the modern world" and the "evangelistic approach to the great non-Christian faiths." The resulting book, *The Christian Message in a Non-Christian World,* responded to both the notion of one religion fulfilling another put forth by Ernest Hocking in the greatly controversial *Re-Thinking Missions* of a decade earlier and Barth's absolute reliance on revelation by calling for "biblical realism." Kraemer's concept would, he explained, encompass both the central thesis that "the Christian revelation as the record of God's self-disclosing revelation in Jesus Christ is absolutely *sui generis*" and the evaluation of "the non-Christian religions" as "all inclusive systems and theories of life." Later in life, Kraemer continued to see the necessity of doing apologetics in an interreligious context as, among other things, the starting point for dialog among people of differing religions.[48] A clear knowledge of Christianity among the religions is useful for living in the modern world, as is the idea that religions can coexist within a state-ordained framework, which had, in part, its seeds in wartime Japan. It is worth keeping Harry Harootunian's provocative suggestion regarding one significance of much of Japanese wartime thought—including, I think, theology—in mind: "contemporary postcolonial discourse is simply a repetition of the Japanese experience in a different historical register, where the outside, Europe's unacknowledged shadow, returns to take reprisals for the injuries inflicted on it by colonialism and imperialism, which the Japanese were the first to recognize and put into question."[49]

Notes

1. These events are drawn from Okino Iwasaburō, *Jinja mondai* [The Shrine Issue], bound with Tagawa Daikichirō, *Nihon to Kirisutokyō* [Japan and Christianity] (Tokyo: Kyōbunkan, 1939), 147–150. The *norito* translation comes from Holtom's reading of Okino, discussed below: D. C. Holtom, *Modern Japan and Shinto Nationalism: A Study of Present-Day Trends in Japanese Religions* (Chicago: University of Chicago Press, 1943), 100–101. For a contemporary English-language portrait of the Omi Brotherhood, see Wm. Merrell Vories, *The Omi Brotherhood in Nippon* (Omi Hachiman: Omi Brotherhood Book Department,

1934). On the story of Vories, Yoshida, and the Omi Brotherhood as a way into the modern history of Christianity in imperial Japan, see Gregory Vanderbilt, "'The Kingdom of God Is Like a Mustard Seed': Evangelizing Modernity between the United States and Japan, 1905–1948" (Ph.D. diss., University of California, Los Angeles, 2005).

2. Okino Iwasaburō, "Jinja sanpai" [Shrine Worship], *Kohan no koe* [Voice at the Lakeside], September 1939, 10–11; Okino, *Jinja mondai,* 147–150. Having been pastor and close friend to Ōishi Seinosuke, the one Christian convicted and executed in the High Treason Incident of 1910–1911, Okino presents a complex attitude to the nation, seeking its cultural dignity while maintaining distance from the emperor-centered ideology.

3. Holtom, 100.

4. Neither this incident nor Yoshida's effort to insulate Doshisha from suspicion appears in its official centennial history: Ueno Naozō, *Dōshisha hyakunenshi* [Doshisha Centennial History] (Kyoto: Doshisha, 1979); the relevant section is Tsūshi-hen, vol. 2, pp. 1094–1120. But Yuasa later provided his own account of this "unprecedented and unthinkable episode," praising Yoshida for his "business sense" and reprinting a lengthy set of proposals Yoshida made for reshaping Doshisha to meet the future that appeared to be coming in 1937. Yuasa Hachirō, "Yoshida Etsuzō-shi to Dōshisha" [Mr. Yoshida Etsuzō and Doshisha], *Doshisha jihō* [Doshisha Newsletter] 12 (October 1964): 63–65.

5. Vories Diary, June 16, 1944, housed at the Vories Museum, Omi Hachiman, Japan. Vories' language here is influenced by the Oxford Group. Emphasis in original.

6. Yoshida Etsuzō, "Kōdai Jingū ni mōdete" [Approaching the Imperial Shrine] and "Reihai" [Worship], *Kohan no koe,* September 1937, frontispiece and 1.

7. Yoshida Etsuzō, "Shūkyō to iu moji" [The Word Religion], *Shin Ōmi,* September 1937, 4. On the formation of the category of "religion," see Isomae Jun'ichi, "Kindai ni okeru 'Shukyō' gainen no keisei katei" [The Formation of the Concept of Religion in the Modern Era], in *Kindai chi no seiritsu* [The Birth of Modern Knowledge], volume 3 of *Iwanami Kōza: Kindai Nihon no bunkashi* [Iwanami Lectures: Cultural History of Modern Japan], ed. Ryūichi Narita et al. (Tokyo: Iwanami, 2001), 163–196.

8. Tagawa, *Nihon to Kirisutokyō,* 74.

9. Tagawa Daikichirō, *Kokka to shūkyō* [State and Religion] (Tokyo: Kyōbunkan, 1938), 128–136.

10. Matsujima Tsunejirō, "Mon to to" [Q & A], *Kohan no koe,* October 1937, 21.

11. Yoshida Etsuzō, "Shintaisei to Nihon no Kirisutokyōdan ni tsuite" [On the New Structure and Japan's Christian Kyōdan], *Kohan no koe,* October 1940, 1.

12. Yoshida Etsuzō, "Shasetsu" [Editorial], *Ōmi Kyōdaisha shūhō* [Omi Brotherhood Weekly Newsletter], March 9, 1934.

13. The problem of Christianity and the "emperor system" has received much attention in the postwar era. A key work is Dohi Akio and Tanaka Masato, eds., *Kindai tennōsei to Kirisutokyō* [The Modern Emperor System and Christianity] (Kyoto: Jinbun Shoin, 1996). I have tried to make sense of it in "Postwar Japanese Christian Historians, Democracy, and the Problem of the 'Emperor-System' State," in *Christianity and the State in Asia: Complicity and Conflict,* ed. Julius Bautista and Francis Lim Khek Gee (New York: Routledge, 2009), 59–78.

14. For a history of theology in Japan, see Charles H. Germany, *Protestant Theologies in Modern Japan* (Tokyo: I.I.S.R. Press, 1966); Furuya Yasuo, ed., *A History of Japanese Theology* (Grand Rapids, MI: W. B. Eerdman, 1997); and Mitsuo Miyata, *Authority and Obedience: Romans 13:1–7 in Modern Japan* (New York: Peter Lang, 2009).

15. Kasahara Yoshimitsu, "'Nihonteki Kirisutokyō' hihan," [Critique of "Christianity on Japanese Terms"], *Kirisutokyō shakai mondai kenkyū* [Study of Christianity and Social Problems] 22 (1974): 114–139.

16. Hara Makoto, *Kokka o koerarenakatta kyōkai: 15-nen sensōka no Nihon Purotesutanto kyōkai* [The Church That Was Unable to Transcend the State: Japanese Protestant Churches during the Fifteen-Year War] (Tokyo: Nihon Kirisuto Kyōdan Shuppankyoku, 2005), 67.

17. Despite the difficulties presented by the gaps noted below surrounding definitions of the nation and of Japan, the phrase *Nihonteki* (on Japanese terms) belonged to the wartime era; of the nearly four hundred uses of the term in the Diet Library's Kindai Digital Library, two-thirds are from the 1940s, and another quarter are from the 1930s.

18. Shimizu Yasuzō, "Tōyōteki Kirisutokyō no teishō" [Advocating Oriental Christianity] and "Shakaiteki Kirisutokyō no teishō" [Advocating Social Christianity], *Kohan no koe* (serialized in 1929 and 1930). What was missing was the "Social Christianity" of Doshisha professor Nakajima Shigeru, with its influences from both Marx and Niebuhr and its activism.

19. Fujiwara Fujio, *Nihon seishin to Kirisutokyō* [The Japanese Spirit and Christianity] (Sakai: Tomoshibisha, 1941); John Owen Gauntlett, Robert King Hall, eds. and trans., *Kokutai no Hongi: Cardinal Principles of the National Entity of Japan* (Cambridge, MA: Harvard University Press, 1949), 96, 146. Original text available at http://www.j-texts.com/showa/kokutaiah.html.

20. Kanzō Uchimura, "Two J's" (1926) and "Japanese Christianity" (1920), in *Uchimura Kanzō zenshū* (Tokyo: Iwanami, 1982), vol. 30, 53–54, and vol. 25, 592.

21. Yanaihara Tadao, "Nihonteki Kirisutokyō," *Kohan no koe,* January 1934, 10–13, 38–40; Yanaihara, "Kirisutokyōteki Nihon," *Kohan no koe,* September 1934,

4–6. Like other Christian intellectuals, Yanaihara published in numerous popular and semi-intellectual periodicals as well as his own newsletters *Tsūshin* and *Kashin*. These were his only contributions to *Voice at the Lakeside*."Ideals of the State," the essay invoking the prophet Isaiah to criticize the Japanese state, was published in *Chūō kōron* in September 1937.

22. Katō Kazuo, "Nihonjin no Kirisuto" [The Christ of the Japanese], *Kohan no koe*, January 1935, 36–39.

23. Katō Kazuo, *Kirisuto* [Christ] (Tokyo: Shin Shichōsha, 1937).

24. While passion play dramas date to the Middle Ages, novelistic lives of Christ had emerged in the West around 1870. Yoshida's and Katō's Jesus also fit with the "historical Jesus," the object of considerable scholarship spurred on by the so-called higher criticism of biblical texts, archaeological discoveries, and philosophical attacks. By this time, novels about Christ in Japanese numbered nearly two hundred.

25. Tagawa and Okino, *Jinja mondai*, 150–152; on "Nihon Shinkō," see Miyata, *Authority and Obedience*, 84–85. Katō was joined at Ise by Matsukura Shigenao, a pastor who had written *Kirisutokyō wo Daijōteki ni miru*, or *Seeing Christianity on Mahayana Terms*. In 1940, the league did not join the Kyōdan in order to deepen its own Christianity on Japanese terms.

26. Yoshida Etsuzō, *Maruko no tsutaeshi Iesu monogatari* [The Story of Jesus as told by Mark] (Omi Hachiman: Ōmi Kyōdaisha, 1939); "Paresuchina o kataru" [Narrating Palestine], *Kohan no koe*, December 1934, 7–14. This journey parallels the trips Japanese Buddhist leaders took to India, as described by Richard M. Jaffe, "Seeking Sakyamuni: Travel and the Reconstruction of Japanese Buddhism," *Journal of Japanese Studies* 30, no. 1 (2004): 65–96.

27. Ebina Danjō, "Shin Nihon seishin no sōshō," *Kohan no koe*, November 1934, 6–10; "Nihon seishin no shinka," *Kohan no koe*, December 1934, 22–27; "Nihon Seishin ni okeru kami no naizai," *Kohan no koe*, April 1935, 28–31. The same contents were also printed as *Shin Nihon seishin* [The New Japanese Spirit] (Omi Hachiman: Ōmi Kyōdaisha Shuppanbu, 1935). One study that makes the important connection between Ebina's thought and social position and Japanese colonialism (including via his disciple and later biographer Watase Tsunekichi, who directed Kumiai Church activities in Korea) is Mun-gil Kim, *Kindai Nihon Kirisutokyō to Chōsen: Ebina Danjō no shisō to kōdō* (Tokyo: Akashi Shoten, 1998). Kim's term of choice for defining Ebina is "*Shintō-teki*" *Kirisutokyō*, with the "on Shintō terms" set off by quotation marks; by this Kim plays down the emphasis on Ebina's Christianity being forged in a Confucian crucible and argues that Ebina wanted to fuse his Christianity with Shintō and thus lost the critical edge that had been present, for example, in the Barmen Declaration, which was issued while Ebina was still alive.

28. An example of criticism of Nitobe is Yuzo Ota, "Mediation between Cultures," in *Nitobe Inazō: Japan's Bridge across the Pacific*, ed. John F. Howes (Boulder, CO: Westview Press, 1995), 237–252.

29. Inoue Tetsujirō and Arima Hiromasa, *Bushidō sōsho* (Tokyo: Hakubunkan, 1905).

30. Araki Sadao, "Heiwa to Bushidō" [Peace and Bushidō], *Kohan no koe*, September 1934, 13–19.

31. Okino Iwasaburō, *Nihon kenkokushi kō: "Kojiki," "Nihon shoki" no yomikata* [On the History of the Founding of the Nation of Japan: Reading the *Kojiki* and *Nihon Shoki*] (Tokyo: Kōseisha, 1939).

32. Kagawa Toyohiko, *Shisen o koete* (Tokyo: Kaizōsha, 1920); translated by Ichiji Fukumoto and Thomas Satchell as *Before the Dawn* (New York: George H. Doran, 1924). Kagawa's 1934 *Christ and Japan* (translated by William L. Axling; New York: Friendship Press, 1934) showed Japanese religious traditions to be both historically and currently bankrupt and to hunger for Christ. Although the debate over whether the eighteenth-century Confucian scholar Nakae Tōju was a hidden Christian (*Kirishitan*) had earlier been mentioned in the pages of *Voice at the Lakeside* (and in Kagawa's book), there is no indication in these texts whether the similar debate over whether the Kokugaku figure Hirata Atsutane had read Catholic texts in Chinese translation—and from them derived ideas about monotheism—was known to these scholars. In any case, to show foreign influence on Hirata would undermine his place in their arguments. Cf. Richard Devine, "Hirata Atsutane and Christian Sources," *Monumenta Nipponica* 36, no. 1 (1981): 37–54.

33. Sano Katsuya, "Kirisutokyō Nihonka no mondai: Nihon seishin to Kirisutokyō no yūgō" [The Issue of the Japanification of Christianity: The Fusion of Christianity and the Japanese Spirit], *Kohan no koe*, January 1938, 2–6, 29.

34. Uoki Tadakazu, "Nihon seishin to Kirisutokyō: Kokugakusha Hirata Atsutane no kotodomo" [The Japanese Spirit and Christianity: On the Kokugaku Scholar Hirata Atsutane], *Kohan no koe*, April 1940, 6–8; Miyata, *Authority and Obedience*, 86–87.

35. Yamabe Kyūkichi, "Kirisutokyō to Nihon seishin," *Kohan no koe*, April–June 1941, 11–13, 13–15, 16–17.

36. Germany, *Theologies*, 169. Germany concludes, however, that "the position of dualism, or the two realms," demonstrated by "the non-resistance of Japanese Barthianism," was, "on the whole within the Japanese situation, one of realism and revelatory of a considerable degree of health within the Christian body." Ibid., 174.

37. Harada Nobuo, *Kaaru Baruto no ningengaku* [Karl Barth's Anthropology] (Tokyo: Shinseidō, 1935), 2, 92; Harada Nobuo, "Baruto Shingaku to Omi Ryōyōin" [Barth's Theology and the Omi Sanatorium], *Kohan no koe*, March 1937,

44–48. Baruto Shingaku Juyōshi Kenkyūkai, ed., *Nihon ni okeru Kaaru Baruto: Haisenmade no juyōshi no shodanmen* [Karl Barth in Japan: Aspects of the History of his Reception in Japan through 1945] (Tokyo: Shinkyō Shuppansha, 2009), including Hirabayashi Takahiro, "Ashida, Hashimoto Saakuru ni yoru Baruto juyō" [Reception of Barth in the Ashida/Hashimoto Circle], 68–73.

38. There is no evidence of exchange with movements like the Mikuni movement, which extrapolated from the homonymy of "Kingdom of God" and "Emperor's Kingdom" to insist that Japan's "holy war" in Asia was biblically ordained. Miyata, *Authority and Obedience,* 83–84.

39. Quoted in Okumura Naohiko, *Voorizu hyōden* [Biography of Vories] (Kamakura: Minatonohito, 2005), 228–229. This is the point that gives Vories' leading biographer great trouble: "Vories himself held firmly to his orthodox Calvinist faith, but this raises the question of whether he was able to convey it to his students."

40. Hiyane Antei, *Kirisutokyō no Nihonteki tenkai* (Tokyo: Kirisutokyō Shisō Sōsho Kankōkai, 1938). Passages from its conclusion were also translated by W. T. Thomas as Antei Hiyane, "National Spirit and the Christian Faith," *Japan Christian Quarterly,* 15 (January 1940): 42–49.

41. Masaharu Anesaki, *History of Japanese Religion, with Special Reference to the Social and Moral Life of the Nation* (London: Kegan Paul, 1930), 406.

42. Hiyane Antei, *Nihon shūkyōshi* [History of Religion in Japan] (Tokyo: Sankyō Shuppansha, 1925); Hiyane Antei, *Shina Kirisutokyō shi* [History of Christianity in China] (Tokyo: Seikatsusha, 1940). Hiyane noted the connections between Catholicism in China and in Japan and devoted a final chapter to the missionary activities of Japanese Protestants including Shimizu. However, he did not allow for comparisons, including in his discussion of the Chinese rites controversy, which had been "resolved" the previous year by papal bull. On "Japanese historicism," see Germany, *Theologies,* 165; Miyata, *Authority and Obedience,* 85–87.

43. Hiyane Antei, "Tōyō shōrai to Kirisutokyō" [The Future of the Orient and Christianity], *Kohan no koe,* February 1942, 4–7.

44. Matsumura Katsumi, "Sokoku Nihon to Kirisutokyō" [Our Homeland Japan and Christianity], *Kohan no koe,* February 1942, 8–10. Such a position was shared by, for example, the pastor Akira Ebisawa, who was then head of the East Asia Division of the Kirisitu Kyōdan, in *Daitōa kensetsu to Nihon Kirisutokyō* [The Construction of East Asia and Japan Christianity] (Tokyo: Kyōbunkan, 1942). On the activities of this division and its notorious letter to the Christians of the "Co-Prosperity Sphere," see Miyata, *Authority and Obedience,* 136–138.

45. Matsumura directed readers to an article he had just published in the intellectual journal *Shisō.* "Nihon Kirisutokyōdan seiritsu no igi to sono kadai"

[Significance of the Establishment of the Japan Christian Kyōdan], *Shisō* [Pensées] 235 (December 1941): 1–14.

46. J. Victor Koschmann, trans., "Japanese Christianity: Between Orthodoxy and Heterodoxy," in *Authority and the Individual in Japan,* ed. J. Victor Koschmann (Tokyo: University of Tokyo Press, 1978), 98.

47. Kagawa Toyohiko, "Ashifumi suru Indo" [Setting Foot in India], *Kohan no koe,* May 1939, 12–16. Gandhi urged Kagawa to accept prison or even death as made necessary by his convictions, so that his nation's honor might be restored, "making Japan live through your death." M. K. Gandhi, *My Non-Violence* (Ahmedabad: Navajivan Publishing, 1960), 85–86.

48. *The Authority of the Faith* (vol. 1) and *Addresses and Other Records* (vol. 8), proceedings of the Meeting of the International Missionary Council, Tambaram, Madras, India, December 12 to 29, 1938 (New York: International Missionary Council, 1939); Hendrik Kraemer, *The Christian Message in a Non-Christian World* (New York: Harper and Brothers, 1938); Hendrik Kraemer, *World Cultures and World Religions: The Coming Dialogue* (Philadelphia: Westminster Press, 1960). See also Timothy Yates, *Christian Mission in the Twentieth Century* (Cambridge, UK: Cambridge University Press, 1994), 94–124.

49. Harry D. Harootunian, *Overcome by Modernity: History, Culture, and Community in Interwar Japan* (Princeton, NJ: Princeton University Press, 2000), 422.

10

Diasporic Korean Christianity in the United States, 1922–1941

David K. Yoo

In October of 1922, Julian S. Park left New York City on a three-week tour of a dozen colleges and universities to visit with Korean and Korean American students. Park, who was a graduate of Methodist-related Baldwin-Wallace College in Ohio and had taken classes at the Presbyterian seminary in Princeton, knew the situation of his fellow students well. The tour christened his duties as the Korean secretary of the Committee on Friendly Relations among Foreign Students of the Young Men's Christian Association (YMCA). The report of Park's trip appeared in the inaugural issue of the *Korean Student Bulletin* (*KSB*) that served as a news, opinion, and information outlet.[1]

The *Korean Student Bulletin* provides access to the perspectives of students and others who appeared in its pages during the years of its publication from 1922 to 1941.[2] The themes of race and religion, migration and exile, and colonialism and independence help frame the discussion of the *KSB* as a marker of the role of religion in the history of Koreans on the mainland and in Hawai'i. The linkages between race and religion emerged as writers wrestled with how to understand their Christian faith in light of the racialization of Koreans within the setting of American race relations. Race represented one of many issues of what might be termed an applied Christianity in which authors explored how to make sense of the circumstances that they faced.

The migration and exile theme took many forms, but the experience of being an international student itself, in its varied forms, constituted a form a migration and exile. Another dimension of this relational theme encompassed the second generation and how its members blurred the line between Korean and Korean American. The linkages between colonialism and independence emerged in the ongoing concern for the fate of Korea under Japanese rule. The *KSB* faithfully reported on people and events in the Korean diaspora, while asking questions about how Christianity related to hopes of freedom and independence.

The *KSB* gave young men and women a space to articulate what constituted a kind of wilderness experience as they faced uncertain and difficult times. Protestant Christianity served as a means of exploring and navigating that wilderness against the shadows cast by colonial oppression, economic depression, and increasing global conflict. The bulletin's networks spanned continents and connected Koreans in places like Los Angeles, Honolulu, and Seoul.[3]

Promoting Friendly Relations

The *Korean Student Bulletin* stated its aim as twofold: "First, it is to serve all the Korean students in this country in a way to bring them into close contact with the Christian influence and to foster the moral and educational interests among them; secondly, to deepen and widen the interest of American Christians in Korea and her people."[4] These goals formed part of a larger effort by the Committee on Friendly Relations to promote international friendship and understanding under the auspices of the YMCA and in cooperation with American Protestant denominations, local churches, and other affiliated organizations. Although the committee did not offer financial aid to students, it did serve as an international network of support that included advising students in their home country as well as placement services to colleges in the United States. Local staff met students once they disembarked at American ports and stations, and escorted them to their respective campuses and helped them to make the initial adjustments to their new environment. Self-supporting students could find information about and introductions to possible employers. The work of the committee situated students within a comprehensive network that included campus organizations and Protestant congregations.[5]

The ministry of the Committee on Friendly Relations extended the missionary impulse by connecting the work overseas to college campuses in the United States. Formed in 1911, the committee, itself under the International Committee of the YMCA, represented a ministry to students that resonated with broader Protestant efforts to work with Asians in the United States with the aim of supporting missions overseas.[6] The Korean Methodist churches in Honolulu and Los Angeles started under such circumstances. The movement between Korea, Hawai'i, and the mainland underscored the relationship between migrants and exiles that very much included students.

Many of the international students, including Koreans, already had attended mission institutions in their home countries, and, through those connections, young people left for America often with the sponsorship of foreign mission as well as indigenous religious organizations. The programs of the committee also reflected the influence of the Student Volunteer Movement that emerged in the late nineteenth century.[7] The YMCA and the YWCA became the catalysts for college and seminarian students to enter foreign missions. The Student Volunteer Movement also hosted large, international conferences called quadrennials that attracted thousands of students during their time in college. Books, pamphlets, and study materials produced under the Student Volunteer Movement banner gained wide usage by students in the United States and abroad.[8] The movement spread to Europe and Asia, and the *KSB* carried news of related events such as the Ninth Quadrennial held in Indianapolis in 1924.[9]

Korean students took an active role in the wide range of programs associated with the Committee on Friendly Relations, including the formation of the Korean Student Federation of North America in 1923. The Korean Student Federation served as an organizing and coordinating body for key events such as the regional summer conferences that brought together international and American students at retreat centers and campgrounds. The conferences and the *KSB* helped create spaces for interaction to take place and for friendships to form.[10] In 1937, nearly 9,000 international students from almost one hundred different countries ventured to the United States. Estimates vary regarding the numbers of international students from Korea; the *KSB* reported numbers ranging from 20 to 250 at different points throughout its publication span in the early 1920s to the early 1940s.[11] One study noted that nearly 900 Korean students had come to the United States during the period from 1899 to 1940.[12] These numbers did not take into account that many laborers floated in and out of student status depending on their ability to pay for their schooling. Nor do these figures include second-generation American-born Koreans.

Regardless of these distinctions, students of Korean ancestry found support in the work of the international arm of the YMCA. Moreover, the work with Koreans represented just part of a much larger effort. The Committee on Friendly Relations helped sponsor a secretary for Chinese, Japanese, Koreans, and Filipinos in addition to those who hailed from non-Asian countries. The secretaries traveled throughout the United States and overseas. Each of the Asian groups also published its own bulletin.[13]

The Committee on Friendly Relations, based in New York City, provided the structure for the work among international students, and some within the YMCA held up a vision in which students, educated and exposed to an American Christian civilization, might return to their home countries to become leading citizens embodying Protestant ideals. The white-collar and capitalist orientation of the organization has been well documented. Captains of industry and American wealth fueled the rapid growth and expansion of the YMCA in the United States and abroad.[14] As such, one could situate the YMCA as part of a larger American imperial project.

At the same time, an internal critique (as well as appreciation) of American culture and society had long formed part of the missionary enterprise.[15] Moreover, the social gospel movement that reached its peak in the late nineteenth century and in the early decades of the twentieth century made an impact on the YMCA by asking how Christianity engaged societal concerns such as race relations, labor unrest, crime and poverty in cities, and international peace. The movement drew from various traditions and represented an effort by Christians to respond to the massive scale of change taking place around them. As one study has pointed out, social gospel advocates attempted to address the dilemmas of adapting a religion of an earlier rural America to the pressures of an emergent industrial nation.[16] The social gospel deeply influenced the student wing of the YMCA under the leadership of its secretary John R. Mott. One can see a reflection of the movement with regard to the work of the YMCA in Asia in terms of its emphasis on cultivating leadership from the countries themselves to guide the work of the associations:

> Our great idea going out to these countries is to leave them as soon as possible; to plant the Association idea in the hearts and minds of native young men in order that they may propagate the Movement themselves, and let us go home as soon as may be. We are putting this burden on the native shoulders. This great work of evangelization is not supremely for British or American or Continental leaders; it is primarily a Chinese, a Japanese, an Indian, a native enterprise.[17]

Mott's directive targeted YMCA endeavors in Asia, but it also applied to students from Asia and of Asian ancestry in the United States. Accordingly, students found a measure of autonomy and freedom within their organizations and networks. Koreans did not shy away from anticolonial discourse regarding their homeland and championing a religious nationalism. Chinese students advocated for their nation as a great civilization deserving of the rights and privileges given to European nations.[18] Moreover, Filipino students spoke out against their in-between status as US nationals barred from access to many facets of American life; on homeland politics, they pointed out that the Philippines merited the same level of independence that Americans enjoyed. Japanese students critiqued the immigration policies of the United States and argued for racial equality to counter discrimination and prejudice directed at Japan.[19] As these perspectives suggest, students from Asia made informed cases for their respective nations, all the while exhibiting a keen awareness of the powerful role of the United States in the international order that included US-Asia relations.

Racial Sensibilities

Students from Korea critiqued and discussed events taking place in Korea, but they also provided commentary on American society and culture. Race and its relationship to religion, both in the United States and within an international context, drew out the observations of students who wrote for the *KSB*. C. C. Hahn of the University of Southern California assessed the positive and negative elements in American civilization. On the plus side of the ledger, Hahn underscored religion, chiefly Christianity, as shaping the character of the nation. Echoing a familiar refrain, Hahn noted that the country's founders came to what would become the United States for religious democracy. Enshrining the separation of church and state meant that the ideal of religious freedom continued to exert its influence. In contrast, widespread economic exploitation coupled with racial prejudice marred American civilization. Hahn focused primarily on immigrants and how their idealized views of the United States so often crumbled under the weight of their actual experience once they arrived in the country and sought to establish their lives. Hahn cited the example by which the United States barred Chinese laborers from entering the country during lean economic times but recruited them when they needed cheap labor. The USC student did not look kindly upon what he termed a "dirty attitude," nor did he excuse the harm that American companies inflicted directly in Asia. In linking race and economics, Hahn juxtaposed the positive elements of Christianity against the corrosive effects of prejudice and greed.[20]

In another essay, written by an attendee of the 1924 Quadrennial International Student Volunteer Convention, the themes of race and religion intersected both with domestic American concerns and more broadly with the issues of international race relations. In both cases, people at the convention sought "to find places where the spirit of Christ has not been the dominant factor in life, and to picture before the students the world of need and its Christian solution." The writer commented on a consciousness that emerged during the event in which attendees realized how the various races of the world connected. Technology drove some of this consciousness as modern transportation and travel brought people into more frequent contact. Some clearly did not welcome such proximity. Delegates experienced the tension between the ideal of living in peace and harmony as Christians and the harsh reality of racial discrimination. Charges of prejudice apparently had made their way through the gathering—unleashing anger, discomfort, and embarrassment. In particular, the author sympathized with the situation in the United States with specific reference to the American South and African Americans.[21]

In extending the international theme, elder statesman and physician Philip Jaisohn (So Chae'pil), contributed an article to the *KSB* in October of 1925 describing his experience attending the conference of the Institute of Pacific Relations in Honolulu. The conference brought together peoples living around the Pacific Ocean with the intent of fostering an exchange of ideas and greater mutual understanding among the participants. Interracial issues posed a central concern as nations jockeyed for economic and military advantage in the region in which stronger countries exploited weaker ones through territorial aggression. Jaisohn could not provide details of the proceedings for reasons of confidentiality, but he mentioned that attendees briefly addressed the plight of Korea. Hugh Cynn represented Korea at the meeting and did so admirably. Despite the complexities of the interracial conditions in the Pacific region, Jaisohn suggested that the answer could be found in the Eighth Commandment: Thou shalt not steal. If nations as well as individuals adhered to this principle, then more peace and justice would be evident in international interracial relations.[22]

Applied Christianity

"A Rule of Life: Comfort the poor, protect and shelter the weak and with all thy might right that which is wrong. Then shall the Lord love thee, and God himself shall be thy great reward."[23] Along with issues of race, the pages of the *KSB* enabled writers to work out meanings of their faith for themselves and for their readers. Protestant Christianity assumed a place of privilege within the bulletin, though often subsumed in the reportage of news and other related activities. Articles about religion revealed a kind of applied Christianity. As they moved from the realm of belief to action, a life of service beyond the self emerged as a major theme based on the example of Jesus.

One essayist reminded readers that, despite the importance of an education, the ultimate goal remained to live life as Christians fully engaged in the world. The challenge set before students entailed the development of Christian character modeled on the life of Jesus. Character in turn led one to a life of service: "The world needs not so much men who will dazzle it with their learning as it needs men and women who will lift it with their useful lives of earnestness and sincerity. The races of the world need more God-fearing earnest toiling men and women living truly that they may live to bless all about them." In calling readers to a life of service, the writer encouraged readers not to heed the pull of materialism and a life of acquisition. Far greater meaning and fulfillment awaited those who looked to Jesus as the guide and rule of life.[24]

Another journalist distinguished between a general belief in human nature or a supreme being to one centered on a personal God in whose image human beings had been created. The writer suggested that faith consisted of a relationship not only with God, but with other human beings.

What is interesting in this schema is how the connection between people necessitated working for social righteousness. The embrace of social change and the betterment of society, while worthy goals, had religion at its source. The appeal to be a blessing to all nations echoed the biblical promise given to Abraham and Sarah in the Hebrew scriptures. The author painted an integrated notion of faith in which faith in a personal God led to a life of service beneficial to other people, communities in which the believer lived, and by extension to the world at large.[25]

That world included a colonized Korea. In addressing the Korean Student Federation, Philip Jaisohn related the situation of Korea to the Christian faith. Jaisohn had been invited to be a speaker at a meeting of the federation during the summer of 1924 in Evanston, Illinois, but he could not be present. He sent his remarks by mail, and *KSB* printed the letter. The bulk of the message was a call to unity, citing the damage done to the cause of independence in Korea by internal divisions and strife. Jaisohn noted that the Korean Student Federation embodied the hope for the future of Korea since students represented a new generation of leadership. The nationalism in the letter is what one might expect from such a figure, but he closed his comments by underscoring the critical place of faith as a foundation for Korea's future. Jaisohn painted Korea's cause as a sacred one because of the just nature of Korea's yearning to be a free and independent nation. In a simple turn of phrase, the physician added: "This simple faith will enable you to face death with courage and receive honor and fortune with humble spirit."[26]

Between Here and There

Philip Jaisohn may have been based in the Philadelphia area, but in his commitments and aspirations he remained part of Korea. Many Koreans in the United States simultaneously and in dynamic fashion occupied migrant and exilic spaces, including those who passed through the pages of the *KSB*. Hugh Cynn continued his transnational ties through frequent travels through the Korean and the international YMCA. Others like Syngman Rhee, based in Hawaiʻi and the mainland, also spoke through the bulletin. The experiences of many less well-known individuals surfaced at different points over the course of the publication of the *KSB*. Second-generation Korean Americans comprised a distinctive subset of those both here and there, even though many of them had never been outside the United States and its territories, while international students from Korea encountered a range of experiences that marked the migration and exile relationship.

Park Sang Ryup left Korea in August of 1926 to begin his journey as an international student, slated to study at Ohio Wesleyan University. In a poignant letter written to his father, Park recounted the experience of being held for a week at the infamous Angel Island Detention Center in San Francisco Bay. He described how he could not sleep the night before the ships' arrival because of his anticipation of finally setting foot on the soil of the country that had inhabited his imagination for so long. The joy Park experienced at entering the bay proved short-lived, and the very fog seemed to say: "Don't come. Our country is too clean to admit a poor Oriental student as you." As he left the ship with immigration officials and went by a small motor boat to the white detention barracks, Park could not help but mark the irony of the beauty of the bay at twilight set against the two armed officials who greeted them at the dock. Approximately one hundred Chinese nationals had been pent up in the prisonlike quarters for months on end, and Park compared the center to an exhibit of undesirables from all over the world. The dehumanization of the process included being identified only by number, and the pain and suffering of those detained found expression in Chinese character poems etched into the very walls of the barracks.[27] How could a Christian nation so enamored of its democracy and liberty treat peoples from other parts of the world in such a fashion? Park's stay lasted a week, and one sensed that he felt fortunate to have gotten out but remained haunted by what he had experienced and seen. He ended the letter by letting his father know that he had arrived safely at Ohio Wesleyan.[28]

Park, like so many international students from Korea, hoped and dreamed of returning to the homelands with an American education. The *KSB* did not often print demographic information about students but rather gave more descriptive listings and news about individuals at various institutions. Of the few numbers available, the KSB reported that 21 Korean students were enrolled during the 1924–1925 academic year. By comparison, there were 36 students from India, 62 students from Japan, and 328 students from China. As US nationals, Filipinos were not counted as foreign students.[29] By 1939, approximately 265 students from Korea had gone to the United States. In 1937, the Committee on Friendly Relations recorded that California for that year had the largest number of foreign students (1,906) but also indicated that American-born Asians accounted for 735 of that number. Demographic data often depended on self-reportage, and many individuals floated in and out of student status depending on finances, health, and other issues. The high mobility and sporadic attendance of some students made it difficult to get accurate assessments of the general student profile. In addition, the fact that students overstayed their visas meant that they avoided bringing attention to their immigration status.[30]

Many young men and women did not realize their aspirations, beset by the realities of student-laborer lives in which they frequently had to interrupt their studies to earn a living. Emily Porcincula Lawsin's study of the *Filipino Student Bulletin* recounts that many students not only did not graduate from colleges and universities, but they also did not return home.[31] Sometimes, but not always differentiated by class, laborers and students illustrated the ambiguous and shifting nature of migration. For Koreans and Filipinos, colonialism and exile added another layer of experience. In calculating whether to stay or to return, colonization muted the pull of family and other ties to the homeland.[32]

Even for those students who received their degrees and went back to Korea, the time in the United States rendered them as transnational peoples in that they belonged to more than one place but perhaps not wholly to any. A biographical article published in 1927 featured L. George Paik, who after a decade in the United States returned to Korea to take up a teaching post at the Chosen Christian College in Seoul. A product of missionary education and sponsorship, Paik had been groomed to play a leading role in Korea's burgeoning Protestant movement. The star student earned an array of degrees from American schools: B.A. (Park College), M.A. and Th.B. (Princeton Seminary), and Ph.D. (Yale University). The article proudly listed Paik's many accomplishments, including his fluency in the Korean, Japanese, Chinese (Mandarin), and English languages as well as his scholarly work in biblical Greek, Latin, Hebrew, and German. Paik represented the elite segment of international students from Korea. The accumulation of cosmopolitan and cultural capital made Paik not only Korean, but a figure who could and did cross many boundaries. He became a leading figure in Korean higher education and a prominent church person in his home country and also in the international arena.[33]

If student-laborers from Korea who traversed the Pacific Ocean and negotiated life in United States provide glimpses into the relationship between migration and exile, then it might seem less likely that this theme would apply to second-generation Korean Americans. As US citizens by birth, the children of immigrants in places like Honolulu and Los Angeles had only a rudimentary grasp of the Korean language and Korean history, and few had ever been to Korea. Nevertheless, the experiences of the second generation underscore another dimension of migration and exile. Every second generation in the United States has had to grapple with their in-betweenness. The ties to ancestry through families and immigrant institutions coexisted with exposure to the larger society through schooling and popular culture.[34] This in-betweenness, however, has not been uniform. Korean Americans encountered an enduring racism reserved for those groups who have more or less been permanently relegated as the racial "other" in the United States, even accounting for the shifting constructions of "race" over time and place.[35]

A report based on the Korean secretary's travel in 1929 included an extended discussion of the second generation, prompted apparently by time spent in the Korean American community in Los Angeles. The American-born and Korean-born students did not have much interaction; the tensions between the two groups stemmed from differences in age, sensibilities, and life experiences. Chinese and Japanese students also faced similar circumstances. The article related that the separation could result in the loss of the soul of Koreanness in the second generation as the distance grew greater between them and Korea. And yet, this drift and potential loss did not stem from the wholesale embrace of American culture by Korean Americans. The commentary implied that racism factored into the situation, creating barriers and limits for the second generation and fostering isolation and an inward focus. The report recommended that the two groups of students seek to interact and to learn from one another and suggested that the YMCA, YWCA, and churches could facilitate interaction and exchange more broadly.[36]

KSB dedicated its May 1930 issue largely to the second generation. Numerous articles offered commentaries on the topic, including a pointed essay by Martha Choy. She did not take kindly to being referred to as a "problem" and especially bristled at critiques by international students: "But my indignation is aroused every time a braggadocio, sweetly deluded into believing himself the epitome of Korean learning and patriotism feels the urge to hand out hackneyed bits of wisdom. 'Tis no learning in him but pedantry; no patriotism, but chauvinism." Choy's reaction stemmed in part from her own assessment of how she had once idealized Korea and the prospect of someday visiting the land of her ancestors. Inspired by the patriotism she witnessed as a child growing up in Hawai'i, Choy had envisioned becoming a Korean Joan of Arc. Time had tempered her adolescent attitudes toward Korea, including the international students she encountered. Given her experience, one might have expected Choy to claim more of an American identity that stood in contrast with the overseas students with whom she differed. If so, Choy did not express such sentiments, and her essay seemed more about clarifying and carving out space for the second generation within an expanded and inclusive sense of what it meant to be Korean. She counseled greater tolerance even as she clearly set forth a defense of the second generation.[37]

Helen Lim provided her own version of how the second generation could integrate a sense of self based on what she saw taking place in Los Angeles. Rather than viewing American-born Koreans as a "problem," Lim instead envisioned the possibility of blending the best of two civilizations. Koreans in the United States represented a repository of Korean identity while the homeland suffered under colonial rule. By this logic, the future of Korea rested with the second generation to the extent that they embodied a Koreanness that would endure beyond their parents. According to Lim, the churches, and in her case the Korean Methodist Church of Los Angeles, held a key place in helping the second generation reach its potential. Lim pointed out that young men and women exercised leadership skills through church life, leading services and taking greater responsibility within the community. Music provided another venue in which the second generation could use their talents to bring recognition to Korean Americans in the eyes of the larger public.[38]

Several years after the special issue, an honors student at Mt. Holyoke College, Anne Kim, penned an insightful essay tackling head on the dilemma faced by second-generation Korean Americans—namely, that they were by no means full-fledged Americans nor were they fully Korean. Kim eloquently expressed the sentiments held by many of her peers: "In this land of freedom, he is not free. He will always have the label of yellow man and be treated as such. If he remains in this 'free and equal' country he will always be patronized and looked down upon by the white man. He will not have equal footing on which he can compete with the white man. . . . As long as he remains in this country he will always be treated as inferior and not as an equal to his white neighbor." Kim's candid words underscored the racialization of Korean Americans and the limits of US citizenship for the second generation in particular. Interestingly, Kim, while recognizing the ways in which a move to Korea would create serious challenges for the American-born, still considered the homeland an outlet for those with ambitions. Drawn by a sense of nationalism coupled with the realities of race relations in the United States, Kim believed Korea to hold possibilities for the second generation. Kim encouraged her readers to creatively approach the circumstances that they faced in order for Korean Americans to move forward.[39]

The future loomed large for every Korean student, with many struggling simply to stay in school as others worked hard to complete their varied programs. A colonized Korea and, in Anne Kim's estimation, an America in which Asians could not get a fair chance each presented young people with daunting barriers. During the end of the run of the *KSB* in the late 1930s and early 1940s, Japan's war with China meant that Korea's people and resources would be pressed into even greater service of the Japanese empire seeking to mold East Asia in its own image. In the United States, the lingering effects of the Great Depression placed Koreans, already on the margins, in a more precarious economic position. In this context, perhaps the most sober commentary on the status of Korean students in the United States came from a Princeton Seminary student named Y. Hahn. Writing in 1940, Hahn specifically addressed fellow students from Korea who understandably may have been tempted to not return home but to make a life in the United States.[40]

Hahn pointed to the need in the homeland for those with resurrection hope to walk the difficult path of sacrificial service because of the example set by Jesus, Mary Magdalene, and the early apostles and martyrs of the church: "Now 'our Jerusalem' is not Los Angeles, Chicago, New York, or Washington, D.C., but it is *Seoul,* the capital of our homeland. Our mission is the re-building of 'our Jerusalem.' Do our friends warn us not to enter the city, as Agabus warned St. Paul with the prophetic sign of binding feet and hands? Let us look beyond the gloomy predictions to the Divine Will which will guide our way toward 'our Jerusalem.'" Hahn understood the pull for migrant students to take exile in the United States, since Christians increasingly faced harassment and violence from Japanese police and spies sent to conduct surveillance and to monitor churches and church-related institutions. The seminarian encouraged people to look to the Risen Lord for courage and hope so that they might be faithful to the calling that they had received.[41]

The migrant and exile relationship encompassed a range of individuals who surfaced in the pages of the *Korean Student Bulletin*, from elder statesmen who as exiles worked diligently on behalf of Korean independence to students, both foreign and native born. Some young men and women enjoyed the privilege of full-time study, but most worked their way through school with interruptions and, in some cases, unrealized dreams. Irrespective of citizenship, generation, or class, all of the writers in the *KSB* could identify with an in-betweenness that marked their condition as Korean/American Christians seeking to find their way in a transnational and troubled world.

Sacred Cause of Liberty

In the golden age of Asia
Korea was one of its lamp-bearers
And that lamp is waiting
To be lighted once again
For the illumination
In the East

—Rabindranath Tagore[42]

Migration and exile, in a geographic and spiritual sense, stemmed in part from the realities of colonialism and the struggle for independence. The hope of a Korea free from Japanese rule rested in the hearts of Koreans spread across continents, spurring concerted action and creating contention and strife. Students occupied an importance place in the workings of independence, as is evident in the ways that the issue found expression within the *KSB*. The fate of Korea elicited varied responses from writers. Many of them saw their homeland within a biblical framework. Korea, like Israel, sought divine deliverance from its oppressors, even as many other peoples throughout history had drawn such an analogy. In addition, conference proceedings, editorial columns, discussion forums, and news stories all demonstrated a dedication to keeping alive Korea's sacred cause of liberty.[43]

The future Christian educator L. George Paik reported his attendance at an interdenominational student conference held in the Chicago area at the end of 1925. Paik noted the full agenda of panels, topics, and resolutions, but one element of the gathering seemed to make a lasting impression. A contingent of Filipino students passionately presented their case for the independence of the Philippines before their colonizers, since the majority of the conference goers were European Americans. These students operated from within a Christian framework to critique religion as complicit with colonialism but also offered an example of a faith-based approach to the concerns of their homeland.[44]

Other writers must have picked up on the sentiments expressed by Paik as they pondered how their faith informed their aspirations and actions for Korea. One columnist in 1931 commented on how the momentum and energy from the March First movement had been waning under the tightening control of the Japanese. The author noted that the change in colonial policy to ease overt controls and restrictions masked more covert and subtle ways that the Japanese operated in Korea. International students, among others, faced an "agonizing" test in working on behalf of Korea's freedom. The writer invoked the language of building the kingdom of God and asked readers whether they possessed the devotion to consecrate their lives to this cause. The very future of the nation depended on it.[45]

While some called for action, others brought their faith and intellects to better understand how they might participate in the larger cause of their homeland. In a symposium hosted by the *KSB*, several students offered their perspectives on Korea's needs. Chyung Yil Hyung, a seminarian in New York, suggested that a greater percentage of Korea's population be given access to education. Only about a third of Korean children went to school, according to Chyung, and hearts and minds could not be cultivated without a foundation in education. In addition, those working on the farms of Korea suffered under high taxes, depressed prices, and difficult working conditions. Along with these educational and agricultural issues, leadership remained a pressing concern for the nation: "We need not only men and women with brain power, but men and women who are spiritual giants, individuals that can lift the crowds above the fog and mist of depression and show them the dawn of the 'Greater Korea.'"[46]

Others in the discussion forum reinforced the idea of leadership. T. H. Chun of the Pacific School of Religion in Berkeley, California, emphasized that leadership entailed a sacrificial love exemplified by Jesus, who laid down his life for others. From a societal standpoint, Chun advanced the idea of a reconstruction of the nation based on a social justice that applied to the political and economic realms.[47] A student from the Teachers College at Columbia University stressed leadership experienced in self-help, promoting unity, and democratic mass education. Moreover, in addressing material concerns of the nation, one should not forget the spiritual and how the two must go hand in hand in moving Korea forward.[48]

Maria Kim of Biblical Seminary also raised the issue of leadership,[49] but in the context of a Korea free to manage its own affairs. Instead of looking to others, Koreans had to fend for themselves and fight. An important part of these efforts included genuine leadership independent in thought but dependent upon God. She also juxtaposed individual initiative and a cooperative spirit. Kim looked to the biblical witness: "As the Israelites in Egypt in their distress cried unto God for deliverance and He raised up Moses as their deliverer, so we Koreans at home and abroad must cry unto God that He would raise up a like leader who will lead us out of bondage unto the promised land of plenty."[50]

It is debatable whether Maria Kim's prayer for a Korean Moses had been answered, but the *KSB* certainly carried news about important leaders within the Korean diaspora. Many of these figures had been influenced by Protestant Christianity and spent significant time in the United States.[51] The bulletin reported on the assassination of patriot Pak Yong-man in China in October of 1928 and its reverberations through the Korean community in Hawai'i.[52] A graduate of the University of Nebraska, Pak advocated a military approach to Korean independence and had established academies on the mainland, in Hawai'i, and in East Asia.[53] In the same issue, an article featured Helen Kim, a leading figure in higher education in Korea.[54] Kim had graduated from Methodist-related Ewha, the prestigious college for women, and then gone on to the United States to continue her studies at Ohio Wesleyan, Boston University, and Columbia University. The *KSB* noted that Kim received her Ph.D. from Teachers College at Columbia in 1931, the first Korean woman to earn an American doctorate.[55] As dean and eventually president of Ewha and a Christian lay leader, Kim worked on broad social reforms in Korea through her alma mater and through the YWCA.

Physician and statesman Philip Jaisohn served as an advisor and role model for both international and native-born students connected to the Korean Student Federation. Jaisohn wrote in the *KSB* about compatriot Ahn Chang-ho (An Ch'ang-ho), who had been imprisoned by the Japanese and died in Seoul in March 1938.[56] Jaisohn had not known Ahn very well, but a connection existed between the two in that Ahn had been inspired by Jaisohn's lectures given at the Independence Club in Korea. Jaisohn noted the contributions that Ahn had made in California through the Korean National Association and the Young Korean Academy.[57] Ahn worked tirelessly for unity and spiritual and moral regeneration among Koreans to lay a foundation for self-rule.[58]

Another person with strong missionary ties was Kim Kiusic (Kim Kyu-sik),[59] former chief delegate of Korea to the Paris Peace Conference in 1919. The *KSB* reported in its May–June 1933 issue that Kim had been touring the country to garner American support for China and Korea in light of Japan's invasion of Manchuria.[60] One of the first families of American Protestant missionaries in Korea, the Underwoods, took the orphaned Kim under its wing and sponsored him to attend Roanoke College in Virginia, a Lutheran-affiliated school. Kim graduated as valedictorian in 1903. He returned to Korea as secretary to Horace G. Underwood and remained active with the Korean YMCA and in missionary-affiliated education. To avoid the Japanese, Kim went into exile and embarked on a long and winding journey of nationalist politics that took him to France, the United States, China, and Mongolia. He also worked across a wide political spectrum from right to left and became a major player in diasporic politics.[61]

Despite these and other able leaders, Korea during the era of the publication of the *KSB* suffered under colonialism without much hope of relief. An incident involving derogatory language used by three Japanese high school male students toward three Korean female students in the southwest region near the city of Kwangju in October 1929 set off demonstrations that spread and that by early 1930 involved nearly 60,000 students in close to two hundred schools. The events in Kwangju formed part of a larger set of student-based nationalist activities that protested curricular issues such as the prohibition against the teaching of the Korean language and Korean history.[62] The *KSB* provided ample print space to cover the events taking place. One response to the events took the form of a heartfelt, unsigned prayer. In its tone and content, the prayer can be read as a lament regarding the Kwangju demonstrations, but it can also be understood as speaking to the larger issue of colonial oppression within the context of Christian faith:

> Father, where is thy justice? Must righteousness ever be crushed in the hands of injustice? Must the will to live that Thou hast given be trampled down so mercilessly? Must humanity succumb to brutality? Must brotherhood suffer under the tyranny of bloodshed?
>
> O Lord, where is thy love that led the people of Israel to the land of milk and honey from the yoke of Egypt? Where is thy wrath that destroyed the wickedness of Sodom and Gomorrah?[63]

Fare Thee Well

As a publication by and for students, the *Korean Student Bulletin* regularly reported news of comings and goings. Perhaps it is fitting that the last issue of the *KSB*, in April 1941, marked the untimely passing of Alexander Hurh, who had served as the secretary for Korean students for the previous seven years.[64] Like many others, Hurh had been educated in Protestant mission schools in Korea. He arrived at the University of Michigan in 1924 to earn both a B.A. and an M.A. in history. Hurh had to work his way through school, and it seems likely that financial pressures forced him to end his postgraduate studies at Columbia University and to take the position as Korean secretary with the Committee on Friendly Relations.[65]

The *KSB* noted that, at the memorial service held in New York City at the Korean Methodist Church on January 4, 1941, both Koreans and Americans filled the sanctuary to capacity and spilled outside the doors of the church. The Korean Methodist Church and Institute had been founded in the early 1920s, and it made sense that the service for Hurh took place at that central gathering place for Koreans in New York City. The church had come into being in the aftermath of the March First movement in 1919, and independence had been woven into its mission from the start. Located near Columbia University on 115th Street, the church had for many years served as a way station for students, political exiles, and the small Korean

American community in the area. The designation of "institute" along with the church signified its more expansive mission.[66]

The confluence of religion and race could be seen in those in attendance at the church that day—students, YMCA staff, church members, former missionaries, and friends. Most if not all in attendance that day shared a Protestant faith, but there nevertheless remained a marker that set Koreans apart from non-Koreans. Race framed the language of the Christian service and witness by underscoring the difference between Hurh and his people from those in the United States. Tributes to Hurh emphasized the ways in which he fostered "mutual understanding and esteem between these two peace loving nations."[67] The workings of religion and race were not lost upon the writers of the *KSB* over the years. They commented on the reality of racism in American society, a reality not easily overcome even within the Christian fold.

Along with religion and race, one sees in the life journey of Alexander Hurh, and with so many of the students, the complexities of migration and exile. Hurh had come to the United States to get an education to return to his homeland, but by the time of his death at age thirty-eight, he had spent almost half of his life outside of Korea.[68] Hurh's position as Korean secretary, however, enabled him to keep abreast of events in the homeland through the steady flow of students from Korea to the United States and back again. Migration and exile were not strange themes to the Christian faith, and students made the connections throughout their journeys.[69]

For all of the students crossing paths with the *Korean Student Bulletin,* Korea's fate as a colonized nation sparked visions of independence that many of them linked to their faith. Some looked to the Israelites held captive in and then delivered from Egypt as a source of hope and encouragement. Others spoke about the pressing need for leadership, asking God to raise up a Moses for Korea. News of important leaders filled the pages of the bulletin over the years, and so did prayers seeking justice for those suffering under the yoke of oppression.

Much had taken place between the day the first Korean secretary, Julian S. Park, left New York City in the autumn of 1922 to tour college and university campuses and the unfortunate death of Korean secretary Alexander Hurh in 1941. The pages of the *Korean Student Bulletin* served as a printed record of the many lives that spanned a Korean diaspora marked in part by the relationships between religion and race, migration and exile, and colonialism and independence. The sorrow surrounding Hurh's passing in January of 1941 mixed with uncertainty in the wake of Pearl Harbor by the year's end. The sober reality of a world at war also brought with it a renewed hope of a free Korea.

Notes

An earlier version of this chapter appeared in *Contentious Spirits: Religion in Korea American History, 1903–1945* (Stanford, CA: Stanford University Press, 2010), chapter 6.

1. "Mr. Yelton Introduces the Korean Secretary" and "Report on College Visitation," *Korean Student Bulletin* (hereafter *KSB*), December 1922.

2. The last regular issue of the *KSB* appears to have been the March–April 1940 issue, though nothing in the issue itself indicated that it would be the end. The date 1941 is listed as the end point because of a special issue in April 1941 in honor of Alexander Hurh, who died of an illness in January 1941. Hurh had served as the Korean secretary.

3. The bulletin had a broad geographic focus since students went to school throughout the United States, but California and Hawai'i still proved to be centers of activity, as reflected in many of the writings discussed in this chapter.

4. "The Bulletin Is," *KSB*, December 1922.

5. "Committee on Friendly Relations among Foreign Students," *KSB*, December 1922.

6. C. Howard Hopkins, *History of the Y.M.C.A. in North America* (New York: Association Press, 1951), 629–630.

7. Michael Parker, *The Kingdom of Character: The Student Volunteer Movement for Foreign Missions, 1886–1926* (Lanham, MD: University Press of America, 1998).

8. H. M. Goodpasture, "Student Volunteer Movement for Foreign Missions," in *Dictionary of Christianity in America*, ed. Daniel G. Reid et al. (Downers Grove, IL: InterVarsity Press, 1990), 1143.

9. "My Impressions of the Ninth Quadrennial International Student Volunteer Convention in Indianapolis," *KSB*, February 1924.

10. Regional groups formed, affiliated with the national work of the Committee on Friendly Relations, like the Korean Christian Students Association of Los Angeles.

11. *KSB*, October 1925; March–April 1939.

12. Warren Y. Kim, *Koreans in America* (Seoul: Po Chin Chai Printing Co., 1971), 22–23.

13. For information on the other Asian groups see Timothy Tseng, "Religious Liberalism, International Politics, and Diasporic Realities: The Chinese Students Christian Association of North America, 1909–1951," *The Journal of America-East Asian Relations* 5, nos. 3–4 (1996): 305–330; David K. Yoo, *Growing Up Nisei: Race, Generation, and Culture among Japanese Americans of California, 1924–1949* (Urbana: University of Illinois Press, 2000), 59–63; Emily Porcincula Lawsin, "Pensionados, Paisanos, and Pinoys: An Analysis of the Filipino Student Bulletin, 1929–1933," *Filipino American National Historical Society Journal* 4 (1996): 33–33P.

14. Hopkins, *Y.M.C.A. in North America*, 6, 594–604. The stories of the intensive and massive fund-raising campaigns in various cities in the United States (and in other locales) suggest the capitalist storehouse that funded the YMCA and other American Protestant ventures at home and abroad.

15. For a helpful study of American Protestant missions, see William R. Hutchison, *Errand to the World: American Protestant Thought and Foreign Missions* (Chicago: University of Chicago Press, 1987).

16. Mark A. Noll, *A History of Christianity in the United States and Canada* (Grand Rapids, MI: W. B. Eerdmans, 1992), 304–307.

17. Mott as quoted in Hopkins, *Y.M.C.A. in North America*, 657. The social gospel in the United States is far more complex than the couple of sentences devoted to the movement here. There is a considerable body of work that has been identified with the movement as well as studies about the movement. Among the secondary literature, see C. Howard Hopkins, *The Rise of the Social Gospel in American Protestantism, 1865–1915* (New Haven: Yale University Press, 1940); Ronald C. White and C. Howard Hopkins, *The Social Gospel: Religion and Reform in Changing America* (Philadelphia: Temple University Press, 1976); and Christopher H. Evans, ed., *The Social Gospel Today* (Louisville: Westminster John Knox Press, 2001).

18. Jun Xing, *Baptized in the Fire of Revolution: The American Social Gospel and the YMCA in China, 1919–1937* (Bethlehem, PA: Lehigh University Press, 1996). This study provides a good case study of how the YMCA's student movement's embrace of the social gospel played out in China during a volatile era.

19. "Foreign Students in U.S.A.," *KSB*, May–June 1937.

20. Chi Chin Hahn, "The Good and Bad Elements of American Civilization," *KSB*, January 1926.

21. "My Impressions of the Ninth Quadrennial International Student Volunteer Convention in Indianapolis," *KSB*, February 1924.

22. Dr. Philip Jaisohn, "Institute of Pacific Relations," *KSB*, October 1925.

23. Attributed to Alfred the Great (c. 849–899), quoted in *KSB*, January 1926.

24. "The Christian Challenge," *KSB*, February 1923.

25. "Faith in a Personal God," *KSB*, April 1923.

26. "Dr. Jaisohn's Letter to the Convention," *KSB*, September 1924.

27. Angel Island serves as a prominent marker in Asian American history of exclusion, racism, and the role of the nation-state. Many studies examine the history of Asian Americans (especially Chinese Americans) and Angel Island, including Sucheng Chan, *Asian Americans: An Interpretive History* (Boston: Twayne, 1991); Ronald Takaki, *Strangers from a Different Shore: A History of Asian Americans* (Boston: Little, Brown, 1989); Him Mark Lai, Genny Lim, and Judy Yung, *Island: Poetry and History of Chinese Immigrants on Angel Island, 1910*–1940 (Seattle: University of Washington Press, 1999); Erika Lee, *At America's Gates: Chinese Immigration during the Exclusion Era* (Chapel Hill: University of North Carolina Press, 2003); and Laurence Yep and Kathy S. Yep, *The Dragon's Child: A Story of Angel Island* (New York: HarperCollins, 2008).

28. "On Entering the U.S.: A Letter from a Korean Student to His Father," *KSB*, November–December 1938. Sang Ryup Park later worked in Los Angeles on the leftist newspaper linked to the Korean National Revolutionary Party, *Korean Independence.*

29. "Number of Foreign Students Admitted to U.S.," *KSB*, October 1925.

30. "Korean Students in America," *KSB,* 1939; "Foreign Students in U.S.A.," *KSB*, May–June 1937.

31. Lawsin, "Pensionados, Paisanos, and Pinoys," 33D–33E.

32. On religion and migration in the Filipino American experience, see Steffi San Buenaventura, "Filipino Folk Spirituality and Immigration: From Mutual Aid to Religion," in *New Spiritual Homes: Religion and Asian Americans*, ed. David K. Yoo (Honolulu: University of Hawai'i Press, 1999), 52–86.

33. "Dr. Paik Returns to Korea to Teach," *KSB*, November 1927.

34. There are many fine studies of second-generation Americans, including Deborah Dash Moore, *At Home in America: Second Generation New York Jews* (New York: Columbia University Press, 1981); Jere Takahashi, *Nisei/Sansei: Shifting Japanese American Identities and Politics* (Philadelphia: Temple University Press, 1997); and Marjorie Lee, "*Hu-Jee:* The Forgotten Second Generation of Chinese America, 1930–1950" (M.A. thesis, University of California, Los Angeles, 1984). For a general overview of US immigration history: Thomas Archdeacon, *Becoming American: An Ethnic History* (New York: Free Press, 1983); Roger Daniels, *Coming to America: A History of Immigration and Ethnicity in American Life* (New York: Harper Perennial, 2002).

35. Joe R. Feagin, *Systemic Racism: A Theory of Oppression* (New York: Routledge, 2006).

36. "The Secretary's Trip to the Pacific Coast," *KSB,* October 1929.

37. "Confessions of an American-Born Korean," *KSB*, May 1930.

38. "Problems of the Second Generation in Los Angeles," *KSB*, May 1930.

39. "Whither American-Born Korean," *KSB*, March–April 1935.

40. "The Sanction of the Christian Worker," *KSB*, March–April 1940.

41. Ibid.

42. The Nobel Laureate's poem appeared in the October 1929 issue of the *KSB* in what appeared to be a copy of a handwritten message from Tagore, dated March 28, 1929.

43. The identification of God and nation is a tradition firmly grounded in the American experience, extending from colonial times to the period under discussion, including the Protestant missionary enterprise. Helpful texts on this theme include Ernest L. Tuveson, *Redeemer Nation: The Idea of America's Millennial Role* (Chicago: University of Chicago Press, 1968); and Robert T. Handy, *A Christian America: Protestant Hopes and Historical Realities* (New York: Oxford University Press, 1971).

44. "Evanston Conference," *KSB*, March 1926.

45. "Meeting the Supreme Test," *KSB*, March 1931.

46. "Mass Education, Improvement of Agriculture, Spiritual Leadership," *KSB*, March 1931.

47. "Love, Faithful Leadership and Economic Justice," *KSB*, March 1931. See also Kenneth M. Wells, *New God, New Nation: Protestants and Self-Reconstruction Nationalism in Korea, 1896–1937* (Honolulu: University of Hawai'i Press, 1990).

48. "Spirit and Matter Must Go Together," *KSB*, March 1931.

49. Biblical Seminary is today New York Theological Seminary. The school was founded in 1900 as a nondenominational Protestant institution. For more information, see http://www.nyts.edu.

50. "Initiative but Cooperative Leadership," *KSB*, March 1931.

51. This intentionally brief discussion of important leaders is meant only to offer a quick composite sketch of those who appeared in the pages of the *KSB* and to provide a few additional details by way of context. Many of these individuals are discussed in previous chapters. Other key leaders, especially those who did not have a connection with the United States and Protestant Christianity, did not get much press. Information about the leaders who appear in the *KSB* (and these others) is available in the literature of Korean and Korean American studies. Some helpful texts include Chong-Sik Lee, *The Politics of Korean Nationalism* (Berkeley: University of California Press, 1963); Bruce Cumings, *Korea's Place in the Sun: A Modern History* (New York: W. W. Norton, 2005); Ki-Baik Lee, *A New History of Korea*, translated by Edward W. Wagner with Edward Schulz (Cambridge, MA: Harvard University Press, 1984); Bong-youn Choy, *Koreans in America* (Chicago: Nelson-Hall, 1977); Warren Y. Kim, *Koreans in America*.

52. "News Items from Hawai'i," *KSB*, December 1928.

53. Choy, *Koreans in America*, 85–87.

54. "An Appreciation of Miss Helen Kim," *KSB*, December 1928.

55. "New Ewha Head," *KSB*, May–June 1939.

56. "Chang Ho Ahn Dies at 61; Champion of Korea's Freedom," *KSB*, February–March 1938; "My Impression of Ahn Chang-Ho," *KSB*, April–May 1938.

57. "My Impression of Ahn Chang-Ho," *KSB*, April–May 1938.

58. Choy, *Koreans in America*, 80–83.

59. Kiusic Kim as well as Kiusic Kimm were anglicized spellings of Kim Kyu-sik, and the spelling here is what appeared in the bulletin.

60. "Dr. Kiusic Kim in America," *KSB*, May–June 1935.

61. Key S. Ryang, "Kim Kyu-Sik as a Common Man and a Political Leader," *Korea Observer* 13, no. 1 (1982): 36–54.

62. Ki-Baik Lee, *History of Korea*, 363–364.

63. "In Defense of Justice: A Prayer," *KSB*, February 1930.

64. Although most records indicate that the last regular issue of the *KSB* appeared in March–April 1940, the tribute to Hurh was published as a special issue in April 1941.

65. *KSB*, April 1941. In the November–December 1934 issue of the *KSB* announcing his appointment, Hurh was identified as a Ph.D. candidate in History at Columbia University.

66. Ellen Lee, *The Planted Seed: History of the English Language Ministry of the Korean Methodist Church and Institute* (New York: Korean Methodist Church and Institute, 1995), 13–17; Warren Y. Kim, *Koreans in America*, 36–37; Choy, *Koreans in America*, 256.

67. Choy, *Koreans in America*, 256.

68. Based on the information in the special issue of the *KSB*, Hurh, by my calculation, had been born in 1903, come to the United States at the age of twenty-one in 1924, and died in 1941 at the age of thirty-eight.

69. *New Korea*, January 9, 1941. The article listed Hurh as thirty-six years old.

11

Protestant Christianity in Reform-Era China

Realities and Representations

David Ownby

For several summers in the mid-1990s, I had the good fortune to carry out fieldwork in rural Henan with a Chinese colleague who taught at the Communist Party School in Zhengzhou, the provincial capital. Although we were working on the resurgence of Chinese popular religion, we immediately noticed that in some parts of rural Henan, Protestant Christian groups were at least as active as those of native popular religions. Consequently, one summer we visited numerous villages where House Church Protestants were very active, and to this day I have vivid memories of my warm reception by the local Christians, who hoped that I would spread the gospel to Canada on my return to Montreal. I toyed with the idea of undertaking a major research project on the growth of Protestantism in the region but eventually abandoned the idea because of logistical, political, and financial difficulties (I did not obtain a grant that I had applied for).

Fifteen years later, it is clear that I missed a historic opportunity. The rise of the Protestant Church in post-Mao China, part of a larger religious revival still under way, has surpassed the expectations of all but the most visionary of Christian believers. Despite decades of efforts by dedicated Western missionaries and Chinese converts since the nineteenth century, there were at most 1 million Chinese Protestants in 1949 when the Communist regime came to power, a number that appears to have remained stable or perhaps suffered a decline during the Maoist period (1949–1976). At present, estimates of the number of Chinese Protestants vary widely, ranging from 20 million (a conservative estimate that includes only the government-approved churches of the Three-Self Protestant movement) to 110 million (an estimate including membership in both Three-Self churches and the unregistered, semilegal House Church movement).[1] If one accepts the high estimate, then roughly 10 percent of China's population would now be Christian (especially considering that China's Catholics number some 20 million), which would represent a major change in China's religious landscape as well as that of world Christianity: China would be the third largest Christian nation in the world in terms of absolute numbers of believers, coming after the United States (225 million) and Brazil (140 million).[2] And even if we err on the side of conservatism and accept a figure of 20 million Chinese Protestants—a number that seems improbably small—Chinese Protestantism would still have expanded by a factor of twenty in thirty-odd years. The rise of Chinese Protestantism from the late 1970s to the present is thus a phenomenon worthy of the attention of sinologists, students of world affairs, Christians and students of Christianity, and the Chinese authorities.

That being said, the Protestant revival in contemporary China is a frustrating topic to try to research for a variety of reasons. First is the ambivalence of the Chinese state on all issues concerning religion. If Chinese authorities have largely abandoned the iconoclastic, aggressively secularizing policies of the Cultural Revolution period in favor of a half-hearted embrace of religion as a force contributing to social harmony, the statist desire for control that has been at the heart of China's politics of religion over the past century remains intact. The Chinese state currently treats religion in much the same way most governments treat alcohol: as harmless or perhaps mildly beneficial if carefully controlled but dangerous without proper regulation or if consumed in excessive quantities. Christianity, which remains a foreign faith in the eyes of China's leaders, is seen to be particularly risky. Consequently, all official state pronouncements about religion—and hence about Protestantism—must be read through the distorting lens of China's ongoing political quest to monitor and regulate religion for statist ends.

Second, state ambivalence toward Protestant Christianity has been institutionalized in the structure and function of the Chinese Christian Council and the Three-Self Protestant movement church. While serving some of the needs of the religious faithful attending Three-Self churches, the established church also hews very closely to the Communist Party line in terms of doctrine (emphasis on social engagement and modernist ecumenical spirit as opposed to evangelical themes such as repentance, salvation, and end-times discourse) and practice (acceptance of regulations that slow church growth and eschew ties with unauthorized Protestant groups). Statements made by Three-Self Protestant movement leaders in journals, on web sites, in seminaries, and from the pulpit cannot be accepted at face value because they inevitably reflect the fact that the church's primary loyalty is to the Chinese Communist Party, rather than to their faith or their faithful.

Third, the House Church Protestant movement, widely acknowledged to be the most vibrant part of the Protestant revival, is a semiunderground phenomenon with its roots in rural China—even if it seems to have spread throughout much of urban China over the past two decades. Although in some parts of China the House Church has become an accepted part of the social fabric, in other areas leaders and even members are regularly harassed and arrested. Consequently, it is not surprising that the House Church movement does not make available detailed information concerning its size, structure, and activities. The public statements they do make (such as "Back to Jerusalem: God's Call to the Chinese Church to Complete the Great Commission")[3] are often more immediately revealing of the ambitions of certain groups within the larger House Church movement than of daily realities.

Fourth, many of those who write about Protestant Christianity from outside China do so from a partisan perspective. Tony Lambert and David Aikman, who have written compelling books about the House Church movement, are both evangelical Christians and predisposed to see the hand of the Holy Spirit at work in the rapid expansion of the House Church and the ultimate salvation of China. Philip Wickeri has written learned tomes about the Three-Self Protestant movement and its leadership at least in part to defend the actions and the theology of the state-sanctioned church. Most of the many web sites that follow the fortunes of Christians in China do so from a point of view of clear advocacy; indeed, many are directly linked to Christian missionary efforts in China.[4] Examples of more neutral scholarship are few and far between, largely because such work would require extensive fieldwork, which is difficult to carry out under current conditions in China.

For all of these reasons, it is extremely difficult, when trying to understand the Protestant revival in China, to see past the spin employed by most of the players to the complex reality on the ground. In preparation for this chapter, I have devoted several months to reading what I could find in English, French, and Chinese on the Protestant revival under way in today's China, including Western journalistic and scholarly studies, Chinese scholarship and statements by Chinese secular and religious authorities, and, finally, materials produced by Chinese missionary organizations such as ChinaAid and the China Soul for Christ Foundation. These varied perspectives, often grounded in divergent objectives (scholars analyze, governments regulate/control, missionaries proselytize), allow us to grasp different aspects of China's Protestant boom but do not provide a comprehensive overview. My general reflections on the state of our knowledge about the Protestant revival in China are as follows.

Western scholarship provides us with basic information, and increasing numbers of scholars are turning their attention to Chinese Protestantism. At the same time, Western studies lag behind the events on the ground in China. This is perhaps inevitable; China is a large country, and the Protestant movement is both fairly new and quite decentralized. There is much fieldwork to be done, and Chinese authorities are not eager to help foreigners working on this topic. At the same time, my impression is that the China field as a whole does not accord religion—and particularly Chinese Christianity—the attention it deserves.

Turning to Chinese-language sources, I was surprised to find that increasing numbers of scholars have taken up the study of the Protestant revival in reform era China. One can read reasonably objective depictions of the House Church and even calls for its legalization. At the same time, neither China's religious authorities (the State Administration for Religious Affairs) nor the head of the state-approved Protestant church (the Chinese Christian Council) publicly acknowledges the dimensions of the Protestant revival, preferring to speak through regulations designed to slow the growth of the church. Religion in general has been granted a more positive role since 2006 in China's campaign to build a harmonious socialist society, but the discursive silence on the subject of the rapid rise of Protestantism is marked.

The refusal by Chinese secular or religious authorities to acknowledge the Protestant revival under way in China combined with the semilegal—and hence somewhat voiceless—status of the House Church, the driving force of the revival, means that the revival has occurred, is occurring, in something of a vacuum. With the exception of preachers and evangelists in China, there has been no person or organization to define or speak for the burgeoning Protestant movement, outline its history, craft its larger narrative, and clarify its relationship to China's social development. Into this vacuum has stepped groups such as the China Soul for Christ Foundation, an organization founded and largely run by Chinese converts from the mainland (with the help of some Christians from Taiwan), now established in North America, who have dedicated themselves to converting all of China to Christ through the production and dissemination of high-quality videos and DVDs depicting the rise of Protestant Christianity in China. These videos link today's Protestants in China with the modern history of the independent Chinese Protestant church (and not with the state-authorized Three-Self Protestant movement church, although China Soul strikes an ecumenical rather a sectarian tone—in other words, the Three-Self church is invited to join the true church), with modern science, and with the achievement of China's true destiny as a Christian nation. To the extent that these videos are available in China—and the organization has made a concerted effort to make them available—they may well provide a sense of self-awareness to a "movement" that to date may not have seen itself as such. Indeed, the work of organizations such as China Soul illustrates the complex, global character of China's Protestant revival, as exiled Christians from China use modern technology and a base abroad to instruct Chinese Protestants in their own history and identity. What China Soul is doing is attempting to turn a representation into a reality.

Western-Language Studies of China's Protestant Revival

Given the newness of the Protestant revival and the attitude of China's authorities toward the rise of the church, it is not surprising that Western literature on the topic is uneven. There is sufficient information available for scholars who wish to appraise the state of the field with an eye toward future research[5] or for journalists in search of further challenges to the rule of China's Communist Party.[6] On the whole, however, the field is at present partisan and fragmented.

As evidence of partisanship, let us look briefly at the two best overviews of China's Protestant revival, written by two Christian journalists: Tony Lambert's *China's Christian Millions*[7] and David Aikman's *Jesus in Beijing*.[8] Lambert, an English evangelical Christian who speaks Chinese and has spent considerable time in China, including a stint with the British Embassy in Beijing, is currently director of China research for OMF International. His *China's Christian Millions* touches on many aspects of the Protestant experience in China since the nineteenth century but focuses on the House Church revival since the Cultural Revolution. Lambert follows the rise—and tribulations—of the House Church in Henan, Anhui, and elsewhere, providing valuable details about the leadership and spread of the movement, as well as the movement's response to frequent harassment and persecution. Aikman, formerly a journalist for *Time* magazine, offers a book that is broadly similar to Lambert's. He too focuses largely on the House Church and bases his work chiefly on personal reporting—several trips carried out in the late 1990s and 2000s. Aikman offers perhaps a bit more history of the Chinese Protestant church than does Lambert, tracing the history of Christian missions in China from much earlier periods and offering a chapter on Chinese "patriarchs" such as Wang Mingdao, Allen Yuan, Samuel Lamb, Moses Xie, and Li Tianen, all of whom were imprisoned in the 1950s for refusing to join the Three-Self church. But most of his narrative focuses on the dramatic rise of the House Church in central China in the post–Cultural Revolution period, although the Three-Self church and even the Catholics are discussed as well.

These books are extremely informative and greatly enriched by the personal contacts between the journalists and leaders and members of the House Church, contacts that might not have been possible had the journalists not identified themselves as evangelical Christians. At the same time, their Christian convictions clearly shape the authors' presentation of the House Church, which they identify as part of a major renewal of world Protestantism (although Lambert takes Aikman to task for his "overly charismatic bias").[9] Lambert and Aikman are free to craft their arguments as they see fit, and since they are publishing at Christian publishing houses with, presumably, a largely Christian readership in mind, it is perhaps not surprising that the books strike a triumphalist tone. At the same time, their focus perhaps leads the authors to overstate the impact of the emergence of "Christian China"—because, after all, even if by some miracle 10 percent of China's population is now Christian, 90 percent still is not. Their focus on Christianity rather than China also leads Lambert and Aikman to overlook crucial questions such as the relations between the Christian minority and the non-Christian majority, except in the context of persecution. In the absence of persecution, do Chinese Protestants see themselves as an embattled minority? Or does their Christian identity readily coexist with other layers of their pre-Christian social world? As the House Church movement spreads into urban areas, Protestantism surely cannot be grafted onto preexisting village solidarities, which might have been the case in rural areas. For all of these reasons, one is forced to conclude that, if Lambert and Aikman are must-reads, they may not be the last word on the subject.

Philip Wickeri offers another version of partisanship. Professor of Evangelism and Mission at the San Francisco Theological Seminary, Wickeri is an active member of the Council of World Mission and Evangelism of the World Council of Churches with historical ties to the Chinese Three-Self Protestant movement church through his work with the Amity Foundation.[10] Wickeri's scholarship takes the Chinese establishment church seriously,[11] both as an expression of a nationalistic desire to build an indigenous Christianity and, from a global theological perspective, a participant in world dialogues concerning the "liberal" church. In other words, he seeks to defend the Three-Self Protestant movement and its leadership from charges that the official church is little more than the lapdog of the Chinese party-state, or at the very least to read church writings and pronouncements carefully, giving them the benefit of the doubt. Although I doubt that many House Church Christians would be swayed by Wickeri's arguments, he documents with great care the difficult task undertaken by the Three-Self Protestant movement to seek to provide a relatively safe haven, in a time of revolution and rapid social change, for members of their flock.[12] Moreover, Wickeri's scholarly and missionary work has been devoted for some decades to the cause of making Chinese Christianity part of world Christianity.

That said, just as Lambert and Aikman embrace China's House Church Protestants as the wave of the future in Christian evangelism, Wickeri defends the liberal ecumenicalism at the heart of Three-Self Protestant movement theology and at least implicitly endorses the difficult political compromises its leadership has had to make over the years as concessions necessary to ensure the survival of the church in China. One focus is just as partisan as the other (and neither addresses the other directly). One of the few doctoral dissertations completed on reform era Protestantism in China, Jason Kindopp's "The Politics of Protestantism in Contemporary China: State Control, Civil Society, and Social Movement in a Single-Party State,"[13] convincingly demonstrates that, at the level of everyday worship and ecclesiastical practice, the Three-Self church does indeed put the interests of the party-state ahead of those of church members. Based on extensive fieldwork and interviews in his Nanjing base (and elsewhere in China), Kindopp confirms the argument that the Three-Self Protestant movement serves the Party first, the church second, and church members last. Organizational policies—from seminary training to appointment of ministers and much else—are designed to assure Party control, to slow the growth of Protestant Christianity, and to bend church growth to state purposes. Kindopp also points out the failure of the Three-Self Protestant movement, and of religious authorities more broadly, to deal effectively with the rise of the House Church and other localized Protestant movements.[14]

In the same way that Kindopp offers a valuable perspective on Wickeri's work on the Three-Self Protestant movement, the historian Lian Xi offers a sobering corrective to the soaring optimism of Lambert and Aikman in his *Redeemed by Fire.*[15] Lambert and Aikman present China's House Church Protestants as heirs to the revivalist traditions that have shaped politics and culture in the modern Anglophone world; Western evangelicals are meant to see their Chinese counterparts above all as understandable and familiar. By contrast, Lian emphasizes the apocalyptic eschatology at the core of indigenous Chinese Protestantism, which he depicts in somber tones as an understandable, if perhaps regrettable, response to the misery of rural China in the nineteenth and twentieth centuries. Most of Lian's book is devoted to the rise of indigenous Chinese Protestantism in the pre-PRC period, but his chapter on the underground church in the post-Mao years stresses the links to today's House Church and the sectarian movements of the past (The True Jesus Church, The Little Flock, and so on). Perhaps because of his use of Public Security Bureau documents, he also emphasizes the violence and recklessness of the more sectarian of the underground churches, problems that Lambert and Aikman mention only in passing. In Lian's eyes, the underground churches may well provide a voice for peasant discontent (he says little about the spread of the House Church into urban areas), but he sees such developments more as cause for concern than for optimism.

More broadly, academic work on the Chinese Protestant revival is largely in its infancy—which is not to question the quality of the pioneering work being carried out. Fenggang Yang, a sociologist of religion at Purdue University, is probably the most influential and most prolific of the scholars involved. His interest in the subject of Chinese Christianity was initially sparked by the surprising number of mainland Chinese who converted to Christianity during the course of their studies in the United States, and, in his well-received *Chinese Christians in America: Conversion, Assimilation, and Adhesive Identities,* he argues that Chinese converts have managed to sinicize Christianity even as their conversion aids their partial assimilation into American society.[16] Subsequently, Yang moved on to the study of Christianity in China proper, focusing particularly on developing the theoretical tools necessary to understand the current religious revival: in "The Red, Black, and Gray Markets of Religion in China" he applies Stark and Bainbridge's religious market model to China, illustrating how the important role played by China's state shapes the religious marketplace;[17] in "Lost in the Market, Saved at McDonald's: Conversion to Christianity in Urban China" he argues that for many urban Chinese Protestantism is a trope for modernity in the post-Mao world.[18] To date, Yang has offered valuable snapshots of various aspects of the Protestant revival in China without delivering an overview. He is, however, one of the principal investigators in a Templeton Foundation–funded study on "The Empirical Study of Religions in China," so we might expect a major publication shortly.[19]

Other work is perhaps more topical. Nanlai Cao examines the Protestants of Wenzhou—the Zhejiang commercial center often closely identified with the rise of Protestantism in post-Mao China—searching for connections between Protestantism and the rise of the market economy.[20] Jason Kindopp and Jacqueline Wenger have written on the differences between the House Church and the Three-Self Protestant movement.[21] Emily Dunn examines Chinese Protestant sectarian conflict on the Internet.[22] Kim-kwong Chan examines missionary work carried out by Chinese Christians within China.[23]

To sum up, when compared with the vast outpouring of scholarship on Chinese politics and economics since the end of the Maoist period, work on Chinese Protestantism—despite the inherent drama of the subject—remains largely underdeveloped. One cannot but agree with Cao Nanlai's terse appraisal:

> Western discourse on Chinese Christianity has been dominated by sensational journalistic accounts of state religious persecution on the one hand, and speculative demographic assessments on the Christian proportion of society on the other. While China historians have contributed a great deal to the understanding of Chinese Christianity today, few social scientists have engaged in fieldword-based research on contemporary China and its changing dynamics.[24]

China's Protestant Revival as Seen in China

Academic research in China has become more open and lively in the reform era, and Christianity has attracted the attention of a number of scholars. One finds articles on the attraction of Christianity for university students, case studies of rural Protestant churches, and even discussion of the House Church movement. Some authors are mildly disapproving of the rise of Protestantism, depicting it as evidence that China's society and culture remain "underdeveloped" in spite of thirty years of impressive GDP growth rates.[25] Others, however, are objective or even approving of the benefits brought by Protestantism, which include better organized, more law-respecting villages and villagers, for instance.[26] One article traces the evolution of a rural church from its founding by Western missionaries in the nineteenth century through its incorporation into the Three-Self Protestant movement in the 1950s and its eventual "amicable divorce" from the movement in the post-Mao era as it opted for Home Church status. The author implies that the Three-Self Protestant movement, in the eyes of rural Protestants, was more trouble than it was worth; in other words he places the "blame," such as there is, on the government and not on the Christians.[27] Another author describes the growth of the House Church in urban Shenyang in the same neutral tone he would use to describe, say, an increase in the number of grocery stores, even as he states that there are "thousands" of small house churches in greater Shenyang.[28] One team of scholars examines the well-known Tanghe China Gospel group, an important part of the Henan House Church movement (which counts perhaps 10 million members), and essentially sides with the House Church, arguing that it has abandoned its former "cultic" posture and that it is now up to the government to come to terms with it in more constructive ways as part of the ongoing development of China's "harmonious society."[29] As evidence of what might be a sign of growing openness toward the House Church, there was even a conference in Beijing in late 2008 that brought together House Church leaders and representatives of the State Council to discuss the history and future of the House Church in China. Three-Self Protestant movement/Chinese Christian Council leaders were not present.[30]

Despite these encouraging academic forays into research on Chinese Christianity, Chinese authorities, both secular and religious, have had relatively little to say about the Protestant revival as such, even as seemingly new state attitudes toward religion have evolved in the post-Mao period. The Chinese authorities' narrative construction of the rise of religion in general in the post-Mao era is built on a small number of basic points, all of which grow organically out of prereform era history. First, China's leaders insist that they have put the bad old days of the Cultural Revolution period behind them; the extreme rejection of all religion is now condemned as theoretically wrongheaded, the violence and physical abuse of clergy as examples of the absence of the rule of law. Second, healthy, respectful state regulation will henceforth take the place of the lawless extremes of the Cultural Revolution period. Third, such proper regulation will guide religion in the right direction so that religion will make a positive contribution to national goals, such as the achievement of a harmonious society. The image of religion as the "opium of the people" has thus given way to a more positive image of (proper) religion as a partner in the ongoing task of nation-building.[31] I have argued elsewhere that, despite its positive tone, state discourse on religion continues to sound familiar themes of control and even domination of religion,[32] but there is no doubt that the authorities' rhetorical embrace of religion combined with the retreat of the Chinese state from daily micromanagement of Chinese society have allowed religion to flourish in the post-Mao period.

The invitation to all recognized religions to contribute positively to the construction of a harmonious socialist society has been extended to China's Christians as members of the larger religious community, even if reminders of the necessity of continued vigilance because of Christianity's foreign origins often accompany the invitation. Otherwise, Chinese authorities have had relatively little to say—at least in public—about the Protestant revival, beyond their more general remarks concerning all sanctioned religions (delivered with appropriate Christian "garnishings" on Christmas and Easter).

The same is largely true, strangely enough, of China's authorized Protestant church, the Three-Self Protestant movement/Chinese Christian Council, or at least insofar as I can determine from a partial reading of its mouthpiece publication, *Tianfeng*, over the past few years. Even in *Tianfeng*, the narrative construction of China's recent Protestant revival is noteworthy chiefly for its public reluctance to acknowledge the significance of the phenomenon and for its insistence on subordinating the religious and Christian revival to the discourse of harmonious social development.

Indeed, perusing *Tianfeng*, one would never suspect that a revival of historical proportions was under way or that authorities were unduly concerned about certain aspects of the revival.[33] Instead, *Tianfeng* conveys messages from national and church leaders to the Protestant faithful and depicts a church that is doing its utmost to obey those messages. A partial translation of the table of contents of the August 2006 issue reflects a typical mixture of official pronouncements by national and church leaders, lessons drawn from the Bible, reflections on Christian practice, theological discussions, and timid investigations of church "problems":

> Twelfth (Enlarged) Meeting of the [Leadership] of the Three-Self Protestant Movement and the Christian Council Opens in Shanghai
> Deborah, Female Prophet
> The Metaphor of the Flock
> Mr. Wu Yaozong's Life of Pursuing and Practicing Love and Truth[34]
> A Brief Discussion of the Direction of the Rural Church in the Construction of Harmonious Society
> The Three-Self Principle and Church Construction
> Study of the Three-Self Protestant Movement and Theological Reconstruction through Contextual Theology

More careful reading of selected articles from the 1990s and 2000s confirms the impression that *Tianfeng* is not the place to look for incisive commentary on developments in Chinese Protestantism. Indeed, pride of place is given to the application of current state policy to the church as reflected in articles such as "Excavate Positive Elements of Love and Harmony from within Christian Teachings; Actively Join in the Construction of Harmonious Society,"[35] "Closing Remarks at the End of the Eighth Meeting of the Representatives of Chinese Christianity,"[36] and "Responses to Readers' Questions Concerning Regulation of Religious Worship Sites."[37] Articles that appear at first glance to be more topical or to be devoted to the church rather than to policy invariably bring the discussion back to the needs of the moment, as seen by China's authorities. An article on the revival of one particular church in Ningbo, for example, cast as a reflection on the impact, over thirty years, of the policy of reform and opening up on Chinese Protestantism, thanks God (and the Chinese Communist Party) that the madness of the Cultural Revolution is over and that things are back on track.[38] Another article, published in April 1994, sounds the familiar theme of the need for vigilance given the foreign character of Christianity and the wrongs China historically suffered at the hands of the foreign missionaries.[39] A February 1994 article titled "A Close Look at the Church in the Hechi Region of Guangxi" paints a somewhat condescending portrait of minority believers and their untrained leaders, all of whom lack "quality."[40]

In sum, whatever changes may have occurred in Chinese society, Chinese journalism, or Chinese Protestantism over the past thirty years, *Tianfeng* remains largely tied to the top-down model of media-as-propaganda as practiced in the People's Republic during the Maoist period. Indeed, Chinese Protestantism as depicted by *Tianfeng* resembles nothing so much as Garrison Keillor's Lake Wobegon, the fictitious Minnesota town where "all the women are strong, all the men are good looking, and all the children are above average." Major issues are simply not addressed. Little is said, for example, about the explosive growth in Protestantism mentioned in other sources; one of the few articles that mentions the number of Protestants in China gave the figure of 16 million—a very low number. No attempt is made to document this figure, to break it down, or to suggest that it is in any way in dispute. It is part of the "narrative construction" of Protestant development in post-Mao China to suggest that numbers of Protestants remain small. Nor was the House Church mentioned in any of the *Tianfeng* articles I read.

In sum, Chinese secular and religious authorities have remained largely silent in the face of the stunning growth of Protestantism in post-Mao China. Whether this silence at the core of state discourse on Protestant expansion is unconscious—that is, authorities simply do not know what to say—or part of a larger design—authorities have no desire to help the Chinese Protestant community achieve greater self-awareness—is difficult to determine. What is clear, however, is that this deafening silence leaves the field wide open for others who would like to speak to and for China's Protestants.

Protestant Voices from the Chinese Diaspora

It is in this context that we turn finally to Chinese Protestant voices in the Chinese diaspora, particularly in North America. Some of these Chinese Christians, like Bob Fu, to be discussed immediately below, had already converted in China and came to North America to avoid persecution, but most converted after their arrival—some having gone into exile for political reasons. Christians who have recently emigrated from China may well have access to information that Western scholar/journalists and even non-Christian Chinese scholars may not, and those that use that information to further the cause of the Chinese church—generally but not always the House Church—can serve as sources for our inquiry.

Bob Fu became a Christian in 1989 while still a university student, after having participated as an activist in the student demonstrations in Tian'anmen Square. Within a few years he came to be a House Church leader in the Beijing area, and he was arrested and briefly imprisoned in 1996. Later that year he escaped to Hong Kong with his pregnant wife, and the couple subsequently immigrated to the United States. Since his arrival in the United States, Fu has worked to keep the fate of China's persecuted House Church Christians in the headlines, and in 2002 he founded the ChinaAid Association "to draw international attention to China's gross human rights violations against house church Christians."[41] ChinaAid is supported financially by organizations such as the National Endowment for Democracy,[42] and its self-proclaimed mission is to "*expose* religious persecution by Communist government against Christians by gathering information inside China and disseminating it to the international community . . . *encourage* Christians and other victims of religious persecution who have been beaten, tortured, or imprisoned for their faith . . . and *equip* leaders on behalf of the persecuted church to help them to advance religious freedom in China . . . through legal and Biblical training."[43]

Like many other advocacy organizations, ChinaAid has adopted the approach of Human Rights Watch and other international lobbying groups in collecting information on persecuted Christians in China and making this information available on their web site and in their publications. The most useful of their publications for our present purposes is the *Chinese Law and Religion Monitor* (*Zongjiao fazhi wenzai* in Chinese; one does not appear to be a direct translation of the other), which began appearing in 2005. The tone of the publication is clear from the very beginning: "The Communist Party of China keeps playing two-hand tactics [*sic*] with the Chinese people and the international community as a whole. On the one hand it makes domestic laws and international commitments 'to protect human rights' including the 'freedom of religious faith'; on the other hand it still promulgates secret documents depriving people of basic human rights such as religious freedom." The articles, translations, and republications printed in *Chinese Law and Religion Monitor* are consistent with the mandate Bob Fu set for the journal from the outset and illustrate the duplicity of Chinese authorities who claim—in public—to embrace "proper religion" but who continue to harass and imprison House Church members when it suits their immediate needs. At the same time, although the tone of *Chinese Law and Religion Monitor* is inevitably somber, it does report good news, including publications and conferences in China that treat the House Church with greater objectivity.[44] Consequently, ChinaAid and its publications are useful both for what they reveal about the ongoing problem of persecution of House Church Christians and also for what we learn about the evolving state discourse on religion. That said, the *China Law and Religion Monitor* is also written with an eye toward the sympathies of the American government and American Christian donors who will support ChinaAid and their efforts to advance the cause of the church in China.

The China Soul for Christ Foundation is another example of organized activity by Chinese Christians in North America, but one that blends politics and proselytism in a somewhat more subtle fashion. Founded in 1998 in California by Yuan Zhiming and a number of fellow Chinese Christians,[45] its goal is the evangelization of China through the diffusion of high-quality videos telling the story of the Christian revival already in progress:

> We deeply feel that it is our responsibility to record truthfully God's amazing grace: how such boundless grace falls upon this ancient country of wide expanse and abundant legacy; how God baptizes hundreds of thousands of His sons and daughters with fire and the Holy Spirit; how His sons and daughters go out weeping and return with songs of joy. . . . To other people, the unique events [occurring in China] are still vague and blurred. Therefore, the TV serial "The Cross," a factual historic record, will expand the tale, from the coming of western missionaries in early days to this present generation.

The work of China Soul is intimately linked to the story of its chief founder, Yuan Zhiming. Born in rural Hebei in 1955, Yuan was a doctoral student in political theory in Beijing University's Department of Philosophy when he was recruited by Su Xiaokang and Xia Jun to contribute to the writing of *Heshang* [translated as both *Deathsong of the River* and *River Elegy*], the television series, critical of traditional Chinese civilization, part of which aired in China in 1988 before authorities pulled it from the airwaves. Together with Xie Xuanjun, a scholar of comparative mythology and culture, Yuan was responsible for the episode titled "Blueness," which argued that civilizations were either open and maritime, and hence "blue," or closed and continental, and hence "yellow." In what translator Richard W. Bodman dubbed "the most 'political' of all the episodes," Yuan and Xie painted China as thoroughly "yellow" and argued that its salvation must come through intellectual engagement with the outside world.[46] The same critical political engagement led Yuan to participate actively in the student demonstrations in 1989, which in turn led authorities to label him a dangerous dissident and to force him into exile.

In the United States, Yuan became a visiting scholar at Princeton University, served as chief editor of the magazine *Democratic China,* and cofounded the organization Chinese Democratic Frontline. In 1991, a year after arriving in the United States, he converted to Christianity, the result of having met and befriended a number of Chinese Christians in the Princeton area. In 1992, he left Princeton to enter the Reformed Theological Seminary in Jackson, Mississippi.

After graduation from the seminary, he served as editor of *Overseas Campus Magazine* (*Haiwai xiaoyuan*), a Chinese-language evangelical publication targeting Chinese intellectuals, particularly those studying outside of China.[47] Yuan also turned his intellectual talents toward Christian subjects by writing Chinese-language books such as *Lao Zi versus the Bible: A Welcome from across Time*[48] and *Laozi in Original Language and Translation,*[49] many of which stressed the compatibility of Chinese culture and Christian teachings. In 1997, he published *China's Confession: God and Five Thousand Years in China,* which became the basis for China Soul's first series of videos.

Inspired by what he describes as a vision from God, Yuan subsequently decided to produce a series of videos based on *China's Confession,* the idea being, according to China Soul's mission statement, to "let vision be transformed into pictures. Let God's light shine upon China, the Land of God. Let history become truthful records." This decision led to the founding of China Soul in 1999. Yuan's team worked for more than two years on the project, ultimately producing, in 2000, a high-quality video in seven episodes of thirty-minute-long videos that, in tone, theme, and production values, recalled many of the features of *Heshang.*

China's Confession (the title in Chinese, *Shenzhou*—"Land of God"—is even more suggestive) begins from the premise that the origins of Chinese civilization are Christian. Borrowing arguments and evidence from themes developed by European Jesuit missionaries in China during the sixteenth and seventeenth centuries, *China's Confession* seeks out evidence from Chinese classical sources suggesting a shared history between China and the ancient Middle East. Such evidence includes origin myths and stories of floods in ancient China as well the etymology of certain Chinese characters that suggests links with biblical themes (the character for "boat," for example, contains graphs meaning "eight people," the same number supposedly on Noah's ark). Most tellingly, *China's Confession* points to evidence of worship of a monotheistic god (Shangdi) as well as a moral code suggestive of Judeo-Christian values. In sum, the basic argument of *China's Confession* is that China is, historically, a Christian nation, and that embrace of Christianity is not a betrayal of Chineseness but rather a return to a lost golden age.

China lost its way with the establishment of the imperial system, continues *China's Confession,* when the emperor took the place of God, and a moral code celebrating ambition and self-advancement at any price took the place of previous emphasis on virtuous behavior. "Throughout the history of China, millions of lives were sacrificed and families scattered in order for one man to dominate the land. . . . Many Chinese folk heroes were praised for their strategic skill, courage and loyalty—their deeds immortalized in books and poems. However, under their virtuous veneers lay deceit, brutality, misguided devotion, and self-righteousness." Here *China's Confession* parts company with the Jesuits, who tended to blame China's fall on "false religions" such as Buddhism and Daoism, and, consistent with the themes developed in *River Elegy*, identifies China's traditional political culture as the source for the suffering of the Chinese people, today and in the past (the title of the last episode of *China's Confession* is "The Ocean Blue").

China's history is thus depicted as an endless cycle of dashed hopes as the spiritual vacuum at the heart of China's political culture kept the Chinese people from putting their obvious talents to proper purposes. Western missionaries are praised for their efforts to bring the gospel to China, as is Sun Yat-sen, the father of modern China *and* a practicing Christian. The reign of Mao Zedong, however, represented the return of traditional treachery, manipulation, and suffering. *China's Confession* praises the reforms launched by Deng Xiaoping but notes at the same time that "China's root problem is spiritual and cannot be solved by an economic boom. It is a festering wound that has brought forth an abundance of social ills." Jesus Christ is the missing ingredient.

One may quibble with or even reject out of hand *China's Confession*'s vision of Chinese history, but as television docudrama, the series is well produced and effective. The images are compelling, the narration measured, the pace and timing professional. If convinced Marxists—or even convinced secularists—may well remain unmoved, the average Chinese viewer—to say nothing of the Chinese Christian viewer—could readily be drawn into a narrative that offers a vision of China's past and future that they will not find in Chinese textbooks or on CTV, and that underscores China's immense potential (if it were to become Christian) at the same time that it replays the glories—and the tragedies—of China's past.

China's Confession was, however, but a prelude for China Soul's next project, *The Cross—Jesus in China* (*Shizijia—Yesu zai Zhongguo*), which is nothing short of masterful. Begun in 2000 and completed in 2003, *The Cross* tells the story of Protestant Christianity, or more particularly Chinese

Protestant Christianity (although Western missionaries are mentioned), in modern and contemporary China. As China Soul describes the goals of the project on its web site: "How did this miracle [the rapid rise of Protestantism in the post-Mao period] come about? How did the Gospel spread so effectively through China under persecution? How were these underground churches formed and managed? . . . What influence has Christianity had on Chinese life, and what impact are Christians having on China's destiny?"

The story is told in four episodes of one hour each. The first episode, "Seeds of Blood," begins with the stories of Wang Mingdao, John Song, and Watchman Nee, early-twentieth-century Chinese Christian preachers who were determined to found a Chinese Protestant church largely independent from foreign influence. The narrative passes quickly to the PRC period and the founding of the Three-Self Protestant church, thus setting the stage for extended interviews with several successors of Wang Mingdao, John Song, and Watchman Nee who were imprisoned beginning in the 1950s for refusing to join the Three-Self Protestant movement. This second generation of independent Protestants includes Allen Yuan, Yang Xinfei, Moses Xie, Samuel Lamb, and Joseph Li, all of whom recount, without rancor, their experiences of persecution and of return to doing the work of the true church when they were released from prison. In some cases, wives and family members of the persecuted Christian leaders speak of the hardships they experienced and the kindness manifested toward them—often anonymously—by fellow believers. One of the final images of the episode shows Allan Yuan, then in his nineties, baptizing new believers in a river somewhere in the outskirts of Beijing.

The second episode, "The Bitter Cup," focuses on the rise of the rural House Church movement, which accelerated during the 1970s. The filmmakers interviewed church leaders as well as activists/preachers and ordinary believers. A related theme is the mounting persecution of the House Church in the wake of the reestablishment of the Three-Self Protestant movement in the early 1980s. One story line is that of a young Christian woman who was arrested for House Church activities three days before she was to be wed. Her fiancé, also a House Church Christian, visited her whenever authorities would allow during the three years the woman was imprisoned, and the couple was married only days after her release. *The Cross* films the wedding, where man and wife both sing Christian hymns, and offers moving interviews with the couple. We also meet numerous House Christians who have been harassed and imprisoned many times and who have no doubt that such practices will continue. Their response? Jesus suffered for his beliefs; why should we expect anything different? The filmmakers cleverly reveal that the persecution of the House Church movement is one of the chief motors of its expansion: activists and missionaries are constantly on the run and spread the gospel as they flee into unexplored territories. We also meet Christian House Church converts in the Daqing oil fields—long heralded as a model enterprise during the Maoist period—on university campuses, and among ethnic minorities.

Episode 3, "The Spring of Life," illustrates the saving power of Christianity in the context of today's China. Several couples recount how Christianity saved their marriages from extramarital affairs, from gambling, and from a variety of social problems, all linked to the "moral vacuum" at the heart of today's Chinese culture. A brilliant and very moving passage focuses on an "underground" orphanage in Sichuan, run by the House Church, which ministers to abandoned children. Intellectuals, artists, and scientists talk about their surprise in finding Jesus and how their faith has helped them in their careers and family lives. Two Christian Chinese Communist Party members are interviewed. A final passage focuses on a Shenyang restaurant (or chain of restaurants) owned and staffed exclusively by Christians. Instead of call girls and karaoke, the restaurant offers hymns (at the table) and a prayer request box where clients leave word of their problems so that the restaurant staff can pray for them.

The final episode, "The Canaan Hymns," recounts the life and musical career of Lü Xiaomin, a Christian convert (she is from a Muslim family) from rural Henan with a middle-school education who, on becoming a Christian, discovered that she had a rare talent for composing hymns—even though she had no musical training at all. Through word of mouth, her songs spread throughout the Chinese Christian community, where they are known as "Canaan Hymns" (*Jia'nan gequ*). There are now some thousand Canaan hymns available, all written by Xiaomin, some of which have been performed by well-known ensembles in Beijing and elsewhere. One of China Soul's projects is to produce karaoke-ready versions of Xiaomin's Canaan Hymns for use in Christian activities throughout China.

To shoot *The Cross*, the China Soul team made more than fifteen trips to China, traveling to more than eighteen provinces and major cities.

They filmed several hundred house churches and underground seminaries. They carried out interviews with nearly one hundred House Church leaders as well as with several hundred ministers and ordinary believers. Such a project was not without risks, but they managed to shoot more than four hundred hours of footage, which they intercut with clips from other sources.

It is difficult to convey in words the impact of *The Cross;* its power is based on the immediacy of the images and the testimony offered by the interviewees. In terms of production values and general professionalism, it is on a par with, say, *60 Minutes.* Moreover, since China Soul is telling a relatively unknown and highly dramatic story, and since they have an overabundance of material, they do not have to oversell. As a result, the tone of *The Cross* is very nearly pitch-perfect. The dignity, the equanimity, the strength of character of the elderly men imprisoned for twenty and more years command attention; the stories told by their family members ring true. Indeed, the entire series, despite being overtly dedicated to the conversion of China to Jesus Christ, conveys a stunning level of authenticity. Watching these episodes, you may not believe that Jesus is the source of the miracles that have changed these people's lives, but you cannot doubt the sincerity of the House Church Christians who expound such beliefs. The videos are professionally edited for maximum impact, but I did not get the sense that they are heavily scripted in the sense that interview subjects had been told what to say or were asked leading questions. At the same time, another striking point about *The Cross* is the virtual absence of anger or rancor—surely the result of politically savvy editing. Despite numerous critical remarks, neither the Communist Party nor the official church is denounced directly or associated with the devil; ministers and believers take great pains to demonstrate their patriotism and their general support for the government (in all matters excepting those of current religious policy). But the message is neither preachy nor self-righteous; *The Cross* paints a joyous portrait of who China's Protestants are, where they came from, and why they are happy. One might call this "proselytism by example," and I personally find it highly effective as a tool of persuasion. The polemics of *China's Confession* and the love-hate relationship with China's past are largely absent from *The Cross,* a vehicle designed—among other things—to show Chinese Protestants that they can be proud of who they are and what they have done, and to encourage them to bring others into the fold.

On the basis of the interviews carried out in the making of *The Cross,* China Soul also put together a series of hourlong interviews with the older generation of persecuted Christians, including Allen Yuan, Samuel Lamb, Epaphras, Joseph Li, Moses Xie, and Yang Xinfei. At roughly the same time, China Soul began to offer on its web site and for sale lectures on a variety of Christian topics by leaders of the Chinese Protestant church in the United States (or at least those leaders associated with Yuan Zhiming and China Soul). These include Yuan Zhiming, "Why I Believe in Jesus" (12 lectures); Fan Xuede, "Why Did I Want to Become a Christian?" (12 lectures); Liu Tongsu and Hou Junli (husband and wife), "Our Testimony on Spreading the Word" (12 lectures); Feng Bingcheng, "Belief, Science, and Human Life" (15 lectures); as well as a lecture series titled "Chinese Scholars in the United States" in which seven such scholars speak of their discovery of Jesus Christ and their work for the church since that discovery. Some of these lectures appear to have been filmed as part of the normal round of evangelistic engagements that make up a big part of the lives of Yuan and his colleagues, who are much in demand in Chinese Christian communities throughout the world. Others may have been put together expressly for diffusion via sales and/or downloads on the China Soul web site. As in the case of *The Cross,* the production values of these interviews and lectures are very high and the content generally compelling and apolitical. The goal is evangelism, not settling accounts with the Three-Self Protestant movement or the Chinese party-state.

After *The Cross,* China Soul produced another series titled *The Gospel,* based not on the Chinese experience but on the life of Jesus and the meaning of his message in world-historical terms. Instead of reshooting the story of Christ from scratch, *The Gospel* uses Franco Zeffirelli's 1977 miniseries *Jesus of Nazareth* as its basic source of images but adds considerable discussion of evidence of the meaning of life from a scientific point of view—and to this end includes interview clips with Steven Hawking and other well-known scientists. This emphasis on science is consistent with themes developed in *River Elegy* and reminds us of the saving power accorded to science by Chinese intellectuals and reformers over the course of the twentieth century. Although I personally find *The Gospel* less compelling than either *The Cross* or *China's Confession,* its message might readily appeal to Chinese intellectuals or university students, groups among which Protestant Christianity appears to have been growing as of late. A future China Soul project is *The Opposite Shore* (*Bi'an*), based on the experiences of Chinese intellectuals who have converted to Christianity in the United States; in Chinese Buddhist texts, *bi'an*/the opposite shore is a metaphor for salvation, which China Soul has cleverly transposed to the United States for the purposes of this production.

The crucial question, for China Soul as well as for this chapter, is the impact its work has had in China, a question that is hard to answer in the absence of considerable fieldwork. On the China Soul web site, we find statements like the following:

> Under a strategic outreach program called "*Send to China*" adopted by its board of directors, CSFC makes its videos available, *free of charge*, as VCDs, to anyone who will bring them to China. We strongly believe that these VCDs will be an effective tool in reaching out to Chinese in their own homes. We also encourage individuals, organizations, bookstores, Bible study groups, and churches in China to duplicate and distribute our videos *free of charge*.

In a June 2009 newsletter, China Soul informed its readers that it had been sending free copies of *China's Confession* and *The Cross* to China for years, noting that "it has been expensive to give these away and pay the postage, but this is God's will, and relies entirely on his grace. We come into this world with nothing, and leave with nothing; how much more is this true about money?!" A September 2009 newsletter again notes that China Soul from the outset abandoned the copyright on its materials for China and removed copy protection from its VCDs (I hardly need add that pirated CDs, DVDs, and VCDs are readily available in China). They estimate that they have given away some US$750,000 worth of material, or some 50,000 sets of materials, which, given the relatively small budgets of China Soul, published in their newsletters, is a considerable sum.

It is difficult to know how many of the 50,000 copies found their way to Christian groups or individuals. The following witness statement, found yet again in China Soul materials, is surely representative of the type of impact they would *like* to have:

> My name is Wang and I am from Hainan. On a Tianya BBS . . . I saw that there were people talking about their reactions on having watched

> *The Cross*, and they greatly praised it. I really wanted to see it, so I asked fellow believers who might have a copy, and learned that XX, with whom I had gone to school, had one, so I asked him to send it express. Yesterday after church, I went with ten or so believers to an isolated mountain in Ding'an county to watch their Christmas play. When we got home everyone was tired, but most of the believers wanted to go to the church to watch *The Cross*. One brother invited one of his fellow students who is not a Christian. So I sang a Canaan hymn . . . and offered an opening prayer, and we quieted down to watch. When we got to the part when Allen Yuan's wife talked about their son being called "cornbread head" by other kids and his asking just once for a regular piece of steamed bread [*mantou*], and the mother's saying she could do nothing about it, the non-Christian began sobbing . . . his whole body was trembling and he could not control himself. Others also started to cry and we knelt down and confessed our sin of not being loyal to God. One girl said that she was serving God to show off; two others admitted that their faith was not solid. I hugged the non-Christian and prayed for him, and asked "do you want to accept Jesus Christ as your savior?" He replied firmly "I do." I asked "Do you confess you are a sinner, and you will let the precious blood of the cross wash away your sins?" He answered, "I confess that I am a sinner." Halleluiah! 2003.12.23

Carol Lee Hamrin, a China scholar and former State Department expert on China with a particular interest in Chinese Christianity, informed me in an email exchange that China Soul's impact is considerable, both on mainland Chinese overseas and on Chinese Christians (House Church and Three-Self Protestant movement) within China. Yuan circulates his films in China before they are made available outside. The Chinese government is, according to Hamrin, very attentive to Yuan and China Soul: *The Cross* was screened at an annual meeting of religious affairs officials in Beijing so as to warn them what to watch out for and to suppress. Yuan himself is still banned from China, as are his films.

The religious revival in China is the unexpected by-product of Deng Xiaoping's decision to favor economic development over Maoist revolution and to pursue this goal by liberalizing China's economy and, to some extent, China's society and culture. The return of religion caught both Chinese authorities and Western China-watchers by surprise, and scholars have been struggling to catch up with events on the ground ever since. This is particularly true of the rise of Chinese Protestantism, given the limited inroads Protestantism had made in China before the Communist Revolution and the heavy control exercised by the Chinese state on the Protestant church after 1949. No one would have believed that there would be 20 million Chinese Protestants by the beginning of the twenty-first century, to say nothing of 100 million or more.

As is clear from this essay, the full story of the rapid rise of Chinese Protestantism has yet to be told, and much of what has been written about it is political, designed either to further the Protestant movement or to contain it. Chinese scholars such as Kang Xiaoguang, who advocate the establishment of a state-supported Confucian church as a first step toward rebuilding an organic relationship between Chinese state and society, recognize the social importance of religion and the positive role that religion can serve in China's future development.[50] Chinese authorities have grasped this point rhetorically, as illustrated by their endorsement of religion as a positive factor in the construction of a harmonious society. At the same time, the Chinese state continues to demand ultimate control over the content of religious belief and the nature of religious organizations, which inevitably weakens their discursive endorsement of religion.

In an increasingly globalized world, where more and more Chinese are connected to the Chinese diaspora and to non-Chinese cultures via the Internet, telephone, emigration, and tourism, the contradictions and half-measures at the heart of PRC discourse on religion are increasingly obvious, particularly to religious believers in China who can compare their experiences with those of fellow believers elsewhere in the world. This is true in the case of Falun Gong and explains, in large measure, the ongoing conflict between Falun Gong and Chinese authorities.[51] This is all the more true of Chinese Protestants, as they can draw on both Chinese and non-Chinese Christian networks outside of China. The innovative missionary work of Yuan Zhiming and China Soul, based on VCDs and the Internet, provides one illustration of how Chinese Protestants, from the safe haven of the United States, have sought to tell the story of Chinese Protestantism to Chinese Protestants in China in such a way as to change the narrative framework of their own religious life by providing their own experiences with a "virtual" history and larger identity. Portraying Chinese Protestants as open, loving, ecumenical, and patriotic, and Chinese Protestantism as an integral part of China's history, both classical and modern, China Soul has crafted an intelligent and persuasive message that Christianity must be an important part of China's future.

Notes

1. On the difficult question of the number of Christians in China, see Tony Lambert, "Counting Christians in China: A Cautionary Report," *International Bulletin of Missionary Research* 27, no. 1 (2006): 6–11. The high numbers come either from House Church Christians or from Chinese official sources, such as Ye Xiaowen, the director of the Chinese State Administration for Religious Affairs, who stated in internal meetings that the number of Christians in China had reached 130 million by the end of 2006, including about 20 million Catholics. See "The Annual Report on Persecution of Chinese House Churches by Province," China Aid Association, January 2007, http://chinaaid.org/pdf/2006_persecution_e.pdf, accessed February 8, 2007.

2. "Christianity Today—General Statistics and Facts of Christianity," http://christianity.about.com/od/denominations/p/christiantoday.htm, accessed September 4, 2012.

3. "Back to Jerusalem," http://www.backtojerusalem.com/, accessed September 4, 2012.

4. See, for example, ChinaAid Association at http://www.chinaaid.org, accessed September 3, 2012; the Church in China at http://www.churchinchina.com, accessed September 4, 2012; the Voice of the Martyrs at http://www.persecution.net, accessed September 4, 2012; and Christian Solidarity Worldwide at http://www.cswusa.com, accessed September 4, 2012.

5. See, for example, Daniel H. Bays, "Chinese Protestant Christianity Today," *The China Quarterly* 174 (2003): 488–504; Ryan Dunch, "Protestant Christianity in China Today: Fragile, Fragmented, Flourishing," in *China and Christianity: Burdened Past, Hopeful Future,* ed. Stephen Uhally, Jr., and Xiaowin Wu (Armonk, NY: M. E. Sharpe, 2001), 195–216; and Alan Hunter and Kim-Kwong Chan, *Protestantism in Contemporary China* (Cambridge, UK: Cambridge University Press, 1993).

6. See, among many others, Robert Marquand, "In China, Pews are Packed: Beijing Is Wary as Christianity Counts Up to 90 Million Adherents," *Christian Science Monitor,* December 24, 2003, 1; Nicholas D. Kristof, "Keeping Faith in China," *New York Times,* June 25, 2006, 4, 13; Annie Cho, "A Crisis in Christian-

ity: Why China's Most Explosive Religious Movement Worships Underground," *Foreign Policy Digest,* 2009, available online at http://www.foreignpolicydigest.org/April-2009/Archive/a-crisis-of-christianity-why-chinas-most-explosive-religious-movement-worships-underground.html, accessed December 15, 2009.

7. Tony Lambert, *China's Christian Millions* (Oxford : Monarch Books, 1999). Reprinted in 2000 and 2006.

8. David Aikman, *Jesus in Beijing: How Christianity Is Transforming China and Changing the Global Balance of Power* (Washington, DC: Regnery Press, 2003).

9. Lambert, *China's Christian Millions,* 281.

10. See Philip Wickeri's website at http://web.sfts.edu/wickeri/cv.htm, accessed January 15, 2010, where we also learn that he was ordained in Nanjing by Bishop Ding Guangxun (K. H. Ting) on behalf of the Jiangsu Christian Council in 1991.

11. See especially his books *Seeking the Common Ground: Protestant Christianity, the Three-Self Movement, and China's United Front* (Maryknoll, NY: Orbis Books, 1988); and *Reconstructing Christianity in China: K. H. Ting and the Chinese Church* (Maryknoll, NY: Orbis Books, 2007).

12. Yihua Xu gives a Chinese perspective on the rise of the Three-Self Protestant movement in his "'Patriotic' Protestants: The Making of an Official Church," in *God and Caesar in China: Policy Implications of Church-State Tensions,* ed. Jason Kindopp and Carol Lee Hamrin (Washington, DC: The Brookings Institute, 2004), 107–121.

13. George Washington University, Department of Political Science, 2004.

14. See Jason Kindopp, "Fragmented yet Defiant: Protestant Resilience under Chinese Communist Party Rule," in *God and Caesar in China,* ed. Jason Kindopp and Carol Lee Hamrin (Washington, DC: The Brookings Institute, 2004), 122–145; and Jason Kindopp, "China's War on 'Cults,'" *Current History* 100, no. 651 (2002): 259–266.

15. Lian Xi, *Redeemed by Fire: The Rise of Popular Christianity in Modern China* (New Haven: Yale University Press, 2009). See also Lian Xi, "The Search for Chinese Christianity in the Republican Period (1912–1949)," *Modern Asian Studies* 38 (2004): 851–898; and Lian Xi, "A Messianic Deliverance for Post-Dynastic China: The Launch of the True Jesus Church in the Early Twentieth Century," *Modern China* 34, no. 4 (2008): 407–441.

16. Fenggang Yang, *Chinese Christians in America: Conversion, Assimilation, and Adhesive Identities* (University Park: Pennsylvania State University Press, 1999). Yang makes similar arguments in his contributions to Fenggang Yang and Tong Carnes, eds., *Asian-American Religions: The Making and Remaking of Borders and Boundaries* (New York: New York University Press, 2004). See also Fenggang Yang and Helen Rose Ebaugh, "Transformations in New Immigrant Religions and

Their Global Implications," *American Sociological Review* 66, no. 2 (2001): 269–288; *Conversion to Christianity among the Chinese* (a special issue of *Sociology of Religion: A Quarterly Review*, 2006). On similar topics, see also Kenneth J. Guest, *God in Chinatown: Religion and Survival in New York's Evolving Immigrant Community* (New York: New York University Press, 2003).

17. Fenggang Yang, "The Red, Black, and Gray Markets of Religion in China," *Sociological Quarterly* 47 (2006): 93–122.

18. Fenggang Yang, "Lost in the Market, Saved at McDonald's: Conversion to Christianity in Urban China," *Journal for the Scientific Study of Religion* 44, no. 4 (2005): 423–441.

19. See Yang's web site at http://www.cla.purdue.edu/religious-studies/directory/?personid=68, accessed September 4, 2012.

20. See Nanlai Cao, "Christian Entrepreneurs and the Post-Mao State: An Ethnographic Account of Church-State Relations in China's Economic Transition," *Sociology of Religion* 68, no. 1 (2007): 45–66; "Boss Christians: The Business of Religion in the 'Wenzhou Model' of Christian Revival," *The China Journal* 59 (2008): 63–87; "Raising the Quality of Belief: *Suzhi* and the Production of an Elite Protestantism," *China Perspectives* 4 (2009): 54–66.

21. Jason Kindopp and Jacqueline E. Wenger, "Official versus Underground Protestant Churches in China: Challenges for Reconciliation and Social Influence," *Review of Religious Research* 46, no. 2 (2004): 169–182.

22. Emily C. Dunn, "Netizens of Heaven: Contesting Orthodoxies on the Chinese Protestant Web," *Asian Studies Review* 31, no. 5 (2007): 447–458.

23. Kim-kwong Chan, "Missiological Implications of Chinese Christianity in a Globalized Context," *Quest* 4, no. 1 (2005): 55–74.

24. Cao, "Raising the Quality of Belief," 54.

25. Li Hongju, Cui Jinxia, Zhang Rong, and Wang Yanlei, "Xiangmin shehui Jidujiao xinyang de yuanyin tanxi: dui Yubei Jiangcun jiaotang de diaocha" [Inquiry into the Reasons for Belief in Christianity in Rural Society: Survey of the Jiang Village Church in Northern Henan], *Zhongguo Nongye Daxue xuebao (Shehui kexue ban)* [Journal of China Agricultural University (Social Sciences Edition)] 57, no. 4 (2004).

26. Yang Hongshan, "Wandong nongcun 'Jidujiaore' diaocha yu sikao" [Fieldwork and Reflections on the "Christianity Craze" in Eastern Anhui], *Jianghuai luntan* [Jianghuai Forum] 4 (1994).

27. Wang Siming and Tian Xiong, "Xiangcun Jidujiao de shijian xingtai: qianru yu lishu—yi Guandong diqu Nancun Jidu jiaohui lishibianqian weili" [The Practical Form of Embedded and Alienated Rural Christianity: A Case Study of Nan Village in Central Shaanxi Province], *Nanjing Shida xuebao (Shehui kexue ban)* [Journal of Nanjing Normal University (Social Science)] 6 (2008): 38–43.

28. Wen Miao, "'Jiating jiaohui' qiaoran xingqi" [The Quiet Rise of the "Home Church"], no. 2 (1994): 33.

29. Li Hongju et al., "Xiangmin shehui Jidujiao xinyang."

30. See the report by Tongsu Liu, an associate of China Soul founder Yuan Zhiming, who was present at the meeting, available on the bulletin board system of *Gongfa pinlun* at http://www.gongfa.com/html/gongfazhuanti/zongjiaoziyou/20090311/302.html, accessed May 21, 2012. The meeting was held on November 21 and 22 in Beijing, organized by the National Institute of Development Studies of the Development Research Center of the State Council. The same bulletin board announced crackdowns on the House Church in June 2009; see http://www.gongfa.org/bbs/viewthread.php?action=printable&tid=3852, accessed September 4, 2012.

31. See Ryan Dunch, "Christianity and 'Adaptation to Socialism,'" in *Chinese Religiosities: Afflictions of Modernity and State Formation*, ed. Mayfair Mei-hui Yang (Berkeley: University of California, 2008), 155–178; and Pittman B. Potter, "Belief in Control: Regulation of Religion in China," *The China Quarterly* 174, no. 2 (2003): 317–337.

32. See David Ownby, "Religious Revival and the Rule of Law in China: An Evaluation of 'Secularization with Chinese Characteristics,'" paper presented at the Conference on Political Change in China, Munk Centre, University of Toronto, March 6–7, 2009.

33. *Tianfeng* is not available in libraries in Montreal, and I consulted only a small percentage of the issues available online. *Tianfeng* may have little to say, but it says it often and at great length.

34. Wu Yaozong is one of the major leaders of the Three-Self Protestant movement, together with Ding Guangxun.

35. "Wajue jidujiao jiaoyi zhong ai yu hexie de jiji yinsu, jiji canyu shehui xiandaihua jianshe," *Tianfeng* 21 (2007).

36. Wang Zuoan, "Zai Zhongguo Jidujiao dibaci daibiao huiyi bimushishang de jianghua," *Tianfeng* 4 (2008).

37. "Jiu Zongjiao huodong changsuo guanli tiaoli da duzhe wen," *Tianfeng* 4 (1994).

38. Fan Aishi, "Zheli shi yi xiao bu, quanguo shi yi da bu: Huimou gaige kaifang jiaohui fusu 30 nian" [What We've Done Here Is But One Small Step; the Country Has Taken a Big Step: Looking Back on Thirty Years of Church Revival since Reform and Opening Up], *Tianfeng* 21 (2008).

39. "'Jiuhua' congti: su Guowuyuan 144 hao 'guiding' yougan" [Bringing up an "Old Subject" Once Again: Reactions on Reading State Council Regulation 144], *Tianfeng* 4 (1994).

40. Yun Caiyang, "Guangxi Hechi diqu jiaohui toushi" [A Close Look at the Church in the Hechi Region of Guangxi], *Tianfeng* 2 (1994).

41. See the ChinaAid web site at http://www.chinaaid.org/qry/page.taf?id=20, accessed November 20, 2009.

42. See http://www.ned.org/where-we-work/asia/china, accessed January 4, 2010.

43. See http://www.chinaaid.org/qry/page.taf?id=97, accessed December 12, 2009. Italics added to emphasize that "expose, encourage, and equip" is a central slogan of ChinaAid.

44. See http://www.chinaaid.org/qry/page.taf?id=135, accessed January 5, 2010.

45. China Soul became a nonprofit organization in 2001. See http://www.chinasoul.org/e/e-about.htm, accessed January 15, 2010. Unless otherwise noted, all information about China Soul comes from their web site, which is available in Chinese (http://www.chinasoul.com/, accessed September 4, 2012) and in English (http://www.chinasoul.org/index.php?lang=en-gb, last modified September 4, 2012). The Chinese-language site contains considerably more information.

46. Xiaokang Su and Luxiang Wang, *Deathsong of the River: A Reader's Guide to the Chinese TV Series "Heshang,"* trans. Richard W. Bodman and Pin P. Wan (Ithaca, NY: Cornell University East Asia Series, 1991), 4, 9.

47. For *Haiwai xiaoyuan* see http://www.oc.org/web/modules/smartsection/category.php?categoryid=199, accessed September 4, 2012.

48. *Laozi vs. Shengjing: kuayue shikong de yinghou* (Taipei: Yuzhouguang, 1997).

49. *Laozi yuanwen yu yiwen,* (Taipei: Yuzhouguang, 1997).

50. See David Ownby, "Kang Xiaoguang: Social Science, Civil Society, and Confucian Religion," *China Perspectives* 4 (2009): 101–111.

51. See David Ownby, *Falun Gong and China's Future* (New York: Oxford University Press, 2008); and James W. Tong, *Revenge of the Forbidden City: The Suppression of the Falungong in China, 1999–2005* (New York: Oxford University Press, 2009).

Selected Bibliography

Ahn Chang-ho. "Nakgwan kwa pigwan" [Optimism and Pessimism]. *Tongkwang* [The East Light] 12 (1927): 3–4.

Aikman, David. *Jesus in Beijing: How Christianity Is Transforming China and Changing the Global Balance of Power.* Washington, DC: Regnery Press, 2003.

Allan, Sarah. *The Way of Water and Sprouts of Virtue.* Albany: State University of New York Press, 1997.

Allen, Ernest, Jr. "When Japan Was 'Champion of the Darker Races': Satokata Takahashi and the Flowering of Black Messianic Nationalism." *The Black Scholar* 240, no. 1 (2001): 21–46.

Allen, Horace N. "Medical Work in Korea." *The Foreign Missionary* 44 (1885): 76.

Anderson, Benedict. *Imagined Communities: Reflections on the Origin and Spread of Nationalism.* London: Verso, 1991.

Anesaki, Masaharu. *History of Japanese Religion, with Special Reference to the Social and Moral Life of the Nation.* London: Kegan Paul, 1930.

Archdeacon, Thomas. *Becoming American: An Ethnic History.* New York: Free Press, 1983.

Aspalter, Christian. "The Taiwanese Economic Miracle: From Sugarcane to High-Technology." In *Understanding Modern Taiwan: Essays in Economics, Politics, and Social Policy,* edited by Christian Aspalter, 1–32. Aldershot, England: Ashgate Publishing Limited, 2001.

Avison, Oliver R. *Annual Report of the Imperial Korean Hospital.* Seoul: Methodist Publishing, 1901.

———. *The Land of the Morning Calm: Reminiscence of Oliver R. Avison, M.D.* Daegu: Taegu University Press, 1988.

Baruto, Shingaku Juyōshi Kenkyūkai, ed. *Nihon ni okeru Kaaru Baruto: Haisen-made no Juyōshi no Shodanmen* [Karl Barth in Japan: Aspects of the History of his Reception in Japan through 1945]. Tokyo: Shinkyō Shuppansha, 2009.

Bays, Daniel H. "Chinese Protestant Christianity Today." *The China Quarterly* 174 (2003): 488–504.

Beck, Ulrich, Anthony Giddens, and Scott Lash. *Reflexive Modernization: Politics, Tradition and Aesthetics in the Modern Social Order.* Cambridge, UK: Polity, 1994.

Bellah, Robert N., Richard Madsen, William Sullivan, Ann Swidler, and Stephen Tipton. *Habits of the Heart.* Berkeley and Los Angeles: University of California Press, 1985.

Berman, Marshall. *All That Is Solid Melts into Air.* New York: Penguin Books, 1982.

Berry, Mary Elizabeth. *Hideyoshi.* Cambridge, MA: Harvard University Press, 1982.

Buchanan, Daniel C. *Japanese Proverbs and Sayings.* Norman: University of Oklahoma Press, 1965.

Buswell, Robert E., and Timothy S. Lee, eds. *Christianity in Korea.* Honolulu: University of Hawai'i Press, 2007.

Cai, Ellen Xiangyu. "The Itinerant Preaching of Three Hoklo Evangelists in Mid-Nineteenth Century Hong Kong." *Itinerario* 33, no. 3 (2009): 113–134.

Caldarola, Carlo. *Christianity: The Japanese Way.* Leiden: E. J. Brill, 1979.

Cao, Nanlai. "Boss Christians: The Business of Religion in the 'Wenzhou Model' of Christian Revival." *The China Journal* 59 (2008): 63–87.

———. "Christian Entrepreneurs and the Post-Mao State: An Ethnographic Account of Church-State Relations in China's Economic Transition." *Sociology of Religion* 68, no. 1 (2007): 45–66.

———. "Raising the Quality of Belief: *Suzhi* and the Production of an Elite Protestantism." *China Perspectives* 4 (2009): 54–66.

Chamberlain, Basil H. *Things Japanese: Being Notes on Various Subjects Connected with Japan.* London: J. Murray, 1905.

Chan, Kim-kwong. "Missiological Implications of Chinese Christianity in a Globalized Context." *Quest* 4, no. 1 (2005): 55–74.

Chan, Sucheng. *Asian Americans: An Interpretive History.* Boston: Twayne, 1991.

Chang, Shirley L. *Taiwan's Brain Drain and Its Reversal.* Taipei: Lucky Bookstore, 1998.

Chang Kyusik. "Dosan Ahn Chang-ho ŭi minjokjuŭi wa simin sahoeron" [Ahn Chang-ho's View of Nationalism and the Theory of Civil Society]. *Dosan sasang yŏn'gu* [Journal of Dosan Ahn Chang-ho Studies] 6 (2000): 49–52.

———. *Ilcheha Han'guk Kidokkyo minjokjuŭi yŏn'gu* [Christian Nationalism in Modern Korea]. Seoul: Hyean Press, 2001.

———. "Ilcheha Kidokkyo kyeyŏl ŭi minjok kyŏngje kŏnsŏlron" [The National Economic Development Theory of Christian Nationalists under Japanese Colonial Rule: The Case of the P'yŏngyang YMCA]. *Han'guk sasang sahak* [The Study of the History of Korean Thought] 15 (2000): 255–291.

Chao, Hsing-Huang. "Mobilizing to Grow: The Persistence and Transformation of the Evangelical Formosan Church of Los Angeles." Ph.D. diss., Purdue University, 1995.

Chen, Carolyn E. "From Filial Piety to Religious Piety: Evangelical Christianity Reconstructing Taiwanese Immigrant Families in the United States." *International Migration Review* 40, no. 3 (2006): 573–602.

———. *Getting Saved in America: Taiwanese Immigration and Religious Experience.* Princeton, NJ: Princeton University Press, 2008.

———. "The Religious Varieties of Ethnic Presence: A Comparison between a Taiwanese Immigrant Buddhist Temple and an Evangelical Christian Church." *Sociology of Religion* 63 (2002): 215–238.

Ching, Leo T. S. *Becoming Japanese: Colonial Taiwan and the Politics of Identity Formation.* Berkeley: University of California Press, 2001.

Cho Ki-joon. *Han'guk chaponjuŭi sŏngrip saron* [Historical Essay on the Establishment of Capitalism in Korea]. Seoul: Daewangsa, 1977.

Cho Man-sik. "Ŏin e i rŭl jum ŭn daegŭmmul" [Internal Division Is Our Greatest Enemy]. *Samchŏnri* [Korean Peninsula] 12 (1931): 7–8.

Choy, Bong-youn. *Koreans in America.* Chicago: Nelson-Hall, 1977.

Clark, Charles Allen. *The Nevius Plan for Mission Work.* Seoul: Christian Literature Society, 1937.

Clark, Donald N. *Living Dangerously in Korea.* Norwalk: East Bridge Press, 2003.

Comaroff, Jean, and John L. Comaroff. "Millennial Capitalism: First Thoughts on a Second Coming." In *Millennial Capitalism and the Culture of Neoliberalism,* edited by Jean Comaroff and John L. Comaroff, 1–56. Durham, NC: Duke University Press, 2001.

———. *Of Revelation and Revolution,* vol. 2. Chicago: University of Chicago Press, 1997.

Cumings, Bruce. *Korea's Place in the Sun: A Modern History.* New York: W. W. Norton, 2005.

Cunningham, David S. *Christian Ethics: The End of the Law.* London: Routledge, 2008.

Daidōji Yūzan. *Budō shoshinshū* [Initiation to the Warrior Way]. Edited by Tetsushi Furukawa. Tokyo: Iwanami Shoten, 1943; original 1720.

Daikichirō Tagawa. *Kokka to shūkyō* [State and Religion]. Tokyo: Kyōbunkan, 1938.

Daniels, Roger. *Coming to America: A History of Immigration and Ethnicity in American Life.* New York: Harper Perennial, 2002.

Davis, Sandra T. W. "Treaty Revision." In *Japan in Transition: Thought and Action in the Meiji Era, 1868–1912,* edited by Hilary Conroy, Sandra T. W. Davis, and Wayne Patterson. London: Associated University Press, 1984.

Dawber, M. A. "The Cooperative Movement and the Church." *Annals of the American Academy of Political and Social Science* 191 (1937): 70–75.

Devine, Richard. "Hirata Atsutane and Christian Sources." *Monumenta Nipponica* 36, no. 1 (1981): 37–54.

Dillon, Nara, and Jean C. Oi, eds. *At the Crossroads of Empires: Middlemen, Social Networks, and State-Building in Republican Shanghai.* Stanford, CA: Stanford University Press, 2008.

Dohi Akio and Tanaka Masato, eds. *Kindai tennōsei to Kirisutokyō* [The Modern Emperor System and Christianity]. Kyoto: Jinbun Shoin, 1996.

Dolan, Jay P. *The American Catholic Experience: A History from Colonial Times to the Present.* Garden City, NY: Doubleday, 1985.

———. *The Immigrant Church: New York's Irish and German Catholics, 1815–1865.* Baltimore: Johns Hopkins University Press, 1975.

Dōshisha Daigaku Jinbun Kagaku Kenkyūjo, ed. *Kumamoto bando kenkyū: Nihon Purotesutantoisumu, genryū to kaiten* [Study of the Kumamoto Band: Japanese Protestantism, Origins and Development]. Tokyo: Misuzu Shogo, 1965.

Douglas, Thomas J. "The Cross and the Lotus: Changing Religious Practices among Cambodian Immigrants in Seattle." In *Revealing the Sacred,* edited by Jane N. Iwamura and Paul Spickard, 159–176. New York: Routledge, 2003.

Duara, Prasenjit. *Rescuing History from the Nation: Questioning Narratives of Modern China.* Chicago: University of Chicago Press, 1997.

Dunch, Ryan. "Christianity and 'Adaptation to Socialism.'" In *Chinese Religiosities: Afflictions of Modernity and State Formation,* edited by Mayfair Mei-hui Yang. Berkeley: University of California, 2008.

———. "Protestant Christianity in China Today: Fragile, Fragmented, Flourishing." In *China and Christianity: Burdened Past, Hopeful Future,* edited by Stephen Uhally, Jr., and Xiaowin Wu. Armonk, NY: M. E. Sharpe, 2001.

Dunn, Emily C. "Netizens of Heaven: Contesting Orthodoxies on the Chinese Protestant Web." *Asian Studies Review* 31, no. 5 (2007): 447–458.

Ebina Danjō. "Gojin no shūyō" [Our Cultivation]. *Shinjin* 1, no. 7 (1901).

———. "Ima wa kitō toki nari" [Now It's Time to Pray]. *Shinjin* 6, no. 10 (1905).

———. "Kirisutokyō to demokurashii" [Christianity and Democracy]. *Shinjin* 21, no. 6 (1920).

———. "Sensō no bi" [The Beauty of War]. *Shinjin* 5, no. 8 (1904).

———. "Shin bushido" [The New Way of the Warrior]. *Shinjin* 3, no. 10 (1902). Reprinted in *Ebina Danjō no sekkyōshuū* [The Collected Sermons of Ebina Danjō]. Tokyo: Shinkyō Shuppansha, 1973.

Espiritu, Yen Le. *Home Bound: Filipino American Lives across Cultures, Communities, and Countries.* Berkeley: University of California Press, 2003.

Evans, Christopher H., ed. *The Social Gospel Today.* Louisville: Westminster John Knox Press, 2001.

Faure, David. *Emperor and Ancestor: State and Lineage in South China.* Stanford, CA: Stanford University Press, 2007.

Feagin, Joe R. *Systemic Racism: A Theory of Oppression.* New York: Routledge, 2006.

Fridell, Wilbur M. "Government Ethics Textbooks in Late Meiji Japan." *Journal of Asian Studies* 29 (1970): 823–833.

Fujitani, Takashi. *Splendid Monarchy: Power and Pageantry in Modern Japan.* Berkeley: University of California Press, 1998.

Fujiwara Fujio. *Nihon seishin to Kirisutokyō* [The Japanese Spirit and Christianity]. Sakai: Tomoshibisha, 1941.

Furuya Yasuo. *Nihon no Kirisutokyō* [Christianity in Japan]. Tokyo: Kyobunkwan, 2003.

Gaonkar, Dilip Parameshwa. "On Alternative Modernities." In *Alternative Modernities,* edited by Dilip Parameshwar Gaonkar, 1–23. Durham, NC: Duke University Press, 2001.

Gauntlett, John Owen, and Robert King Hall, eds. and trans. *Kokutai no Hongi: Cardinal Principles of the National Entity of Japan.* Cambridge, MA: Harvard University Press, 1949.

Germany, Charles H. *Protestant Theologies in Modern Japan.* Tokyo: I.I.S.R. Press, 1966.

Gibson, John Campbell. *Mission Problems and Mission Methods in South China.* New York: Revell, 1901.

Giddens, Anthony. *Modernity and Self-Identity: Self and Society in the Late Modern Age.* Stanford, CA: Stanford University Press, 1991.

Gilley, Sheridan, and Brian Stanley, eds. *Cambridge History of Christianity,* vol. 8. Cambridge, UK: Cambridge University Press, 2005.

Gluck, Carol. *Japan's Modern Myths: Ideology in the Late Meiji Period.* Princeton, NJ: Princeton University Press, 1985.

Goethe, Johann Wolfgang. *Hermann and Dorothea.* In *The Harvard Classics,* translated by Ellen Frothingham. New York: P. F. Collier and Son, 1909–1914.

Gold, Thomas, Doug Guthrie, and David Wank, eds. *Social Connections in China: Institutions, Culture, and the Changing Nature of Guanxi.* Cambridge, UK: Cambridge University Press, 2002.

Goodpasture, H. M. "Student Volunteer Movement for Foreign Missions." In *Dictionary of Christianity in America,* edited by Daniel G. Reid et al. Downers Grove, IL: InterVarsity Press, 1990.

Gordon, Andrew. *A Modern History of Japan from Tokugawa Times to the Present.* New York: Oxford University Press, 2003.

Gregg, George A. "Educating Hand and Brain." *The Korea Mission Field,* June 1912, 171–175.

Guest, Kenneth J. *God in Chinatown: Religion and Survival in New York's Evolving Immigrant Community.* New York: New York University Press, 2003.

Guo, Xuezhi. "Dimensions of *Guanxi* in Chinese Elite Politics." *The China Journal* 46 (2001): 69–90.

Habermas, Jürgen. *The Structural Transformation of the Public Sphere.* Cambridge, MA: The MIT Press, 1989.

Hall, Robert King, ed. *Kokutai no Hongi: Cardinal Principles of the National Entity of Japan.* Cambridge, MA: Harvard University Press, 1949.

Handy, Robert T. *A Christian America: Protestant Hopes and Historical Realities.* New York: Oxford University Press, 1971, 1984.

Hane, Mikiso. *Peasants, Rebels, and Outcastes: The Underside of Modern Japan.* New York: Pantheon Books, 1982.

Harada Nobuo. *Kaaru Baruto no ningengaku* [Karl Barth's Anthropology]. Tokyo: Shinseidō, 1935.

Harootunian, Harry. *Overcome by Modernity: History, Culture, and Community in Interwar Japan.* Princeton, NJ: Princeton University Press, 2000.

Harrington, Fred Harvey. *God, Mammon, and the Japanese.* Madison, Milwaukee, London: The University of Wisconsin Press, 1966.

Harvey, David. *The Limits to Capital.* Oxford: Basil Blackwell Publishing, 1982.

Hayashi, Brian Masaru. *For the Sake of Our Japanese Brethren: Assimilation, Nationalism, and Protestantism among the Japanese of Los Angeles, 1895–1942.* Stanford, CA: Stanford University Press, 1995.

Hayek, Friedrich von. *Law, Legislation and Liberty.* New York: Routledge and Kegan Paul, 1976.

———. *The Road to Serfdom.* London: George Routledge, 1944.

Hee, Kang Nae. *Neoliberalism and Culture: Labor Society to Culture Society.* Seoul: Munwa Kwa Haksa, 2000.

Hiyane Antei. *Kirisutokyō no Nihonteki tenkai* [National Spirit and the Christian Faith]. Tokyo: Kirisutokyō Shisō Sōsho Kankōkai, 1938.

———. *Nihon shūkyōshi* [History of Religion in Japan]. Tokyo: Sankyō Shuppansha, 1925.

———. *Shina Kirisutokyō shi* [History of Christianity in China]. Tokyo: Seikatsusha, 1940.

Holtom, D. C. *Modern Japan and Shinto Nationalism: A Study of Present-Day Trends in Japanese Religions.* Chicago: University of Chicago Press, 1943.

Hong Yŏng-ki. *Kyohoe sŏnt'aek ŭi chokŏn* [Conditions for Choosing a Church]. Seoul: Kyohoe Sŏngjang Yŏn'guso, 2004.

Hood, George A. *Mission Accomplished? The English Presbyterian Mission in Lingtung, South China: A Study of Interplay between Mission Methods and Their Historical Contexts.* Frankfurt, Germany: Peter Lang, 1986.

Hopkins, C. Howard. *History of the Y.M.C.A. in North America.* New York: Association Press, 1951.

———. *The Rise of the Social Gospel in American Protestantism, 1865–1915.* New Haven: Yale University Press, 1940.

Howes, John F. "Two Types: Kagawa and Uchimura." *Theology Today* 23, no. 1 (1966): 88–97.

Hulbert, Homer B. *The History of Korea.* Seoul: Methodist Publishing House, 1905.

Hunter, Alan, and Kim-Kwong Chan. *Protestantism in Contemporary China.* Cambridge, UK: Cambridge University Press, 1993.

Hurst, G. Cameron, III. "Death, Honor, and Loyalty: The Bushidō Ideal." *Philosophy East and West* 40 (1990): 511–527.

Hutchison, William R. *Errand to the World: American Protestant Thought and Foreign Missions.* Chicago: University of Chicago Press, 1987.

Hwang, Il-do. "Representative of Korean Christianity: Onnuri Community Church." *Sindonga* 577 (2007): 152–165.

Issei Sekioka. "Ebina Danjō ni okeru sekaishugi to Nihonshugi [Ebina Danjō on Internationalism and Japanism]." *Kirisutokyō shakai mondai kenkyū* 44 (1995): 26–48.

Ito, Yushi. *Yamaji Aizan and His Time: Nationalism and Debating Japanese History.* Kent, UK: Global Oriental, 2007.

Iwai, Shuma. "Japanese Christianity in the Meiji Era: An Analysis of Ebina Danjo's Perspective on Shintoistic Christianity." *Transformation: An International Journal of Holistic Mission Studies* 25, no. 4 (2008): 195–204.

Jae, Yoo-Kyong, ed. *Sermons of Sixteen Korean Protestant Pastors.* Seoul: The Christian Literature Society of Korea, 2004.

Jaffe, Richard M. "Seeking Sakyamuni: Travel and the Reconstruction of Japanese Buddhism." *Journal of Japanese Studies* 30, no. 1 (2004): 65–96.

Jennings, J. Nelson. *Theology in Japan: Takakura Tokutaro, 1885–1934.* New York: University Press of America, 2005.

Kagawa Toyohiko. *Before the Dawn* [English title of *Shisen o koete*]. Translated by Ichiji Fukumoto and Thomas Satchell. New York: George H. Doran Company, 1924.

———. *Brotherhood Economics.* New York: Harper and Brothers, 1936.

———. "Christianity and Race Prejudice: A Japanese Plea." *The Friend* 65 (1925).

———. *Kagawa Toyohiko zenshū* [The Collected Works of Kagawa Toyohiko]. Tokyo: Kirisuto Shinbunsha, 1962–1964.

———. *Meditations on the Cross.* Translated by Helen F. Topping and Marion R. Draper. Chicago/New York: Willett, Clark and Company, 1935.

Kang, Eun Ryung. "A Study on Cultural Trend and Youth Community of Mega-Sized Churches in South Korea." M.A. thesis, Yonsei University, 2005.

Kanshi Imanaka. "Ebina Danjō to sono shisō [Ebina Danjō and His Thought]." *Kirisutokyō shakai mondai kenkyū* 23 (1975): 1–27.

Kanter, Rosabeth Moss. "Commitment and Social Organization: A Study of Commitment Mechanisms in Utopian Communities." *American Sociological Review* 33 (1968): 499–517.

Kasahara Yoshimitsu. "Nihonteki Kirisutokyō' hihan [Critique of "Christianity on Japanese Terms"]." *Kirisutokyō shakai mondai kenkyū* [Study of Christianity and Social Problems] 22 (1974): 114–139.

Kassel, Marleen. *Tokugawa Confucian Education: The Kangien Academy of Hirose Tanso: 1782–1856.* Albany: State University of New York Press, 1996.

Kayama Hisao. "Kagawa Toyohiko to 'Kami no kuni' [Kagawa Toyohiko and the Kingdom of God]." *Kagawa Toyohiko kenkyū* 48 (2004).

Kearney, Reginald. *African American Views of the Japanese: Solidarity or Sedition.* Albany: State University of New York Press, 1998.

Kim, Jim Yong. "The Role of Christianity in the Economic Modernization of South Korea." Ph.D. diss., Florida State University, 1984.

Kim, Moon Sun. "Analysis on the Fast Growth of Protestant Churches in Korea: Cases Studies on Large and Small Churches." M.A. thesis, Ewha University, 1996.

Kim, Warren Y. *Koreans in America.* Seoul: Po Chin Chai Printing Co., 1971.

Kim, Young Il. "A Study on the Move of Young Christian Populations to the Mega Churches." M.A. thesis, Yonsei University, 2001.

Kim Dong-no. "National Identity and Class Interest in Peasant Movements during the Colonial Period." Unpublished paper, Yonsei University, 2004.

Kim In-soo, trans. *Alrenuisaui sŏngyo oigyopyeonji* [Horace H. Allen, M.D.'s Missionary and Diplomatic Letters]. Seoul: Institute of Studies of the Korean Church History Presbyterian College and Theological Seminary, 2007.

———. *Heronuisaui seongyopyeonji* [John W. Heron, M.D.'s Missionary Letters]. Seoul: Institute of Studies of the Korean Church History Presbyterian College and Theological Seminary, 2007.

Kim Jin-gyun and Jung Keun-sik, eds., *Kŭndae chuch'e wa sikminji kyuyul kwonryŏk* [Modern Subjects and Colonial Disciplinary Power]. Seoul: Munhwa Kwa Haksa, 1997.

Kim Sang-tae. "Kŭnhyŏndae P'yŏngyangdo ch'ulsin sahoe chidoch'ŭng yŏn'gu" [Research on the Class of Social Leaders from the P'yŏngyang Region during the Modern Period]. Ph.D. diss., Seoul National University, 2002.

———. *Yebae wa hyŏndae munhwa* [Worship Service and Modern Culture]. Seoul: Taehan Kidokkyosŏhoe, 2005.

Kim Sŏng-gŏn. *Chonggyo wa sahoe* [Religion and Society]. Taejŏn: Mun'gyŏng Ch'ulp'ansa, 1997.

Kim Wŏn-mo, trans. *Alrenŭi ilki* [Allen's Diary]. Seoul: Kunkuk University Press, 1991.

Kim Yŏng-chae. *Han'guk kyohoesa* [The History of the Korean Church]. Seoul: Reformed Press Interactive, 1992.

Kindopp, Jason. "China's War on 'Cults.'" *Current History* 100, no. 651 (2002): 259–266.

———. "Fragmented Yet Defiant: Protestant Resilience under Chinese Communist Party Rule." In *God and Caesar in China,* edited by Jason Kindopp and Carol Lee Hamrin, 122–145. Washington, DC: The Brookings Institute, 2004.

Kindopp, Jason, and Jacqueline E. Wenger. "Official versus Underground Protestant Churches in China: Challenges for Reconciliation and Social Influence." *Review of Religious Research* 46, no. 2 (2004): 169–182.

Koga, Rev. Sumio, comp. *"A Centennial Legacy": History of the Japanese Christian Missions in North America 1877–1977,* vol. 1. Chicago: Nobart, Inc., 1977.

Koschmann, J. Victor, trans. "Japanese Christianity: Between Orthodoxy and Heterodoxy." In *Authority and the Individual in Japan,* edited by Victor J. Koschman. Tokyo: University of Tokyo Press, 1978.

Kraemer, Hendrik. *The Christian Message in a Non-Christian World.* New York: Harper and Brothers, 1938.

———. *World Cultures and World Religions: The Coming Dialogue.* Philadelphia: Westminster Press, 1960.

Kurien, Prema. "'We Are Better Hindus Here': Religion and Ethnicity among Indian Americans." In *Religions in Asian America,* edited by Pyong Gap Min and Jung Ha Kim, 99–120. Walnut Creek, CA: Altamira Press, 2002.

Kuroda Shirō. *Watakushi no Kagawa Toyohiko kenkyū* [My Research on Kagawa Toyohiko]. Tokyo: Kirisuto Shinbunsha, 1983.

Lagerwey, John. *China: A Religious State.* Hong Kong: Hong Kong University Press, 2010.

Lai, Him Mark, Genny Lim, and Judy Yung. *Island: Poetry and History of Chinese Immigrants on Angel Island, 1910*–1940. Seattle: University of Washington Press, 1999.

Lambert, Tony. *China's Christian Millions.* Oxford: Monarch Books, 1999.

———. "Counting Christians in China: A Cautionary Report." *International Bulletin of Missionary Research* 27, no. 1 (2006): 6–11.

Lande, Aasulv. *Meiji Protestantism in History and Historiography: A Comparative Study of Japanese and Western Interpretation of Early Protestantism in Japan.* New York: Peter Lang, 1989.

Lawsin, Emily Porcincula. "Pensionados, Paisanos, and Pinoys: An Analysis of the Filipino Student Bulletin, 1929–1933." *Filipino American National Historical Society Journal* 4 (1996), 33–33P.

Lee, Chong-sik. *The Politics of Korean Nationalism.* Berkeley: University of California Press, 1963.

Lee, Ellen. *The Planted Seed: History of the English Language Ministry of the Korean Methodist Church and Institute.* New York: Korean Methodist Church and Institute, 1995.

Lee, Erika. *At America's Gates: Chinese Immigration during the Exclusion Era.* Chapel Hill: University of North Carolina Press, 2003.

Lee, Eun Young. "Neoliberalism and a New Protestant Ethic: The Transformation of Korean Mega-Churches since the 1990s." M.A. thesis, Yonsei University, 2007.

Lee, Joseph Tse-Hei. *The Bible and the Gun: Christianity in South China, 1860–1911.* New York and London: Routledge, 2003.

———. "Christianity in Contemporary China: An Update." *Journal of Church and State* 49, no. 2 (2007): 277–304.

———. "The Overseas Chinese Networks and Early Baptist Missionary Movement across the South China Sea." *The Historian* 63, no. 4 (2001): 752–768.

Lee, Ki-Baik. *A New History of Korea.* Translated by Edward W. Wagner with Edward Schulz. Cambridge, MA: Harvard University Press, 1984.

Lee, Marjorie. "*Hu-Jee:* The Forgotten Second Generation of Chinese America, 1930–1950." M.A. thesis, University of California, Los Angeles, 1984.

Lee Kwang-in. "Kaehwagi kwansŏ chipang kwa Kaesinkyo" [Northwest Korea and Protestant Christianity in the Later Chosŏn Dynasty]. *Han'guk kaehwa sasang yŏn'gu* [Studies on Ideas of Enlightenment in the Later Chosŏn Dynasty]. Seoul: Iljogak, 1979.

Lee Seong-jeon. *Miguk sŏngyosawa Han'guk kŭndae kyoyuk* [American Missionaries and Modern Education in Korea]. Translated by Seo Jeong-min and Minako Kamiyama. Seoul: Han'guk Kidokkyo Yŏk'sa Yŏn'guso, 2007.

Li Hongju, Cui Jinxia, Zhang Rong, and Wang Yanlei. "Xiangmin shehui Jidujiao xinyang de yuanyin tanxi: dui Yubei Jiangcun jiaotang de diaocha" [Inquiry into the Reasons for Belief in Christianity in Rural Society: Survey of the Jiang Village Church in Northern Henan]. *Zhongguo Nongye Daxue xuebao (Shehui kexue ban)* [Journal of China Agricultural University (Social Sciences Edition)] 57, no. 4 (2004).

Li Longqian. *Ming Qing Guangdong shehui jingji yanjiu* [Studies on Guangdong Society and Economy in the Ming and Qing Eras]. Shanghai: Guji Chubanshe, 2006.

Lian, Xi. "A Messianic Deliverance for Post-Dynastic China: The Launch of the True Jesus Church in the Early Twentieth Century." *Modern China* 34, no. 4 (2008): 407–441.

———. *Redeemed by Fire: The Rise of Popular Christianity in Modern China.* New Haven: Yale University Press, 2009.

———. "The Search for Chinese Christianity in the Republican Period (1912–1949)." *Modern Asian Studies* 38 (2004): 851–898.

Lien, Pei-te, and Tony Carnes, "The Religious Demography of Asian American Boundary Crossing." In *Asian American Religions: The Making and Remaking of Borders and Boundaries,* edited by Fenggang Yang, 67–87. New York and London: New York University Press, 2004.

Lim, Hyun-Chin, and Jin-Ho Jang. "Neo-Liberalism in Post-Crisis South Korea: Social Conditions and Outcomes." *Journal of Contemporary Asia* 36, no. 4 (2006): 443–445.

Ling, Oi-Ki. "Bible Women." In *Pioneer Chinese Christian Women: Gender, Christianity, and Social Mobility,* edited by Jessie G. Lutz, 246–266. Bethlehem, PA: Lehigh University Press, 2010.

Liu Yihui. "*Liu shi jiapu* jiaodian: Chaoshan Jidujiao bentuhua shiliao juyu" [Commentaries on *The Liu Family Genealogy:* Historical Sources on the Localization of Christianity in Chaoshan]. *Shantou Daxue xuebao* [Journal of Shantou University] 19 (2003): 115–117.

Lutz, Jessie G., and Rolland Ray Lutz. *Hakka Chinese Confront Protestant Christianity 1850–1900.* Armonk, NY: M. E. Sharpe, 1998.

Ma, Zhao. "Down the Alleyway: Courtyard Tenements and Women's Networks in Early Twentieth-Century Beijing." *Journal of Urban History* 36, no. 2 (2010): 151–172.

Madsen, Richard. *China's Catholics: Tragedy and Hope in an Emerging Civil Society.* Berkeley: University of California Press, 1998.

Maekawa Shinjirō. *Zetsudai naru jinkaku* [Tremendous Character]. Tokyo: Seikokai Shuppan Sha, 1929.

Mann, C. *Catherine Maria Ricketts of Brighton and China.* London: Women's Missionary Association of the Presbyterian Church of England, 1924.

Marriott, Victor. *Kagawa and Cooperatives.* Chicago: Kingdom of God Fellowship, 1936.

McCullough, Helen Craig. *The Tale of the Heike.* Stanford, CA: Stanford University Press, 1988.

Millard, Thomas F. "Japanese Immigration into Korea." *Annals of the American Academy of Political and Social Science* 34, no. 2 (1909): 183–189.

Miller, Donald E. *Reinventing American Protestantism.* Berkeley: University of California Press, 1997.

Min, Pyong Gap. "Religion and the Maintenance of Ethnicity among Immigrants: A Comparison of Indian Hindus and Korean Protestants." In *Immigrant Faiths: Transforming Religious Life in America,* edited by Karen I. Leonard et al., 99–122. Walnut Creek, CA: AltaMira Press, 2005.

Minear, Richard H. *Japanese Tradition and Western Law: Emperor, State, and Law in the Thought of Hozumi Yatsuka.* Cambridge, MA: Harvard University Press, 1970.

Mission Council, comp. *The Congregational Rolls for Use in the Swatow Mission.* Shantou: Mission Press, 1885.

Miyata, Mitsuo. *Authority and Obedience: Romans 13:1–7 in Modern Japan.* New York: Peter Lang, 2009.

Moffett, Samuel. "Policy and Methods for the Evangelization of Korea." In *Sources of Korean Christianity 1832–1945,* edited and translated by Sung-Deuk Oak, 121–128. Seoul: Han'guk Kidokkyo Yŏk'sa Yŏn'guso, 2004.

Moore, Deborah Dash. *At Home in America: Second Generation New York Jews.* New York: Columbia University Press, 1981.

Mullins, Mark R. "Christianity as a Transnational Social Movement: Kagawa Toyohiko and the Friends of Jesus." *Japanese Religions* 32, no. 1 (2007): 69–87.

———. *Christianity Made in Japan: A Study of Indigenous Movements.* Honolulu: University of Hawai'i Press, 1998.

Mutō Tomio. *Kagawa Toyohiko zenshū daijesuto* [Digest of Toyohiko Kagawa's Collected Works]. Tokyo: Kirisuto Shinbunsha, 1966.

Myers, Ramon H., and Mark R. Peattie, eds. *The Japanese Colonial Empire, 1895–1945.* Princeton, NJ: Princeton University Press, 1984.

Najita, Tetsuo. *Visions of Virtue in Tokugawa Japan.* Chicago: University of Chicago Press, 1987.

Nelson, John. "Social Memory as Ritual Practice: Commemorating Spirits of the Military Dead at Yasukuni Shinto Shrine." *Journal of Asian Studies* 62, no. 2 (2003): 443–467.

Nevius, John L. "Mission Work in Central Shantung." In *Sources of Korean Christianity,* edited by Sung-deuk Oak, 113. Seoul: Institute for Korean Church History, 2004.

Niebuhr, Reinhold. "The Political Confusion of Dr. Kagawa." *Radical Religion* 1, no. 2 (1936): 6–7.

Nitobe, Inazō. *Bushido: The Soul of Japan.* Philadelphia: Leeds and Biddle, 1900.

Noll, Mark A. *A History of Christianity in the United States and Canada.* Grand Rapids, MI: W. B. Eerdmans, 1992.

Oh Ki-young. "P'yŏngyang sahoe danche kaegwan" [Overview of NGOs in P'yŏngyang]. *Pyŏlgŏngon* [Another World] 32 (1930): 43–44.

Okino Iwasaburō. *Nihon kenkokushi kō: "Kojiki," "Nihon shoki" no yomikata* [On the History of the Founding of the Nation of Japan: Reading the *Kojiki* and *Nihon shoki*]. Tokyo: Kōseisha, 1939.

Okumura Naohiko. *Voorizu hoyden* [Biography of Vories]. Kamakura: Minatonohito, 2005.

O'Neil, Kevin. "Brain Drain and the Gain: The Case of Taiwan." Migration Policy Institute, 2003. http://www.migrationinformation.org/Feature/display.cfm?ID=155.

Ota, Yuzo. "Kagawa Toyohiko: A Pacifist?" In *Pacifism in Japan: The Christian Socialist Tradition,* edited by Nobuya Bamba and John F. Howes, 169–197. Vancouver: University of British Columbia Press, 1978.

———. "Mediation between Cultures." In *Nitobe Inazō: Japan's Bridge across the Pacific,* edited by John F. Howes, 237–252. Boulder, CO: Westview Press, 1995.

Ownby, David. *Falun Gong and China's Future.* New York: Oxford University Press, 2008.

———. "Kang Xiaoguang: Social Science, Civil Society, and Confucian Religion." *China Perspectives* 4 (2009): 101–111.

———. "Religious Revival and the Rule of Law in China: An Evaluation of 'Secularization with Chinese Characteristics.'" Paper presented at the Conference on Political Change in China, Munk Centre, University of Toronto, March 6–7, 2009.

Ozaki, Yukio. *The Autobiography of Ozaki Yukio: The Struggle for Constitutional Government in Japan.* Translated by Fujiko Hara and edited by Marius Jansen. Princeton, NJ: Princeton University Press, 2001.

Paik, George. *The History of Protestant Missions in Korea, 1832–1910.* Seoul: Yonsei University Press, 1970.

Pak, Ung Kyu. *Millennialism in the Korean Protestant Church.* New York: Peter Lang, 2005.

Pak Yŏng-sin. "Han'guk kŭndae sahoe pyŏndong kwa Kidokkyo" [The Transformation of Modern Korean Society and Protestantism]. *Kidokkyo sasang* 313 (1984): 122–132.

Park, Chung-shin. *Protestantism and Politics in Korea.* Seattle and London: University of Washington Press, 2003.

Park, Hyŏng-woo. *Chejungwŏn.* Seoul:, 2002.

Park, Yunjae. "Early Colonial Laws on Medical Practitioners and the Japanese Colonial Rule." In *Japanese Studies around the World 2002,* 338–345. Kyoto: International Research Center for Japanese Studies, 2002.

———. *Han'guk kŭndaeŭihak ŭi kiwon* [The Origin of the Modern Korean Medical System]. Seoul: Hyean, 2005.

Parker, Michael. *The Kingdom of Character: The Student Volunteer Movement for*

Foreign Missions, 1886–1926. Lanham, MD: University Press of America, 1998.

Phan, Peter, ed. *Christianities in Asia*. Chichester: Wiley-Blackwell, 2011.

Potter, Pittman B. "Belief in Control: Regulation of Religion in China." *The China Quarterly* 174, no. 2 (2003): 317–337.

Powles, Cyril H. "Bushidō: Its Admirers and Its Critics." In *Nitobe Inazō: Japan's Bridge across the Pacific*, edited by John F. Howes, 107–118. Oxford, UK: Westview Press, 1995.

Pyle, Kenneth. *The New Generation in Meiji Japan: Problems of Cultural Identity, 1885–1895*. Stanford, CA: Stanford University Press, 1969.

Rhodes, Harry A. *History of the Korea Mission Presbyterian Church U.S.A., 1884–1934*. Seoul: Chosen Mission Presbyterian Church, 1934.

Richman, Karen. "The Protestant Ethic and the Dis-Spirit of Vodou." In *Immigrant Faiths: Transforming Religious Life in America*, edited by Karen I. Leonard et al., 165–288. Walnut Creek, CA: AltaMira Press, 2005.

Ro, Bong Rin, and Marlin L. Nelson. *Korean Church Growth Explosion*. Seoul: Saengmyŏngŭi Malssŭmsa, 1995.

Ro, Kil-myung. "New Religions and Social Change in Modern Korea History." *Review of Korean Studies* 2002:31–62.

Rodgers, Daniel T. *The Work Ethic in Industrial America, 1850–1920*. Chicago: University of Chicago Press, 1978.

Rubinstein, Murray A. "Actors: Protestant Missionaries." In *Handbook of Christianity in China*, vol. 2: *1800 to the Present*, edited by R. G. Tiedemann, 133–192. Leiden: E. J. Brill, 2010.

———. *The Other Taiwan: 1945 to the Present*. Armonk, NY: M. E. Sharpe, 1994.

Ryang, Key S. "Kim Kyu-Sik as a Common Man and a Political Leader." *Korea Observer* 13, no. 1 (1982): 36–54.

Saiga Hiroyoshi. *Saigō nanshūoū: daijinkan no ikan* [Venerable Man of the South Saigō: Magnificent Example of the Great Character]. Tokyo: Shizendō Shoten, 1919.

San Buenaventura, Steffi. "Filipino Folk Spirituality and Immigration: From Mutual Aid to Religion." In *New Spiritual Homes: Religion and Asian Americans*, edited by David K. Yoo, 52–86. Honolulu: University of Hawai'i Press, 1999.

Sanneh, Lamin. *Disciples of All Nations: Pillars of World Christianity*. New York: Oxford University Press, 2005.

Sassen, Saskia. "America's Immigration Problem." In *Globalization and Its Discontents*, 31–54. New York: The New Press, 1998.

Saunders, Kenneth. "The Passing of Paternalism in Missions." *The Journal of Religion* 2, no. 5 (1922): 466–475.

———. "Toyohiko Kagawa: The St. Francis of Japan." *Pacific Affairs* 4, no. 4 (1931): 308–317.

Scheiner, Irwin. *Christian Converts and Social Protest in Meiji Japan.* Berkeley: University of California Press, 1970.

Schildgen, Robert D. *Toyohiko Kagawa: An Apostle of Love and Social Justice.* Berkeley: Centenary Books, 1988.

Schmid, Andre. *Korea between Empires.* New York: Columbia University Press, 2002.

Sennett, Richard. *The Corrosion of Character: The Personal Consequences of Work in the New Capitalism.* New York: W. W. Norton and Company, 2001.

Sewell, William H. *Logics of History.* Chicago: University of Chicago Press, 2005.

Shaffer, Robert. "Opposition to Internment: Defending Japanese American Rights during World War II." *The Historian* 61, no. 3 (1999): 597–620.

Shimazu, Naoko. *Japanese Society at War Death, Memory and the Russo-Japanese War.* Cambridge, UK: Cambridge University Press, 2009.

Shin, Jang-Sup, and Ha-Joon Jang. *Restructuring Korea Inc.* New York: Routledge Curzon, 2003.

Shin, Michael D. 2009. "The Spectre of Yi Kwang-su." Unpublished manuscript.

Shin, Michael D., and Pang Kie Chung. *Landlord, Peasants, Intellectuals in Modern Korea.* Ithaca, NY: Cornell East Asia Program, 2005.

Skya, Walter A. *Japan's Holy War: The Ideology of Radical Shinto Ultranationalism.* Durham, NC: Duke University Press, 2009.

Sŏ Tong-chin. *Chayuŭi ŭiji chagiŭi kyebalŭi ŭiji* [The Will to Freedom: The Will to Self-Empowerment]. Seoul: Tol Pegae, 2009.

Speicher, Jacob. *The Conquest of the Cross in China.* New York: Fleming H. Revell, 1907.

Spickard, Paul. *Almost All Aliens: Immigration, Race, and Colonialism in American History and Identity.* New York: Routledge, 2007.

———. *Japanese Americans: The Formation and Transformations of an Ethnic Group.* New York: Twayne Publishers, 1996.

Standaert, Nicholas. "New Trends in the Historiography of Christianity in China." *The Catholic Historical Review* 1997:573–613.

Su, Xiaokang, and Wang Luxiang. *Deathsong of the River: A Reader's Guide to the Chinese TV Series "Heshang."* Translated by Richard W. Bodman and Pin P. Wan. Ithaca, NY: Cornell University East Asia Series, 1991.

Sumiya Mikio. *Kagawa Toyohiko.* Tokyo: Iwanami Shoten, 1995.

Swallen, W. L. "Types of Korean Christian Character." *Missionary Review of the World,* March 1902, 191–195.

Swanson, Allen J. *The Church in Taiwan: Profile 1980: A Review of the Past and a Projection for the Future.* Pasadena, CA: William Carey Library, 1981.

Tagawa Daikichirō. *Kokka to shūkyō* [State and Religion]. Tokyo: Kyōbunkan, 1938.

Takahashi, Jere. *Nisei/Sansei: Shifting Japanese American Identities and Politics.* Philadelphia: Temple University Press, 1997.

Takaki, Ronald. *Strangers from a Different Shore: A History of Asian Americans.* Boston, MA: Little, Brown, 1989.

Take Kuniyasu. "Ebina Danjō no sensō ron" [Ebina Danjō's Arguments on War]. *Kirisutokyō shakai mondai kenkyū* 23 (1975): 44–82.

Takeda, Kiyoko. "Japanese Christianity: Between Orthodoxy and Heterodoxy." In *Authority and the Individual in Japan,* translated and edited by J. Victor Koschmann, 82–107. Tokyo: University of Tokyo Press, 1978.

Takenaka, Masao. *Reconciliation and Renewal in Japan.* New York: Student Volunteer Movement for Christian Missions and Friendship Press, 1957.

———. "Relations of Protestantism to Social Problems in Japan, 1900–1941." Ph.D. diss., Yale University, 1955.

Tanaka, Stefan. *Japan's Orient.* Berkeley: University of California Press, 1995.

Taylor, Charles. "Modern Social Imaginaries." *Public Culture* 14 (2002): 91–124.

Thornton, Arland, and Hui-Shen Lin. *Social Change and the Family in Taiwan.* Chicago: University of Chicago Press, 1994.

Tocqueville, Alexis de. *Democracy in America.* New York: HarperCollins, 2000.

Tong, James W. *Revenge of the Forbidden City: The Suppression of the Falungong in China, 1999–2005.* New York: Oxford University Press, 2009.

Tseng, Timothy. "Religious Liberalism, International Politics, and Diasporic Realities: The Chinese Students Christian Association of North America, 1909–1951." *The Journal of America—East Asian Relations* 5, nos. 3–4 (1996): 305–330.

Tsunajima Kakichi. *Gyakkyō no fukuin* [The Gospel of Adversity]. Tokyo: Keiseisha, 1924.

———. *Hai-Nichi mondai to Kirisutokyō* [The Anti-Japanese Problem and Christianity]. Tokyo: Keiseisha, 1917.

Tucker, John. "Tokugawa Intellectual History and Prewar Ideology: The Case of Inoue Tetsujirō, Yamaga Sokō, and the Forty-Seven Rōnin." *Sino-Japanese Studies* 14 (2002): 35–70.

Tuveson, Ernest L. *Redeemer Nation: The Idea of America's Millennial Role.* Chicago: University of Chicago Press, 1968.

Uemura Masahisa. *Uemura Masahisa zenshū* [The Collected Works of Uemura Masahisa], vol. 1. Tokyo: Uemura Zenshū Kankōkai, 1931–1934.

Underwood, Horace G. "An Object Lesson in Self-Support." *Missionary Review of the World,* June 1900, 443–449.

Underwood, Horace H. "Industrial Training in the Far East." *Missionary Review of the World,* September 1918, 673–680.

———. *Modern Education in Korea.* New York: International Press, 1926.

Unsworth, J. K. "Gandhi and Kagawa: Two Spiritual Forces of the East." *The Churchman,* October 1926, 10–11.

Van Compernolle, Timothy J. *The Uses of Memory: The Critique of Modernity in the Fiction of Higuchi Ichiyō.* Cambridge, MA: Harvard University Press, 2006.

Vanderbilt, Gregory. "Postwar Japanese Christian Historians, Democracy, and the Problem of the 'Emperor-System' State." In *Christianity and the State in Asia: Complicity and Conflict,* edited by Julius Bautista and Francis Lim Khek Gee, 59–78. New York: Routledge, 2009.

Vinton, C. C. "To-day in Korean Missions." *Missionary Review of the World,* August 1906, 571–574.

Vories, Wm. Merrell. *The Omi Brotherhood in Nippon.* Omi Hachiman: Omi Brotherhood Book Department, 1934.

Wada Yōichi, ed. *Dōshisha no shisōkatachi* [Dōshisha's Thinkers]. Kyoto: Dōshisha Daigaku Seikyō Shuppanbu, 1965–1973.

Wang Siming and Tian Xiong. "Xiangcun Jidujiao de shijian xingtai: qianru yu lishu—yi Guandong diqu Nancun Jidu jiaohui lishibianqian weili [The Practical Form of Embedded and Alienated Rural Christianity: A Case Study of Nan Village in Central Shaanxi Province]. *Nanjing Shida xuebao (Shehui kexue ban)* [Journal of Nanjing Normal University (Social Science)] 6 (2008): 38–43.

Warner, R. Stephen. "The Place of the Congregation in American Religious Configuration." In *New Perspectives in the Study of Congregations,* edited by James P. Wind and James W. Lewis, 54–99. Chicago: University of Chicago Press, 1994.

Wei Zhiyuan. "Yanzao tanghui bainian shiluo" [An Overview of the History of the Yanzao Church]. In *Yanzao tanghui bainian jiniankan* [A Special Issue on the Hundredth Anniversary of the Yanzao Church]. Yanzao, Guangdong Province: Yanzao Presbyterian Church, 1949.

Weller, Robert P. "Identity and Social Change in Taiwanese Religion." In *Taiwan: A New History,* edited by Murray A. Rubinstein, 339–365. Armonk, NY: M. E. Sharpe, 1994.

Wells, Kenneth M. *New God, New Nation: Protestants and Self-Reconstruction Nationalism in Korea, 1896–1937.* Honolulu: University of Hawai'i Press, 1990.

White, Ronald C., and C. Howard Hopkins. *The Social Gospel: Religion and Reform in Changing America.* Philadelphia: Temple University Press, 1976.

Wi, Jo Kang. "Church and State Relations in the Japanese Colonial Period." In *Christianity in Korea,* edited by Robert E. Buswell and Timothy S. Lee, 97–115. Honolulu: University of Hawai'i Press, 2006.

Wickeri, Philip. *Reconstructing Christianity in China: K. H. Ting and the Chinese Church.* Maryknoll, NY: Orbis Books, 2007.

———. *Seeking the Common Ground: Protestant Christianity, the Three-Self Movement, and China's United Front.* Maryknoll, NY: Orbis Books, 1988.

Wiest, Jean-Paul. "Lineage and Patterns of Conversion in Guangdong," *Ch'ing-shih wen-t'i* 4, no. 7 (1982): 1–32.

Williams, Raymond. *Politics of Modernism.* London: Verso Press, 2007.

Woodson, Carter G. *The Works of Francis J. Grimké.* Washington, DC: The Associated Publishers, 1942.

Wright, Robert. *A World Mission: Canadian Protestantism and the Quest for a New International Order, 1918–1939.* Montreal and Kingston: McGill-Queen's University Press, 1991.

Xie Yufang. "Xie shi jiapu [The Xie Family Genealogy]." Unpublished manuscript, 1983.

Xing, Jun. *Baptized in the Fire of Revolution: The American Social Gospel and the YMCA in China, 1919–1937.* Bethlehem, PA: Lehigh University Press, 1996.

Xu, Yihua. "'Patriotic' Protestants: The Making of an Official Church." In *God and Caesar in China: Policy Implications of Church-State Tensions,* edited by Jason Kindopp and Carol Lee Hamrin, 107–121. Washington, DC: The Brookings Institute, 2004.

Yang, Fenggang. *Chinese Christians in America: Conversion, Assimilation, and Adhesive Identities.* University Park: Pennsylvania State University Press, 1999.

———. "Lost in the Market, Saved at McDonald's: Conversion to Christianity in Urban China." *Journal for the Scientific Study of Religion* 44, no. 4 (2005): 423–441.

———. "The Red, Black, and Gray Markets of Religion in China." *Sociological Quarterly* 47 (2006): 93–122.

Yang, Fenggang, and Tong Carnes, eds. *Asian-American Religions: The Making and Remaking of Borders and Boundaries.* New York: New York University Press, 2004.

Yang, Fenggang, and Helen Rose Ebaugh. "Transformations in New Immigrant Religions and Their Global Implications." *American Sociological Review* 66, no. 2 (2001): 269–288.

Yang, Li-Shou, Arland Thornton, and Thomas Fricke. "Religion and Family Formation in Taiwan: The Decline of Ancestral Authority." In *Family, Religion, and Social Change in Diverse Societies,* edited by Sharon K. Houseknecht and Jerry G. Pankhurst, 121–146. New York: Oxford University Press, 2000.

Yang, Mayfair Mei-Hui. *Gifts, Favors, and Banquets: The Art of Social Relationships in China.* Ithaca, NY: Cornell University Press, 1994.

Yasuo, Furuya, ed. *A History of Japanese Theology.* Grand Rapids, MI: W. B. Eerdman, 1997.

Yates, Charles S. "Saigo Takamori in the Emergence of Meiji Japan." *Modern Asian Studies* 28, no. 3 (1994): 449–474.

Yep, Laurence, and Kathy S. Yep. *The Dragon's Child: A Story of Angel Island.* New York: HarperCollins, 2008.

Yi Chin-ku. "Kaesin'gyo wa sŏngjangjuŭi ideollogi" [Protestantism and Growth Orientation]. *Tangdae pip'yŏng* 12 (2000): 225–240.

Yi Kwang-su. "Minjok kaejoron" [A Treatise on National Reconstruction]. *Kaebyŏk* 23 (1922).

Yi Man-yŏl. *Han'guk Kidokkyo munhwa undong sa* [The Cultural History of the Christian Movement in Korea]. Seoul: The Christian Literature Society, 1987.

———. *Han'guk Kidokkyo uiryosa* [A History of Christian Medical Work in Korea]. Seoul: Acanet, 2003.

Yi Man-yŏl and Oak Sung-Deuk, trans. *Eondeoudeu jaryojip 1* [Horace G. Underwood Papers 1]. Seoul: Yonsei University Press, 2005.

———. *Eondeoudeu jaryojip 2* [Horace G. Underwood Papers 2]. Seoul: Yonsei University Press, 2006.

———. *Eondeoudeu jaryojip 3* [Horace G. Underwood Papers 3]. Seoul: Yonsei University Press, 2007.

———. *Eondeoudeu jaryojip 5* [Horace G. Underwood and Lillias Horton Underwood Papers 5]. Seoul: Yonsei University Press, 2010.

Yi Wŏn-kyu. *Kidokkyoŭi wigiwa hŭimang* [Crisis and Hope of Protestantism]. Seoul:_Taehan Kidokkyosŏhoe, 2003.

Yokoyama Haruichi. *Kagawa Toyohiko den* [The Life of Kagawa Toyohiko]. Tokyo: Keiseisha, 1959.

———. *Toyohiko Kagawa and His Works.* Tokyo: Friends of Jesus, 1961.

Yoo, David K. *Contentious Spirits: Religion in Korea American History, 1903–1945.* Stanford, CA: Stanford University Press, 2010.

———. *Growing Up Nisei: Race, Generation, and Culture among Japanese Americans of California, 1924–1949.* Urbana: University of Illinois Press, 2000.

Young, Ahn Byoung, and Yim Hyuk Baek, eds. *Globalization and Neoliberalism: Philosophy, Reality and Korea's Response.* Seoul: Nanam, 2000.

Yuki, Kō. *Watakushi no Uchimura Kanzō ron* [My Interpretation of Uchimura Kanzō]. Tokyo: Kyobunkwan, 1978.

Yun, T. H. "What Shall We Eat." *The Korean Mission Field,* January 1918, 11–12.

Yun Kyung-ro. *Han'guk kŭndaesa ŭi Kidokkyo sajak ihae* [Understanding the Achievement of Christianity in Modern Korea]. Seoul: Yukminsa, 1992.

Contributors

Kyusik Chang is professor in the Department of History at Chung-ang University. The focus of his research is the modern intellectual history of Korea. He is the author of *Ilcheha Han'guk Kidokkyo minjokchuŭi yŏn'gu* [Christian Nationalism in Modern Korea] (Seoul: Hye'an, 2001).

Carolyn Chen is associate professor of Sociology and Asian American Studies at Northwestern University. She is the author of *Getting Saved in America: Taiwanese Immigration and Religious Experience* (Princeton University Press, 2008) and coeditor of *Sustaining Faith Traditions: Race, Religion and Ethnicity among the Latino and Asian American Second Generation* (NYU Press, 2012).

Eun Young Lee Easley is an independent scholar. She received her M.A. in cultural anthropology from Yonsei University in 2007 and was a Freeman Fellow at Williams College in 2005. She is now working in energy market analysis with a continuing interest in the social economics of Korean Christianity.

Joseph Tse-Hei Lee is professor of History at Pace University. His research focuses on church-state relations in modern China. Among his publications are *The Bible and the Gun: Christianity in South China, 1860–1900* (Routledge, 2003; Chinese edition, 2010) and two coedited works, *Marginalization in China: Recasting Minority Politics* (Palgrave Macmillan, 2009) and *China's Rise to Power: Conceptions of State Governance* (Palgrave Macmillan, 2012).

Mark R. Mullins is professor of Japanese Studies in the School of Asian Studies, University of Auckland, New Zealand. His teaching and research focus on religion in modern societies. He is the author and coeditor of a number of studies, including *Christianity Made in Japan* (University of Hawai'i Press, 1998), *Religion and Social Crisis in Japan* (Palgrave Macmillan, 2001), and *Handbook of Christianity in Japan* (Brill, 2003). He is currently engaged in research and writing on neonationalism and contemporary Japanese religions.

David Ownby is professor in the Department of History at Université de Montréal. His most recent book is *Falun Gong and the Future of China* (Oxford, 2008).

Albert L. Park is assistant professor of History at Claremont McKenna College. His teaching and research focus on the modern history of Korea and East Asia, in particular the relationship between economic structures and religious and cultural trends and developments. While finishing his book manuscript *Building a Heaven on Earth: Religion, Activism and Protest in Japanese Occupied Korea,* he is also working on his next project, which looks at the intersection between design, social activism, and democracy in South Korea.

Yunjae Park is associate professor in the Department of History at Kyung Hee University. He is the author of *Han'guk kŭndaeŭhak ŭi kiwŏn* [The Origin of the Modern Korean Medical System] (Seoul: Hye'an, 2005).

Gregory Vanderbilt is an independent scholar. He earned a Ph.D. in history from UCLA in 2005. He is the translator of Mitsuo Miyata's *Authority and Obedience: Romans 13:1–7 in Modern Japan* (Peter Lang, 2009). He is completing a history of Christianity in imperial Japan based on the experience of the Omi Brotherhood and is planning projects on the history of people with Hansen's Disease in Japan and on the American anthropologist John Embree.

Garrett L. Washington is visiting assistant professor in the Department of History at The College of Wooster. He was formally a Mellon Postdoctoral Fellow and Visiting Assistant Professor at Oberlin College and Case Western Reserve University. He is a historian of modern Japanese religion specializing in the study of religious spaces, discourse, and activism. His work has appeared in *Japanese Studies.*

David K. Yoo is professor of Asian American Studies and Director of the Asian American Studies Center at the University of California, Los Angeles. He is the author of *Contentious Spirits: Religion in Korean American History, 1903–1945* (Stanford, 2010).

Index

An **f**, **m**, **n**, **t** after a page number indicates a **f**igure, **m**ap, **n**ote, **t**able on that page.

Production Notes for
Park and Yoo / Encountering Modernity:
Christianity in East Asia and Asian

Jacket design by Julie Matsuo-Chun.

Interior design and composition by Josie Herr
with text and display in Minion Pro.

Printing and binding by Sheridan Books, Inc.

Printed on 60 lb. House White, 444 ppi.